SUBSTANCE ABUSE ASSESSMENT, INTERVENTIONS AND TREATMENT

EMERGING TARGETS
FOR DRUG ADDICTION TREATMENT

SUBSTANCE ABUSE ASSESSMENT, INTERVENTIONS AND TREATMENT

Additional books in this series can be found on Nova's website under the Series tab.

Additional e-books in this series can be found on Nova's website under the e-book tab.

EMERGING TARGETS FOR DRUG ADDICTION TREATMENT

JUAN CANALES
EDITOR

publishers

New York

NOTICE TO THE READER

The Publisher has taken reasonable care in the preparation of this book, but makes no expressed or implied warranty of any kind and assumes no responsibility for any errors or omissions. No liability is assumed for incidental or consequential damages in connection with or arising out of information contained in this book. The Publisher shall not be liable for any special, consequential, or exemplary damages resulting, in whole or in part, from the readers' use of, or reliance upon, this material. Any parts of this book based on government reports are so indicated and copyright is claimed for those parts to the extent applicable to compilations of such works.

Independent verification should be sought for any data, advice or recommendations contained in this book. In addition, no responsibility is assumed by the publisher for any injury and/or damage to persons or property arising from any methods, products, instructions, ideas or otherwise contained in this publication.

This publication is designed to provide accurate and authoritative information with regard to the subject matter covered herein. It is sold with the clear understanding that the Publisher is not engaged in rendering legal or any other professional services. If legal or any other expert assistance is required, the services of a competent person should be sought. FROM A DECLARATION OF PARTICIPANTS JOINTLY ADOPTED BY A COMMITTEE OF THE AMERICAN BAR ASSOCIATION AND A COMMITTEE OF PUBLISHERS.

Additional color graphics may be available in the e-book version of this book.

Library of Congress Cataloging-in-Publication Data

Emerging targets for drug addiction treatment / editor, Juan Canales.
p. cm.
Includes index.
ISBN 978-1-62081-913-5 (hardcover)
1. Drug addiction--Treatment. I. Canales, Juan.
RC563.E44 2012
362.29--dc23

2012017839

Published by Nova Science Publishers, Inc. †New York

CONTENTS

INTRODUCTION

Addiction is a devastating disorder that poses an important challenge to public health institutions and gravely compromises social wellbeing. The market for illicit drug use has reached global proportions and the use of drugs remains at epidemic levels in many countries. Drug addiction can have serious neurological and neuropsychological consequences, including neurotoxicity, long-lasting neurotransmitter depletion, alterations in cognition and decision-making, mood disturbances and aggressive behaviour. At the present time, psychosocial treatments for drug addiction are partially effective and medications currently available to manage the disorder are non-specific, contributing mainly to attenuate some of the symptoms associated with drug withdrawal, such as anhedonia, dysphoria, anxiety and depression. As far as treatment is concerned, relapse represents the greatest challenge of all. Non-substance-related addictions, also referred to as behavioral addictions, including pathological gambling, compulsive shopping/buying, sexual addiction and computer/internet addiction, are on the rise and also compromise people's health. Non-substance-related addictive behaviours are still poorly understood and the state of research for treatments in this area is in a very early stage of development.

In *Emerging Targets for Drug Addiction Treatment* I present a collection of state-of-the-art, authoritative overviews in the field of treatment for drug and behavioral addictions. Both clinical and basic research perspectives are integrated in the book, covering recent findings in the field of stimulant, cannabis and opioid abuse, as well as non-drug addictions, with an emphasis in novel pharmacological interventions and potential receptor targets recently identified. The intended audience of this exciting selection is broad, encompassing clinicians, researchers and graduate students who seek advanced knowledge and up-to-date information in this rapidly moving field of enquiry.

Juan J. Canales, *D.Phil.*
Editor

In: Emerging Targets for Drug Addiction Treatment   ISBN 978-1-62081-913-5
Editor: Juan Canales   ©2012 Nova Science Publishers, Inc.

Chapter 1

PHARMACOLOGICAL TREATMENTS FOR COCAINE ADDICTION

*Laurent Karila**

Addiction Research and Treatment Center, Paul Brousse Hospital,
Paris Sud-11 University, France

ABSTRACT

Cocaine remains the second most commonly used illicit drug in the world. Cocaine addiction is a chronic, relapsing disorder characterized by repetitive and compulsive drug-seeking behavior and cocaine use despite negative consequences. This disease is a significant public health problem with somatic, psychiatric, psychological, legal and social complications. Despite many years of research, there is no currently specific pharmacotherapy, with established efficacy for the treatment of cocaine addiction, which is approved by regulatory authorities. Recent studies have identified various mechanisms implicated in cocaine addiction. Several promising pharmacological treatments have been suggested such as medications affecting the glutamate, GABA, acetylcholine, dopamine systems, agonist replacement therapy and cocaine vaccine. Abstinence initiation and relapse prevention are the main goals of cocaine addiction treatment. Combination of pharmacological agents and behavioral therapies is the optimal therapeutic strategy for cocaine use disorders.

1. EPIDEMIOLOGICAL DATA

Cultivation of leaves from the coca plant is concentrated in Peru, Colombia and Bolivia. Cocaine is a crystalline alkaloid, found in the Erythroxylum Cocacoca or Novogranatense [1]. The 2010 production of pure cocaine is comprised between 786 and 1054 tons, which is quite similar to 2009. Cocaine found in Europe appears to be transited through Argentina, Brazil, Ecuador, Venezuela, Mexico, Caribbean islands and West Africa. The main points of entry to Europe for cocaïne are Spain, Netherlands, Portugal and Belgium. Germany, France and the

---

* Email: laurent.karila@gmail.com.

United Kingdom are known to be important transit or destination countries. Cocaine remains the most trafficked drug in the world after cannabis and cannabis [2]. Since 2009, cocaine purity has declined. Its mean value in the samples tested ranged between 25 % and 43 % in most of the European countries. The mean retail price of cocaine ranged between 45 and 80 euros per gram in Europe [3]. Cocaine remains the second most commonly used illicit drug in the world even if there is an increase of the production of synthetic drugs or legal highs. This drug has become an essential part of the world drug scene with a consumption that varies among countries [2]. According to the European Monitoring Centre for Drugs and Drug Addiction (EMCDDA), 14.5 million Europeans have used cocaine at least once in their life, on average 4.3 % of adults aged 15–64 years. Four million Europeans have used the drug in the last year (1.2 %). For last month cocaine use, it represents about 1.5 million Europeans (0.5 % of the adult population). Eight million young adults aged 15–34 years (5.9 %) have used cocaine at least once in their life. It is particularly high among young European males [3]. Lifetime prevalence of cocaine use among 15- to 16-year- old school students is 1 to 2 % in most of the european countries, while it is 5 % in France and the United Kingdom. Furthermore, 5% of cocaine users will develop a substance dependence during the first year of use, and 20% of these will become long-term cocaine-dependent patients [4]. In agreement with these epidemiological data, the number of patients entering drug treatment for primary cocaine use has been increasing in Europe for several years [3] [5].

2. CLINICAL DATA

Cocaine hydrochloride (powder form) is well absorbed by intranasal and intravenous routes. The alkaline form, freebase or crack cocaine, can be smoked. Intranasal cocaine powder requires 5 to 10 minutes to produce psychostimulant effects whereas the smoked form is instantaneous [6]. Cocaine addiction is a chronic, relapsing disorder characterized by repetitive and compulsive drug-seeking behavior and drug use despite negative psychological, physical and social consequences. The multifactorial disorder leads to a cycle of addiction : cocaine-induced euphoria, acute stimulant withdrawal, cue-induced craving (friends, dealers, places), loss of control, poor decision making, cocaine-seeking behavior with legal risks taken and cocaine administration [6] [7, 8]. The DSM-V work group is recommending that this disorder be subsumed into a new disorder, Cocaine-Use Disorder, with the following criteria (see www.dsm5.org, last access january 12nd, 2012).

A maladaptive pattern of substance use leading to clinically significant impairment or distress, as manifested by 2 (or more) of the following, occurring within a 12-month period:

1. recurrent cocaine use resulting in a failure to fulfill major role obligations at work, school, or home (e.g., repeated absences or poor work performance related to substance use; substance-related absences, suspensions, or expulsions from school; neglect of children or household)
2. recurrent substance use in situations in which it is physically hazardous (e.g., driving an automobile or operating a machine when impaired by substance use)

3. continued substance use despite having persistent or recurrent social or interpersonal problems caused or exacerbated by the effects of the substance (e.g., arguments with spouse about consequences of intoxication, physical fights)

4. tolerance, as defined by either of the following:

    a. a need for markedly increased amounts of the substance to achieve intoxication or desired effect

    b. markedly diminished effect with continued use of the same amount of the substance

5. withdrawal, as manifested by either of the following:

    a. the characteristic withdrawal syndrome for the substance (refer to Criteria A and B of the criteria sets for Withdrawal from the specific substances)

    b. the same (or a closely related) substance is taken to relieve or avoid withdrawal symptoms

6. the substance is often taken in larger amounts or over a longer period than was intended

7. there is a persistent desire or unsuccessful efforts to cut down or control substance use

8. a great deal of time is spent in activities necessary to obtain the substance, use the substance, or recover from its effects

9. important social, occupational, or recreational activities are given up or reduced because of substance use

10. the substance use is continued despite knowledge of having a persistent or recurrent physical or psychological problem that is likely to have been caused or exacerbated by the substance (e.g., current cocaine use despite recognition of cocaine-induced depression, or continued drinking despite recognition that an ulcer was made worse by alcohol consumption)

11. Craving or a strong desire or urge to use a specific substance.

Cocaine addiction is a significant public health problem. Regular, intranasal, smoked or intravenous, use can be associated with cardiovascular, neurological and psychiatric problems. The risk of accidents and of transmission of infectious diseases are also evident (unprotected sex, sharing of straws, crack pipes, syringes) [9] [10]. There is also considerable heterogeneity among cocaine users, including occasional users, socially integrated regular users, abusers, dependent users [11]. Cocaine use is strongly linked with alcohol, cannabis, benzodiazepines or opiates use.

2. PHARMACOLOGICAL TREATMENTS

Cocaine increases synaptic levels of dopamine [12], norepinephrine [13] and serotonin [14]. Cocaine reward is attributable mostly to increased dopamine in the meso-cortico-limbic system [15]. Other neurotransmitter systems including glutamate, GABA, endocannabinoid, acetylcholine and corticotrophin-releasing hormone are influenced by cocaine [16-18] [19-21]. These systems interact with and modulate the reward, motivation, and memory pathways in the brain [22].

Despite many years of research, there is no currently specific pharmacotherapy with established efficacy for the treatment of cocaine addiction, nor is any pharmacological agents approved by regulatory authorities for such treatment. Recent reviews on pharmacological agents for cocaine addiction have been published [23-28] but it is a quickly evolving area with new clinical trials frequently reported. New insights into the effects of cocaine on the brain reward system have resulted in several promising relapse prevention medications [29]. Recent studies have identified various neuronal mechanisms implicated in cocaine addiction [29] and have suggested several promising pharmacological treatments such as medications affecting the glutamatergic, GABAergic, acetylcholine, dopamine systems, agonist replacement therapy and cocaine vaccine [23]. Abstinence initiation and relapse prevention are the main goals of cocaine addiction treatment. Combination of pharmacological agents and behavioral therapies is the optimal therapeutic strategy for this addictive disease [30].

2.1. Abstinence Initiation

2.1.1. N-Acetylcysteine

N-Acetyl Cysteine (NAC) is a glutamate prodrug. As a mucolytic agent, also available as a nutritional supplement, it is used in chronic pulmonary conditions, in cystic fibrosis and to treat paracetamol acute intoxication. A double blind placebo-controlled clinical trial was conducted in non-treatment seeking cocaine-dependent patients. Well tolerated, NAC may decrease cocaine related withdrawal symptoms and craving [31].

A 4-week open-label pilot study has shown that 3 doses of NAC (1200, 2400 or 3600 mg/day (mg/d)) were well tolerated in cocaine-dependent patients. The two higher doses of medication were correlated with treatment retention levels. Of the subjects that finished the study, most terminated or reduced cocaine use during the treatment [32]. In a double-blind, placebo-controlled crossover trial, participants treated with NAC completed a cue-reactivity procedure that involved collecting psychophysical and subjective data in response to slides depicting cocaine and cocaine use. NAC patients reported less desire to use, less interest in response to cocaine images and watched cocaine slides for less time. NAC plays a role in the inhibition of cocaine cue reactivity [33]. Repeated administration, during 4 days, of NAC (1200–2400 mg/d) to cocaine-dependent participants produced decreased craving following an experimenter-delivered intraveinous injection of cocaine [34]. A 8-week randomized controlled trial is actually conducted with NAC (1200 - 2400 mg/d) with a weekly cognitive behavioral therapy (CBT) throughout the study (see clinicaltrials.gov).

2.1.2. Vigabatrin

Vigabatrin or Gamma-Vinyl GABA is an atypical antiepileptic. Three open-label studies involving cocaine-dependent outpatients have shown that this GABA agent (1.5-3 g/d) was well tolerated with no reported ophtalmologic adverse effects [35-37]. A recent 9-week randomized, double-blind, placebo-controlled trial with vigabatrin (1 to 3 g/d), involving 103 cocaine-dependent treatment-seeking mexican parolees, has also shown that the medication was safe and well tolerated. The retention rate was 62% in the vigabatrin arm and a better achieved full end of the trial abstinence was found in this arm [38].

2.1.3. Modafinil

Modafinil is a non-amphetamine stimulant approved for the treatment of narcolepsy with or without cataplexy [39-42]. Modafinil is known to not have a significant addictive liability [43-45]. However, a brain imaging study evaluating the effects of modafinil (200 or 400 mg given orally) has shown a potential for abuse and maybe dependence on modafinil in vulnerable populations [46]. A recent study found preclinical evidence for the addictive potential of modafinil. Wuo-Silva and colleagues have also suggested that similar neural substrates were involved in the psychomotor/rewarding effects of modafinil and cocaine [47]. Modafinil has stimulant-like subjective effects in humans [48, 49] and may decrease the symptoms of cocaine withdrawal [50] and cocaine craving. It does not appear to produce euphoria or cocaine craving [51, 52]. Laboratory studies found no significant adverse interactions between modafinil and cocaine in humans [50, 53, 54]. Patients taking modafinil (400 mg/d) in a randomized, double-blind clinical trial had significantly less cocaine use measured by urine toxicology [55]. A study also showed that modafinil could decrease self-administration of smoked cocaine base in habitual crack users [56]. Modafinil (200 or 400 mg/d) was examined in a recent randomized, double blind, placebo-controlled study involving 210 cocaine-dependent outpatients. No significant differences were observed between the 2 groups in their change in the average weekly cocaine non-use days. As a secondary outcome, modafinil significantly decreased cocaine craving. The medication was also effective for increasing cocaine non-use days in participants without comorbid alcohol dependence [57]. It could suggest a target subgroup of cocaine-dependent patients [26]. A recent meta-analysis found that the proportion of patients achieving sustained cocaine abstinence was higher with modafinil, at a statistical trend of significance, than with placebo [58]. New therapeutic strategies for cocaine addiction could be medications enhancing cognitive function and attenuating drug reward [59]. Modafinil is a mild psychostimulant with pro-cognitive effects. It improves attention and enhances performance in a variety of cognitive tasks [60, 61]. Hypersomnia during withdrawal syndrome might amplify stimulant-induced euphoria, which reinforces stimulant use and could increase the likelihood for relapse. Cocaine users reported poor sleep and fatigue in the first 3 weeks of abstinence. A 16-day inpatient, randomized, double-blind, placebo-controlled trial found that sleep normalization by morning-dosed modafinil (400 mg/d) might actually improve clinical outcome in this addictive disease [62]. Controlled clinical trials of modafinil are ongoing at this time (see clinicaltrials.gov).

2.1.4. Varenicline

Cocaine has non-dopaminergic effects on acetylcholine, suggesting that this neurotransmitter mauy play a role in cocaine addiction [20]. Varenicline, a partial agonist for the alpha4-beta2 nicotinic acetylcholine receptor subtypes, is approved for smoking cessation and relapse prevention [63]. A 9-week double blind placebo controlled study has tested the potential efficacy of varenicline (2mg/d) in a population of cocaine-dependent patients. A small to moderate effect for this pharmacological agent on cocaine use was found in this preliminary study [64]. Cocaine reward seemed to be reduced. Future studies of varenicline for cocaine addiction may be warranted.

2.1.5. Antidepressants

A meta-analysis of 37 studies with 3551 participants do not support the efficacy of antidepressants (desipramine, imipramine, fluoxetine) in the treatment of cocaine addiction [65]. Depressed cocaine-dependent subjects received either mirtazapine (45 mg/d) or placebo for 12 weeks. Mirtazapine is superior to placebo in improving sleep in patients with comorbid depression and cocaine dependence, but is not more effective than placebo in reducing cocaine use [66]. Promising findings from preclinical research on the effects of cocaine on serotonin lead to examination of selective serotonin reuptake inhibitors (SSRIs) as potential treatments for cocaine dependence with mixed results. A 33-week randomized, double-blind, placebo-controlled clinical trials involving 145 cocaine and opioid dependent treated with methadone outpatients found no efficacy of fluoxetine [67]. A double blind controlled trial found that Citalopram (20 mg/d) combined with CBT and contingency management showed a significant reduction in cocaine-positive urines during treatment compared to placebo treated subjects [68].

2.2. Relapse Prevention Medication

A key feature of successful pharmacological treatment of psychostimulant addiction is the prevention of relapse following abstinence.

2.2.1. Disulfiram

Disulfiram, an acetylaldehyde dehydrogenase inhibitor and a dopamine beta-hydroxylase inhibitor, is approved for alcohol dependence [69]. This pharmacological agent could be useful in patients who have cocaine addiction alone or comorbid cocaine and alcohol addiction [70, 71]. Several clinical studies have reported that disulfiram (250-500 mg/d) reduces cocaine use and improves abstinence in patients with comorbid alcohol use disorders [72, 73]. The decrease of cocaine use was still present one year after treatment [74]. Patients taking disulfiram (250 mg/d) alone or in combination with naltrexone (100 mg/d) were most likely to achieve combined abstinence from cocaine and alcohol than placebo-treated patients [75]. Furthermore, disulfiram efficacy to reduce cocaine use also has been observed in non alcohol abuser patients or in opiate-dependent and receiving opiate agonist maintenance treatment (e.g méthadone, buprenorphine) [76, 77]. The dose-related efficacy of disulfiram (62,5; 125 or 250 mg/d) for treating cocaine dependence in 161 methadone-stabilized cocaine-dependent participants was evaluated in a 14-week, double blind, randomized, placebo-controlled clinical trial. Cocaine positive urines increased over time in the 62.5 and 125 mg disulfiram groups. So, it may be contraindicated to prescribe this pharmacological agent for cocaine addiction at doses inferior to 250 mg/d [78].

Disulfiram is rarely used in clinical settings due to the potential for medically serious drug interactions between alcohol and disulfiram in cocaine-dependent individuals [79]. The most frequent side effects of disulfiram in randomized clinical trials include anxiety, fatigue, headache and sleepiness. Disulfiram at doses inferior or equal to 250 mg/d led to only mild interactions with alcohol. This médication has an acceptable side-effect profile for the treatment of cocaine dependence with or without alcohol dependence (79). A double-blind, placebo-controlled assessment of the safety of potential interactions between intravenous cocaine (30 mg), ethanol (0.4 g/kg), and oral disulfiram (0, 250, and 500 mg/d) was conducted in treated cocaine-dependent research volunteers. Disulfiram did not enhance the cardiovascular effects of cocaine and may have reduced the subjective high from cocaine. The severity of disulfiram–ethanol réaction (hypotension, tachycardia, nausea, and flushing) was related to disulfiram dose. The trial with 500 mg/d was stopped prematurely due to safety concerns. This study suggests that the risks of the moderate use of cocaine and ethanol in individuals treated with moderate doses of disulfiram (≤250 mg/d) may not be problematic [80]. Future studies should target subgroup of cocaine-dependent patients with disulfiram.

2.2.2. Topiramate

Topiramate is an anticonvulsant and a medication also used to prevent migraine headaches. Based on its effects on glutamate and GABA neurotransmission, it may be a promising pharmacological agent for relapse prevention [81]. A significant decrease of cocaine craving intensity and duration was found in a 12-week open-label pilot study with increasing doses of topiramate (25 to 300 mg/d) in cocaine-dependent outpatients. This effect was only seen in 25% of the sample [82].

A 13-week randomized, double-blind, placebo-controlled, clinical trial was conducted in 40 cocaine-dependent outpatients who received topiramate (up to 200 mg/d) with twice weekly cognitive behavioral therapy. Over the first eight weeks of the study, there was less cocaine use than the placebo arm and 59% of the patients maintained continuous abstinence for at least 3 weeks. After the eight weeks, the topiramate group was more likely to be abstinent from cocaine compared to the placebo arm [83]. Evidence for topiramate in the treatment of cocaine is promising but limited by small sample size [84]. Other studies are necessary.

2.2.3. Baclofen

Baclofen is a GABA agonist used to reduce muscle spasticity in neurological diseases (multiple sclerosis or medullar lesions). Studies found anti-craving properties of Baclofen (20-40 mg/d) for cocaine [85, 86]. Baclofen 60 mg/day decreased cocaine self-administration in non-opioid-dependent, non-treatment-seeking cocaine-dependent patients [87]. However, 2 randomized placebo controlled trial with baclofen 60 mg/d in cocaine-dependent outpatients found no significant difference between the 2 groups [88] [89]. Despite the fact that there is no evidence to use baclofen for initiation abstinence, baclofen should be tested at higher doses for relapse prevention [27]. The main targets could be heavy cocaine use and severity of the disease [88, 89].

2.2.4. Dextroamphetamine (D-Amphetamine)

Agonist replacement therapy may be an interesting option in the treatment of cocaine addiction [90]. This pharmacological strategy uses a drug from the same pharmacological family as the abused drug to suppress withdrawal and craving [91, 92]. D-amphetamine is a potential pharmacological agent such as disulfiram, methylphenidate, or modafinil [23]. D-amphetamine sustained release formulation (15 to 60 mg/d) was evaluated in cocaine-dependent or in cocaine-heroin-dependent patients in 3 double blind, placebo-controlled studies. Cocaine use decreased at the higher doses (30-60 mg/d) [93-95]. Pretreatment with 15 mg oral d-amphetamine did not increase stimulant self-administration [96]. This pharmacologial agent attenuated some of the subject-rated effects of cocaine [97]. Prolonged d-amphetamine treatment may be necessary to produce a sustained reduction in the reinforcing effects of cocaine [98]. Further research for the use of d-amphetamine for cocaine dependence is needed [99].

2.2.5. Cocaine Vaccine

A promising relapse prevention therapy is a vaccine capable of stimulating the production of cocaine-specific antibodies [30, 100]. Vaccines have great potential to help the patient achieve and sustain abstinence and have advantages over conventional medications in that they would have no direct psychoactive effects and no abuse liability. Their effects may improve patient adherence to treatment [101]. The goal of using cocaine-selective antibodies is to block the compound peripherally and to prevent it from crossing the blood–brain barrier. TA-CD vaccine is a cocaine conjugate that stimulates the production of antibodies against cocaine [102]. The first controlled clinical trial of an anti-cocaine vaccine, using 34 cocaine abusers, over one year, was coonducted in 2002. Three different doses were given three times at monthly intervals. The vaccine was well tolerated. Cocaine-specific IgG cocaine antibodies were induced in a time- and dose-dependent manner [103]. An open label, dose-escalation trial found that the vaccine was well tolerated. The more the dose was high, the more the levels of antibodies were high in the serum. A less euphoric effect was found if participants did take cocaine. Cocaine specific antibodies persisted at least 6 months.

Booster vaccinations in a few subjects increased the antibody titers [104]. A 24-week, phase IIb, randomized, double-blind, placebo-controlled trial was conducted in 115 cocaine-dependent methadone-maintained outpatients. A significant decreased cocaine use was found in patients attaining high antibody levels (superior or equal to 43 microg/mL), but only 38% of the subjects reached these IgG levels. Patients had only 2 months of adequate cocaine blockade [105]. A multi-site, Phase IIb clinical trial with this vaccine in 300 subjects is currently underway [106]. The TA-CD vaccine decreased smoked cocaine acute effects in subjects generating sufficient antibody in a laboratory study conducted by Haney and colleagues [107]. Interception of cocaine by enzyme or antibody delivered with viral gene transfer may be a novel strategy for relapse preventing in recovering cocaine users [108]. A new vaccine by covalently linking a cocaine analog to the capsid proteins of noninfectious, disrupted adenovirus vector was developed. Preclinical evidence found that this novel cocaine vaccine evokes high-titer anticocaine antibodies in mice sufficient to completely reverse, on a persistent basis, the hyperlocomotor activity induced by intravenous administration of cocaine [109]. It also was found that it blocks cocaine psychostimulant and reinforcing effects [110].

CONCLUSION

Cocaine has become an essential part of the world drug scene with a consumption that varies among countries. This drug is associated with a significant morbidity and mortality. Despite many years of clinical research, no pharmacological treatment has proven its efficacy in treating cocaine addiction. However, various recent controlled clinical studies brought to the forefront some very promising medications, especially the glutamate (e.g N-acetylcysteine, modafinil), GABA (topiramate, vigabatrin, baclofen), acetylcholine (varenicline), dopamine (disulfiram), serotonin (citalopram) agents, which act on the various neurobiological circuits modified by acute and chronic cocaine exposure. Among future promising medications, anti-cocaine vaccine seems to be an innovative treatment especially for relapse prevention that can also be combined with other anticraving medications against drug addiction. The combination of pharmacological agents and psychosocial treatments (e.g. motivational therapy, CBT, contingency management) during abstinence intiation and relapse prevention could be the perfect therapeutic platform to bring some hope for significant improvement in the treatment of cocaine addiction. Recovery programs should be flexible and involve individual and family education on recovery and the nature of addictive disease. Clinical trials with new medications are actually underway.

STATEMENT OF INTEREST

Dr Laurent Karila receives consulting fees from Sanofi Aventis, BMS Otsuka, Lundbeck, Gillead, Shering Plough, Eutherapie, Astra Zeneca Pharmaceuticals

REFERENCES

[1]   Cocaine: pharmacology, addiction, and therapy. *Adv. Alcohol Subst. Abuse.* 1986 Winter;6 (2): 1-184.
[2]   UNODC. World drug report 2011, *United Nations Office on Drugs and Crime*, Vienna. 2011.
[3]   EMCDDA. European Monitoring Center for Drugs and Drug Abuse: Annual report 2011: *The state of the drug problem in Europe. last access the january 12th,* 2012 on www.emcdda.europa.eu. 2011.
[4]   Wagner FA, Anthony JC. From first drug use to drug dependence; developmental periods of risk for dependence upon marijuana, cocaine, and alcohol. *Neuropsychopharmacology* 2002; 26: 479-88.
[5]   Karila L, Beck F, Legleye S, Reynaud M. [Cocaine: from recreational use to dependence]. *Rev. Prat.* 2009 Jun 20; 59 (6): 821-5.
[6]   Dackis CA, O'Brien CP. Cocaine dependence: a disease of the brain's reward centers. *J. Subst. Abuse Treat.* 2001 Oct; 21 (3): 111-7.
[7]   Dackis CA. Recent advances in the pharmacotherapy of cocaine dependence. *Curr. Psychiatry Rep.* 2004 Oct; 6 (5): 323-31.
[8]   Dackis CA, Gold MS. Addictiveness of central stimulants. *Adv. Alcohol Subst. Abuse.* 1990; 9 (1-2): 9-26.
[9]   Haas C, Karila L, Lowenstein W. [Cocaine and crack addiction: a growing public health problem]. *Bull. Acad. Natl. Med.* 2009 Apr; 193 (4): 947-62; discussion 62-3.
[10]   Karila L, Lowenstein W, Coscas S, Benyamina A, Reynaud M. [Complications of cocaine addiction]. *Rev. Prat.* 2009 Jun 20; 59 (6): 825-9.
[11]   Wu LT, Pan JJ, Blazer DG, Tai B, Brooner RK, Stitzer ML, et al. The construct and measurement equivalence of cocaine and opioid dependences: a National Drug Abuse

Treatment Clinical Trials Network (CTN) study. *Drug Alcohol Depend.* 2009 Aug 1; 103 (3): 114-23.

[12] Kuhar MJ, Ritz MC, Boja JW. The dopamine hypothesis of the reinforcing properties of cocaine. *Trends Neurosci.* 1991 Jul; 14 (7): 299-302.

[13] Sofuoglu M, Sewell RA. Norepinephrine and stimulant addiction. *Addict Biol.* 2009 Apr; 14 (2): 119-29.

[14] Hamon M. [Neurobiological mechanisms of dependence: implication of serotonin]. *Bull. Acad. Natl. Med.* 2002; 186 (2): 307-15; discussion 15-7.

[15] Cami J, Farre M. Drug addiction. *N. Engl. J. Med.* 2003 Sep 4; 349 (10): 975-86.

[16] Uys JD, LaLumiere RT. Glutamate: the new frontier in pharmacotherapy for cocaine addiction. *CNS Neurol. Disord. Drug Targets.* 2008 Nov; 7 (5): 482-91.

[17] Lhuillier L, Mombereau C, Cryan JF, Kaupmann K. GABA(B) Receptor-Positive Modulation Decreases Selective Molecular and Behavioral Effects of Cocaine. *Neuropsychopharmacology.* 2006 May 17.

[18] Arnold JC. The role of endocannabinoid transmission in cocaine addiction. Pharmacol Biochem Behav. 2005 Jun; 81 (2): 396-406.

[19] Wiskerke J, Pattij T, Schoffelmeer AN, De Vries TJ. The role of CB1 receptors in psychostimulant addiction. *Addict. Biol.* 2008 Jun; 13 (2): 225-38.

[20] Williams MJ, Adinoff B. The role of acetylcholine in cocaine addiction. *Neuropsychopharmacology.* 2008 Jul; 33 (8): 1779-97.

[21] Lee B, Tiefenbacher S, Platt DM, Spealman RD. Role of the hypothalamic-pituitary-adrenal axis in reinstatement of cocaine-seeking behavior in squirrel monkeys. *Psycho-pharmacology (Berl).* 2003 Jul; 168 (1-2): 177-83.

[22] Lingford-Hughes A, Nutt D. Neurobiology of addiction and implications for treatment. *Br. J. Psychiatry.* 2003; 182: 97-100.

[23] Karila L, Gorelick D, Weinstein A, Noble F, Benyamina A, Coscas S, et al. New treatments for cocaine dependence: a focused review. *Int. J. Neuropsychopharmacol.* 2008 May; 11 (3): 425-38.

[24] Kampman KM. New medications for the treatment of cocaine dependence. *Ann. Ist Super Sanita.* 2009; 45 (2): 109-15.

[25] Penberthy JK, Ait-Daoud N, Vaughan M, Fanning T. Review of treatment for cocaine dependence. *Curr. Drug. Abuse Rev.* 2010 Mar; 3 (1): 49-62.

[26] Karila L, Reynaud M, Aubin HJ, Rolland B, Guardia D, Cottencin O, et al. Pharmacological treatments for cocaine dependence: is there something new? *Curr. Pharm. Des.* 2011; 17 (14): 1359-68.

[27] Shorter D, Kosten TR. Novel pharmacotherapeutic treatments for cocaine addiction. *BMC Med.* 2011; 9: 119.

[28] Somaini L, Donnini C, Raggi MA, Amore M, Ciccocioppo R, Saracino MA, et al. Promising medications for cocaine dependence treatment. *Recent Pat. CNS Drug Discov.* 2011 May 1; 6 (2): 146-60.

[29] Kampman KM. What's new in the treatment of cocaine addiction? *Curr. Psychiatry Rep.* 2010 Oct; 12 (5): 441-7.

[30] Karila L, Reynaud M. [Therapeutic approaches to cocaine addiction]. *Rev. Prat.* 2009 Jun 20; 59 (6): 830-4.

[31] LaRowe SD, Mardikian P, Malcolm R, Myrick H, Kalivas P, McFarland K, et al. Safety and tolerability of N-acetylcysteine in cocaine-dependent individuals. *Am. J. Addict.* 2006 Jan-Feb; 15 (1): 105-10.

[32] Mardikian PN, LaRowe SD, Hedden S, Kalivas PW, Malcolm RJ. An open-label trial of N-acetylcysteine for the treatment of cocaine dependence: a pilot study. *Prog. Neuropsychopharmacol. Biol. Psychiatry.* 2007 Mar 30; 31 (2): 389-94.

[33] LaRowe SD, Myrick H, Hedden S, Mardikian P, Saladin M, McRae A, et al. Is cocaine desire reduced by N-acetylcysteine? *Am. J. Psychiatry.* 2007 Jul; 164 (7): 1115-7.

[34] Amen SL, Piacentine LB, Ahmad ME, Li SJ, Mantsch JR, Risinger RC, et al. Repeated N-Acetyl Cysteine Reduces Cocaine Seeking in Rodents and Craving in Cocaine-Dependent Humans. *Neuro Psycho Pharmacology.* 2010 Dec 15.

[35] Brodie JD, Figueroa E, Dewey SL. Treating cocaine addiction: from preclinical to clinical trial experience with gamma-vinyl GABA. *Synapse.* 2003 Dec 1; 50 (3): 261-5.

[36] Fechtner R, Khouri A, Figueroa E, Ramirez M, Federico M, Dewey S, et al. Short-term treatment of cocaine and/or methamphetamine abuse with vigabatrin: ocular safety pilot results. *Arch. Ophthalmol.* 2006; 124: 1257-62.

[37] Brodie JD, Figueroa E, Laska EM, Dewey SL. Safety and efficacy of gamma-vinyl GABA (GVG) for the treatment of methamphetamine and/or cocaine addiction. *Synapse.* 2005 Feb; 55 (2): 122-5.

[38] Brodie JD, Case BG, Figueroa E, Dewey SL, Robinson JA, Wanderling JA, et al. Randomized, double-blind, placebo-controlled trial of vigabatrin for the treatment of cocaine dependence in Mexican parolees. *Am. J. Psychiatry.* 2009 Nov; 166 (11): 1269-77.

[39] Arnulf I, Derenne JP. [Modafinil (Midiodal): wakefulness stimulant in narcoleptic patients]. *Presse Med.* 2000 Jun 10; 29 (20): 1131-2.

[40] Billiard M, Besset A, Montplaisir J, Laffont F, Goldenberg F, Weill JS, et al. Modafinil: a double-blind multicentric study. *Sleep.* 1994 Dec; 17 (8 Suppl): S107-12.

[41] Laffont F, Mayer G, Minz M. Modafinil in diurnal sleepiness. A study of 123 patients. *Sleep.* 1994 Dec; 17 (8 Suppl): S113-5.

[42] Bastuji H, Jouvet M. Successful treatment of idiopathic hypersomnia and narcolepsy with modafinil. *Prog. Neuropsychopharmacol. Biol. Psychiatry.* 1988; 12 (5): 695-700.

[43] Jasinski DR. An evaluation of the abuse potential of modafinil using methylphenidate as a reference. *J. Psychopharmacol.* 2000 Mar; 14 (1): 53-60.

[44] Jasinski DR, Kovacevic-Ristanovic R. Evaluation of the abuse liability of modafinil and other drugs for excessive daytime sleepiness associated with narcolepsy. *Clin. Neuropharmacol.* 2000 May-Jun; 23 (3): 149-56.

[45] Vosburg SK, Hart CL, Haney M, Rubin E, Foltin RW. Modafinil does not serve as a reinforcer in cocaine abusers. *Drug Alcohol Depend.* 2010 Jan 15; 106 (2-3): 233-6.

[46] Volkow ND, Fowler JS, Logan J, Alexoff D, Zhu W, Telang F, et al. Effects of modafinil on dopamine and dopamine transporters in the male human brain: clinical implications. *Jama.* 2009 Mar 18; 301 (11): 1148-54.

[47] Wuo-Silva R, Fukushiro DF, Borcoi AR, Fernandes HA, Procopio-Souza R, Hollais AW, et al. Addictive potential of modafinil and cross-sensitization with cocaine: a preclinical study. *Addict. Biol.* 2011 Oct; 16 (4): 565-79.

[48] Rush CR, Kelly TH, Hays LR, Baker RW, Wooten AF. Acute behavioral and physiological effects of modafinil in drug abusers. *Behav. Pharmacol.* 2002 Mar; 13 (2): 105-15.

[49] Rush CR, Kelly TH, Hays LR, Wooten AF. Discriminative-stimulus effects of modafinil in cocaine-trained humans. *Drug Alcohol Depend.* 2002 Aug 1; 67 (3): 311-22.

[50] Dackis CA, Lynch KG, Yu E, Samaha FF, Kampman KM, Cornish JW, et al. Modafinil and cocaine: a double-blind, placebo-controlled drug interaction study. *Drug Alcohol. Depend.* 2003 May 1; 70 (1): 29-37.

[51] Ballon JS, Feifel D. A systematic review of modafinil: Potential clinical uses and mechanisms of action. *J. Clin. Psychiatry.* 2006 Apr; 67 (4): 554-66.

[52] O'Brien CP, Dackis CA, Kampman K. Does modafinil produce euphoria? *Am. J. Psychiatry.* 2006 Jun; 163 (6): 1109.

[53] Donovan JL, DeVane CL, Malcolm RJ, Mojsiak J, Chiang CN, Elkashef A, et al. Modafinil influences the pharmacokinetics of intravenous cocaine in healthy cocaine-dependent volunteers. *Clin. Pharmacokinet.* 2005; 44 (7): 753-65.

[54] Malcolm R, Swayngim K, Donovan JL, DeVane CL, Elkashef A, Chiang N, et al. Modafinil and cocaine interactions. *Am. J. Drug Alcohol Abuse.* 2006; 32 (4): 577-87.

[55] Dackis CA, Kampman KM, Lynch KG, Pettinati HM, O'Brien CP. A double-blind, placebo-controlled trial of modafinil for cocaine dependence. *Neuropsychopharmacology.* 2005 Jan; 30 (1): 205-11.

[56] Hart CL, Haney M, Vosburg SK, Rubin E, Foltin RW. Smoked cocaine self-administration is decreased by modafinil. *Neuropsychopharmacology.* 2008 Mar; 33 (4): 761-8.

[57] Anderson AL, Reid MS, Li SH, Holmes T, Shemanski L, Slee A, et al. Modafinil for the treatment of cocaine dependence. *Drug Alcohol Depend.* 2009 Sep 1; 104 (1-2): 133-9.

[58] Castells X, Casas M, Perez-Mana C, Roncero C, Vidal X, Capella D. Efficacy of psychostimulant drugs for cocaine dependence. *Cochrane Database Syst. Rev.* 2010 (2): CD007380.

[59] Sofuoglu M. Cognitive enhancement as a pharmacotherapy target for stimulant addiction. *Addiction.* 2010 Jan; 105 (1): 38-48.

[60] Muller U, Steffenhagen N, Regenthal R, Bublak P. Effects of modafinil on working memory processes in humans. *Psychopharmacology (Berl).* 2004 Dec; 177 (1-2): 161-9.

[61] Turner DC, Robbins TW, Clark L, Aron AR, Dowson J, Sahakian BJ. Cognitive enhancing effects of modafinil in healthy volunteers. *Psychopharmacology (Berl).* 2003 Jan; 165 (3): 260-9.

[62] Morgan PT, Pace-Schott E, Pittman B, Stickgold R, Malison RT. Normalizing effects of modafinil on sleep in chronic cocaine users. *Am. J. Psychiatry.* 2010 Mar; 167 (3): 331-40.

[63] Crunelle CL, Miller ML, Booij J, van den Brink W. The nicotinic acetylcholine receptor partial agonist varenicline and the treatment of drug dependence: a review. *Eur. Neuropsychopharmacol.* 2010 Feb; 20 (2): 69-79.

[64] Plebani JG, Lynch KG, Yu Q, Pettinati HM, O'Brien CP, Kampman KM. Results of an initial clinical trial of varenicline for the treatment of cocaine dependence. *Drug Alcohol Depend.* 2011 Sep 16.

[65] Pani PP, Trogu E, Vecchi S, Amato L. Antidepressants for cocaine dependence and problematic cocaine use. *Cochrane Database Syst. Rev.* 2011; 12: CD002950.

[66] Afshar M, Knapp CM, Sarid-Segal O, Devine E, Colaneri LS, Tozier L, et al. The Efficacy of Mirtazapine in the Treatment of Cocaine Dependence with Comorbid Depression. *Am. J. Drug Alcohol Abuse.* 2012 Jan 5.

[67] Winstanley EL, Bigelow GE, Silverman K, Johnson RE, Strain EC. A randomized controlled trial of fluoxetine in the treatment of cocaine dependence among methadone-maintained patients. *J. Subst. Abuse Treat.* 2011 Jan 24.

[68] Moeller FG, Schmitz JM, Steinberg JL, Green CM, Reist C, Lai LY, et al. Citalopram combined with behavioral therapy reduces cocaine use: a double-blind, placebo-controlled trial. *Am. J. Drug Alcohol Abuse.* 2007; 33 (3): 367-78.

[69] Barth KS, Malcolm RJ. Disulfiram: an old therapeutic with new applications. CNS Neurol Disord Drug Targets. 2010 Mar; 9 (1): 5-12.

[70] O'Shea B. Disulfiram revisited. *Hosp. Med.* 2000 Dec; 61 (12): 849-51.

[71] Barth KS, Malcolm RJ. Disulfiram: An Old Therapeutic with New Applications. *CNS Neurol. Disord. Drug Targets.* 2009 Oct 7.

[72] Higgins ST, Budney AJ, Bickel WK, Hughes JR, Foerg F. Disulfiram therapy in patients abusing cocaine and alcohol. *Am. J. Psychiatry.* 1993 Apr; 150 (4): 675-6.

[73] Carroll KM, Nich C, Ball SA, McCance E, Rounsavile BJ. Treatment of cocaine and alcohol dependence with psychotherapy and disulfiram. *Addiction.* 1998 May; 93 (5): 713-27.

[74] Carroll KM, Nich C, Ball SA, McCance E, Frankforter TL, Rounsaville BJ. One-year follow-up of disulfiram and psychotherapy for cocaine-alcohol users: sustained effects of treatment. *Addiction.* 2000 Sep; 95 (9): 1335-49.

[75] Pettinati HM, Kampman KM, Lynch KG, Xie H, Dackis C, Rabinowitz AR, et al. A double blind, placebo-controlled trial that combines disulfiram and naltrexone for treating co-occurring cocaine and alcohol dependence. *Addict. Behav.* 2008 May; 33 (5): 651-67.

[76] George TP, Chawarski MC, Pakes J, Carroll KM, Kosten TR, Schottenfeld RS. Disulfiram versus placebo for cocaine dependence in buprenorphine-maintained subjects: a preliminary trial. *Biol. Psychiatry.* 2000 Jun 15; 47 (12): 1080-6.

[77] Petrakis IL, Carroll KM, Nich C, Gordon LT, McCance-Katz EF, Frankforter T, et al. Disulfiram treatment for cocaine dependence in methadone-maintained opioid addicts. *Addiction.* 2000 Feb; 95 (2): 219-28.

[78] Oliveto A, Poling J, Mancino MJ, Feldman Z, Cubells JF, Pruzinsky R, et al. Randomized, double blind, placebo-controlled trial of disulfiram for the treatment of cocaine dependence in methadone-stabilized patients. *Drug Alcohol Depend.* 2011 Jan 15; 113 (2-3): 184-91.

[79] Malcolm R, Olive MF, Lechner W. The safety of disulfiram for the treatment of alcohol and cocaine dependence in randomized clinical trials: guidance for clinical practice. *Expert Opin. Drug Saf.* 2008 Jul; 7 (4): 459-72.

[80] Roache JD, Kahn R, Newton TF, Wallace CL, Murff WL, De La Garza R, 2nd, et al. A double-blind, placebo-controlled assessment of the safety of potential interactions

between intravenous cocaine, ethanol, and oral disulfiram. *Drug Alcohol Depend.* 2011 Dec 1; 119 (1-2): 37-45.

[81] Shinn AK, Greenfield SF. Topiramate in the treatment of substance-related disorders: a critical review of the literature. *J. Clin. Psychiatry.* 2010 May; 71 (5): 634-48.

[82] Reis AD, Castro LA, Faria R, Laranjeira R. Craving decrease with topiramate in outpatient treatment for cocaine dependence: an open label trial. *Rev. Bras. Psiquiatr.* 2008 Jun; 30 (2): 132-5.

[83] Kampman KM, Pettinati H, Lynch KG, Dackis C, Sparkman T, Weigley C, et al. A pilot trial of topiramate for the treatment of cocaine dependence. *Drug Alcohol Depend.* 2004 Sep 6; 75 (3): 233-40.

[84] Minozzi S, Amato L, Davoli M, Farrell M, Lima Reisser AA, Pani PP, et al. Anticonvulsants for cocaine dependence. *Cochrane Database Syst. Rev.* 2008 (2): CD006754.

[85] Ling W, Shoptaw S, Majewska D. Baclofen as a cocaine anti-craving medication: a preliminary clinical study. *Neuropsychopharmacology.* 1998 May; 18 (5): 403-4.

[86] Brebner K, Childress AR, Roberts DC. A potential role for GABA(B) agonists in the treatment of psychostimulant addiction. *Alcohol Alcohol.* 2002 Sep-Oct; 37 (5): 478-84.

[87] Haney M, Hart CL, Foltin RW. Effects of baclofen on cocaine self-administration: opioid- and nonopioid-dependent volunteers. *Neuropsychopharmacology.* 2006 Aug; 31 (8): 1814-21.

[88] Shoptaw S, Yang X, Rotheram-Fuller EJ, Hsieh YC, Kintaudi PC, Charuvastra VC, et al. Randomized placebo-controlled trial of baclofen for cocaine dependence: preliminary effects for individuals with chronic patterns of cocaine use. *J. Clin. Psychiatry.* 2003 Dec; 64 (12): 1440-8.

[89] Kahn R, Biswas K, Childress AR, Shoptaw S, Fudala PJ, Gorgon L, et al. Multi-center trial of baclofen for abstinence initiation in severe cocaine-dependent individuals. *Drug Alcohol Depend.* 2009 Jul 1; 103 (1-2): 59-64.

[90] Stoops WW, Blackburn JW, Hudson DA, Hays LR, Rush CR. Safety, tolerability and subject-rated effects of acute intranasal cocaine administration during atomoxetine maintenance. *Drug Alcohol Depend.* 2008 Jan 1; 92 (1-3): 282-5.

[91] Grabowski J, Shearer J, Merrill J, Negus SS. Agonist-like, replacement pharma-cotherapy for stimulant abuse and dependence. *Addict. Behav.* 2004 Sep; 29 (7): 1439-64.

[92] Gorelick DA. The rate hypothesis and agonist substitution approaches to cocaine abuse treatment. *Adv. Pharmacol.* 1998; 42: 995-7.

[93] Grabowski J, Rhoades H, Stotts A, Cowan K, Kopecky C, Dougherty A, et al. Agonist-like or antagonist-like treatment for cocaine dependence with methadone for heroin dependence: two double-blind randomized clinical trials. *Neuropsychopharmacology.* 2004 May; 29 (5): 969-81.

[94] Grabowski J, Rhoades H, Schmitz J, Stotts A, Daruzska LA, Creson D, et al. Dextroamphetamine for cocaine-dependence treatment: a double-blind randomized clinical trial. *J. Clin. Psychopharmacol.* 2001 Oct; 21 (5): 522-6.

[95] Shearer J, Wodak A, van Beek I, Mattick RP, Lewis J. Pilot randomized double blind placebo-controlled study of dexamphetamine for cocaine dependence. *Addiction.* 2003 Aug; 98 (8): 1137-41.

[96] Stoops WW, Vansickel AR, Lile JA, Rush CR. Acute d-amphetamine pretreatment does not alter stimulant self-administration in humans. *Pharmacol. Biochem. Behav.* 2007 May; 87 (1): 20-9.

[97] Rush CR, Stoops WW, Hays LR. Cocaine effects during D-amphetamine maintenance: a human laboratory analysis of safety, tolerability and efficacy. *Drug Alcohol Depend.* 2009 Jan 1; 99 (1-3): 261-71.

[98] Czoty PW, Martelle JL, Nader MA. Effects of chronic d-amphetamine administration on the reinforcing strength of cocaine in rhesus monkeys. *Psychopharmacology (Berl).* 2010 May; 209 (4): 375-82.

[99] Castells X, Casas M, Vidal X, Bosch R, Roncero C, Ramos-Quiroga JA, et al. Efficacy of central nervous system stimulant treatment for cocaine dependence: a systematic review and meta-analysis of randomized controlled clinical trials. *Addiction.* 2007 Dec; 102 (12): 1871-87.

[100] Moreno AY, Janda KD. Immunopharmacotherapy: vaccination strategies as a treatment for drug abuse and dependence. *Pharmacol. Biochem. Behav.* 2009 Apr; 92 (2): 199-205.

[101] Orson FM, Kinsey BM, Singh RA, Wu Y, Gardner T, Kosten TR. The future of vaccines in the management of addictive disorders. *Curr. Psychiatry Rep.* 2007 Oct; 9 (5): 381-7.

[102] Heading CE. TA-CD. Xenova. *IDrugs.* 2002 Nov; 5 (11): 1070-4.

[103] Kosten T, Rosen M, Bond J, Settles M, Roberts J, Shields J, et al. Human therapeutic cocaine vaccine: Safety and immunogenicity. *Vaccine.* 2002; 20: 1196-204.

[104] Martell BA, Mitchell E, Poling J, Gonsai K, Kosten TR. Vaccine pharmacotherapy for the treatment of cocaine dependence. *Biol. Psychiatry.* 2005 Jul 15; 58 (2): 158-64.

[105] Martell BA, Orson FM, Poling J, Mitchell E, Rossen RD, Gardner T, et al. Cocaine vaccine for the treatment of cocaine dependence in methadone-maintained patients: a randomized, double-blind, placebo-controlled efficacy trial. Arch Gen Psychiatry. 2009 Oct; 66 (10): 1116-23.

[106] Shen X, Kosten TR. Immunotherapy for Drug Abuse. *CNS Neurol. Disord. Drug Targets.* 2012 Jan 10.

[107] Haney M, Gunderson EW, Jiang H, Collins ED, Foltin RW. Cocaine-specific antibodies blunt the subjective effects of smoked cocaine in humans. *Biol. Psychiatry.* 2009 Jan 1; 67 (1): 59-65.

[108] Brimijoin S. Interception of Cocaine by Enzyme or Antibody Delivered with Viral Gene Transfer: A Novel Strategy for Preventing Relapse in Recovering Drug Users. *CNS Neurol. Disord. Drug Targets.* 2012 Jan 10.

[109] Hicks MJ, De BP, Rosenberg JB, Davidson JT, Moreno AY, Janda KD, et al. Cocaine Analog Coupled to Disrupted Adenovirus: *A Vaccine Strategy to Evoke High-titer Immunity Against Addictive Drugs. Mol. Ther.* 2011 Jan 4.

[110] Wee S, Hicks MJ, De BP, Rosenberg JB, Moreno AY, Kaminsky SM, et al. Novel Cocaine Vaccine Linked to a Disrupted Adenovirus Gene Transfer Vector Blocks Cocaine Psychostimulant and Reinforcing Effects. *Neuropsychopharmacology.* 2011 Sep 14.

In: Emerging Targets for Drug Addiction Treatment
Editor: Juan Canales

ISBN 978-1-62081-913-5
©2012 Nova Science Publishers, Inc.

Chapter 2

STIMULANTS:
NEUROIMAGING AND TREATMENTS

*Joanne C. Lin and Bruce R. Russell**
School of Pharmacy, University of Auckland, New Zealand

ABSTRACT

Psychostimulant abuse is an epidemic of global proportion; the associated medical, social and economic consequences have become a major problem worldwide. Stimulant drugs such as cocaine and amphetamine have approved medical use but are well documented to cause addiction. Recent advances in neuroimaging techniques have enabled research into the effects of stimulants on the human brain; positron emission tomography and magnetic resonance imaging studies confirm that stimulant addiction results in structural, functional and neurochemical damage. This chapter provides a review of neuroimaging research in human cocaine and methamphetamine users, and trials of medications for stimulant addiction with an emphasis on agonist replacement therapy and medications modulating related neurotransmitter systems.

1. INTRODUCTION

Drug addiction, or dependence, is one of the most pervasive, costly and challenging health and social problems [1]. The associated cost to society is prodigious when medical, economic, criminal and social factors are combined. The estimated overall costs of substance abuse in the USA, related health and crime consequences, loss of productivity, foster care and other social problems, exceed $600 billion annually which includes $181 billion for illicit drugs [2], while public expenditure on all aspects of drug phenomena in Europe was estimated at €34 billion in 2005 [3]. Addiction is defined as a chronic relapsing brain disorder characterised by a maladaptive pattern of substance use (the terms 'addiction' and 'dependence' will be used interchangeably throughout this chapter).

---

* Email: b.russell@auckland.ac.nz

DSM-IV Diagnostic Criteria for Alcohol and Drug Dependence

Tolerance	A need for markedly increased amounts of the substance to achieve intoxication or desired effect; or markedly diminished effect with continued use of the same amount of the substance.
Withdrawal	The characteristic withdrawal syndrome for a substance; or the same (or a closely related) substance is taken to relieve or avoid withdrawal symptoms.
Impaired control	The substance is often taken in larger amounts or over a longer period than was intended. A persistent desire or unsuccessful efforts to cut down or control substance use.
Time spent	A great deal of time is spent in activities necessary to obtain the substance, use the substance, or recover from its effects.
Neglect of activities	Important social, occupational, or recreational activities are given up or reduced because of substance use.
Continued use despite problems	The substance use is continued despite knowledge of having a persistent or recurrent physical or psychological problem that is likely to have been caused or exacerbated by the substance.

The diagnostic criteria for addiction have evolved over the past three decades with a shift from the emphasis and necessary criteria of tolerance and withdrawal to other factors more focused on compulsive use [4]. The Diagnostic and Statistical Manual of Mental Disorders 4th edition (DSM-IV) outlines seven criteria and states that addiction is as a "maladaptive pattern of substance use, leading to clinically significant impairment or distress as manifested by three or more of the following occurring in the same 12-month period" [5]. The number of criteria met by drug users can vary with the severity of addiction, the stage of the addiction process and the substance being used [6]. From a psychiatric perspective, drug addiction includes aspects of impulse control and compulsive disorders. Impulse control disorders are characterised by tension or arousal before committing an impulsive act, and pleasure, gratification or relief at the time of committing the act which may or may not be accompanied by feelings of regret, self-reproach or guilt [5]. In contrast, compulsive disorders are characterised by anxiety and stress beforehand, and relief from the stress by performing the compulsive behaviour. As an individual moves from impulsive to compulsive behaviour, there is a shift from positive reinforcement driving the motivated behaviour to negative reinforcement [7]. Drug addiction has been conceptualised as a disorder that evolves from impulsivity to compulsivity, and this shift often occurs either when there is increased access to the drug or when a more rapid route of administration is employed.

The onset and intensity of the 'high' and the subsequent dysphoria are dependent on the route of administration; for example, smoking cocaine is associated with a more rapid and intense high and dysphoria than the intranasal and oral routes [8-10]. All drugs of abuse act on the central nervous system and largely affect dopamine, noradrenaline and serotonin, as well as acetylcholine, glutamate and γ-amino butyric acid (GABA) [11]. Of these, dopamine has been consistently associated with reinforcing effects and is involved in the regulation of movement, reward, cognition, psychosis and numerous other functions [12]. Although different drugs of abuse have different acute mechanisms of action, there is evidence that they all converge on a common pathway in the limbic system [13-17]. Research has focused on the mesolimbic dopamine pathway, which projects from the ventral tegmental area (VTA) to the nucleus accumbens (NAc), amygdala, hippocampus and prefrontal cortex (18). The VTA-NAc pathway, along with other limbic regions, mediate the positive emotional effects of natural rewards, such as food, water and social interactions [19, 20]. It is also one of the most important substrates for the acute rewarding effects of all drugs of abuse. Drugs of abuse cause excessive release of dopamine, often surpassing the magnitude and duration of dopamine release that is triggered by natural rewards [21]. While dopamine increases induced by natural rewards undergo habituation, those produced by drugs of abuse do not [22]. This chapter will focus on cocaine and amphetamines – psychostimulants that have high abuse potential and are well documented to produce addiction. It will outline findings from studies of dependent participants using various neuroimaging techniques, as well as trials of pharmacological agents to treat amphetamine addiction.

2. STIMULANTS

Stimulant drugs such as cocaine, amphetamine and methamphetamine are approved for medical use, but also have considerable abuse potential [4]. These drugs act by increasing the amount of synaptic monoamine neurotransmitters in the synaptic cleft by blocking the reuptake of dopamine, noradrenaline and serotonin [23]; amphetamines also enhance the release of these neurotransmitters [24].

2.1. Cocaine

Cocaine, derived from the coca plant (*Erythroxylon coca*), has been a popular recreational drug for decades and has a long history of misuse. The powdered hydrochloride salt form can be snorted or dissolved in water then injected. 'Crack' is the street name given to cocaine that has been processed to make a rock crystal, which, when heated, produces vapours that are inhaled [25]. It was used early on as a local anaesthetic for ophthalmological work and today, the only accepted medical uses are local anaesthesia and vasoconstriction for some ear, nose and throat surgeries [26]. After the opiates and heroin, cocaine is the most problematic drug worldwide and the United Nations Office on Drugs and Crime estimated the prevalence of cocaine use in 2008 to be 0.3-0.4% of the adult population, or between 15 and 19 million people [27].

Cocaine acts by blocking synaptic reuptake mechanisms; this prevents reabsoprtion of the neurotransmitters dopamine and noradrenaline, resulting in higher concentrations of neurotransmitter in the synaptic cleft which then bind to postsynaptic receptors [28]. Acute administration of cocaine is associated with feelings of energy, decreased fatigue, a sense of wellbeing and increased confidence and talkativeness while prolonged cocaine use can cause depletion of neurotransmitters, which may account for the depression and craving associated with the cessation of drug use.

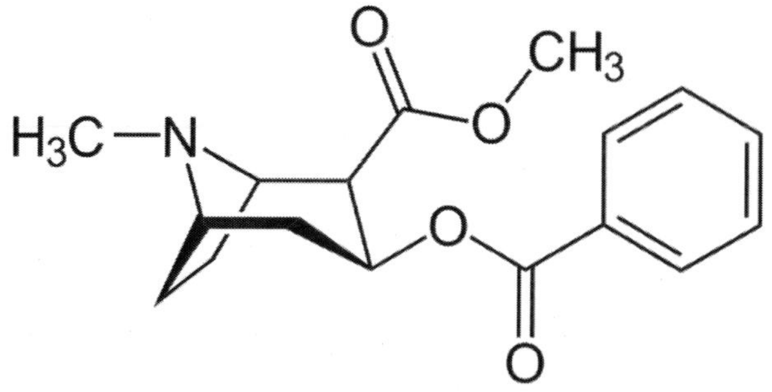

Figure 1. Chemical structure of cocaine.

2.2. Amphetamine-Type Stimulants

Amphetamine-type stimulants refer to a group of synthetic substances comprised of simple phenethylamines (primarily amphetamine, methamphetamine and methcathinone) and substituted phenethylamines i.e. the ecstasy-group substances (3, 4-methylenedioxymethamphetamine or MDMA and its analogues). While ecstasy-group substances are chemically related to the amphetamines, they differ structurally in terms of the methylenedioxy (-O-CH$_2$-O-) group attached to the ring of the phenethylamine molecule. In this respect, they more closely resemble the structure of mescaline – a hallucinogenic substance and, as a result, increase serotonin release and inhibit its reuptake to a greater extent than dopamine; their pharmacological effects are a blend of those seen following amphetamine and mescaline administration. It has been claimed that dependence on MDMA is unlikely to become a serious problem because the decrease in pleasurable or rewarding effects and contrasting increase in unpleasant effects following frequent drug use would diminish the incentive to use the drug in a manner that could give rise to dependence. This phenomenon occurs with the classical hallucinogens such as lysergic acid diethylamide or LSD, which have not proven to cause dependence to the same extent as drugs such as alcohol and the opioids [29]. Therefore, this chapter will primarily focus on simple phenethylamines D-amphetamine (or dexamphetamine) and methamphetamine; MDMA addiction will not be discussed. Amphetamines were originally synthesised for the treatment of asthma and used by the military for their anti-fatigue properties [30]. After the Second World War, an epidemic of methamphetamine abuse occurred in Japan when military stockpiles of amphetamines were released to the Japanese market [31]. Amphetamines are currently approved for use as adjuncts for short-term weight loss and in the treatment of narcolepsy and attention deficit-hyperactivity disorder (ADHD).

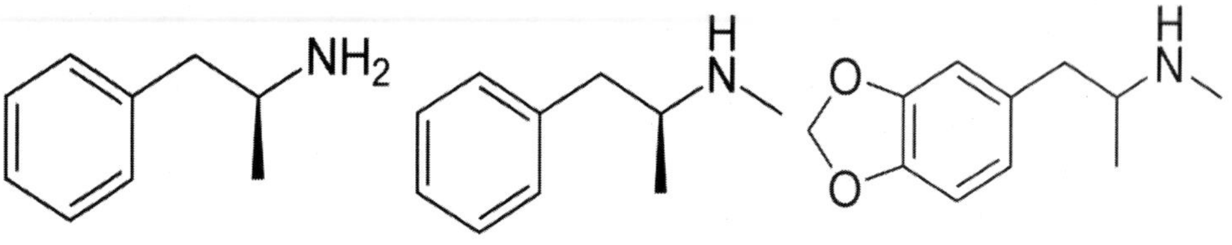

Figure 2. From left to right: the chemical structures of dexamphetamine, methamphetamine and MDMA.

Unlike the coca leaf or opium poppy, the manufacture of illicit amphetamines is not affected by geographical or environmental factors; laboratories can operate anywhere and be relocated. Furthermore, amphetamines can be synthesised from a variety of starting materials using a range of methods, consequently they are the second most commonly used illicit drugs. The global number of users is likely to exceed the number of opiate and cocaine users combined [27].

Similarly to cocaine, amphetamines increase synaptic concentrations of monoamines and have greater effects on noradrenaline than dopamine or serotonin [32]; however, the primary neuropharmacological action responsible for the psychostimulant and reinforcing effects appears to be the dopamine system [4]. In addition to blocking monoamine reuptake, amphetamines also stimulate the presynaptic release of neurotransmitters [28] and inhibit monoamine oxidase [33]. The stimulant effects of amphetamines are similar to those produced by cocaine, with a much longer duration of action due to an unusually long half-life – 1.1 hours when smoked, to 12.2 hours when used intravenously [34]. By contrast, the half-life of cocaine ranges from 48 to 75 minutes [35].

3. NEUROIMAGING

Neuroimaging encompasses a wide variety of techniques that enable assessment of the structure, function and pharmacology of the brain, and includes techniques that use X-rays (computed tomography or computed axial tomography), infrared light (diffuse optical imaging and event-related optical signal), magnetic fields and radioactively labelled chemicals.

This chapter will focus primarily on one radiotracer technique – positron emission tomorgraphy (PET)–and one magnetic resonance imaging (MRI) technique, with four different modalities–functional MRI (fMRI), structural MRI, diffusion tensor imaging (DTI) and proton magnetic resonance spectroscopy (MRS).

3.1. Positron Emission Tomography

Radiotracer studies are used in the measurement of molecular targets such as receptors, transporters and enzymes; they are the only techniques that allow for the direct assessment of blood flow, metabolism or neurochemical reactions in a particular region of the living brain. PET is a molecular imaging technique that has been used to capture markers of brain activity such as drug uptake, oxygen use, regional blood flow and the rate of glucose metabolism. The underlying technical principle involves a radiotracer administered into the blood stream that emits high-energy gamma-rays when a positron combines with an electron. The disintegration of particles from the positron-emitting radiotracer is recorded by sensors placed around the head, and reconstructed images reflect the location and concentration of the isotope for a given place. PET can locate activity changes in spatial resolution of 6 mm for all part parts of the brain and, although it is progressively being replaced by fMRI, PET remains necessary for molecular, receptor, neurotransmitter and gene imaging [36]. PET can be used to study drugs of abuse in a number of ways [37]:

1. Using radiolabelled drug to ascertain drug distribution in the brain and other organs
2. Using tracer doses of drug (where only a small fraction of binding sites is occupied) to investigate local concentrations of drug binding sites
3. Determining the degree of binding site occupancy by a drug
4. Measuring competitive binding between a radiolabelled drug and endogenous neurotransmitter
5. Examining the effects of drugs of abuse on other neurotransmitter systems
6. Investigating the activity of enzymes that transform the radiolabelled drug into a labelled product that is 'metabolically trapped' in tissues

A number of radiotracers are available to image neurochemistry relating to drug addiction, including ^{3}H-SCH23390 for dopamine D_1 receptors, ^{11}C-raclopride for D_2 receptors and ^{11}C-methylphenidate or ^{11}C-WIN35428 (a cocaine analogue) for dopamine transporters. SCH23390 has also been shown to interact potently with serotonin 5-HT$_2$ receptors as well as D_2 receptors [38]. Levels of monoamine oxidase A (MAO-A) and monoamine oxidase B (MAO-B) can also be measured with PET radiotracers ^{11}C-clorgyline and ^{11}C-deprenyl respectively. MAO-A is located predominantly within neurons while MAO-B is largely localised to glial cells and is involved in the metabolism of dopamine [39]. 2-^{18}F-fluoro-2-deoxy-D-glucose (FDG) can be used to measure brain glucose metabolism [40], which is considered a marker of brain function. PET has been used extensively in both preclinical and clinical research and can also be used for functional imaging during tasks; however, only human PET studies of dopaminergic function and cerebral metabolism in drug addiction will be discussed.

3.1.1. Cocaine

The role of dopamine in the psychostimulant actions of cocaine have been thoroughly investigated by animal studies, therefore PET studies of cocaine addiction have predominantly been centred around dopaminergic transmission. An early study by Volkow et al. [41] assessed the effects of chronic cocaine use on postsynaptic dopamine receptors in cocaine users with ^{18}F-N-methylspiroperidol (NMS). The ratio index represents the slope of the ratio of radioactivity in the striatum to radioactivity in the cerebellum, and is used as an index of postsynaptic dopamine receptor availability. Analysis of ratio index values found that non-detoxified cocaine users showed lower than normal uptake of NMS in the striatum but values of the participants who had been detoxified for four to five weeks did not differ from controls, suggesting that decreased receptor availability may be temporary and associated with the period of time since last cocaine use.

Volkow et al. [42], [43] then investigated the patterns of regional brain metabolism and D_2 receptor availability using FDG and NMS respectively, to determine whether regional brain function may be related to cocaine dependence and withdrawal. Participants in the early trial were studied within one to four weeks after their last dose of cocaine. Recently abstinent users displayed higher glucose metabolism rates than both longer abstinent users and controls, particularly in the orbitofrontal cortex and basal ganglia regions; however, no differences were observed between the longer abstinent group and controls. The selectivity of changes in glucose metabolism suggested that the regional metabolic abnormalities seen in cocaine users during the detoxification phase may be related to alterations in dopamine activity [42]. In the later trial, cocaine users exhibited significantly lower NMS uptake, indicating decreases in D_2

receptor availability, which persisted for up to three months after drug withdrawal. Correlational analysis showed that these decreases were significantly associated with lower metabolic rate in several frontal brain regions, most prominently in the orbitofrontal cortex and the cingulate gyri, suggesting that dopamine dysregulation of regions involved in motivational drive and affect may result in the loss of control that is responsible for drug-taking behaviour [43].

The relationship between dopamine transporter occupancy, blockade by cocaine and the subsequent subjective effects has also been evaluated. Volkow et al. [44] tested the ability to block or attenuate the high elicited by prior dopamine transporter blockade by administering two doses of methylphenidate 60 minutes apart and comparing responses in healthy drug-naïve male participants. Although pre-treatment with methylphenidate significantly reduced ligand binding, no association was found between the level of transporter occupancy and the subjective perception of a 'high'. However, a negative correlation was observed when transporter occupancy was close to 100% suggesting that greater than 80% transporter blockade needs to be achieved in order to prevent the high induced by cocaine [44]. These findings were extended in another study using ^{11}C-cocaine to measure the direct relationship between dopamine transporter blockade and the subjective effects of cocaine in current cocaine users [45]. Intravenous cocaine administration (0.3-0.6 mg/kg) resulted in 60-77% dopamine transporter blockade, and the magnitude of self-reported 'high' correlated with the degree of transporter occupancy in the striatum. Furthermore, the temporal course of self-reported feelings of 'high' paralleled that of cocaine concentration within the striatum, a region implicated in the regulation of motivation and reward. These findings suggest that a substitution medication for cocaine addiction would only be effective if given at doses that achieve almost complete dopamine transporter blockade [45]. The results of studies evaluating the potential for methylphenidate as a pharmacological substitute for stimulant addiction will be discussed further in later sections of this chapter.

The mechanisms involved in craving and the role of drug-related cues in addiction and relapse have also been investigated using FDG. Long-term cocaine users showed regional increases in metabolism within the cortex and medial temporal lobe when presented with cocaine-related cues [46]. Furthermore, there was a significant correlation between self-reported craving and regional glucose metabolism in the dorsolateral prefrontal cortex, medial temporal lobe – particularly in the amygdala – and cerebellum that was not seen in healthy control participants, suggesting that the effects of such cocaine-related stimuli are dependent upon a history of cocaine use. These regions correspond to a distributed neural network that links emotional and cognitive aspects of memory; therefore it is possible that the association between environmental cues and cocaine craving is mediated by this network [46]. Similar findings were observed in a later study by Bonson et al. [47] using neutral and cocaine-related visual cues and an evocative cocaine-related script. Cocaine-related stimuli elicited increased self-reported feelings of craving in cocaine users, which correlated with greater brain activations in the left amygdala/rhinal cortex, left lateral orbitofrontal cortex, right superior frontal cortex and left posterior insula. These results suggest that induction of drug craving involves a neural network which assigns incentive motivational value to environmental stimuli via activation of regions that process information about memories and emotions [47]. The identification of specific regional activation associated with craving may be important for directing future investigations into the mechanisms and therapeutic targets for relieving craving in drug addiction [46].

3.1.2. Methamphetamine

In animals, methamphetamine administration is well known to cause damage to dopamine terminals [48], and post-mortem data from human methamphetamine abusers indicate deficits in striatal dopamine markers [49]. McCann et al. [50] carried out the first PET study in living humans using ^{11}C-WIN35428 to investigate decrements in striatal dopamine transporter density in abstinent methamphetamine and methcathinone users. Results were compared to control participants and patients with early Parkinson's disease. Analysis revealed a significantly reduced density of ^{11}C-WIN35428-labelled dopamine transporter binding sites in the caudate nucleus and putamen of participants with a history of methamphetamine and methcathinone use compared to controls, though these decreases were not as pronounced as those observed in Parkinson's patients. A later longitudinal study using the dopamine transporter radioligand ^{11}C-methylphenidate provided evidence that losses in dopamine transporter density recover with abstinence [51]. Abstinent methamphetamine users were tested within six months of last methamphetamine use and again at least nine months later if they remained drug-free [52]. The results showed significantly higher ^{11}C-methylphenidate binding in the caudate and putamen of methamphetamine users following protracted abstinence suggesting significant recovery of dopamine transporter density in those who stayed drug free for at least nine months after the initial testing session. Furthermore, the period between test sessions positively correlated with dopamine transporter binding, indicating that the recovery of transporter binding may be, in part, a function of the duration of abstinence [51].

Previous PET studies of methamphetamine users have reported losses in dopamine transporters; however, the first study to investigate D_2 receptor density was carried out by Volkow et al. [53] using ^{11}C-raclopride. PET measures of D_2 receptors predominantly reflect levels of postsynaptic receptors [54]. Estimates of D_2 receptor availability in methamphetamine users were significantly lower than those in controls in the caudate and putamen, which may reflect receptor down regulation in response to high extracellular dopamine content secondary to the acute pharmacological effects of methamphetamine, as well as a methamphetamine-induced loss of dopamine transporters [49]. Reductions in D_2 receptor numbers have been reported in users of other drugs, including cocaine, alcohol and heroin, which suggest that reduced D_2 receptor density is not specific to any type of drug addiction but may underlie a common abnormality in addiction or be a common predisposing factor.

Because striatal D_2 receptor levels have been associated with metabolic rates in the orbitofrontal cortex of cocaine users [43], the authors investigated whether a similar dopaminergic dysfunction underlies the compulsive behaviour seen in methamphetamine users. D_2 receptor availability in the putamen of the methamphetamine group correlated significantly with metabolism in the orbitofrontal cortex, which may reflect dopamine-mediated striatal regulation of orbitofrontal activity via striato-thalamo-cortical pathways [55]. These findings are in accordance with previous findings in cocaine users, suggesting that D_2 receptor-mediated dysregulation of the orbitofrontal cortex may underlie a common mechanism for loss of control and compulsive behaviour in drug addiction.

The first study of the non-dopamine neurons in human methamphetamine users was carried out using FDG to assess changes in regions other than those innervated by dopamine [56]. Compared to control participants, global metabolic rate was significantly higher in methamphetamine users, particularly in the parietal cortex, and analysis of relative measures also showed significantly lower metabolism in the thalamus and striatum. The patterns of hypometabolism in the striatum closely reflect those of dopamine transporter reduction, and the authors propose that hypermetabolism in the parietal cortex – which is not significantly innervated by dopamine – is the result of methamphetamine-induced effects on circuits other than those modulated by dopamine i.e. glutamate and serotonin. These findings provide evidence that methamphetamine induces persistent metabolic changes in brain regions neuroanatomically connected with dopamine as well as in regions that are not innervated by dopamine.

Chronic methamphetamine use is often accompanied by psychiatric symptoms during intoxication or withdrawal; symptoms include psychosis and anxiety and mood disturbances, which can reflect neurochemical abnormalities detectable by PET. The relationship between dopamine transporter density and clinical characteristics was investigated in abstinent methamphetamine users with ^{11}C-WIN35428 [57]. In comparison to controls, methamphetamine users showed significantly lower dopamine transporter binding potentials in the caudate/putamen, nucleus accumbens and the prefrontal cortex. Moreover, significant correlations were observed between dopamine transporter binding potential and clinical measures in the caudate/putamen and nucleus accumbens but not the prefrontal cortex i.e. decreased dopamine transporter density in the caudate/putamen and nucleus accumbens was associated with increased durations of methamphetamine use and greater scores on the positive symptoms subscale of the Brief Psychiatric Rating Scale. These results show parallels between reduced dopamine transporter density in the brain, which was associated with the duration of methamphetamine use, and symptoms of a chronic psychotic state in methamphetamine users. However, transporters are only one part of the dynamics of the dopamine transmission and further study is needed to elucidate the causal mechanisms of methamphetamine-induced psychosis. London et al. [58] conducted a study to investigate whether dysfunction in certain regions may underlie negative affect in recently abstinent methamphetamine users.

The Beck Depression Inventory and State-Trait Anxiety Inventory were used to rate depression and anxiety, respectively, on the day of the PET examination; results were correlated with regional glucose metabolism measure using FDG. Methamphetamine users showed significantly higher self-ratings of depression and anxiety than control participants, and relative regional glucose metabolism also differed in several areas – lower in the anterior cingulate and insula, and higher in the lateral orbitofrontal area, middle and posterior cingulate, amygdala, ventral striatum and cerebellum. Self-reported depressive symptoms correlated significantly with relative glucose metabolism in limbic regions, and ratings of state and trait anxiety correlated negatively with glucose metabolism in the anterior cingulate cortex and left insula. Trait anxiety was also negatively associated with glucose metabolism in the orbitofrontal cortex and positively associated with amygdala activity. These results identified brain substrates of affective dysfunction in recently abstinent methamphetamine users, which may provide potential targets for pharmacological intervention in the treatment of addiction [58].

3.2. Magnetic Resonance Imaging

MRI includes a variety of techniques that do not use ionising radiation but instead use a powerful magnetic field to align the atoms in the body which are then exposed to a beam of radio waves. MRI detects radio signals emitted by the atoms, which differ based on proton composition of tissue and has been an invaluable tool for providing insight into the structure, function and biochemistry of the human brain, in both clinical settings and research.

3.2.1. Functional MRI

fMRI has the ability to detect small magnetic fields induced by increases in blood oxygen that occur in areas of heightened neuronal activity [59]. The most common form of fMRI measures changes in magnetic fields associated with the ratio of oxygenated to deoxygenated haemoglobin, referred to as the blood oxygenation level-dependent or BOLD contrast [60]. During activation of a brain region, this ratio changes as increased delivery of diamagnetic oxygenated blood into that region temporarily surpasses the consumption, consequently decreasing the amount of paramagnetic deoxygenated haemoglobin. Having lower levels of deoxygenated haemoglobin in a region of the brain alters the T2*-weighted magnetic resonance signal and results in less rapid signal decay [61]. The recorded signal is stronger; hence, deoxygenated haemoglobin is sometimes considered an endogenous contrast enhancing agent. This small signal increase – typically about 1% or less – serves as a marker of functional activation and can vary depending on the strength of the applied field [59, 61]. The magnitude of the signal is dependent upon the changes in blood flow and volume within a tissue, as well the change in local oxygen tension so there is no straightforward relationship between signal change and a single physiological parameter [61]. Although, unlike PET, fMRI cannot report absolute changes such as units of blood flow, it allows for visualisation of neural activities with higher spatial and temporal resolution than PET or single-photon emission computed tomography (SPECT) by monitoring changes in blood flow-induced signals in real time. Advances in gradient coil technology have allowed ultra-fast imaging, in which complete cross-sectional images are recorded in 50-100 ms, permitting multi-slice recording of the entire brain within seconds. Different task-related stimuli can be presented to a participant during fMRI and can localise changes in basic functions including primary sensory areas, areas involved in simple motor tasks or higher-order areas responsible for cognitive function. The haemodynamic response to repeated stimuli over a typical experimental time course is recorded as a series of low resolution images which are then mapped onto high-resolution anatomical images and analysed.

3.2.1.1. Cocaine

Functional neuroimaging in cocaine dependence indicates prefrontal deficits, suggesting that cocaine users show attentional biases toward drug-related stimuli, poor inhibitory control and compromised behavioural monitoring and evaluation [62]. Attentional control has been assessed using Stroop tasks where irrelevant information requires participants to engage cognitive control to inhibit a prepotent response and execute a task-relevant response [63]. Typical versions of the Stroop task present words in different font colours and require participants to ignore the word name and respond to the font colour (colour-word Stroop). 'Emotional' Stroop tasks present drug-related colour words, or drug-related pictures surrounded by coloured borders and require participants to ignore the picture and respond to the border colour (colour-word drug Stroop) [64].

The neural mechanisms underlying attentional biases have not been extensively studied. Goldstein et al. [65] conducted an imaging study using with the colour-word drug Stroop to investigate the role of the anterior cingulate and orbitofrontal cortices in the processing of salient cues. The task produced bilateral activation of the anterior cingulate cortex, a region frequently implicated in cognitive dysfunction. Hypoactivation was observed in the rostral anterior cingulate and medial orbitofrontal cortices of cocaine users for drug-related words compared to neutral words, which correlated with more errors committed for drug-related words. These results suggest that the abovementioned regions may contribute to different aspects of drug-related responses. Brewer et al. [66] used the colour-word Stroop to investigate the relationship between regional brain activation and treatment outcomes using behavioural therapy. During the Stroop task, cocaine users activated similar brain regions as those reported in non-addicted individuals – the anterior cingulate cortex, dorsolateral prefrontal cortex, parietal lobe, insula and striatum; however, activation in corticostriatal regions were correlated with reported abstinence and cocaine-free urine toxicology. These findings suggest that the neurocircuitry underlying cognitive control may play a role in behavioural treatment outcomes and that neural activation patterns during cognitive tasks can be predictors of treatment response. Attention switching studies assess switching between externally presented stimuli (e.g. between sensory modalities or between competing stimuli in one modality) [67] or between task sets (e.g. between mathematical operations and language-based operations) [68]. Attentional control of thoughts may be particularly relevant to drug abuse as perseverative thinking is characteristic of many clinical conditions including drug dependence [62]. Garavan [69] operationalised attentional control of thoughts in a task which required participants to switch between items held in working memory. Using such a task, Kübler et al. [70] found evidence of impaired attention switching in cocaine users. These impairments manifested as hypoactivity in the cingulate and prefrontal areas and putamen, while other task-related cortical areas, such as the dorsolateral prefrontal and anterior frontal cortices [71] were unaffected. This finding provides evidence for the neurological basis of impairment in disengaging attention from drug-related thoughts that characterises drug-seeking behaviour and/or contribute to the maintenance of addiction [62, 70].

Frontal lobe functions are thought to be involved in the control and regulation of behaviour in cocaine users [72]. A key function of this region is to control behaviour via inhibitory processes that suppress or terminate prepotent responses [73]. The failure to develop adequate inhibitory control and/or the loss of previously learned inhibitory control may have profound effects on the ability of an individual to gate prepotent behaviours, such as cocaine use [74]. The GO-NOGO task requires the suppression of prepotent behaviours and has been conducted with and without varying working memory demands to assess inhibitory control in active cocaine users [74, 75]. In both studies, cocaine users showed a compromised ability to exert control over strong prepotent urges that was associated with reduced activity in the anterior cingulate cortex, insular regions and the left inferior frontal gyrus. These data demonstrate that midline areas of the anterior cingulate are critical for cognitive control and are less responsive in cocaine users, suggesting that addiction may be accompanied by a disruption of brain structures that are critical for higher-order cognitive control. With higher working memory demands, increased activity was observed in the left cerebellum of cocaine users, which may indicate a compensatory response to diminished prefrontal activation. The results indicate that cocaine users experience difficulty in inhibiting actions, particularly when working memory demands increase, which is the case during cue-induced craving [47]. This provides support for the importance of cognitive functions in maintaining abuse or predisposing users towards relapse. Improving our understanding of the neural activity associated with stress and stress-induced drug craving could be beneficial for the development of treatments to prevent relapse in cocaine dependence.

3.2.1.2. Methamphetamine

fMRI has also been used to assess the neural substrates of cognitive function relevant to methamphetamine addiction; impairments have been observed in tasks of decision making and cognitive control. Cognitive impairment may contribute to and promote maintenance of the maladaptive actions associated with drug-seeking behaviour and addiction [76]. The orbitofrontal cortex plays a vital role in stimulus-reinforcement association learning and the correction of these associations when contingencies change [77]. Decision making, which involves balancing expectations with stimulus-associated rewards or reinforcing possibilities, is one of three behavioural functions affected by orbitofrontal and dorsolateral cortex dysregulation [78]. The decision making process itself involves several cognitive and non-cognitive functions [79], such as attention, working memory [80], contingency approximation [81, 82], hypothesis testing [82], impulsivity [83, 84] and risk taking [85]. Paulus et al. [79] used a two-choice prediction task to investigate whether methamphetamine users in early abstinence showed altered decision making rules. Analysis revealed that methamphetamine users relied more heavily on an outcome-dependent strategy (win-stay/lose-shift) and the magnitude of these behavioural differences decreased with increasing duration of abstinence. This increased use of win-stay/lose-shift strategy supports the hypothesis that methamphetamine users are more driven by the immediately preceding outcome, even in situations without a priori advantageous or disadvantageous response bias. Furthermore, methamphetamine users displayed more task-related activation in the bilateral prefrontal, parietal and insular cortices but showed no activation in the left prefrontal, bilateral ventromedial prefrontal and right orbitofrontal cortices. The discrepancies in task-related activation between methamphetamine users and controls are consistent with previous studies, which show those areas are essential in the decision making process [85, 86]. A further study using the two-choice prediction task investigated whether methamphetamine users exhibited altered sensitivity to different degrees of success or failure, as well as the influence of stimulus presentation on response during decision making [87]. Recently abstinent methamphetamine users were found to be no more or less sensitive to success or failure than controls. The increase in win-stay/lose-shift consistent responses by methamphetamine users was independent of success rate, rather a result of an increased response to the previous stimulus and not due to altered processing of success or failure. Irrespective of error rate, methamphetamine users showed diminished task-related activation in the bilateral inferior prefrontal and dorsolateral prefrontal cortices, as well as in the bilateral parietal cortex and left superior temporal gyrus. While control participants showed success-related patterns of activation in the left insula, middle frontal gyrus, precuneus and inferior parietal lobe, activation in these areas of methamphetamine users was inversely related to the degree of outcome predictability i.e. highest activation when the outcome was most unpredictable. These findings are consistent with the idea that stimulant addiction is a state where stimuli exert a strong influence on response selective, regardless of associated outcomes [76].

Paulus et al. [88] conducted the first study using fMRI to predict relapse in substance-dependent participants. Performance on the two-choice prediction task was assessed in recently abstinent methamphetamine users, and participants were followed up one year after the imaging session. As hypothesised, methamphetamine users who relapsed during the follow-up period showed less activation in the dorsolateral prefrontal, parietal and temporal cortices and the insula – a network of structures involved in decision making. fMRI activation patterns within the right insular, posterior cingulate and temporal cortices correctly predicted 20 of 22 participants who did not relapse and 17 of 18 participants who did; upon regression analysis, activation in the right middle frontal and middle temporal gyri and posterior cingulate were identified as the best predictors of time to relapse. These results suggest that functional neuroimaging may prove a valuable clinical tool for assessing susceptibility to relapse.

Chronic methamphetamine use is also associated with structural deficits in the frontal and basal ganglia regions that play an important role in inhibitory control, which is closely related to impulsivity. Impulsivity has been operationalised in terms of the inability to inhibit prepotent actions – people who are impulsive have difficulty inhibiting action, whereas people who are not impulsive find it easier to do so [89]. 'Delay discounting', the relationship between the delay and value of reinforcers, has been hypothesised to be the basis of impulsivity [90]. Rewards and punishments are more potent reinforcers when they are immediate rather than delayed; this may be particularly relevant to addiction as the rewarding effects of drug use are relatively immediate and the consequent adverse effects tend to be delayed, and drug users tend to devalue or discount future rewards. The ventromedial prefrontal cortex, including the orbitofrontal cortex, is indirectly involved in the valuation of delayed rewards. Monterosso et al. [91] and Hoffman et al. [92] combined the Delay Discounting Task with fMRI to assess this phenomenon in current and recently abstinent methamphetamine users. Behaviourally, methamphetamine users showed more delay discounting than control participants – the control group was approximately indifferent in choosing between $20 immediately and $28 delayed by one month, whereas the methamphetamine users group was approximately indifferent in choosing between $20 immediately and $47 delayed by one month, showing a greater than normal willingness to trade reward amount for immediacy [91]. Analysis revealed significantly different neural recruitment among methamphetamine users because control participants displayed minimal recruitment during 'easy choice' blocks, while recruitment during 'easy choice' blocks in methamphetamine users was close to the level observed in 'hard choice' blocks which may indicate inefficiency of cortical processing related to decision making. Control participants displayed more robust cortical activation in the anterior cingulate, dorsal anterior cingulate and right dorsolateral prefrontal cortices – the anterior part of a brain system that connects working memory, spatially-directed attention [93, 94] and cognitive control [95]. Interestingly, amygdala activation in methamphetamine users during choice of delayed rewards was associated with a greater degree of discounting, which may represent the aversive nature of picking the deferred option. The authors suggest that methamphetamine users who discount more heavily may be at greater risk of relapse, therefore heavy discounting may provide a target for pharmacological and psychosocial intervention aimed at changing the magnitude of preference for immediate rewards [91].

3.2.2. Structural MRI

The investigation of structural changes in the brain using MRI has become increasingly important for the study of addiction. Pathological changes resulting in cell loss manifest as loss of brain tissue or atrophy, which can be detected by structural MRI [96]. Methods of analysing brain atrophy include visual inspection by experienced radiologists or manual measurement of structures of interest; traditionally, the most commonly employed method was region of interest (ROI)-based volumetric analysis. ROI-based analysis requires manual delineation of the regions and can be very accurate; however, the process is time consuming and researchers must have the requisite anatomical knowledge. More recently, with the advancement of MRI, automated techniques have been developed to enable the rapid exploratory assessment of atrophy across large study groups and circumvent the need for manual delineation and subjective visual inspection. Voxel-based morphometry (VBM) is one such automated tool that is used to investigate changes in brain tissue concentration [97, 98], thus allowing assessment of damage within a structure even if its overall size has not changed. The process involves spatial normalisation of individual data – typically high resolution T1-weighted volumetric images – to the same stereotactic space, extracting and smoothing the grey matter and then performing statistical analysis across all voxels in the image to localise group differences which can then be used to infer the presence of atrophy or tissue expansion [96, 97]. Although VBM can be used to investigate both grey and white matter density, the majority of VBM studies in clinical populations focus on grey matter changes. Abnormalities in white matter may be assessed more accurately with other imaging techniques discussed below.

3.2.2.1. Cocaine

In addition to the functional abnormalities associated with cocaine use, structural abnormalities have also been reported. An early volumetric analysis of the prefrontal lobe of abstinent polysubstance users found that participants displayed significantly lower prefrontal lobe volume with increasing years of cocaine use [99]; however, as participants were polysubstance users, with all participants reporting alcohol use and half of the participants reporting 2-15 year histories of heroin use, these results may not be attributable to cocaine alone. Another study evaluated the relationship between age, and frontal and temporal lobe volumes in young male cohorts of cocaine and methamphetamine users [100]. A significant negative correlation was observed between age and total temporal volume of cocaine users, but not in methamphetamine users or controls. Further segmentation of brain regions into grey and white matter revealed that the negative correlation was predominantly induced by a significant age-related decline in grey matter volume. The magnitude of euphoric effects of cocaine has previously been negatively associated with ventricular-brain ratio [101], suggesting that reductions in cortical grey matter volumes may be related to a diminished capacity to experience the cocaine-induced 'high'. Therefore, it is possible that utilising cortical grey matter volumes as a marker of individual susceptibility to the euphoric effects of drugs of abuse may be of relevance to the development of pharmacotherapy for addiction [100].

Franklin et al. [102] carried out the first VBM study in cocaine-dependent participants to determine whether cocaine use is associated with structural changes within regions involved in decision-making processes and autonomic arousal. Analysis revealed significant decreases in grey matter density in the ventromedial orbitofrontal, anterior cingulate, anteroventral insular and superior temporal cortices of cocaine-dependent participants, which may reflect decreased neuronal content. No areas of increased grey matter or white matter differences were observed. Abnormalities in these particular regions may contribute to interrupted or imbalanced cognitive processing and may underlie the characteristic behavioural patterns associated with cocaine addiction [102]. Another study utilised VBM to relate functional impairments to possible structural abnormalities in short-term abstinent cocaine users, with a priori regions based on fMRI data from the same group. Lower grey matter density was observed in the frontal cortex of cocaine users – the cingulate gyrus, lateral prefrontal cortex, and medial and lateral aspects of the orbitofrontal cortex, but no group differences were seen in white matter. These areas overlap with findings from PET studies which showed less activation in the right lateral prefrontal cortex during the Iowa Gambling [103] and Stroop Interference Tasks [104], and greater activation in the cingulate gyrus, suggesting a relationship between structural integrity and functional performance. Recently, Hanlon et al. [105] carried out the first study to directly compare cognitive performance and neuro-structural integrity in recently abstinent cocaine users with both current users and non-drug-using controls. Current users showed significantly lower cortical and subcortial tissue density relative to controls but tissue density of abstinent users did not differ from healthy levels. Furthermore, cortical grey matter density correlated with performance in several tests of cognitive function with superior performance by abstinent users compared to current users. Considered together, the results suggest that individuals who are able to remain abstinent for a period more than one month may have more cortical grey matter and greater cognitive ability than individuals who continue drug use, indicating grey matter normalisation with protracted abstinence.

Sim et al. [106] conducted a study using an optimised VBM technique to study cerebellar structural abnormalities in cocaine users. Optimised VBM [107] incorporates additional spatial processing steps to improve image registration and segmentation to increase sensitivity and reduce voxel misclassification errors compared to standard VBM methods. Cocaine users showed lower grey matter density in the bilateral premotor cortex, right orbitofrontal cortex, bilateral temporal cortex, left thalamus and cerebellum compared to controls, as well as significantly lower white matter density in the cerebellum. The changes in grey and white cerebellar density correlated with deficits in executive function and decreased motor performance, suggesting that the cerebellum is vulnerable to cocaine-induced effects and such deficits may contribute to neuropsychological deficits and motor dysfunction.

Tensor-based morphometry (TBM) is a more recent voxel-based method for estimating changes in brain structure [108], and has been shown to provide methodological improvements over VBM. The Jacobian determinant is one of the main TBM metrics that directly measures tissue growth or atrophy [109]; the main advantage of TBM is that it can be applied directly to Jacobian determinants without the need for tissue segmentation or spatial smoothing [110, 111]. A recent study failed to detect any cocaine-related volume differences in any brain structure with both TBM and VBM [112]. The authors suggest that this lack of difference may be due to variations in cohorts and demographic factors as well as analysis methods. Evidence from studies using other MRI modalities suggests that cocaine use is associated with relatively limited damage to myelin and axonal injury and some gliosis [113-115]. While demyelination and axonal loss can result in reduced tissue volume, gliosis has the opposite effect; therefore, the lack of overall volumetric changes seen here may not be surprising.

3.2.2.2. Methamphetamine

The strongest evidence for stimulant-associated changes in brain structure, and possible stimulant-induced neurotoxicity, has been drawn from studies relating to methamphetamine use. Bartzokis et al. [100] carried out the first controlled study to measure structural differences in methamphetamine users compared to cocaine users and controls. Both methamphetamine and cocaine users displayed significantly smaller temporal lobe volumes but only cocaine users showed a significant age-related decline. The reduction in temporal lobe volume was localised to grey matter suggesting that these drugs may be associated with region- and drug-specific reductions in brain volume that exceed 'normal' age-related loss of cortical grey matter. In a later trial, high-resolution MRI was combined with computational brain-mapping techniques to determine the pattern of structural brain changes associated with chronic methamphetamine use in the cortex, hippocampus, white matter and ventricles [116]. Analysis revealed that methamphetamine-dependent participants had lower grey matter in the cingulate, limbic and paralimbic regions, as well as smaller hippocampal volumes, which correlated with memory performance on a word-recall task, and significant white matter hypertrophy. The authors suggest that chronic methamphetamine use is associated with a selective pattern of cerebral deterioration, particularly in the medial temporal lobe and limbic cortices, and white matter hypertrophy may reflect adaptive glial changes or altered myelination in response to chronic drug exposure [116]. Chang et al. [117] carried out a study in short-term abstinent methamphetamine users and proposed that evaluation of striatal structures may provide insights into methamphetamine-induced brain injury. Methamphetamine users showed enlarged bilateral putamen and globus pallidus but uncompromised cognitive performance relative to controls. However, poor cognitive performance and high cumulative lifetime methamphetamine use were associated with smaller striatal structures, suggesting that striatal enlargement occurs only during early phases of drug dependence as a compensatory response to methamphetamine-induced injury and greater cumulative methamphetamine use eventually leads to reduced striatal volume and poorer cognitive performance [117].

In accordance with previous findings, significantly larger striatal volumes were observed in abstinent methamphetamine users in a study examining the separate and combined effects of methamphetamine dependence and HIV infection on brain morphology [118]. The caudate nucleus, lenticular nucleus and nucleus accumbens showed significant methamphetamine-associated increases, with a larger increase in the nucleus accumbens of younger methamphetamine users without HIV. Significant increases in parietal lobe volume of methamphetamine users were also observed, which correlated with more severe cognitive impairment; however, lower cortical volumes were observed in HIV-positive individuals which also correlated with cognitive impairment suggesting that larger parietal lobe volumes are unlikely to represent an adaptive compensatory mechanism to methamphetamine-induced neurotoxicity as proposed for striatal volume increases.

A study by Kim et al. [119] was the first to use VBM with methamphetamine-dependent participants to assess grey matter density, as well as the first to compare short-term and long-term abstinent users. Significant differences in grey matter were observed between three groups – the short-term abstinent group had lower right middle frontal grey matter density than the long-term abstinent group who had lower grey matter density than healthy controls. This pattern of results was also observed for performance during the Wisconsin Card Sorting Task – a task that assesses the ability to identify abstract categories and shift cognitive sets, and has been used as a measure of frontal lobe damage [120]. The short-term abstinent group committed the greatest number of total errors relative to long-term abstinent users and controls. The authors proposed that decreases in grey matter density may be related to microscopic neuronal injury from methamphetamine-induced ischaemic changes or dopaminergic neurotoxicity, and that deficits in prefrontal grey matter density may partially recover with long-term abstinence [119]. A more recent study by Schwartz et al. [121] used VBM to relate regional grey matter differences and whole brain segmentation volumes to performance on the Delay Discounting Task. Recently abstinent methamphetamine users displayed higher impulsivity in the task, and had reduced grey matter density in the bilateral insula, which has not previously been reported, and in the left middle frontal gyrus, which has been associated with impaired cognitive control. Length of abstinence was associated grey matter density in several regions – positively correlated with the bilateral amygdala and putamen, and negatively correlated with cortical density in the right middle frontal gyrus which suggests that abstinence from methamphetamine may result in volumetric changes or that volumes in these regions are predictive of the ability to maintain abstinence [121].

There appears to be considerable variability in reports of the location and nature of anatomical changes associated with methamphetamine use, further investigation will lead to better understanding and development of treatment for methamphetamine-induced damage.

3.2.3. Diffusion Tensor Imaging

DTI measures diffusivity of water molecules and shows the preferential orientation of movement in white matter tissue [122]. It provides information about the microstructure and organisation of white matter which is not available with other imaging methods, and allows for quantitative assessment of the integrity of anatomical connectivity in white matter. Isotropic diffusion describes diffusion in the absence of barriers where water molecules undergo Brownian motion in all directions, whereas anisotropic diffusion refers to diffusion where water molecules exhibit directional preference. High anisotropy is observed in organised structures such as fibres in white matter since water diffusion is restricted along the length of tracts. Decreased anisotropy may imply greater diffusivity of water related to white matter pathology or loss of fibre integrity. Fractional anisotropy (FA) is the most commonly used index for quantifying anisotropy [123]; it is a scalar measure ranging from 0 to 1, where 0 indicates isotropic diffusion and 1 represents anisotropic diffusion. FA is mathematically related to the diffusivity values – eigenvalues – of the diffusion tensor along three principal directions. Animal studies have suggested that individual eigenvalues are more specific markers of myelination and axonal morphology than FA or mean diffusivity [124, 125]. Diffusivities perpendicular to axonal fibres are rarely considered separately, and are usually averaged. It has been shown that demyelination increases diffusion perpendicular to the direction of the tract (radial diffusion, $\lambda_2 + \lambda_3/2$ or $\lambda\perp$) with minimal effect on diffusion along the tract (axial diffusion or λ_1); conversely, axonal damage results in decreased λ_1 with relatively little effect on $\lambda\perp$ [124]. Changes in diffusion eigenvalues could potentially be used to differentiate myelin loss and axonal injury. Diffusion data can also be used to trace brain pathways by calculating the orientation of maximum diffusion at each point and using these orientation estimates to reconstruct a pathway that corresponds to the underlying fibre pathway [126]. To date, no tractography studies have been carried in participants with stimulant addiction.

3.2.3.1. Cocaine

Cocaine dependence is associated with white matter abnormalities which occur in multiple locations; however, it has been suggested that investigating white matter hyperintensities is neither specific nor sensitive enough to identify subtle abnormalities in frontal white matter [127]. Therefore, Lim et al. [127] carried out the first study to show that cocaine dependence may be associated with compromised white matter microstructure *in vivo*. The effects of cocaine were determined in different levels of the frontal and temporal lobes, as well as the corpus callosum. Cocaine-dependent participants showed significantly lower FA in frontal white matter at the anterior-commissure-posterior commissure (AC-PC) plane. Compromised white matter integrity was predominantly observed in the inferior frontal brain regions, and no significant changes in white matter integrity were observed in the temporal lobes or corpus callosum. Disrupted connectivity in inferior frontal regions is consistent with hypothesised anatomical circuits, implicating the orbitofrontal cortex in addiction-related phenomena such as craving and compulsive-repetitive behaviours [77, 128]. In a later study by Moeller et al. [129], reduced FA in the anterior corpus callosum was negatively correlated with impulse control and positively correlated with the ability to discriminate between 'target' and 'distracter' stimuli in a memory task. These findings are consistent with prior theories suggesting frontal cortical involvement in impaired inhibitory control in cocaine dependence [73], but may also suggest reduced corpus callosum function manifested as impaired interhemispheric communication rather than damage to the prefrontal cortex [129].

To gain a more specific understanding of the underlying pathology of white matter changes in cocaine dependence, studies have examined diffusion eigenvalues [114, 115, 130]. Higher $\lambda_\perp$ has consistently been observed in frontal and parietal regions, as well as the corpus callosum of cocaine users. Measures of white matter integrity also correlated with decision-making deficits in the Iowa Gambling Task, suggesting that compromised white matter integrity may be related to functional impairments in decision making [130].

Studies have also combined DTI with other imaging techniques to allow for concurrent evaluation of the macrostructural and microstructural correlates of cocaine dependence. Lim et al. [131] showed that cocaine dependence was associated with significantly lower FA in inferior frontal white matter with trends toward smaller white and grey matter volumes in the same region. A later study by Romero et al. [132] also found significantly lower FA values in the bilateral inferior frontal white matter, along with higher FA values in the anterior cingulate white matter of cocaine-dependent participants. Macrostructural analysis also revealed a loss in inferior frontal and anterior cingulate white matter volume [132].

Although white matter abnormalities have been identified in cocaine-dependent participants, the relationship between white matter integrity and treatment outcome is not well understood. Xu et al. [133] directly investigated how measures of white matter integrity related to treatment outcomes in cocaine-dependent participants seeking behavioural therapy. Pre-treatment white matter integrity was assessed in participants who received eight weeks of behavioural therapy; DTI parameters were then correlated with measures of treatment outcome. Multiple DTI measures were correlated with self-reported and urine toxicology-based measures of abstinence, showing that worse white matter integrity at treatment onset is associated with poorer abstinence-based outcomes [133]. Further research into the neurobiological characteristics of successfully abstinent participants showed distinct differences between abstinent cocaine users and controls, as well as among short-, mid- and long-term abstinent subgroups. Higher FA in the right anterior thalamic radiation and right anterior cingulum, and lower FA in the left superior longitudinal fasciculus was associated with longer abstinence, suggesting that FA differences across abstinence durations may reflect dynamic patterns of brain changes in addiction and recovery [134].

3.2.3.2. Methamphetamine

The first DTI study of methamphetamine-dependent participants was carried out by Chung et al. [135], exploring the changes in frontal white matter integrity of long-term abstinent users. Frontal executive function was also assessed using the Wisconsin Card Sorting Task. Methamphetamine users displayed significantly lower FA in three regions of interest – the left and right frontal white matter at the AC-PC plane and the right frontal white matter above the AC-PC plane. Methamphetamine users also committed more errors during the task but only the right frontal white matter above the AC-PC plane negatively correlated with task errors, supporting the hypothesis that frontal white matter integrity may underlie impaired executive function seen in methamphetamine-dependent participants. In a later trial, Tobias et al. [136] used FA as a possible index of gliosis and investigated white matter abnormalities of methamphetamine users during early abstinence. Methamphetamine users displayed significantly lower FA in the right prefrontal white matter above the AC-PC plane, in the midline genu of the corpus callosum, bilateral midcaudal superior corona radiata and right perforant fibres. Changes in FA appear to be limited to late-myelinating structures and, considered together with evidence from previous studies using different MRI modalities (structural MRI, MRS and PET), these findings suggest that frontal white matter and late-myelinating regions are more vulnerable to the effects of methamphetamine.

Kim et al. [137] also assessed the relationship between white matter integrity and impaired cognitive function using the Wisconsin Card Sorting Task in short-term abstinent methamphetamine users. This was the first study to evaluate microstructural abnormalities specifically in the corpus callosum using diffusion eigenvalues. Methamphetamine users displayed significantly lower FA values in the genu of the corpus callosum, as well as lower λ_1 but higher λ_2 and λ_3. Methamphetamine users also performed significantly worse in the task and demonstrated a significant negative correlation between FA and total errors in the genu. There was also a significant positive correlation between λ_2 in the genu and total errors, but not with λ_3. This interesting finding might suggest that λ_2 is more closely related to myelin integrity and is the main source of FA reduction in the genu of the corpus callosum, which, in turn, is associated with impairment of frontal cognitive function [137]. The relationship between behavioural regulation (i.e. cognitive control) and white matter microstructure has also been investigated in long-term abstinent methamphetamine users using the Stroop task [138]. FA and diffusion eigenvalues were obtained in the corpus callosum and correlated with behavioural measures. No group differences were observed in DTI indices in the corpus callosum; however, behavioural analysis revealed that methamphetamine users exhibited greater Stroop interference compared to control participants, which manifested as longer reaction times. Greater Stroop interference significantly correlated with lower FA in the genu of methamphetamine users suggesting that disruptions in white matter integrity may contribute to maladaptive decision making [138]. The basal ganglia have not been previously investigated with DTI; a recent study evaluated the diffusion tensor properties of white matter and subcortical brain regions in a cohort of chronic methamphetamine users [139]. In comparison to controls, methamphetamine users exhibited significantly lower FA in the frontal white matter, as well as higher λ_1 and $\lambda\perp$ in the left caudate. The apparent diffusion coefficient (ADC) describes the three-dimensional mobility of water in brain tissue, with higher values indicating greater diffusivity. Although a higher ADC was observed in the left caudate, this was not associated with any measures of drug exposure; however, the significantly higher ADCs observed in the left and right putamen were associated with earlier initiation of methamphetamine use, greater amounts of methamphetamine used per day and higher cumulative lifetime dose. It is somewhat surprising that methamphetamine users exhibited normal FA within striatal structures but higher diffusivity values; the authors proposed that this reflects increased water content and diffusion in the basal ganglia, which may also be related to inflammatory processes or decreased myelination [139].

Sub-analyses for gender differences have been carried out in some of the abovementioned studies. Results from Chung et al. [135] revealed that lower FA values in frontal white matter and more errors in the Wisconsin Card Sorting Task were found only in male participants relative to control participants of the same gender, suggesting that frontal white matter in males may be more vulnerable to the effects of methamphetamine. However, due to the small number of female participants in the trial, these findings cannot be considered as evidence that methamphetamine use is not harmful to females. In contrast, Salo et al. [138] reported no effect of gender on methamphetamine-induced FA changes in the genu of the corpus callosum and Tobias et al. [136] reported significantly lower FA in all but one of the white matter regions examined in female methamphetamine users but no such difference males. These results suggest that methamphetamine-induced effects can be observed in both males and females, and argue against the possible neuroprotective effects of oestrogen [135]; however, further studies are needed to examine gender differences in white matter microstructure.

3.2.4. Magnetic Resonance Spectroscopy

Proton MRS is a non-invasive imaging technique that allows for the measurement of chemical products without the use of radiotracers. MRS provides a snapshot of the neurochemical environment within a defined volume of interest and, although it provides less sensitivity than other imaging techniques, MRS has the potential for tracking disease and/or treatment progression. The spectral output of MRS depends on the energy absorbed by specific organic molecules, which is determined by the number of hydrogen atoms (protons) in the compound, as well as in the surrounding environment. The most commonly investigated metabolites include *N*-acetylaspartate (NAA), choline (Cho), creatine (Cr) and *myo*-inositol (MI), along with amino acids glutamate, glutamine and GABA. These compounds form a range of markers for cellular integrity and function. With the exception of the water peak, which is frequently suppressed during acquisition, the NAA signal is the most prominent peak on the spectrum (at 2.02 ppm). It is considered a marker of neuronal viability and therefore a measure of the effects of drug use. The Cho peak (at 3.2 ppm) represents a number of choline-containing compounds and indicates cellular density and cell wall turnover [140]; consequently the signal increases with increasing membrane synthesis. It has been suggested that Cho is a marker of glial density and therefore may be an appropriate marker to track neuronal changes associated with drug use and abstinence [141].

The Cr peaks (at 3.03 and 3.94 ppm) are considered markers of high energy metabolism [142] and the first peak is often used as an internal reference metabolite for other peaks as its concentration is assumed to be relatively constant. However, data have shown that Cr is not homogeneously distributed across the brain and the assumption that the concentration remains constant may be incorrect under both normal conditions and pathological states [143]. The significance of the MI (at 3.56 ppm) is not well understood but it has been proposed to be a glial marker [144]; elevation of MI in conditions associated with neuronal loss has been interpreted as a sign of gliosis [145]. The neurotransmitters GABA, glutamate and glutamine maintain a balance between excitation and inhibition, in addition to regulating neuronal energy metabolism [146]. At 1.5 T glutamate and glutamine peaks overlap (at 2.34 and 2.36 ppm) and cannot be separated without specialised spectral editing and are often considered as a 'Glx complex'. At 3.0 T, glutamate can be adequately separated from glutamine to provide identification [147]. Similarly, the GABA peak (at 3.03 ppm) is obscured by Cr and other macromolecules [148]. Despite the preponderance of evidence for the role of abnormal glutamate and GABA neurotransmission in drug addiction [149, 150], most spectroscopic studies have focused on metabolites that are comparatively easier to resolve [151].

3.2.4.1. Cocaine

One of the first *in vivo* proton MRS studies was carried out in a group of long-term abstinent cocaine users, measuring concentrations of NAA, Cho, Cr, MI and Glx [152]. Significantly increased Cr and MI were observed in the temporoparietal white matter of abstinent cocaine users with no change in NAA or other metabolites. These findings are suggestive of abnormalities in the non-neuronal cells of subcortical brain regions with no significant neuronal damage; however, it is possible that biochemical evidence associated with neuronal damage may be detected in brain regions not evaluated in this study. In a later study, Chang et al. [153] examined the persistent cerebral metabolite abnormalities of abstinent cocaine users and also determined whether these changes were different in male and female users. A significant decrease in NAA and increase in MI was seen in the midfrontal grey matter of all cocaine-dependent participants, while only elevated MI was seen in the frontal white matter. Gender effects were also observed; males displayed higher levels of Cho in the grey matter as well as elevated Cr levels in the white matter, while females showed significantly higher MI/Cr in the white matter. Higher elevation of MI in female participants suggests stronger glial reactive processes compared to males and differences in cocaine-induced brain injury. Li et al. [113] investigated the effects of cocaine use on metabolites in the basal ganglia and thalamic region of current users and observed significantly decreased NAA in the thalamic region only.

The results pertaining to NAA have not been consistent throughout the literature, which may be due in part to different regions being investigated. However, the predominant view regarding NAA suggests that levels of NAA may be dynamic and reflective of ongoing processes within neurons, as reductions in NAA observed in neurological disease and brain injury are known to be reversible [154, 155]. Moreover, decrements in NAA content associated with cocaine use may be a result of primary neuronal loss or damage, a reduction in synaptic density or the direct effects of cocaine on neuronal activity and subsequent depletion of monoamine neurotransmitters [113, 151]. Yang et al. [156] investigated glutamate within the anterior cingulate cortex, suggesting that it may improve understanding of frontal lobe alterations and the functional significance of glutamate in cocaine addiction. The study demonstrated significantly lower glutamate/Cr in the rostral anterior cingulate cortex of cocaine-dependent participants which correlated with years of cocaine use but no significant differences in other metabolites.

These findings suggest that glutamate dysfunction is associated with cocaine use and provide support for interventions aimed at normalising glutamatergic transmission and function for the treatment of cocaine addiction. Two studies have demonstrated that cocaine-dependent participants have significantly lower GABA levels in the occipital [157] and prefrontal [158] regions compared to controls. The finding of low GABA within the prefrontal cortex is of particular significance as frontal lobe functions including switching of attention and inhibitory control have been found to be impaired of cocaine-dependent participants. Consequently, the GABA system has been a target for pharmacological treatment in cocaine addiction.

3.2.4.2. Amphetamine

MRS studies investigating the effects of dexamphetamine on brain metabolites have not been from a drug abuse perspective; typically, dexamphetamine has been acutely administered to provide a lithium-sensitive model of mania [159-161]. The doses in these studies do not reflect chronic regimens of amphetamine administration so will not be discussed further.

3.2.4.3. Methamphetamine

Ernst et al. [162] carried out the first MRS study in methamphetamine-dependent participants to examine metabolite abnormalities. Methamphetamine-dependent participants showed a significant reduction of NAA and total Cr in the basal ganglia and significantly increased Cho and MI in the frontal grey matter. These findings have been corroborated by other researchers; Nordahl et al. [163] and Salo et al. [164] observed significantly decreased NAA/Cr levels as well as increased Cho/Cr levels in anterior cingulate regions.

A study of the basal ganglia found reduced Cr/Cho with no change in NAA/Cho in the bilateral basal ganglia; the reduction in Cr/Cho was attributed to abnormal Cr levels [165]. Linear regression analyses between metabolite concentrations and measures of drug exposure and cognitive function were also carried out in the aforementioned studies. Ernst et al. [162] demonstrated an inverse relationship between NAA in the frontal white matter and the logarithm of cumulative lifetime methamphetamine use, while the reduction in NAA correlated with reduced levels of attentional control in a Stroop interference test [164]. Decreased levels of Cr/Cho correlated with a longer duration of methamphetamine use as well as the severity of residual psychotic symptoms resulting from methamphetamine use [165]. Although these studies were carried in abstinent methamphetamine users, relatively fewer studies have used MRS to track the neuronal changes associated with drug abstinence. Nordahl et al. [141] recruited abstinent methamphetamine users and for the purposes of analyses, participants were divided into recently abstinent and distantly abstinent users. All methamphetamine users showed significantly lower levels of NAA/Cr within the anterior cingulate cortex regardless of abstinence duration; however, levels of Cho/NAA in the same region were significantly higher in participants who had recently initiated abstinence compared to participants who had been abstinent for longer than one year, suggesting that Cho can normalise with drug abstinence.

In contrast, Sung et al. [166] found no significant differences in NAA between groups relative to abstinence duration; however, grey matter NAA positively correlated with abstinence duration whereas NAA in white matter did not, suggesting that methamphetamine-induced damage in the grey matter only may recover with prolonged abstinence. Findings from the earlier trial by Nordahl et al. [141] have recently been extended to a larger sample size. With increased statistical power, Salo et al. [167] confirmed the earlier finding of Cho normalisation within the anterior cingulate cortex as a function of drug abstinence, observing abnormally high Cho/NAA values in the short-term abstinent group but no difference between the long-term abstinent group and controls. Evidence of NAA/Cr normalisation was also observed. Considered together with the evidence of improved cognitive function across periods of drug abstinence, these findings suggest that brain metabolites and function may not show signs of normalisation until an extended period of abstinence has been maintained. These results highlight the need for longitudinal follow-up studies to improve understanding of methamphetamine-induced neurotoxicity and elucidate the mechanisms underlying these changes, as well as comparison to studies in current methamphetamine users to gain a better understanding of the timeline of these effects.

Few studies have extended their investigations beyond NAA, Cho, Cr and MI; however, research has found that the effects of methamphetamine are related to glutamate as well as dopamine and serotonin, and that glutamate may be implicated in the oxidative stress-mediated neurotoxicity associated with methamphetamine use [168]. The first study to assess the effects of abstinence from chronic methamphetamine on the Glx complex was carried out in a cross-sectional sample of participants with longitudinal follow-up of a subset of participants, five months later [169].

At baseline, participants with short periods of abstinence showed the lowest levels of Glx in frontal grey matter which positively correlated with duration of abstinence; after five months of abstinence, Glx in the frontal grey matter showed a trend towards correlating inversely with the duration of abstinence, suggesting normalisation over time. Interestingly, participants who reported symptoms of craving had lower levels of Glx in the frontal cortex than those who did not. These findings suggest dynamic abnormalities relating to Glx in recently abstinent methamphetamine users with depletion of the glutamatergic system and progressive normalisation with prolonged abstinence.

Further studies are needed to evaluate glutamate and glutamine separately and further determine whether the severity of the hypoglutamatergic state robustly correlates with craving and withdrawal symptoms. More recently, Sailasuta et al. [170] investigated levels of glutamate in short-term abstinent methamphetamine users, hypothesising that any changes in brain glutamate due to methamphetamine use will be detectable with MRS and persist beyond drug cessation. Significant elevations of glutamate were observed in the frontal white matter of abstinent methamphetamine users with a concurrent reduction in NAA. Although the findings of these two studies are not concordant, they both offer support for glutamatergic dysfunction associated with methamphetamine use and provide an impetus for further research into the role of glutamate in drug abuse.

4. PHARMACOLOGICAL TREATMENT FOR STIMULANT ADDICTION

Behavioural interventions are the current mainstay of stimulant addiction treatment; cognitive behavioural therapy has been effective in decreasing cocaine use and preventing relapse but the success rates are low. Behavioural treatment must be tailored to the needs of the individual and often require a combination of treatment, social support and supplementary services [25]. Research into effective pharmacological treatments is a fast-evolving area and efforts have intensified over the last decade; therefore only pharmacological agents for addiction treatment will be discussed in this chapter.

Currently, there is no pharmacological therapy with established efficacy for the treatment of cocaine and amphetamine dependence; however, animal models of addiction and increased understanding of the neurocircuitry and neuropharmacological mechanisms implicated in stimulant dependence have provided several potential targets for therapy. Pharmacological treatments for stimulant addiction have been selected based on research into the neurobiological mechanisms involved in different stages of the addiction cycle, animal models and medications approved for other indications that overlap with specific components of addiction [171].

Cocaine and methamphetamine share a number of similarities; pharmacologically they both block the reuptake of dopamine at the synaptic cleft of neurons in the reward pathway and produce comparable mood-altering effects and physiological effects. Amphetamines also stimulate the release and inhibit the breakdown of neurotransmitters. Consequently, there is considerable overlap between agents trialled for treatment of cocaine and methamphetamine dependence. As pharmacological treatments for cocaine addiction were discussed in Chapter One, this chapter will focus on agents that have been evaluated in clinical trials for amphetamine addiction and are broadly classified into agonist replacement therapy and drugs affecting monoamine, GABA and glutamate systems.

4.1. Agonist Replacement Therapy

Some research indicates that agonist replacement (or substitution) therapy may be a promising approach for the treatment of addiction. The underlying principle of agonist replacement therapy is using a drug from the same pharmacological family to partially replace the effects of the abused drug, thereby stabilising the patient [172]. This approach has been successfully used for the treatment of opiate and nicotine dependence. Dexamphetamine and methylphenidate are dopaminergic agents that have been trialled as agonist replacement therapy in cocaine and amphetamine addiction. Dexamphetamine promotes the release of dopamine, noradrenaline and serotonin while methylphenidate has affinity for dopamine and noradrenaline transporters, but not the serotonin transporter and, although both agents have some abuse liability (methylphenidate is reported to have less), research with both agents have yielded promising results.

To date, there have been a small number of randomised controlled trials of dexamphetamine maintenance treatment for amphetamine-dependent participants. A small open-label pilot study by Shearer et al. [173] was carried out to determine the feasibility of conducting a trial providing dexamphetamine to dependent users. Amphetamine-dependent participants were randomised to receive weekly counselling or counselling plus immediate-release dexamphetamine (up to 60 mg/day) over 12 weeks. No difference in amphetamine use was observed between groups; however, the dexamphetamine-treatment group was significantly more likely to attend counselling, receiving twice as many sessions as the control group. Although this study was underpowered, the results suggest that substitution therapy is potentially beneficial in problematic amphetamine use. More recently, Longo et al. [174] conducted a randomised, double-blind, placebo-controlled trial of sustained-release dexamphetamine in methamphetamine users. Treatment was administered under a flexible dosing regimen (up to 110 mg/day) over 12 weeks, with 4 sessions of cognitive behavioural therapy over the trial duration. Analysis revealed significantly higher retention rates and longer time to dropout in the dexamphetamine-treated group, as well as lower self-reported dependence. These results show that maintenance treatment with once daily sustained-release dexamphetamine can engage and maintain methamphetamine-dependent participants in treatment and support further investigation of maintenance pharmacotherapy as an intervention for methamphetamine addiction. The role of methylphenidate substitution therapy in amphetamine addiction is relatively less well established than in cocaine addiction; only one study has been carried out. A 20-week randomised study of sustained-release methylphenidate (54 mg/day), aripiprazole (15 mg/day) and placebo in intravenous amphetamine users yielded promising results for methylphenidate [175]. The trial was discontinued due to one active medication being significantly worse than placebo; however, interim analysis showed that methylphenidate treatment was associated with a significant reduction in amphetamine use. The authors suggest that sustained-release methylphenidate may be superior to the immediate-release formulation as users may start to experience cravings for amphetamine as soon as the effects of the substitute drug wear off [175].

4.2. Dopamine-Modulating Agents

Because the addictive qualities of methamphetamine are thought to be primarily mediated by enhancement of dopaminergic activity in the mesolimbic system of the brain, clinical research has been dedicated to developing pharmacotherapeutic strategies targeting the dopamine system.

Atypical antipsychotics have been investigated as treatments for methamphetamine addiction because of their ability to block dopamine and/or serotonin receptors. Risperidone was shown to attenuate the discriminative-stimulus effects of dexamphetamine as well as some of the self-reported drug effects [176], and therefore may decrease the drive to use methamphetamine in early recovery. In an open-label pilot study, participants received treatment with risperidone (average dose 3.6 mg/day) over four weeks [177]. Participants who completed the trial significantly decreased their methamphetamine use and urinalysis showed that less than 3% of weekly urine screens were positive. Although the sample size of this study was small and lacked a control group, the results suggest that risperidone may be a candidate for the treatment of methamphetamine addiction and warrants further investigation. A study evaluating long-acting injectable risperidone in methamphetamine addiction has been completed (see http://clinicaltrials.gov, identifier NCT00284206) but currently, no results are available.

In laboratory studies, aripiprazole (10 and 20 mg) has been shown to significantly attenuate the discriminative-stimulus, cardiovascular and subject-rated effects of dexamphetamine [178, 179], suggesting that partial D_2 agonists have potential as pharmacotherapy in the management of stimulant dependence. However, the results of a more recent trial were in support of the abovementioned trial by Tiihonen et al. [175] where aripiprazole treatment was associated with a significantly higher number of methamphetamine-positive urine samples than placebo. A randomised, double-blind, placebo-controlled inpatient pharmacology study was carried out to assess potential interactions between intravenous methamphetamine (15 and 30 mg) and oral aripiprazole (15 mg), as well as the effects of aripiprazole on abstinence-related craving and cue-induced craving [180]. Analysis revealed that aripiprazole had no effect on cue-induced methamphetamine craving or daily baseline craving over the treatment period and was associated with increased craving independent of methamphetamine dosing, as well as significantly increased subjective ratings of 'euphoria' and 'amphetamine-like effects' and decreased 'bad effects' on rating scales. The findings indicate that aripiprazole increased some of the rewarding and stimulant effects of methamphetamine and is unlikely to be efficacious for facilitating abstinence from methamphetamine, but its efficacy using lower doses and/or its role in relapse prevention should nevertheless be investigated.

4.3. GABA-Modulating Agents

Modulation of the GABA system, particularly $GABA_B$ receptors, is of great interest for the potential treatment of drug dependence – GABA has been shown to exert an inhibitory effect on the tonic activity of dopamine neurons in the ventral tegmental area [181] and the nucleus accumbens [182].

Medications that promote GABAergic activity may be promising medications for the treatment of cocaine and methamphetamine dependence. Results from preclinical and early clinical studies supported the use of GABA-modulating medications in the treatment of cocaine addiction; therefore it was suggested that, by extension, they may also be effective in methamphetamine addiction.

4.3.1. Baclofen

Baclofen is the only $GABA_B$ agonist available for human use. In animals, baclofen attenuates cocaine-induced dopamine release in the nucleus accumbens [183] and intravenous self-administration [184-186]. Heinzerling et al. [187] conducted a randomised, double-blind placebo-controlled trial comparing two GABAergic agents to placebo in methamphetamine-dependent participants. Treatment consisted of baclofen (60 mg/day), gabapentin (2400 mg/day) or placebo for 16 weeks along with thrice-weekly relapse prevention sessions. Analysis revealed no effects for either medication relative to placebo in retention, adherence, craving, depressive symptoms or urine drug screens. However, post-hoc analysis showed that only baclofen had a significant effect of treatment in participants, with higher rates of medication adherence. These authors suggested that, while gabapentin did not appear to be effective for treating methamphetamine addiction, baclofen may have a small effect and concluded that further studies of baclofen and other GABAergic medications may be warranted.

4.3.2. Gabapentin

Urschel et al. [188] carried out an open-label trial, which was recently extended to a double-blind, placebo-controlled trial of a propriety combination of gabapentin with flumazenil (a benzodiazepine antagonist) in methamphetamine-dependent participants [189]. The combination of medication (gabapentin up to 1200 mg/day, flumazenil 0.1-0.3 mg) was administered over 30 days with weekly psychosocial treatment based on the Matrix™ model. In accordance with the previous trial, participants in the active medication group reported less methamphetamine use and decreased craving. The authors suggest that this combination of medications may offer potential benefit in reducing craving and increasing engagement in psychosocial treatment amongst methamphetamine-dependent individuals.

4.3.3. Vigabatrin

Vigabatrin (γ-vinyl-GABA) is an atypical antiepileptic medication used for the treatment of epilepsy and seizures. It is a specific and irreversible suicide inhibitor of GABA transaminase that acts to increase GABA neurotransmission. In animals, vigabatrin has been shown to reduce cocaine-induced dopamine release in the nucleus accumbens by 25% [190]. However, vigabatrin has been associated with the development of unacceptable visual field abnormalities [191], which may limit its clinical use. An early study by Brodie et al. [192] assessed the safety and efficacy of vigabatrin in participants who were dependent on methamphetamine alone, methamphetamine and cocaine, and cocaine alone. Eighteen of the 30 participants completed the 9-week trial; 15 of the completers were methamphetamine- and cocaine-free for more than 4 weeks. Vigabatrin treatment was not associated with any visual field defects; therefore the authors concluded that it may be an appropriate candidate for the treatment of methamphetamine and/or cocaine addiction. However, a recent double-blind, placebo-controlled laboratory study found that, although vigabatrin was well tolerated, it was not efficacious for attenuating the positive subjective effects of methamphetamine and may have the potential to elevate cardiovascular parameters [193]. To date, no randomised controlled clinical trials have been undertaken to determine whether vigabatrin is effective for the treatment of methamphetamine addiction.

4.4. Glutamate-Modulating Agents

The glutamatergic system is involved in drug addiction; glutamate levels increase in the nucleus accumbens during reinstatement, and glutamate receptor activation is necessary for reinstatement of drug-seeking behaviour [194]. Therefore medications that inhibit glutamatergic activity may also be valuable for the treatment of addiction. Modafinil is chemically and pharmacologically distinct from amphetamine-like and other central nervous system stimulants. It is currently approved for the management of narcolepsy, obstructive sleep apnoea/hypoapnoea syndrome or idiopathic hypersomnia [195, 196]. It has a complex neurobiological mechanism of action involving both dopamine- and glutamate-enhancing effects – modafinil increases the release of glutamate in the hippocampus and ventromedial and ventrolateral areas of the thalamus, which may contribute to its vigilance-enhancing effects [197, 198]. There is some evidence that the effects of modafinil are mediated by adrenergic α_1-receptors. A recent PET study shows that modafinil binds to the dopamine transporter, thus possesses similar properties to methylphenidate [199], and is well tolerated with a low overdose risk [200]. A recent randomised, double-blind outpatient study evaluated the subjective and reinforcing effects of modafinil (200, 400 and 600 mg) in cocaine users and found no abuse liability in this population [201]; however, these results should be interpreted with caution. A PET study using ^{11}C-raclopride and ^{11}C-cocaine to measure the effects of modafinil (200 and 400 mg) on dopamine transporters and extracellular dopamine levels found that modafinil blocked dopamine transporters and increased dopamine in regions of the human brain – including the nucleus accumbens. Because drugs that increase dopamine in the nucleus accumbens have the potential for abuse, these results highlight the need for increased awareness of potential abuse and dependence on modafinil in vulnerable populations [199]. Modafinil has weak stimulant properties and has therefore been cited as a putative treatment to decrease stimulant seeking and craving. The rationale to use modafinil in methamphetamine withdrawal treatment was guided, in part, by some of the most prominent features of the methamphetamine withdrawal syndrome – hypersomnolence and fatigue [202]. Modafinil, with its wake-promoting properties, was identified as a medication with the potential to alleviate these symptoms during the withdrawal phase [203]. It may also be a cognitive enhancer in methamphetamine-dependent participants and improve the response to behavioural therapies. A trial by McGregor et al. [203] was the first to evaluate modafinil for safety and tolerability. The 10-day open-label trial compared modafinil (400 mg/day) and mirtazapine (60 mg/day) against 'treatment as usual' with pericyazine in inpatient methamphetamine withdrawal. Modafinil-treated participants had lower withdrawal scores and appeared to experience a significantly milder withdrawal syndrome and less sleep disturbance than mirtazapine- and pericyazine-treated patients. Moreover, participants taking modafinil also reported less fatigue, agitation, anxiety, irritability, tension and frequency of methamphetamine craving. Another small 16-week single-blind trial investigated the efficacy of modafinil (up to 200 mg/day) combined with weekly cognitive behavioural therapy for treatment of methamphetamine addiction among HIV-positive gay men. Ten participants successfully completed the trial, and six of these reduced their methamphetamine use by over 50% [204]. In a more recent trial, participants were randomly assigned to receive 200 mg/day of modafinil or placebo under double-blind conditions for 10 weeks [205]. Treatment retention and medication adherence were equivalent between groups and there were no differences in methamphetamine abstinence, craving or severity of dependence, though compliant patients in the modafinil group tended to provide more negative urine samples over the treatment period. These results suggest that although modafinil may not be efficacious as an anti-craving agent, it appears to be safe and non-reinforcing, and warrants further investigation in larger trials and/or higher doses.

4.5. Serotonin- and Noradrenaline-Modulating Agents

The neurotransmitter deficit model [206] has guided focus toward medications with the potential to raise synaptic concentrations of one or more of three neurotransmitters affected by methamphetamine – dopamine, serotonin and noradrenaline. Although dopamine agonists have not been investigated in methamphetamine addiction, studies of direct and indirect dopamine agonists in cocaine addiction have yielded largely negative results; consequently serotonin and noradrenaline have become the neurotransmitters of interest.

4.5.1. Selective Serotonin Reuptake Inhibitors

Early work in animals demonstrated that lesions or neurotoxins inhibiting serotonergic signalling caused increased self-administration of amphetamine [207, 208], suggesting that selective serotonin reuptake inhibitors (SSRIs) may be useful for decreasing the reinforcing effects of methamphetamine. However, trials of SSRIs such as fluoxetine [209] and paroxetine [210], as well as the tricyclic antidepressant imipramine [211] have shown no clear efficacy for reducing methamphetamine use. In a larger randomised double-blind, placebo-controlled trial, sertraline – a potent SSRI with a strong safety profile – was combined with contingency management using a counselling platform of Matrix™ model relapse prevention groups [212]. Participants were randomised to one of four conditions for 12 weeks – sertraline (100 mg/day) plus contingency management, sertraline only (100 mg/day), placebo plus contingency management and placebo only. There were no statistically significant effects for the medication or behavioural therapies in retention, drug craving, depression or medication adherence. In fact, sertraline treatment without contingency management appeared to increase methamphetamine use, as indicated by a greater number of methamphetamine-positive urine samples and the reduced likelihood of achieving three consecutive weeks of drug abstinence compared to those in contingency management conditions. These findings support the use of contingency management for the treatment of methamphetamine addiction; however, they suggest that sertraline, and possibly SSRIs as a class, are ineffective and may be contraindicated for methamphetamine addiction.

4.5.2. Mirtazapine

Mirtazapine is noradrenergic and serotonergic antidepressant; it enhances noradrenergic and $5-HT_{1A}$-mediated serotonergic neurotransmission by causing the blockade of inhibitory α_2-adrenergic autoreceptors on noradrenaline and $5-HT_2$ and $5-HT_3$ serotonin neurons. The sedative and anxiolytic properties may be mediated by antagonist effects at $5-HT_2$ and $5-HT_3$ receptors, and/or histamine H_1 receptors [213]. A pilot study of mirtazapine for the treatment of amphetamine addiction showed significantly improved withdrawal scores in participants receiving mirtazapine (15-60 mg titrated according to response), as well as significant improvements in the hyperarousal and anxiety subscales [214]. The abovementioned open-label trial by McGregor et al. [203] comparing mirtazapine and modafinil to placebo, found that mirtazapine (60 mg/day) was safe and well tolerated by participants. Mirtazapine treatment was associated with higher withdrawal scores compared to modafinil; however, mirtazapine-treated participants performed better than the 'treatment as usual group', with lower withdrawal scores and overall severity of symptoms. In a later double-blind, randomised placebo-controlled trial by Cruickshank et al. [215], mirtazapine was used in the management of methamphetamine withdrawal in an outpatient setting. Treatment was administered at a lower dose and shorter period than previous trials – 30 mg/day for 14 days, and both mirtazapine and placebo groups were offered narrative therapy counselling in conjunction with treatment. No significant differences were observed between the mirtazapine and placebo groups in retention rate or other symptom measures, suggesting that despite benefits in other settings, mirtazapine does not improve retention or alleviate withdrawal in the outpatient setting within a period of two weeks. More recently, a 12-week randomised, placebo-controlled trial combined mirtazapine (30 mg/day) with weekly counselling in methamphetamine-dependent men who have sex with men. Mirtazapine significantly reduced methamphetamine use and was associated with decreases in sexual risk, but no difference was observed in depression scores, suggesting that its effects of methamphetamine use are independent of its effects on depression [216]. Although there is no clear evidence for the efficacy of mirtazapine in the management of methamphetamine dependence, the differences in treatment setting and doses suggest that it may be a useful pharmacotherapy in certain populations.

4.5.3. Bupropion

Bupropion is an antidepressant that is also approved as a treatment for smoking cessation. It is a monoamine uptake-inhibitor with stimulant-like effects in animals but does not alter serotonergic neurotransmission. Instead, it inhibits the reuptake of dopamine and noradrenaline, and reduces firing of dopamine and noradrenaline neurons – an effect consistent with an increase in synaptic levels of monoamine that inhibits neuronal firing via an autoreceptor-mediated negative feedback mechanism [217]. It also blocks transporters for dopamine and noradrenaline which enhances dopaminergic neurotransmission – an effect that may ameliorate symptoms of methamphetamine withdrawal. Newton et al. [218] conducted a single-blind, placebo-controlled trial in methamphetamine users to assess the effects of bupropion treatment (300 mg/day for 6 days) on methamphetamine-induced subjective effects and craving. Bupropion treatment was associated with a reduced drug effect and feelings of being 'high' after intravenous methamphetamine administration, as well as reduced cue-induced craving. These data provided rationale for further evaluation of bupropion for the treatment of methamphetamine dependence. Bupropion was then tested for efficacy for increasing weeks of abstinence in a 12-week double-blind, placebo-controlled trial [219]. Participants were randomised to receive either sustained-release bupropion (300 mg/day) or placebo. There was no difference between the bupropion and placebo groups in the probability of a 'non-use week' during the 12-week treatment period; however, subgroup analysis revealed that male participants with low baseline use treated with bupropion were more likely to have a methamphetamine-free week. These results suggest that bupropion may be efficacious for the treatment of methamphetamine-dependent participants who exhibit low-to-moderate levels of use. In a further trial, treatment with sustained-release bupropion (300 mg/day) was compared to placebo for efficacy in reducing methamphetamine use, increasing retention and reducing the severity of depressive symptoms and cravings [220]. Treatment with bupropion was associated with significantly reduced cigarette smoking but did not result in any significant differences in severity of depressive symptoms, craving or retention and was no more effective than placebo in reducing methamphetamine use. Post-hoc analysis showed that bupropion reduced methamphetamine use more than placebo amongst participants with low use at baseline. These findings are consistent with the trial by Elkashef et al. [219], demonstrating greater efficacy in participants with low-to-moderate use. Evidence from these trials may warrant further investigation of bupropion in the treatment of methamphetamine dependence among light levels of use.

4.6. Opioid Antagonists

Although the reinforcing effects of stimulants are principally mediated via the mesocorticolimbic dopamine system, other neurotransmitter systems – such as μ-opioid receptors located on mesolimbic dopamine neurons – modulate dopamine [221]. The important functional interactions between the dopamine and opioid systems in stimulant abuse are evident in preclinical and clinical studies. For example, chronic cocaine administration in rats has been shown to increase brain μ-opioid receptor binding in reward-relevant regions, such as the amygdala and nucleus accumbens; this effect appears to be mediated by dopamine receptors [222, 223]. Furthermore, a PET study in chronic cocaine users demonstrated an increase in μ-opioid receptor binding in limbic areas, which correlated with self-reported cocaine craving [224]. Evidence suggests that this dopaminergic-opioid interaction may provide a potential target for pharmacological intervention.

Naltrexone, a μ-opioid receptor antagonist, has been shown to attenuate the subjective effects of dexamphetamine in dependent patients, as well as decrease craving [225], suggesting that naltrexone may be useful as an adjunct pharmacotherapy for treating amphetamine dependence. This provided the rationale for a clinical trial evaluating the efficacy of naltrexone for preventing relapse in amphetamine-dependent participants [226]. In a double-blind, placebo controlled trial, amphetamine-dependent participants were randomly assigned to either placebo or naltrexone (50 mg) treatment for 12 weeks with weekly relapse prevention therapy. Analysis revealed a significantly higher number of amphetamine-negative urine samples in the naltrexone group compared to placebo, as well as a decrease in craving scores and self-reported amphetamine use. Therefore, naltrexone appears to be a very promising medication for treating amphetamine dependence.

CONCLUSION

Stimulant addiction is an increasing worldwide public health problem. Despite many years of clinical research, no pharmacological agent has proven to be robustly successful; consequently the development of effective treatments for stimulant addiction is now a priority. Recent advances in understanding the underlying neurobiological mechanisms of addiction have led to a number of potentially promising medications. However, knowledge about the effects of stimulants and the differences between drug-dependent participants and healthy non-drug users is critical for the identification of possible pharmacotherapies. Neuroimaging techniques can be used to examine the effects of pharmacological interventions and can provide a link between their mechanisms of action and behavioural responses; however, few trials of potential therapies have been guided by findings from imaging studies.

The convergence of evidence from preclinical and clinical trials in addition to neuroimaging studies may provide more insight into the putative effectiveness of potential pharmacotherapies. For example, preclinical studies confirm that baclofen blocks drug-motivated behaviour by inhibiting dopamine release in the ventral striatum and medial prefrontal cortex; however, this mechanism in humans is less well described. Using arterial spin-labelled perfusion fMRI, Franklin et al. [227] examined the effects of baclofen treatment

(80 mg/day for 3 weeks) on cerebral blood flow to reward-relevant areas in smokers. Baclofen significantly modulated blood flow in regions involved in motivational behaviour – the ventral striatum, orbitofrontal cortex and the superior, inferior and ventral medial cortices. The ability to identify the modulatory effects of potential pharmacotherapies on regions involved in addictive processes could improve our understanding of the underlying mechanisms and inform medication selection and/or development.

Chronic drug abuse is also associated with cognitive impairment; these impairments can interfere with behavioural therapy, leading to poor treatment retention and subsequent outcomes. Therefore cognitive remediation strategies using medicines may become an important part of treatment. Modafinil has been used as a cognitive enhancer; however, its mechanism is complex and involves several neurotransmitter systems. Ghahremani et al. [228] used fMRI determine the effects of modafinil (200 mg) on neural function and learning in methamphetamine-dependent participants. Modafinil enhanced learning performance to levels similar to those seen in control participants, which was accompanied by greater activation in bilateral insula/ventrolateral prefrontal and anterior cingulate cortices – regions important for learning and cognitive control. The identification and evaluation of other cognitive-enhancing medications for treating stimulant addiction may be carried out using a range of MRI methods. For example, MRS could be used to assess changes induced by methamphetamine abuse over time or PET could be used to investigate functional and structural amelioration (or deterioration) following drug withdrawal and abstinence. Moreover, combined with pharmacological treatment, neuroimaging may prove to be an invaluable tool for longitudinal follow-up studies of drug addiction.

REFERENCES

[1]   Altman J, Everitt BJ, Glautier S, Markou A, Nutt D, Oretti R, et al. The biological, social and clinical bases of drug addiction: commentary and debate. *Psychopharmacology (Berl)*. 1996 Jun; 125 (4): 285-345.

[2]   Office of National Drug Control Policy. The economic costs of drug abuse in the United States, 1992–2002. Washington, DC: *Executive Office of the President2004 Contract No.*: 207303.

[3]   EMCDDA. Towards a better understanding of drug-related public expenditure in Europe. Luxembourg: *Publications Office of the European Union* 2008.

[4]   Koob GF, Le Moal M. Neurobiology of addiction: *Elsevier Academic*, 2006; 2006.

[5]   American Psychiatric Association. Diagnostic and Statistical Manual of Mental Disorders, Fourth Edition, Text Revision (DSM-IV-TR). *American Psychiatric Association*, editor. Washington, DC: American Psychiatric Press; 2000.

[6]   Chung T, Martin CS. Classification and course of alcohol problems among adolescents in addictions treatment programs. *Alcohol Clin. Exp. Res.* 2001 Dec; 25 (12): 1734-42.

[7]   Koob GF. Allostatic view of motivation: implications for psychopathology. *Nebr. Symp. Motiv.* 2004; 50: 1-18.

[8]   Paly D, Jatlow P, Van Dyke C, Raul Jeri F, Byck R. Plasma cocaine concentrations during cocaine paste smoking. *Life Sci.* 1982; 30 (9): 731-8.

[9]   Van Dyke C, Barash PG, Jatlow P, Byck R. Cocaine: plasma concentrations after intranasal application in man. *Science*. 1976 Feb 27; 191 (4229): 859-61.

[10]   Van Dyke C, Jatlow P, Ungerer J, Barash PG, Byck R. Oral cocaine: plasma concentrations and central effects. *Science*. 1978 Apr 14; 200 (4338): 211-3.

[11]   Volkow ND, Li T-K. Drug addiction: the neurobiology of behaviour gone awry. *Nat. Rev. Neurosci*. 2004; 5 (12): 963-70.

[12]   Stahl SM, Muntner NI. Essential psychopharmacology: *Neuroscientific basis and clinical applications*. New York, NY, US: Cambridge University Press; 2008.

[13]   Koob GF, Le Moal M. Drug addiction, dysregulation of reward, and allostasis. *Neuropsychopharmacology*. 2001 Feb; 24 (2): 97-129.

[14]   Nestler EJ. Molecular basis of long-term plasticity underlying addiction. *Nat. Rev. Neurosci*. 2001 Feb; 2 (2): 119-28.

[15]   Di Chiara G, Bassareo V, Fenu S, De Luca MA, Spina L, Cadoni C, et al. Dopamine and drug addiction: the nucleus accumbens shell connection. *Neuropharmacology*. 2004; 47 Suppl 1:227-41.

[16]   Volkow ND, Fowler JS, Wang GJ, Swanson JM, Telang F. Dopamine in drug abuse and addiction: results of imaging studies and treatment implications. *Arch. Neurol*. 2007 Nov; 64 (11): 1575-9.

[17]   Wise RA. Dopamine, learning and motivation. *Nat. Rev. Neurosci*. 2004 Jun; 5 (6): 483-94.

[18]   Hyman SE, Malenka RC, Nestler EJ. Neural mechanisms of addiction: the role of reward-related learning and memory. *Annu. Rev. Neurosci*. 2006; 29: 565-98.

[19]   Kelley AE, Berridge KC. The neuroscience of natural rewards: relevance to addictive drugs. *J. Neurosci*. 2002 May 1; 22 (9): 3306-11.

[20]   Tobler PN, Fiorillo CD, Schultz W. Adaptive coding of reward value by dopamine neurons. *Science*. 2005 Mar 11; 307 (5715): 1642-5.

[21]   Wise RA. Brain reward circuitry: insights from unsensed incentives. *Neuron*. 2002 Oct 10; 36 (2): 229-40.

[22]   Di Chiara G. Nucleus accumbens shell and core dopamine: differential role in behavior and addiction. *Behav. Brain Res*. 2002 Dec 2; 137 (1-2): 75-114.

[23]   Koob GF, Nestler EJ. The neurobiology of drug addiction. *J. Neuropsychiatry Clin. Neurosci*. 1997 Summer; 9 (3): 482-97.

[24]   Raiteri M, Bertollini A, Angelini F, Levi G. d-Amphetamine as a releaser or reuptake inhibitor of biogenic amines in synaptosomes. *Eur. J. Pharmacol*. 1975 Nov; 34 (1): 189-95.

[25]   NIDA. Cocaine2010.

[26]   Barash PG. Cocaine in clinical medicine. Washington, DC: *NIDA Monograph No. 131*977.

[27]   UNODC. World Drug Report: *United Nations Publication*, Sales No. E.10.XI.132010.

[28]   Freye E. Pharmacology and abuse of cocaine, amphetamines, ecstasy and related designer drugs: a comprehensive review on their mode of action, treatment of abuse and intoxication. *SpringerLink, editor*. London: Springer, 2009; 2009.

[29]   Kalant H. The pharmacology and toxicology of "ecstasy" (MDMA) and related drugs. *CMAJ*. 2001 Oct 2; 165 (7): 917-28.

[30] Caldwell JA, Smythe NK, Leduc PA, Caldwell JL. Efficacy of Dexedrine for maintaining aviator performance during 64 hours of sustained wakefulness: a simulator study. *Aviat. Space Environ. Med.* 2000 Jan; 71 (1): 7-18.

[31] Anglin MD, Burke C, Perrochet B, Stamper E, Dawud-Noursi S. History of the methamphetamine problem. *J. Psychoactive Drugs.* 2000 Apr-Jun; 32 (2): 137-41.

[32] Rothman RB, Baumann MH, Dersch CM, Romero DV, Rice KC, Carroll FI, et al. Amphetamine-type central nervous system stimulants release norepinephrine more potently than they release dopamine and serotonin. *Synapse.* 2001 Jan; 39 (1): 32-41.

[33] Robinson JB. Stereoselectivity and isoenzyme selectivity of monoamine oxidase inhibitors. Enantiomers of amphetamine, N-methylamphetamine and deprenyl. *Biochem. Pharmacol.* 1985 Dec 1; 34 (23): 4105-8.

[34] Cook CE, Jeffcoat AR, Hill JM, Pugh DE, Patetta PK, Sadler BM, et al. Pharmacokinetics of methamphetamine self-administered to human subjects by smoking *S*-(+)-methamphetamine hydrochloride. *Drug Metab. Dispos.* 1993 Jul-Aug; 21 (4): 717-23.

[35] Wilkinson P, Van Dyke C, Jatlow P, Barash P, Byck R. Intranasal and oral cocaine kinetics. *Clin. Pharmacol. Ther.* 1980 Mar; 27 (3): 386-94.

[36] Phelps ME. Positron emission tomography provides molecular imaging of biological processes. *Proc. Natl. Acad. Sci. USA.* 2000 August 1, 2000; 97 (16): 9226-33.

[37] Gatley SJ, Volkow ND, Wang GJ, Fowler JS, Logan J, Ding YS, et al. PET imaging in clinical drug abuse research. *Curr. Pharm. Des.* 2005; 11 (25): 3203-19.

[38] Bischoff S, Heinrich M, Sonntag JM, Krauss J. The D1 dopamine receptor antagonist SCH 23390 also interacts potently with brain serotonin (5-HT$_2$) receptors. *Eur. J. Pharmacol.* 1986; 129 (3): 367-70.

[39] Hitzemann R, Volkow N, Fowler J, Wang GJ. *Neuroimaging and Substance Abuse. Biol. Psychiatry*: John Wiley and Sons, Ltd; 2003. p. 523-35.

[40] Fowler JS, Volkow ND, Wang GJ, Ding YS. 2-deoxy-2-[^{18}F]fluoro-D-glucose and alternative radiotracers for positron emission tomography imaging using the human brain as a model. *Semin. Nucl. Med.* 2004 Apr; 34 (2): 112-21.

[41] Volkow ND, Fowler JS, Wolf AP, Schlyer D, Shiue CY, Alpert R, et al. Effects of chronic cocaine abuse on postsynaptic dopamine receptors. *Am. J. Psychiatry.* 1990 Jun; 147 (6): 719-24.

[42] Volkow ND, Fowler JS, Wolf AP, Hitzemann R, Dewey S, Bendriem B, et al. Changes in brain glucose metabolism in cocaine dependence and withdrawal. *Am. J. Psychiatry.* 1991 May; 148 (5): 621-6.

[43] Volkow ND, Fowler JS, Wang GJ, Hitzemann R, Logan J, Schlyer DJ, et al. Decreased dopamine D2 receptor availability is associated with reduced frontal metabolism in cocaine abusers. *Synapse.* 1993 Jun; 14 (2): 169-77.

[44] Volkow ND, Wang GJ, Fowler JS, Gatley SJ, Ding YS, Logan J, et al. Relationship between psychostimulant-induced "high" and dopamine transporter occupancy. *Proc. Natl. Acad. Sci. USA.* 1996 Sep 17; 93 (19): 10388-92.

[45] Volkow ND, Wang GJ, Fischman MW, Foltin RW, Fowler JS, Abumrad NN, et al. Relationship between subjective effects of cocaine and dopamine transporter occupancy. *Nature.* 1997 Apr 24; 386 (6627): 827-30.

[46] Grant S, London ED, Newlin DB, Villemagne VL, Liu X, Contoreggi C, et al. Activation of memory circuits during cue-elicited cocaine craving. *Proc. Natl. Acad. Sci. USA.* 1996 Oct 15; 93 (21): 12040-5.

[47] Bonson KR, Grant SJ, Contoreggi CS, Links JM, Metcalfe J, Weyl HL, et al. Neural systems and cue-induced cocaine craving. *Neuropsychopharmacology.* 2002 Mar;26(3):376-86.

[48] Seiden LS, Sabol KE. Methamphetamine and methylenedioxymethamphetamine neurotoxicity: possible mechanisms of cell destruction. *NIDA Res. Monogr.* 1996;163:251-76.

[49] Wilson JM, Kalasinsky KS, Levey AI, Bergeron C, Reiber G, Anthony RM, et al. Striatal dopamine nerve terminal markers in human, chronic methamphetamine users. *Nat. Med.* 1996 Jun; 2 (6): 699-703.

[50] McCann UD, Wong DF, Yokoi F, Villemagne V, Dannals RF, Ricaurte GA. Reduced striatal dopamine transporter density in abstinent methamphetamine and methcathinone users: evidence from positron emission tomography studies with [11C]WIN-35,428. *J. Neurosci.* 1998 Oct 15; 18 (20): 8417-22.

[51] Volkow ND, Chang L, Wang GJ, Fowler JS, Franceschi D, Sedler M, et al. Loss of dopamine transporters in methamphetamine abusers recovers with protracted abstinence. *J. Neurosci.* 2001 Dec 1; 21 (23): 9414-8.

[52] Volkow ND, Chang L, Wang GJ, Fowler JS, Leonido-Yee M, Franceschi D, et al. Association of dopamine transporter reduction with psychomotor impairment in methamphetamine abusers. *Am. J. Psychiatry.* 2001 Mar; 158 (3): 377-82.

[53] Volkow ND, Chang L, Wang GJ, Fowler JS, Ding YS, Sedler M, et al. Low level of brain dopamine D_2 receptors in methamphetamine abusers: association with metabolism in the orbitofrontal cortex. *Am. J. Psychiatry.* 2001 Dec; 158 (12): 2015-21.

[54] Hume SP, Lammertsma AA, Myers R, Rajeswaran S, Bloomfield PM, Ashworth S, et al. The potential of high-resolution positron emission tomography to monitor striatal dopaminergic function in rat models of disease. *J. Neurosci. Methods.* 1996 Aug; 67 (2): 103-12.

[55] Haber SN, Kunishio K, Mizobuchi M, Lynd-Balta E. The orbital and medial prefrontal circuit through the primate basal ganglia. *J. Neurosci.* 1995 Jul; 15 (7 Pt 1): 4851-67.

[56] Volkow ND, Chang L, Wang G-J, Fowler JS, Franceschi D, Sedler MJ, et al. Higher cortical and lower subcortical metabolism in detoxified methamphetamine abusers. *Am. J. Psychiatry.* 2001 March 1, 2001; 158 (3): 383-9.

[57] Sekine Y, Iyo M, Ouchi Y, Matsunaga T, Tsukada H, Okada H, et al. Methamphetamine-related psychiatric symptoms and reduced brain dopamine transporters studied with PET. *Am. J. Psychiatry.* 2001 Aug; 158 (8): 1206-14.

[58] London ED, Simon SL, Berman SM, Mandelkern MA, Lichtman AM, Bramen J, et al. Mood disturbances and regional cerebral metabolic abnormalities in recently abstinent methamphetamine abusers. *Arch. Gen. Psychiatry.* 2004 January 1, 2004; 61 (1): 73-84.

[59] Laureys S, Peigneux P, Goldman S. *Brain Imaging. Biol. Psychiatry*: John Wiley and Sons, Ltd; 2003. p. 155-66.

[60] Ogawa S, Lee TM, Kay AR, Tank DW. Brain magnetic resonance imaging with contrast dependent on blood oxygenation. *Proc. Natl. Acad. Sci. USA.* 1990 Dec; 87 (24): 9868-72.

[61]   Gore JC. Principles and practice of functional MRI of the human brain. *J. Clin. Invest.* 2003 Jul; 112 (1): 4-9.

[62]   Garavan H, Hester R. The role of cognitive control in cocaine dependence. *Neuropsychol. Rev.* 2007 Sep; 17 (3): 337-45.

[63]   MacLeod CM. Half a century of research on the Stroop effect: an integrative review. *Psychol. Bull.* 1991 Mar; 109 (2): 163-203.

[64]   Hester R, Dixon V, Garavan H. A consistent attentional bias for drug-related material in active cocaine users across word and picture versions of the emotional Stroop task. *Drug Alcohol Depend.* 2006 Feb 28; 81 (3): 251-7.

[65]   Goldstein RZ, Tomasi D, Rajaram S, Cottone LA, Zhang L, Maloney T, et al. Role of the anterior cingulate and medial orbitofrontal cortex in processing drug cues in cocaine addiction. *Neuroscience.* 2007 Feb 23; 144 (4): 1153-9.

[66]   Brewer JA, Worhunsky PD, Carroll KM, Rounsaville BJ, Potenza MN. Pretreatment brain activation during stroop task is associated with outcomes in cocaine-dependent patients. *Biol. Psychiatry.* 2008 Dec 1; 64 (11): 998-1004.

[67]   Guzy LT, Axelrod S. Interaural attention shifting as response. *J. Exp. Psychol.* 1972 Oct; 95 (2): 290-4.

[68]   Monsell S. Task switching. *Trends Cogn. Sci.* 2003 Mar; 7 (3): 134-40.

[69]   Garavan H. Serial attention within working memory. *Mem. Cognit.* 1998 Mar; 26 (2): 263-76.

[70]   Kübler A, Murphy K, Garavan H. Cocaine dependence and attention switching within and between verbal and visuospatial working memory. *Eur. J. Neurosci.* 2005 Apr; 21 (7): 1984-92.

[71]   Kübler A, Murphy K, Kaufman J, Stein EA, Garavan H. Co-ordination within and between verbal and visuospatial working memory: network modulation and anterior frontal recruitment. *Neuroimage.* 2003 Oct; 20 (2): 1298-308.

[72]   Volkow ND, Ding YS, Fowler JS, Wang GJ. Cocaine addiction: hypothesis derived from imaging studies with PET. *J. Addict Dis.* 1996; 15 (4): 55-71.

[73]   Jentsch JD, Taylor JR. Impulsivity resulting from frontostriatal dysfunction in drug abuse: implications for the control of behavior by reward-related stimuli. *Psychopharmacology (Berl).* 1999 Oct; 146 (4): 373-90.

[74]   Kaufman JN, Ross TJ, Stein EA, Garavan H. Cingulate hypoactivity in cocaine users during a GO-NOGO task as revealed by event-related functional magnetic resonance imaging. *J. Neurosci.* 2003 Aug 27; 23 (21): 7839-43.

[75]   Hester R, Garavan H. Executive dysfunction in cocaine addiction: evidence for discordant frontal, cingulate, and cerebellar activity. *J. Neurosci.* 2004 Dec 8; 24 (49): 11017-22.

[76]   Robbins TW, Everitt BJ. Drug addiction: bad habits add up. *Nature.* 1999 Apr 15; 398 (6728): 567-70.

[77]   Rolls ET. The orbitofrontal cortex and reward. *Cereb Cortex.* 2000 Mar; 10 (3): 284-94.

[78]   London ED, Ernst M, Grant S, Bonson K, Weinstein A. Orbitofrontal cortex and human drug abuse: functional imaging. *Cereb Cortex.* 2000 Mar; 10 (3): 334-42.

[79]   Paulus MP, Hozack NE, Zauscher BE, Frank L, Brown GG, Braff DL, et al. Behavioral and functional neuroimaging evidence for prefrontal dysfunction in methamphetamine-dependent subjects. *Neuropsychopharmacology.* 2002 Jan; 26 (1): 53-63.

[80] Bechara A, Damasio AR, Damasio H, Anderson SW. Insensitivity to future consequences following damage to human prefrontal cortex. *Cognition.* 1994 Apr-Jun; 50 (1-3): 7-15.

[81] Tversky A, Sattath S, Slovic P. Contingent weighting in judgment and choice. *Psychol. Rev.* 1988; 95 (3): 371-84.

[82] Elliott R, Dolan RJ. Activation of different anterior cingulate foci in association with hypothesis testing and response selection. *Neuroimage.* 1998 Jul; 8 (1): 17-29.

[83] Green L, Myerson J, Ostaszewski P. Amount of reward has opposite effects on the discounting of delayed and probabilistic outcomes. *J. Exp. Psychol. Learn Mem. Cogn.* 1999 Mar; 25 (2): 418-27.

[84] Monterosso J, Ainslie G. Beyond discounting: possible experimental models of impulse control. *Psychopharmacology (Berl).* 1999 Oct; 146 (4): 339-47.

[85] Rogers RD, Everitt BJ, Baldacchino A, Blackshaw AJ, Swainson R, Wynne K, et al. Dissociable deficits in the decision-making cognition of chronic amphetamine abusers, opiate abusers, patients with focal damage to prefrontal cortex, and tryptophan-depleted normal volunteers: evidence for monoaminergic mechanisms. *Neuropsychopharmacology.* 1999 Apr; 20 (4): 322-39.

[86] Rogers RD, Owen AM, Middleton HC, Williams EJ, Pickard JD, Sahakian BJ, et al. Choosing between small, likely rewards and large, unlikely rewards activates inferior and orbital prefrontal cortex. *J. Neurosci.* 1999 Oct 15; 19 (20): 9029-38.

[87] Paulus MP, Hozack N, Frank L, Brown GG, Schuckit MA. Decision making by methamphetamine-dependent subjects is associated with error-rate-independent decrease in prefrontal and parietal activation. *Biol. Psychiatry.* 2003 Jan 1; 53 (1): 65-74.

[88] Paulus MP, Tapert SF, Schuckit MA. Neural activation patterns of methamphetamine-dependent subjects during decision making predict relapse. *Arch. Gen. Psychiatry.* 2005 Jul; 62 (7): 761-8.

[89] Gordon DL, Schachar RJ, Tannock R. Impulsivity and Inhibitory Control. *Psychological Science.* 1997; 8 (1): 60-4.

[90] Ainslie G. Specious reward: a behavioral theory of impulsiveness and impulse control. *Psychological Bulletin.* 1975 Jul; 82 (4): 463-96.

[91] Monterosso JR, Ainslie G, Xu J, Cordova X, Domier CP, London ED. Frontoparietal cortical activity of methamphetamine-dependent and comparison subjects performing a delay discounting task. *Human Brain Mapping.* 2007 May; 28 (5): 383-93.

[92] Hoffman WF, Schwartz DL, Huckans MS, McFarland BH, Meiri G, Stevens AA, et al. Cortical activation during delay discounting in abstinent methamphetamine dependent individuals. *Psychopharmacology (Berl).* 2008 Dec; 201 (2): 183-93.

[93] Owen AM, McMillan KM, Laird AR, Bullmore E. N-back working memory paradigm: a meta-analysis of normative functional neuroimaging studies. *Hum. Brain Mapp.* 2005 May; 25 (1): 46-59.

[94] Ricciardi E, Bonino D, Gentili C, Sani L, Pietrini P, Vecchi T. Neural correlates of spatial working memory in humans: a functional magnetic resonance imaging study comparing visual and tactile processes. *Neuroscience.* 2006 Apr 28; 139 (1): 339-49.

[95] Cole MW, Schneider W. The cognitive control network: Integrated cortical regions with dissociable functions. *Neuroimage.* 2007 Aug 1; 37 (1): 343-60.

[96] Whitwell JL. Voxel-based morphometry: an automated technique for assessing structural changes in the brain. *The Journal of Neuroscience.* 2009 August 5, 2009; 29 (31): 9661-4.

[97] Ashburner J, Friston KJ. Voxel-based morphometry--the methods. *Neuroimage.* 2000 Jun; 11 (6 Pt 1): 805-21.

[98] Wright IC, McGuire PK, Poline JB, Travere JM, Murray RM, Frith CD, et al. A voxel-based method for the statistical analysis of gray and white matter density applied to schizophrenia. *Neuroimage.* 1995 Dec; 2 (4): 244-52.

[99] Liu X, Matochik JA, Cadet JL, London ED. Smaller volume of prefrontal lobe in polysubstance abusers: a magnetic resonance imaging study. *Neuropsychopharmacology.* 1998 Apr; 18 (4): 243-52.

[100] Bartzokis G, Beckson M, Lu PH, Edwards N, Rapoport R, Wiseman E, et al. Age-related brain volume reductions in amphetamine and cocaine addicts and normal controls: implications for addiction research. *Psychiatry Res.* 2000 Apr 10; 98 (2): 93-102.

[101] Morgan MJ, Cascella NG, Stapleton JM, Phillips RL, Yung BC, Wong DF, et al. Sensitivity to subjective effects of cocaine in drug abusers: relationship to cerebral ventricle size. *Am. J. Psychiatry.* 1993 Nov; 150 (11): 1712-7.

[102] Franklin TR, Acton PD, Maldjian JA, Gray JD, Croft JR, Dackis CA, et al. Decreased gray matter concentration in the insular, orbitofrontal, cingulate, and temporal cortices of cocaine patients. *Biol. Psychiatry.* 2002; 51 (2): 134-42.

[103] Bolla KI, Eldreth DA, London ED, Kiehl KA, Mouratidis M, Contoreggi C, et al. Orbitofrontal cortex dysfunction in abstinent cocaine abusers performing a decision-making task. *Neuroimage.* 2003; 19 (3): 1085-94.

[104] Bolla K, Ernst M, Kiehl K, Mouratidis M, Eldreth D, Contoreggi C, et al. Prefrontal cortical dysfunction in abstinent cocaine abusers. *J. Neuropsychiatry Clin. Neurosci.* 2004 November 1, 2004; 16 (4): 456-64.

[105] Hanlon CA, Dufault DL, Wesley MJ, Porrino LJ. Elevated gray and white matter densities in cocaine abstainers compared to current users. *Psychopharmacology (Berl).* 2011 Jun 22.

[106] Sim ME, Lyoo IK, Streeter CC, Covell J, Sarid-Segal O, Ciraulo DA, et al. Cerebellar gray matter volume correlates with duration of cocaine use in cocaine-dependent subjects. *Neuropsychopharmacology.* 2007 Oct; 32 (10): 2229-37.

[107] Good CD, Johnsrude IS, Ashburner J, Henson RN, Friston KJ, Frackowiak RS. A voxel-based morphometric study of ageing in 465 normal adult human brains. *Neuroimage.* 2001 Jul; 14 (1 Pt 1): 21-36.

[108] Ashburner J, Friston KJ. Nonlinear spatial normalization using basis functions. *Hum. Brain Mapp.* 1999; 7 (4): 254-66.

[109] Chung MK, Dalton KM, Davidson RJ. Tensor-based cortical surface morphometry via weighted spherical harmonic representation. *IEEE Trans Med. Imaging.* 2008 Aug; 27 (8): 1143-51.

[110] Hua X, Leow AD, Parikshak N, Lee S, Chiang MC, Toga AW, et al. Tensor-based morphometry as a neuroimaging biomarker for Alzheimer's disease: an MRI study of 676 AD, MCI, and normal subjects. *Neuroimage.* 2008 Nov 15; 43 (3): 458-69.

[111] Kim J, Avants B, Patel S, Whyte J, Coslett BH, Pluta J, et al. Structural consequences of diffuse traumatic brain injury: a large deformation tensor-based morphometry study. *Neuroimage.* 2008 Feb 1; 39 (3): 1014-26.

[112] Narayana PA, Datta S, Tao G, Steinberg JL, Moeller FG. Effect of cocaine on structural changes in brain: MRI volumetry using tensor-based morphometry. *Drug Alcohol Depend.* 2010; 111 (3): 191-9.

[113] Li S-J, Wang Y, Pankiewicz J, Stein EA. Neurochemical adaptation to cocaine abuse: reduction of N-acetyl aspartate in thalamus of human cocaine abusers. *Biol. Psychiatry.* 1999; 45 (11): 1481-7.

[114] Ma L, Hasan KM, Steinberg JL, Narayana PA, Lane SD, Zuniga EA, et al. Diffusion tensor imaging in cocaine dependence: Regional effects of cocaine on corpus callosum and effect of cocaine administration route. *Drug Alcohol Depend.* 2009; 104 (3): 262-7.

[115] Moeller FG, Hasan KM, Steinberg JL, Kramer LA, Valdes I, Lai LY, et al. Diffusion tensor imaging eigenvalues: Preliminary evidence for altered myelin in cocaine dependence. *Psychiat. Res.-Neuroim.* 2007; 154 (3): 253-8.

[116] Thompson PM, Hayashi KM, Simon SL, Geaga JA, Hong MS, Sui Y, et al. Structural abnormalities in the brains of human subjects who use methamphetamine. *J. Neurosci.* 2004 June 30, 2004; 24 (26): 6028-36.

[117] Chang L, Cloak C, Patterson K, Grob C, Miller EN, Ernst T. Enlarged striatum in abstinent methamphetamine abusers: a possible compensatory response. *Biol. Psychiatry.* 2005 May 1; 57 (9): 967-74.

[118] Jernigan TL, Gamst AC, Archibald SL, Fennema-Notestine C, Mindt MR, Marcotte TL, et al. Effects of methamphetamine dependence and HIV infection on cerebral morphology. *Am. J. Psychiatry.* 2005 August 1, 2005; 162 (8): 1461-72.

[119] Kim SJ, Lyoo IK, Hwang J, Chung A, Hoon Sung Y, Kim J, et al. Prefrontal grey-matter changes in short-term and long-term abstinent methamphetamine abusers. *The Int. J. Neuropsychopharmacol.* 2006; 9 (02): 221-8.

[120] Anderson SW, Damasio H, Jones RD, Tranel D. Wisconsin Card Sorting Test performance as a measure of frontal lobe damage. *J. Clin. Exp. Neuropsychol.* 1991 Nov; 13 (6): 909-22.

[121] Schwartz DL, Mitchell AD, Lahna DL, Luber HS, Huckans MS, Mitchell SH, et al. Global and local morphometric differences in recently abstinent methamphetamine-dependent individuals. *Neuroimage.* 2010 May 1; 50 (4): 1392-401.

[122] Basser P, J, Jones D, K. Diffusion-tensor MRI: theory, experimental design and data analysis - a technical review. *NMR Biomed.* 2002; 15 (7-8): 456-67.

[123] Basser PJ. Inferring microstructural features and the physiological state of tissues from diffusion-weighted images. *NMR Biomed.* 1995 Nov-Dec; 8 (7-8): 333-44.

[124] Song SK, Sun SW, Ramsbottom MJ, Chang C, Russell J, Cross AH. Dysmyelination revealed through MRI as increased radial (but unchanged axial) diffusion of water. *Neuroimage.* 2002 Nov; 17 (3): 1429-36.

[125] Song SK, Yoshino J, Le TQ, Lin SJ, Sun SW, Cross AH, et al. Demyelination increases radial diffusivity in corpus callosum of mouse brain. *Neuroimage.* 2005 May 15; 26 (1): 132-40.

[126] Mori S, Crain BJ, Chacko VP, van Zijl PC. Three-dimensional tracking of axonal projections in the brain by magnetic resonance imaging. *Ann. Neurol.* 1999 Feb; 45 (2): 265-9.

[127] Lim KO, Choi SJ, Pomara N, Wolkin A, Rotrosen JP. Reduced frontal white matter integrity in cocaine dependence: a controlled diffusion tensor imaging study. *Biol. Psychiatry*. 2002 Jun 1; 51 (11): 890-5.

[128] Volkow ND, Fowler JS. Addiction, a disease of compulsion and drive: involvement of the orbitofrontal cortex. *Cereb Cortex*. 2000 Mar; 10 (3): 318-25.

[129] Moeller FG, Hasan KM, Steinberg JL, Kramer LA, Dougherty DM, Santos RM, et al. Reduced anterior corpus callosum white matter integrity is related to increased impulsivity and reduced discriminability in cocaine-dependent subjects: diffusion tensor imaging. *Neuropsychopharmacology*. 2005 Mar; 30 (3): 610-7.

[130] Lane SD, Steinberg JL, Ma L, Hasan KM, Kramer LA, Zuniga EA, et al. Diffusion tensor imaging and decision making in cocaine dependence. *PLoS ONE*. 2010; 5 (7): e11591.

[131] Lim KO, Wozniak JR, Mueller BA, Franc DT, Specker SM, Rodriguez CP, et al. Brain macrostructural and microstructural abnormalities in cocaine dependence. *Drug and Alcohol Dependence*. 2008; 92 (1-3): 164-72.

[132] Romero MJ, Asensio S, Palau C, Sanchez A, Romero FJ. Cocaine addiction: diffusion tensor imaging study of the inferior frontal and anterior cingulate white matter. *Psychiatry Res*. 2010 Jan 30; 181 (1): 57-63.

[133] Xu J, DeVito EE, Worhunsky PD, Carroll KM, Rounsaville BJ, Potenza MN. White matter integrity is associated with treatment outcome measures in cocaine dependence. *Neuropsychopharmacology*. 2010; 35 (7): 1541-9.

[134] Bell RP, Foxe JJ, Nierenberg J, Hoptman MJ, Garavan H. Assessing white matter integrity as a function of abstinence duration in former cocaine-dependent individuals. *Drug Alcohol Depend*. 2011 Apr 1; 114 (2-3): 159-68.

[135] Chung A, Lyoo IK, Kim SJ, Hwang J, Bae SC, Sung YH, et al. Decreased frontal white-matter integrity in abstinent methamphetamine abusers. *Int. J. Neuropsychopharmcol*. 2007 Dec; 10 (6): 765-75.

[136] Tobias MC, O'Neill J, Hudkins M, Bartzokis G, Dean AC, London ED. White-matter abnormalities in brain during early abstinence from methamphetamine abuse. *Psychopharmacology (Berl)*. 2010 Mar; 209 (1): 13-24.

[137] Kim I-S, Kim Y-T, Song H-J, Lee J-J, Kwon D-H, Lee HJ, et al. Reduced corpus callosum white matter microstructural integrity revealed by diffusion tensor eigenvalues in abstinent methamphetamine addicts. *Neurotoxicology*. 2009; 30 (2): 209-13.

[138] Salo R, Nordahl TE, Buonocore MH, Natsuaki Y, Waters C, Moore CD, et al. Cognitive control and white matter callosal microstructure in methamphetamine-dependent subjects: a diffusion tensor imaging study. *Biol. Psychiatry*. 2009 Jan 15; 65 (2): 122-8.

[139] Alicata D, Chang L, Cloak C, Abe K, Ernst T. Higher diffusion in striatum and lower fractional anisotropy in white matter of methamphetamine users. *Psychiat. Res.-Neuroim.*2009; 174 (1): 1-8.

[140] Miller BL, Changl L, Booth R, Ernst T, Cornford M, Nikas D, et al. In vivo ^{1}H MRS choline: Correlation with in vitro chemistry/histology. *Life Sci*. 1996; 58 (22): 1929-35.

[141] Nordahl TE, Salo R, Natsuaki Y, Galloway GP, Waters C, Moore CD, et al. Methamphetamine users in sustained abstinence: a proton magnetic resonance spectroscopy study. *Arch. Gen. Psychiatry*. 2005 Apr; 62 (4): 444-52.

[142] Tedeschi G, Bertolino A, Righini A, Campbell G, Raman R, Duyn JH, et al. Brain regional distribution pattern of metabolite signal intensities in young adults by proton magnetic resonance spectroscopic imaging. *Neurology.* 1995 Jul; 45 (7): 1384-91.

[143] Jansen JFA, Backes WH, Nicolay K, Kooi ME. [1]H MR spectroscopy of the brain: absolute quantification of metabolites. *Radiology.* 2006 Aug; 240 (2): 318-32.

[144] Brand A, Engelmann J, Leibfritz D. A ^{13}C NMR study on fluxes into the TCA cycle of neuronal and glial tumor cell lines and primary cells. *Biochimie.* 1992 Sep-Oct; 74 (9-10): 941-8.

[145] Chang L, Ernst T, Poland RE, Jenden DJ. In vivo proton magnetic resonance spectroscopy of the normal aging human brain. *Life Sci.* 1996; 58 (22): 2049-56.

[146] Behar KL, Rothman DL. In vivo nuclear magnetic resonance studies of glutamate-gamma-aminobutyric acid-glutamine cycling in rodent and human cortex: the central role of glutamine. *J. Nutr.* 2001 Sep; 131 (9 Suppl): 2498S-504S; discussion 523S-4S.

[147] Haley AP, Knight-Scott J. Proton Magnetic Resonance Spectroscopy (^{1}H MRS): A Practical Guide for the Clinical Neuroscientist. In: Cohen RA, Sweet LH, editors. *Brain Imaging in Behavioral Medicine and Clinical Neuroscience*: Springer New York; 2011. p. 83-91.

[148] Behar KL, Rothman DL, Spencer DD, Petroff OA. Analysis of macromolecule resonances in 1H NMR spectra of human brain. *Magn. Reson. Med.* 1994 Sep; 32 (3): 294-302.

[149] Gass JT, Olive MF. Glutamatergic substrates of drug addiction and alcoholism. *Biochem. Pharmacol.* 2008 Jan 1; 75 (1): 218-65.

[150] Torregrossa MM, Kalivas PW. Microdialysis and the neurochemistry of addiction. *Pharmacol. Biochem. Behav.* 2008 Aug; 90 (2): 261-72.

[151] Licata SC, Renshaw PF. Neurochemistry of drug action: insights from proton magnetic resonance spectroscopic imaging and their relevance to addiction. *Ann. N. Y. Acad. Sci.* 2010 Feb; 1187: 148-71.

[152] Chang L, Mehringer CM, Ernst T, Melchor R, Myers H, Forney D, et al. Neuro-chemical alterations in asymptomatic abstinent cocaine users: A proton magnetic resonance spectroscopy study. *Biol. Psychiatry.* 1997; 42 (12): 1105-14.

[153] Chang L, Ernst T, Strickland T, Mehringer CM. Gender effects on persistent cerebral metabolite changes in the frontal lobes of abstinent cocaine users. *Am. J. Psychiatry.* 1999 May; 156 (5): 716-22.

[154] Cendes F, Andermann F, Dubeau F, Matthews PM, Arnold DL. Normalization of neuronal metabolic dysfunction after surgery for temporal lobe epilepsy. Evidence from proton MR spectroscopic imaging. *Neurology.* 1997 Dec; 49 (6): 1525-33.

[155] De Stefano N, Matthews PM, Arnold DL. Reversible decreases in N-acetylaspartate after acute brain injury. *Magn. Reson. Med.* 1995 Nov; 34 (5): 721-7.

[156] Yang S, Salmeron BJ, Ross TJ, Xi Z-X, Stein EA, Yang Y. Lower glutamate levels in rostral anterior cingulate of chronic cocaine users -- A ^{1}H-MRS study using TE-averaged PRESS at 3 T with an optimized quantification strategy. *Psychiat. Res.-Neuroim.* 2009; 174 (3): 171-6.

[157] Hetherington H, Pan J, Telang F, Pappas N, Volkow N. Reduced brain GABA levels in cocaine abusers. *Proc. Intern. Soc. Magn. Reson. Med.* 2000; 523.

[158] Ke Y, Streeter CC, Nassar LE, Sarid-Segal O, Hennen J, Yurgelun-Todd DA, et al. Frontal lobe GABA levels in cocaine dependence: a two-dimensional, J-resolved magnetic resonance spectroscopy study. *Psychiatry Res.* 2004 Apr 30; 130 (3): 283-93.

[159] McGrath BM, McKay R, Dave S, Seres P, Weljie AM, Slupsky CM, et al. Acute dextro-amphetamine administration does not alter brain *myo*-inositol levels in humans and animals: MRS investigations at 3 and 18.8 T. *Neurosci. Res.* 2008 Aug; 61 (4): 351-9.

[160] Silverstone PH, O'Donnell T, Ulrich M, Asghar S, Hanstock CC. Dextro-amphetamine increases phosphoinositol cycle activity in volunteers: an MRS study. *Hum. Psychopharmacol.* 2002 Dec; 17 (8): 425-9.

[161] Silverstone PH, Rotzinger S, Pukhovsky A, Hanstock CC. Effects of lithium and amphetamine on inositol metabolism in the human brain as measured by ^{1}H and ^{31}P MRS. *Biol. Psychiatry.* 1999 Dec 15; 46 (12): 1634-41.

[162] Ernst T, Chang L, Leonido-Yee M, Speck O. Evidence for long-term neurotoxicity associated with methamphetamine abuse: A ^{1}H MRS study. *Neurology.* 2000 Mar 28; 54 (6): 1344-9.

[163] Nordahl TE, Salo R, Possin K, Gibson DR, Flynn N, Leamon M, et al. Low N-acetyl-aspartate and high choline in the anterior cingulum of recently abstinent methamphetamine-dependent subjects: a preliminary proton MRS study. Magnetic resonance spectroscopy. *Psychiatry Res.* 2002 Nov 30; 116 (1-2): 43-52.

[164] Salo R, Nordahl TE, Natsuaki Y, Leamon MH, Galloway GP, Waters C, et al. Attentional control and brain metabolite levels in methamphetamine abusers. *Biol. Psychiatry.* 2007; 61 (11): 1272-80.

[165] Sekine Y, Minabe Y, Kawai M, Suzuki K, Iyo M, Isoda H, et al. Metabolite alterations in basal ganglia associated with methamphetamine-related psychiatric symptoms. A proton MRS study. *Neuropsychopharmacology.* 2002 Sep; 27 (3): 453-61.

[166] Sung YH, Cho SC, Hwang J, Kim SJ, Kim H, Bae S, et al. Relationship between N-acetyl-aspartate in gray and white matter of abstinent methamphetamine abusers and their history of drug abuse: a proton magnetic resonance spectroscopy study. *Drug Alcohol Depend.* 2007 Apr 17; 88 (1): 28-35.

[167] Salo R, Buonocore MH, Leamon M, Natsuaki Y, Waters C, Moore CD, et al. Extended findings of brain metabolite normalization in MA-dependent subjects across sustained abstinence: A proton MRS study. *Drug Alcohol Depend.* 2011; 113 (2-3): 133-8.

[168] Yamamoto BK, Bankson MG. Amphetamine neurotoxicity: cause and consequence of oxidative stress. *Crit. Rev. Neurobiol.* 2005; 17 (2): 87-117.

[169] Ernst T, Chang L. Adaptation of brain glutamate plus glutamine during abstinence from chronic methamphetamine use. *J. Neuroimmune Pharmacol.* 2008 Sep; 3 (3): 165-72.

[170] Sailasuta N, Abulseoud O, Hernandez M, Haghani P, Ross BD. Metabolic abnormalities in abstinent methamphetamine dependent subjects. *Substance Abuse: Research and Treatment.* 2010; 4 (1): 9-20.

[171] Koob GF, Kenneth Lloyd G, Mason BJ. Development of pharmacotherapies for drug addiction: a Rosetta Stone approach. *Nat. Rev. Drug Discov.* 2009; 8 (6): 500-15.

[172] Grabowski J, Shearer J, Merrill J, Negus SS. Agonist-like, replacement pharmacotherapy for stimulant abuse and dependence. *Addict Behav.* 2004 Sep; 29 (7): 1439-64.

[173] Shearer J, Wodak A, Mattick RP, Van Beek I, Lewis J, Hall W, et al. Pilot randomized controlled study of dexamphetamine substitution for amphetamine dependence. *Addiction.* 2001 Sep; 96 (9): 1289-96.

[174] Longo M, Wickes W, Smout M, Harrison S, Cahill S, White JM. Randomized controlled trial of dexamphetamine maintenance for the treatment of methamphetamine dependence. *Addiction.* 2009;9999(9999).

[175] Tiihonen J, Kuoppasalmi K, Fohr J, Tuomola P, Kuikanmaki O, Vorma H, et al. A comparison of aripiprazole, methylphenidate, and placebo for amphetamine dependence. *Am. J. Psychiatry.* 2007 Jan; 164 (1): 160-2.

[176] Rush CR, Stoops WW, Hays LR, Glaser PE, Hays LS. Risperidone attenuates the discriminative-stimulus effects of d-amphetamine in humans. *J. Pharmacol. Exp. Ther.* 2003 Jul; 306 (1): 195-204.

[177] Meredith CW, Jaffe C, Yanasak E, Cherrier M, Saxon AJ. An open-label pilot study of risperidone in the treatment of methamphetamine dependence. *J. Psychoactive Drugs.* 2007 Jun; 39 (2): 167-72.

[178] Lile JA, Stoops WW, Vansickel AR, Glaser PE, Hays LR, Rush CR. Aripiprazole attenuates the discriminative-stimulus and subject-rated effects of D-amphetamine in humans. *Neuropsychopharmacology.* 2005 Nov; 30 (11): 2103-14.

[179] Stoops WW, Lile JA, Glaser PEA, Rush CR. A low dose of aripiprazole attenuates the subject-rated effects of *d*-amphetamine. *Drug Alcohol Depend.* 2006 Sep 15; 84 (2): 206-9.

[180] Newton TF, Reid MS, De La Garza R, Mahoney JJ, Abad A, Condos R, et al. Evaluation of subjective effects of aripiprazole and methamphetamine in methamphetamine-dependent volunteers. *Int. J. Neuropsychopharmcol.* 2008 Dec; 11 (8): 1037-45.

[181] Wood PL. Actions of GABAergic agents on dopamine metabolism in the nigrostriatal pathway of the rat. *J. Pharmacol. Exp. Ther.* 1982 Sep; 222 (3): 674-9.

[182] Pycock C, Horton R. Evidence for an accumbens-pallidal pathway in the rat and its possible gabaminergic control. *Brain Res.* 1976 Jul 16; 110 (3): 629-34.

[183] Fadda P, Scherma M, Fresu A, Collu M, Fratta W. Baclofen antagonizes nicotine-, cocaine-, and morphine-induced dopamine release in the nucleus accumbens of rat. *Synapse.* 2003 Oct; 50 (1): 1-6.

[184] Brebner K, Phelan R, Roberts DC. Effect of baclofen on cocaine self-administration in rats reinforced under fixed-ratio 1 and progressive-ratio schedules. *Psychopharmacology (Berl).* 2000 Feb; 148 (3): 314-21.

[185] Roberts DC, Andrews MM, Vickers GJ. Baclofen attenuates the reinforcing effects of cocaine in rats. *Neuropsychopharmacology.* 1996 Oct; 15 (4): 417-23.

[186] Shoaib M, Swanner LS, Beyer CE, Goldberg SR, Schindler CW. The GABA_B agonist baclofen modifies cocaine self-administration in rats. *Behav. Pharmacol.* 1998 May; 9 (3): 195-206.

[187] Heinzerling KG, Shoptaw S, Peck JA, Yang X, Liu J, Roll J, et al. Randomized, placebo-controlled trial of baclofen and gabapentin for the treatment of methamphetamine dependence. *Drug and Alcohol Dependence.* 2006; 85 (3): 177-84.

[188] Urschel HC, 3rd, Hanselka LL, Gromov I, White L, Baron M. Open-label study of a proprietary treatment program targeting type A gamma-aminobutyric acid receptor

dysregulation in methamphetamine dependence. *Mayo. Clin. Proc.* 2007 Oct; 82 (10): 1170-8.

[189] Urschel HC, 3rd, Hanselka LL, Baron M. A controlled trial of flumazenil and gabapentin for initial treatment of methylamphetamine dependence. *J. Psychopharmacol.* 2011 Feb; 25 (2): 254-62.

[190] Morgan AE, Dewey SL. Effects of pharmacologic increases in brain GABA levels on cocaine-induced changes in extracellular dopamine. *Synapse.* 1998 Jan; 28 (1): 60-5.

[191] Lawden MC, Eke T, Degg C, Harding GFA, Wild JM. Visual field defects associated with vigabatrin therapy. *J. Neurol. Neurosurg. Psychiatry.* 1999 December 1, 1999; 67 (6): 716-22.

[192] Brodie JD, Figueroa E, Dewey SL. Treating cocaine addiction: From preclinical to clinical trial experience with γ-vinyl GABA. *Synapse.* 2003; 50 (3): 261-5.

[193] De La Garza R, 2nd, Zorick T, Heinzerling KG, Nusinowitz S, London ED, Shoptaw S, et al. The cardiovascular and subjective effects of methamphetamine combined with gamma-vinyl-gamma-aminobutyric acid (GVG) in non-treatment seeking methamphetamine-dependent volunteers. *Pharmacol. Biochem. Behav.* 2009 Nov; 94 (1): 186-93.

[194] Uys JD, LaLumiere RT. Glutamate: the new frontier in pharmacotherapy for cocaine addiction. *CNS Neurol. Disord. Drug Targets.* 2008 Nov;7(5):482-91.

[195] Bastuji H, Jouvet M. Successful treatment of idiopathic hypersomnia and narcolepsy with modafinil. *Progress in Neuro-Psychopharmacology and Biological Psychiatry.* 1988; 12 (5): 695-700.

[196] Billiard M, Besset A, Montplaisir J, Laffont F, Goldenberg F, Weill JS, et al. Modafinil: a double-blind multicentric study. *Sleep.* 1994 Dec; 17 (8 Suppl): S107-12.

[197] Perez de la Mora M, Aguilar-Garcia A, Ramon-Frias T, Ramirez-Ramirez R, Mendez-Franco J, Rambert F, et al. Effects of the vigilance promoting drug modafinil on the synthesis of GABA and glutamate in slices of rat hypothalamus. *Neurosci. Lett.* 1999 Jan 15; 259 (3): 181-5.

[198] Ferraro L, Antonelli T, O'Connor WT, Tanganelli S, Rambert F, Fuxe K. The antinarcoleptic drug modafinil increases glutamate release in thalamic areas and hippocampus. *Neuroreport.* 1997 Sep 8; 8 (13): 2883-7.

[199] Volkow ND, Fowler JS, Logan J, Alexoff D, Zhu W, Telang F, et al. Effects of modafinil on dopamine and dopamine transporters in the male human brain: clinical implications. Jama. 2009 Mar 18;301(11):1148-54.

[200] Robertson P, Jr., Hellriegel ET. Clinical pharmacokinetic profile of modafinil. *Clin. Pharmacokinet.* 2003; 42 (2): 123-37.

[201] Vosburg SK, Hart CL, Haney M, Rubin E, Foltin RW. Modafinil does not serve as a reinforcer in cocaine abusers. *Drug Alcohol Depend.* 2010 Jan 15; 106 (2-3): 233-6.

[202] McGregor C, Srisurapanont M, Jittiwutikarn J, Laobhripatr S, Wongtan T, White JM. The nature, time course and severity of methamphetamine withdrawal. *Addiction.* 2005 Sep; 100 (9): 1320-9.

[203] McGregor C, Srisurapanont M, Mitchell A, Wickes W, White JM. Symptoms and sleep patterns during inpatient treatment of methamphetamine withdrawal: a comparison of mirtazapine and modafinil with treatment as usual. *J. Subst. Abuse Treat.* 2008 Oct; 35 (3): 334-42.

[204] McElhiney MC, Rabkin JG, Rabkin R, Nunes EV. Provigil (modafinil) plus cognitive behavioral therapy for methamphetamine use in HIV+ gay men: a pilot study. *Am. J. Drug Alcohol Abuse.* 2009; 35 (1): 34-7.

[205] Shearer J, Darke S, Rodgers C, Slade T, van Beek I, Lewis J, et al. A double-blind, placebo-controlled trial of modafinil (200mg/day) for methamphetamine dependence. *Addiction.* 2009; 104 (2): 224-33.

[206] Rothman RB, Partilla JS, Dersch CM, Carroll FI, Rice KC, Baumann MH. Methamphetamine dependence: medication development efforts based on the dual deficit model of stimulant addiction. *Ann. N. Y. Acad. Sci.* 2000 Sep; 914: 71-81.

[207] Leccese AP, Lyness WH. The effects of putative 5-hydroxytryptamine receptor active agents on D-amphetamine self-administration in controls and rats with 5,7-dihydroxytryptamine median forebrain bundle lesions. *Brain Res.* 1984 Jun 11; 303 (1): 153-62.

[208] Lyness WH, Friedle NM, Moore KE. Increased self-administration of d-amphetamine after destruction of 5-hydroxytryptaminergic neurons. *Pharmacol. Biochem. Behav.* 1980 Jun; 12 (6): 937-41.

[209] Batki S, Moon J, Bradley M, Hersh D, Smolar S, Mengis M, et al., editors. Fluoxetine in methamphetamine dependence—a controlled trial: preliminary analysis. *CPDD 61st Annual Scientific Meeting*; 1999; Acapulco.

[210] Piasecki MP, Steinagel GM, Thienhaus OJ, Kohlenberg BS. An exploratory study: the use of paroxetine for methamphetamine craving. *J. Psychoactive Drugs.* 2002 Jul-Sep; 34 (3): 301-4.

[211] Galloway GP, Newmeyer J, Knapp T, Stalcup SA, Smith D. A controlled trial of imipramine for the treatment of methamphetamine dependence. *Journal of Substance Abuse Treatment.* 1996; 13 (6): 493-7.

[212] Shoptaw S, Huber A, Peck J, Yang X, Liu J, Jeff D, et al. Randomized, placebo-controlled trial of sertraline and contingency management for the treatment of methamphetamine dependence. *Drug and Alcohol Dependence.* 2006; 85 (1): 12-8.

[213] Anttila SAK, Leinonen EVJ. A review of the pharmacological and clinical profile of mirtazapine. *CNS Drug Reviews.* 2001; 7 (3): 249-64.

[214] Kongsakon R, Papadopoulos KI, Saguansiritham R. Mirtazapine in amphetamine detoxification: a placebo-controlled pilot study. *Int. Clin. Psychopharmacol.* 2005 Sep; 20 (5): 253-6.

[215] Cruickshank CC, Montebello ME, Dyer KR, Quigley A, Blaszczyk J, Tomkins S, et al. A placebo-controlled trial of mirtazapine for the management of methamphetamine withdrawal. *Drug Alcohol Rev.* 2008 May; 27 (3): 326-33.

[216] Colfax GN, Santos GM, Das M, Santos DM, Matheson T, Gasper J, et al. Mirtazapine to reduce methamphetamine use: a randomized controlled trial. *Arch. Gen. Psychiatry.* 2011 Nov; 68 (11): 1168-75.

[217] Stahl SM, Pradko JF, Haight BR, Modell JG, Rockett CB, Learned-Coughlin S. A review of the neuropharmacology of bupropion, a dual norepinephrine and dopamine reuptake inhibitor. *Prim. Care Companion J. Clin. Psychiatry.* 2004; 6 (4): 159-66.

[218] Newton TF, Roache JD, De La Garza R, 2nd, Fong T, Wallace CL, Li S-H, et al. Bupropion reduces methamphetamine-induced subjective effects and cue-induced craving. *Neuropsychopharmacology.* 2006 Jul; 31 (7): 1537-44.

[219] Elkashef AM, Rawson RA, Anderson AL, Li S-H, Holmes T, Smith EV, et al. Bupropion for the treatment of methamphetamine dependence. *Neuropsychopharmacology.* 2007; 33 (5): 1162-70.

[220] Shoptaw S, Heinzerling KG, Rotheram-Fuller E, Steward T, Wang J, Swanson AN, et al. Randomized, placebo-controlled trial of bupropion for the treatment of methamphetamine dependence. *Drug Alcohol Depend.* 2008 Aug 1; 96 (3): 222-32.

[221] Llorens-Cortes C, Pollard H, Schwartz JC. Localization of opiate receptors in substantia nigra evidence by lesion studies. *Neurosci. Lett.* 1979 May; 12 (2-3): 165-70.

[222] Unterwald EM. Regulation of opioid receptors by cocaine. *Ann. N. Y. Acad. Sci.* 2001 Jun; 937: 74-92.

[223] Azaryan AV, Coughlin LJ, Buzas B, Clock BJ, Cox BM. Effect of chronic cocaine treatment on mu- and delta-opioid receptor mRNA levels in dopaminergically innervated brain regions. *J. Neurochem.* 1996 Feb; 66 (2): 443-8.

[224] Gorelick DA, Kim YK, Bencherif B, Boyd SJ, Nelson R, Copersino M, et al. Imaging brain mu-opioid receptors in abstinent cocaine users: time course and relation to cocaine craving. *Biol. Psychiatry.* 2005; 57 (12): 1573-82.

[225] Jayaram-Lindstrom N, Konstenius M, Eksborg S, Beck O, Hammarberg A, Franck J. Naltrexone attenuates the subjective effects of amphetamine in patients with amphetamine dependence. *Neuropsychopharmacology.* 2008 Jul; 33 (8): 1856-63.

[226] Jayaram-Lindstrom N, Hammarberg A, Beck O, Franck J. Naltrexone for the treatment of amphetamine dependence: a randomized, placebo-controlled trial. *Am. J. Psychiatry.* 2008 Nov; 165 (11): 1442-8.

[227] Franklin TR, Wang Z, Sciortino N, Harper D, Li Y, Hakun J, et al. Modulation of resting brain cerebral blood flow by the GABA B agonist, baclofen: A longitudinal perfusion fMRI study. *Drug Alcohol Depend.* 2011; 117 (2): 176-83.

[228] Ghahremani DG, Tabibnia G, Monterosso J, Hellemann G, Poldrack RA, London ED. Effect of modafinil on learning and task-related brain activity in methamphetamine-dependent and healthy individuals. *Neuropsychopharmacology.* 2011 Apr; 36 (5): 950-9.

In: Emerging Targets for Drug Addiction Treatment
Editor: Juan Canales

ISBN 978-1-62081-913-5
©2012 Nova Science Publishers, Inc.

Chapter 3

IMMUNOTHERAPEUTIC VACCINES FOR SUBSTANCE ABUSE

Frank M. Orson[1-4], Berma M. Kinsey[1,2], Muthu Ramakrishnan[1,2], Angel Lopez[1,2] and Xiaoyun Shen[1,2]*

[1]Veterans Affairs Medical Center, Baylor College of Medicine,
[2]Departments of Medicine, [3]Pathology,
[4]Molecular Virology and Microbiology, Houston, Texas, US

ABSTRACT

The scourge of substance abuse has evolved under the pressure of both criminalization and treatment of the addicts. However, it has not declined dramatically with this effort, but rather has been magnified in many parts of the world, especially in developing countries with increasing wealth, social fragmentation, and transportation access. Pharmacological interventions have been helpful for treating tobacco and opiate abuse, although at considerable expense, but they have not been successful for treating people suffering from addiction to stimulants like cocaine and methamphetamine. As a result, novel therapeutic approaches are needed. Conjugate drug vaccine-induced specific antibody blockade of abused drugs has become increasingly appealing in recent years as one such nonpharmacological approach. In this review, the design, theory, animal experimentation, and clinical work underlying the development of anti-drug vaccines will be discussed.

* Email: forson@bcm.edu

1. INTRODUCTION

Substance abuse results in a multiplicity of problems for individuals, their families, and the communities where they live, often causing severe medical and economic complications, even without considering the political and criminal problems that arise on the societal scale. Management of the individual addicted to a drug is often limited by complicated pharmacological and behavioral issues. A distinct approach to this problem which can address some of these difficulties is the use of conjugated drug vaccines that can elicit blocking antibody responses for many of these substances. Alcohol, not further discussed here, is one substance not amenable to this approach, however, since the ethanol molecule is too small (46 grams/mole molecular weight) to be effectively recognized by antibodies, as well as the fact that when it is used, ethanol is in too high a concentration for binding a significant fraction by a practically achievable antibody response, even if it were able to be bound. On the other hand, cocaine, methamphetamine, and heroin (and other opioids), which will be discussed in detail in this review, are of sufficient molecular size to be able to be bound by antibodies, and are pharmacologically active at concentrations that can be inhibited by reasonably achievable antibody responses to highly stimulatory vaccines [1]. A cocaine conjugate vaccine has been studied in a double blind, placebo controlled, clinical trial which showed significant activity against cocaine, and high antibody responses to the vaccine were associated with a reduction in cocaine use. Phencyclidine (and other designer drugs), as well as nicotine, can also be targeted by vaccines, but will not be discussed in this review.

2. CONJUGATE VACCINES

The creation of substance abuse vaccines necessarily requires the conjugation of the drug to a carrier molecule in order for the immune system recognize and respond to the drug with specific antibody production. Methamphetamine, with a molecular weight (MW) of 149 grams/mole, is near the minimum size required for reasonable antibody binding in solution phase. Other molecules like cocaine (MW 303) and morphine (MW 285) provide more potential binding interactions with antibody combining sites, and produce generally higher antibody responses with better affinity to conjugate vaccine immunization. There are numerous issues in the design of conjugate vaccines that can influence the outcome in terms of the quantity and quality of the antibody responses, and although not completely determined as of now, some general principles have been established by a number of labs involved in this work. It is clear, for example, that routine adjuvants and carriers often fail to elicit adequately robust responses in a substantial percentage of humans [2, 3], and as a result, investigations with more stimulatory carriers, linker structure, and innate immune system activating adjuvants are a central area of interest at the present time.

3. ANTIBODY BINDING

Recognition of small molecules in solution by antibodies has some features that are different from the more typical protein antigen targets for immunoglobulin molecules. Drug molecules are sufficiently small that they can ordinarily interact only with a single combining site, unlike multiepitope proteins that can be crosslinked to form immune complexes. This provides some advantages for the vaccine approach to substance abuse therapy, but has some liabilities as well. A principal advantage of the single site interaction is that the antibody molecule itself does not respond structurally to the binding interaction, and thus does not have an increased affinity for Fc receptors on the reticuloendothelial system cells that ordinarily help clear immune complexes from the bloodstream. As a result, the antibodies continue in circulation after binding the drug, and when the drug is gradually released and metabolized, the antibodies remain in circulation and are able to rebind the drug when there is a subsequent dose administered. The half-life of the IgG molecule (about 22 days in humans), for example, is essentially unchanged by drug binding [4]. Other antibody isotypes (see further discussion in Antibody Responses below) are not relevant to this discussion due either to the quantity of antibody produced (IgM, IgD, IgE) or the location of maximum production (IgA in the gut).

On the other hand, binding to a single site results in a lower binding strength to the drug than would binding of both IgG sites to a single antigen molecule (e.g., a protein) with two or more available epitopes [5]. The strength of binding interaction with a single site is called the intrinsic binding affinity while with interactions to more than one site by an antibody molecule is called the binding avidity [6]. In the simplest terms, the interaction of a drug and a single combining site can be described by the Law of Mass Action,

$$A+B \underset{k_d}{\overset{k_a}{\Leftrightarrow}} AB,$$

in which the on rate (k_a) and the off rate (k_d) describe the binding and dissociation rate constants that are dependent on the concentration of the reactants. Their ratio (k_d/k_a) determines the equilibrium dissociation constant (K_D) which is often used as a measure of antibody quality (tightness of binding), and is often also correlated with the relative specificity of binding. Using this approach, one can calculate the quantity of antibody needed for binding most of the drug molecules in solution depending on the dose of the drug and the quality of the antibody (Figure 1).

As can be appreciated in the figure, poor antibody affinities (e.g., a dissociation constant of 1000 nM or more) cannot bind a high proportion of 0.5 μM drug at concentrations of antibody below 50 mg/mL. However, antibodies with a K_D of 100 nM or less will bind more than 80% of the drug at equilibrium. The amount of antibody required to affect the usual recreational doses of cocaine, morphine, and heroin is substantially higher than that required for more typical vaccines used for protection against microbes and microbial toxins. For example, complete protection is afforded by a response to tetanus toxoid vaccine that sustains an antibody concentration of 1-2 μg/mL or more [7].

Affinity Effects on Binding at 0.5 μM

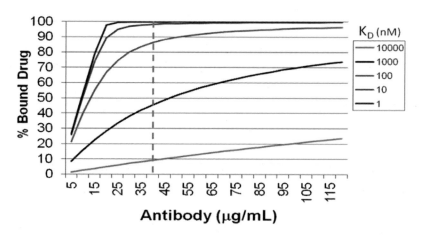

Figure 1. Influence of Antibody Quality on Drug Binding. The proportion of a drug bound at a concentration of 0.5 μM is plotted against the quantity of antibody present in solution. Each curve represents the binding pattern for antibodies with the average dissociation constant specified (nanomolar units).

As shown in Figure 2, however, the amount of antibody required to bind a large fraction of the dose of drug achieving a peak concentration of 0.5 μM (e.g., from a 30 mg dose of smoked cocaine [8]), is about 40 μg/mL. Smaller amounts of antibody (e.g., 20 μg/mL or less) are simply inadequate to have a substantial effect, since the number of binding sites present can only bind a modest fraction of the drug molecules present, and will thus fail to significantly inhibit the effects of the drug dose. These theoretical conclusions are supported by the clinical study of a cocaine vaccine [3], as discussed in more detail in the later section on cocaine vaccines. Another aspect of binding that needs to be mentioned is the rate of binding of the antibody to the target drug molecule. For small molecules, the on rate of binding is generally very fast, such that most drug in a solution that can be bound will be in less than a minute [9, 10].

As shown in Figure 2, the binding kinetics of an antibody with typical characteristics of a "good" affinity antibody (on rate (k_a) of 1 x 10^5 M/sec, K_D of 10 nM) with the number of binding sites approximately matching the 0.5 μM drug concentration at the peak from a typical recreational dose of cocaine [8, 11]. The number of antibody binding sites is slightly higher than the drug concentration to be able to show the curve for free antibody binding sites distinctly. The figure shows that more than 50% of the drug is bound within 25 seconds, and binding is coming close to equilibrium by 100 seconds with more than 80% of the drug bound. This is an especially important issue for substance abuse drugs, since the uptake into the brain from the bloodstream occurs within minutes, as has been shown in many pharmacological studies, e.g., for cocaine and methamphetamine [11]. Fast binding by antibodies is essential to have an impact, therefore, on the rush effect of these drugs, which is closely tied to the development of addiction [12, 13]. The determining factor for equilibrium binding affinity is therefore largely influenced by the off rates of antibody dissociation from the drug, which can vary widely, as shown for monoclonal antibodies [14].

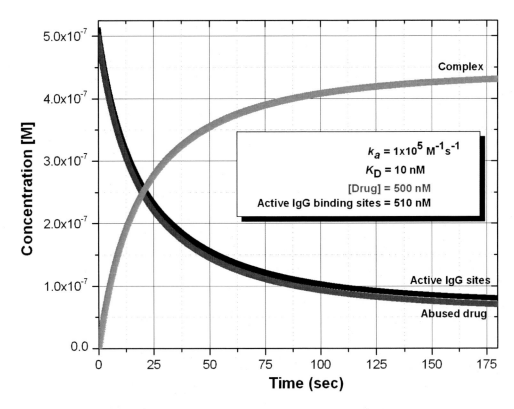

Figure 2. Kinetics of drug binding by antibody in solution. The figure plots the theoretical concentration of drug, free antibody combining sites, and bound drug/antibody complex over time from initial mixing, assuming the conditions specified in the inset for rate, affinitity, drug concentration and antibody combining site concentration.

A further issue that has not yet been fully explored is the fact that in physiological fluids (i.e., plasma in this case), the effective binding affinity of specific proteins for small molecules can be modified due to other serum components [15]. With regard to cocaine, for example, the affinity of both monoclonal and polyclonal antibodies is reduced by a factor of about 10 (Muthu, manuscript in preparation), likely due predominantly to the interaction of cocaine with alpha-1-acid glycoprotein [16], since purified IgG molecules and purified albumin do not show this effect. Thus it is very important to have a high average affinity in the stimulated polyclonal antibodies in order to retain most of the drug in circulation in that early time period after administration to slow its entry into the brain. Slowing the entry of drug into the brain may be as important as reducing the total entry, since, for example, it is well known that cocaine orally delivered by chewing coca leaves has a much lower risk of addiction [17] than other routes (e.g. coca paste smoking [18]), even with the substantial blood concentration of the drug that results from the traditional practice of chewing coca leaves in the Andes [19].

4. ANTIBODY INHIBITION OF DRUG ACTION

Simple blockade of drug effects by antibody sequestration in the bloodstream can certainly explain some aspects of antibody inhibition of pharmacological function. Measurement of the quantity of drug that enters the brain and that which is in the bloodstream demonstrates this principle to some extent. However, the drug and the antibody-drug complex are in equilibrium, with binding and release of the drug occurring constantly, reflecting the on and off rates. In the absence of inflammation, an antibody cannot pass through the blood-brain barrier due to its large size [20], therefore leakage of free drug into the brain does occur, and this continuous process of entry of reduced amounts of drug at a slow rate (compared to the same dose of drug in the absence of antibody) can have a substantially different result in terms of physical and psychological responses to the pharmacological action of the drug. With methamphetamine, for example, the use of long acting preparations of the drug permit its use in the treatment of ADD and ADHD without eliciting the high associated with abuse of the drug in its pure form [21]. The rush associated with the rapid increase in occupancy fraction of the receptors is prevented by the slow absorption from the long acting formulation.

As an additional example, cocaine delivered by the chewing of coca leaves has been used by indigenous populations in the Andes for thousands of years with no significant addictive effects, while slowly resulting in brain concentrations that are comparable to those rapidly achieved by recreational doses of crack cocaine [22]. A similar process will occur when there is a high fractional binding of the street drug by antibodies: a small amount of the drug does gain entry into the brain initially, which increases slowly over time as antibody bound drug is released to reestablish equilibrium conditions when free drug is transported into tissues. Additionally, free drug that is metabolized to components poorly bound by antibodies causes bound drug molecules to be released from the antibody pool "sponge" which reestablishes equilibrium conditions. Drug bound to antibodies does not appear to be metabolized at the same rate as free drug, as suggested by Brimijoin, et al. [23], and demonstrated in direct studies of cocaine with antibody and highly active optimized butyrylcholinesterase (Brimijoin, Orson, manuscript in preparation). Thus antibody binding of drug can reduce both the total amount of drug entering the CNS and the rate of occupancy of drug receptors, thereby contributing to inhibition of the excessive pleasure sensation elicited by the drug, which is closely related to the addictive potential for these substances [24].

5. MORPHINE

Morphine was the first drug of abuse for which a conjugate vaccine was developed. This occurred in the early 1970s [25], but shortly after the vaccine was demonstrated to be effective in rodents and monkeys, drug substitution with a long acting opiate, methadone, became the established treatment for opiate addiction [26] in the United States and Europe. At that time, rates of addiction in less developed countries were lower and not perceived as serious a problem as other issues. As a result, further development of the vaccine was not pursued. With changes in social conditions in China and Southeast Asia, and in the former Soviet Block countries as well as India, addiction to opiates has again become a major societal problem, not because of the addicts themselves and the criminal enterprises they support, but additionally because of the transmission of infectious diseases, especially the human immunodeficiency virus [27-29]. Since methadone, buprenorphine, and naltrexone treatment programs are relatively expensive, the use of these pharmaceutical interventions for opiate addiction has been less successful in regions with rapidly increasing numbers of addicts, particularly China, Russia, and India. As a result, the need for alternative therapies, including vaccines, has become well recognized.

Conjugate vaccines for heroin must produce antibodies that are capable of binding morphine, heroin, 6-acetylmorphine, and 6-glucuronylmorphine. Although heroin (3,6-diacetylmorphine) itself is an inactive prodrug (the 3-hydroxyl group must be present for opiate activity of the molecule), it is rapidly deacetylated to active metabolites including morphine itself and especially 6-acetylmorphine [30]. Heroin metabolism, however, occurs in the brain as well as in the periphery, and so antibodies from vaccines should be capable of binding all these compounds. Fortunately, construction of conjugate vaccines with linkers at the 6 hydroxyl position allows such recognition of active compounds to occur [31]. Vaccines constructed with 6-succinylmorphine produce antibodies capable of blocking morphine activity as measured by in vivo nociception assays [32], as well as self administration studies, which are thought to better correlate with addiction behavior in humans [33]. One concern for morphine/heroin vaccines is that antibodies might block all opiate drugs and thus be a problem for vaccinated patients who may have subsequent need for pain medications after injury or surgery. In fact, however, there are many synthetic opiates available which are sufficiently different in structure that binding to anti-morphine antibodies will not occur, and thus not interfere with pain relief pharmacology. Unfortunately, however, abuse of prescription opiates (i.e., some of these same synthetic drugs) has become a major problem in the United States and Europe [34], and morphine/heroin specific vaccines will not help address abuse of these substances. Potentially, vaccines for individual synthetic compounds could be designed, but moving from one opiate to another, if they are readily available, would circumvent the effectiveness of specific vaccines. In this sense, where practical and available, substitution agents like methadone and buprenorphine will be preferable to the vaccine approach, as this mechanism is independent of the specific opiate.

6. COCAINE

Of the illegal substances of abuse for which vaccine approaches are feasible, work on cocaine is the most advanced. Cocaine abuse has become a major societal problem in the developed world over the past several decades, but especially in the past 30 years when addiction reached into the broader society [35]. Unfortunately, for those truly addicted to the drug, pharmacological treatments have been largely ineffective, and nonpharmacological treatments have shown only partial effectiveness [36]. However, certain aspects of cocaine metabolism make it the most attractive target for vaccine use. Figure 3 shows the major metabolites of cocaine, which retain no significant stimulatory activity. Of particular note is that benzoylecgonine, while only different from cocaine itself by hydrolysis of the methyl ester group to a hydroxyl group, binds poorly to antibodies induced by vaccines against cocaine itself [37]. This is fortunate, because the hydrolysis of the methyl ester occurs both spontaneously and by enzymatic action, and benzoylecgonine has a longer circulatory halflife than cocaine [38], and thus could compete for antibody binding sites if it were significantly recognized.

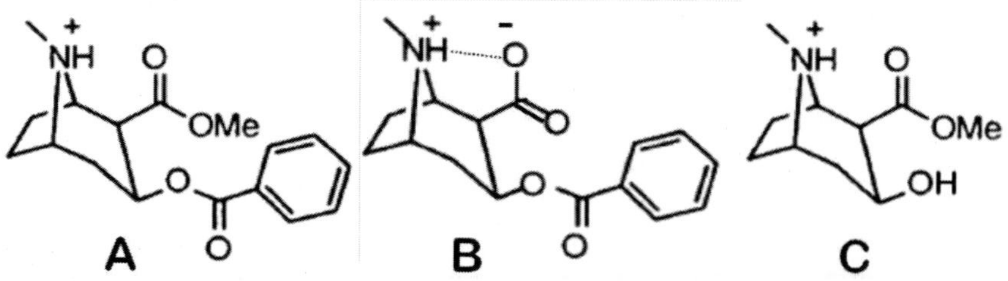

Figure 3. Major metabolites of cocaine. The figure shows cocaine itself (A), benzoylecgonine (B), and ecgonine methyl ester (C). The absence of the methyl ester in benzoyl ecgonine allows for a zwitter ion balance of charges that reduces anti-cocaine antibody binding considerably. Hydrolysis of benzoic acid from ecgonine methyl ester similarly produces a nonbinding product.

Similarly, ecgonine and benzoic acid, the other major metabolic pathway products through the butyrylcholinesterase enzyme present in plasma, are not bound by anti-cocaine antibodies either.

Thus, the short half-life of cocaine, its lack of active metabolites in quantity, and the lack of antibody binding to the metabolites make this drug an excellent target for an immunotherapeutic vaccine. Animal studies with cocaine conjugate vaccines were begun more than 15 years ago, and rapidly demonstrated that adequate concentrations of antibody could inhibit the pharmacological effects of the drug, including stimulation of locomotor activity [37, 39] and reinstatement of cocaine self administration [40, 41]. In the conjugate vaccine that progressed to human trials, the succinlynorcocaine hapten has no charge on the nitrogen, and it was thought this might reduce the binding affinity of the elicited antibodies. However, studies of monoclonal antibodies showed that high binding affinity for cocaine was feasible and depended more on the hydrophobic aspects of the molecule [42]. In addition, later animal studies demonstrated that levels of antibodies induced with this linkage were in fact higher than when other linkers were used (Orson, unpublished). Progress to human studies was considerably slower, but then laboratory studies in people demonstrated that vaccine-induced antibodies could, at peak levels, block the subjective effects of controlled administration (smoked) of up to 50 mg cocaine [43], paving the way for outpatient clinical trials. The first clinical trial of a cocaine vaccine was completed at Yale using succinlynorcocaine conjugated to cholera toxin b as the carrier protein [3]. In this trial, patients dually addicted to opiates and cocaine were selected because it was felt that treatment of the opiate addiction with methadone would enable a high level of retention for the subjects in a cocaine vaccine trial, in contrast to the likelihood of a high dropout rate for cocaine addicts not otherwise engaged in a program with the clinics [44]. This approach was successful, so that the 82% of the subjects completed the study with minimal missed urine samples collected three times per week [3]. Antibody responses showed a high degree of variability, with 30% showing IgG anti-cocaine responses above the 40 μg/mL quantity estimated to be adequate for blocking ordinary recreational doses of cocaine. On the other hand about 25% of the subjects had low responses, less than 20 μg/mL. Interestingly, this group of patients tended to have the presence of IgM capable of binding cocaine, although of relatively low quantity and affinity (Orson, manuscript in preparation). The reasons and effects on the immune response of the IgM are under investigation at present, but may represent a T independent response to the drug elicited during cocaine abuse, perhaps from contaminant materials. Nonetheless, the quantity of IgM, along with its low affinity dictated that this antibody isotype could not inhibit the pharmacological effects of the drug.

In order to analyze the study data properly, it is important to understand that one cannot expect that the vaccine could have any direct influence on cocaine function without an adequate IgG antibody response. As a result, the cocaine usage of high and low responders was compared, excluding those few patients who stopped using cocaine entirely shortly after entering the study (presumably in response to the counseling provided to all participants), since they could not have experienced any effect of the vaccine in the absence of ongoing drug use before the development of the antibody response. Figure 4 shows the antibody levels at time points from 8 weeks through the end of the study for subjects with more than 40% negative urine samples versus those with mostly positive tests, indicating frequent cocaine usage. The differences in antibody levels between the groups were highly significant after 12 weeks, indicating that the levels of antibody were likely related to the reduced cocaine use. Interviews with the patients suggested that many subjects felt that the drugs they obtained in this period were of poor quality and that this contributed to their reduced use.

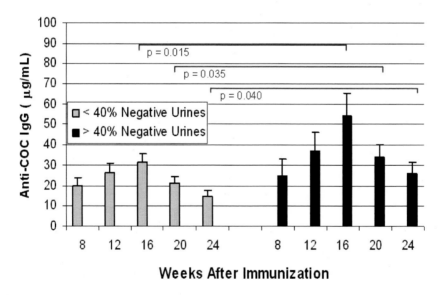

Figure 4. High anti-cocaine IgG correlated with negative urine tests. Subjects immunized with CTB-succinylnorcocaine were analyzed for IgG antibodies recognizing cocaine according to whether total numbers of urine tests in the 8-20 week period were more than 40% negative or not for new cocaine use. Comparison of IgG anti-cocaine levels showed that the subjects with fewer positive urines in this period had significantly higher specific antibody levels.

Importantly, it was also noted that although a few patients increased their cocaine consumption to try to overcome the antibody blockade, most did not. There were no significant treatment-related adverse events in the trial. As a result, the optimal candidates for the vaccine approach would be patients who had already stopped or was motivated and ready to quit substance abuse, so that any subsequent temporary relapse to use from a situational exposure to cocaine consumption would not cause them to suffer the marked increase in craving that would otherwise result and cause relapse. Nonetheless, it is not necessary for a subject to discontinue drug use before receiving the vaccine doses in order to generate antibody responses, since drug use alone is insufficient to inhibit immune responses. Antibodies have been demonstrated to develop while drug is being administered in both animal studies [45] and human studies [3].

7. Methamphetamine

Methamphetamine abuse is well established in the United States [46], but it has now become an increasing problem in many parts of the world. This appears to be especially true in the Far East [47], but it has been recognized in other countries as well. Methamphetamine increases energy, and produces a sense of well-being and euphoria that makes this substance highly addictive. Moreover, once established, the addiction is very difficult to overcome. These effects are mediated through transporter interactions for multiple neurotransmitters, including dopamine, norepinephrine, serotonin, histamine, and gamma-aminobutyric acid, causing the release of monoamines from synaptic vesicles [48]. Due to this multiplicity of effects, methamphetamine is likely to be less amenable to specific drug antagonists, or even a substitute agonist agent, than other drugs of abuse. Since methamphetamine is a small molecule (149 daltons), and cheaply produced, with both domestic and international sources of the drug being distributed in underground networks, an effective vaccine would be very valuable for the individual addict, as well as for society at large.

However, methamphetamine's small molecular size has a daunting implication for vaccine development: its binding to antibodies is necessarily restricted to fewer potential contact interactions than are available on other molecules. Although high affinity monoclonal antibodies have been produced that recognize methamphetamine [49], achieving a high average affinity in a polyclonal antibody response to a vaccine will require improved immunization conditions (e.g., more powerful adjuvants or modified hapten structures) than with other drug conjugate vaccines. Alternatively, if high affinity polyclonal responses are problematic, it may be necessary to produce substantially higher amounts of antibody in the response in order to effectively block methamphetamine. Further complicating this issue, and in distinct contrast to cocaine, the metabolic degradation of methamphetamine is very limited, which contributes to its relatively long half-life of about 9-15 hours in humans, depending in part on the pH of the urine. In fact much of the drug is eliminated unchanged in the urine, and about half is demethylated to amphetamine, which is also an active CNS stimulant in its own right [50], while other minor metabolites are inactive. Despite these limitations, considerable progress has been made in the development of a methamphetamine conjugate vaccine. Initially, in work that is still ongoing, monoclonal antibodies were produced that recognized the drug [51], and these could potentially be used directly for treatment, especially in the context of treating methamphetamine overdoses [49], although chronic therapy would be prohibitively expensive [52] due to the processing necessary for the repeated use of therapeutic biological reagents. Using a highly active carrier for succinylmethamphetamine (the outer membrane protein complex of Neisseria meningitidis), very high levels of antibody were achieved in the mouse that enabled an effective blockade of methamphetamine activity, as measured by locomotor assays (Orson, manuscript in preparation). Interestingly, similar high level antibody responses were achieved as well with a modified hapten, in which the molecule (Figure 5) was stabilized by attachment of the methylamine group to the benzene ring (methyltetraisoquinoline).

Other studies have also demonstrated that some blockade of methamphetamine activity by active immunization can be achieved [53]. A linker attached to the phenyl ring of methamphetamine was used to conjugate the drug to fused peptides (a tetanus toxoid peptide sequence for T cell help and complement fragment C5a which binds to dendritic cells). The amount of antibody produced was sufficient to cause rats to self-administer more drug to overcome the blocking antibodies by saturating the binding sites. Bound drug persisted in circulation, which became completely clear of the drug only 34 days after methamphetamine administration was stopped. With substantially the higher levels of antibody elicited in our lab, a correlation with the degree of inhibition of single dose methamphetamine was observed in locomoter assays, approximating that seen with monoclonal antibody infusions.

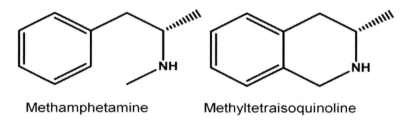

Methamphetamine   Methyltetraisoquinoline

Figure 5. Stabilized derivative of Methamphetamine. Methamphetamine (left structure) has free rotation around the both carbons and the nitrogen of the side chain. Methyltetraisoquinoline is a rigid structure.

Additional studies, using controlled place preference and/or self-administration assays will be useful in establishing the effects of such conjugate vaccines for methamphetamine.

CONCLUSION

Conjugate vaccines for methamphetamine, cocaine, and heroin/morphine need to be further enhanced to ensure high level antibody responses in a majority of recipients in order to achieve effective clinical outcomes. A cocaine vaccine has been characterized in human subjects and a large followup Phase IIb study is in progress. Morphine vaccines will be applicable to heroin and morphine, but with the emergence of a prescription opiate in the developed world, a vaccine for this opiod will likely have its best applicability in developing countries, particularly in the Far East and Russia. Methamphetamine conjugate vaccines will need to elicit even higher levels of antibody for optimal inhibition of drug effects due in part to methamphetamine's long half life, limited metabolism, and small molecular size. The application of vaccines against drug abuse will benefit addicts who want to get off their habit, especially in conjunction with therapy and rehabilitation, and thereby help rid society of a devastating problem.

REFERENCES

[1]   Kinsey BM, Jackson DC, Orson FM: Anti-drug vaccines to treat substance abuse. *Immunology and cell biology* 2009, 87 (4): 309-314.

[2]   Cerny EH, Cerny T: Vaccines against nicotine. *Human vaccines* 2009, 5 (4).

[3]   Martell BA, Orson FM, Poling J, Mitchell E, Rossen RD, Gardner T, Kosten TR: Cocaine Vaccine for the Treatment of Cocaine Dependence: A Randomized Double-Blind Placebo-Controlled Efficacy Trial *Arch. Gen. Psych.* 2009, 66: 1116-1123.

[4]   Schmidt DH, Kaufman BM, Butler VP, Jr.: Persistence of hapten-antibody complexes in the circulation of immunized animals after a single intravenous injection of hapten. *The Journal of experimental medicine* 1974, 139 (2): 278-294.

[5]   Orson FM, Kinsey BM, Singh RAK, Wu Y, Gardner T, Kosten TR: Substance Abuse Vaccines. *Annals of the New York Academy of Sciences* 2008, 1141: 257-269.

[6]   Day ED: *Advanced Immunochemistry*. Second edition. New York: Wiley-Liss; 1990.

[7]   Stevens RH, Saxon A: Reduced in vitro production of anti-tetanus toxoid antibody after repeated in vivo immunization with tetanus toxoid. *J. Immunol.* 1979, 122 (2): 592-598.

[8]   Jenkins AJ, Keenan RM, Henningfield JE, Cone EJ: Correlation between pharmacological effects and plasma cocaine concentrations after smoked adminis-tration. *J. Anal. Toxicol.* 2002, 26 (7): 382-392.

[9]   Barbet J, Rougon-Rapuzzi G, Cupo A, Delaage MA: Structural requirements for recognition of vasopressin by antibody; thermodynamic and kinetic characteristics of the interaction. *Mol. Immunol.* 1981, 18 (5): 439-446.

[10]   Smith TW, Skubitz KM: Kinetics in interactions between antibodies and haptens. *Biochemistry* 1975, 14 (7): 1496-1502.

[11]   Newton TF, De La Garza R, 2nd, Kalechstein AD, Nestor L: Cocaine and methamphetamine produce different patterns of subjective and cardiovascular effects. *Pharmacology, biochemistry, and behavior* 2005, 82 (1): 90-97.

[12]   Gorelick DA: The rate hypothesis and agonist substitution approaches to cocaine abuse treatment. *Adv. Pharmacol.* 1998, 42: 995-997.

[13]   Wakabayashi KT, Weiss MJ, Pickup KN, Robinson TE: Rats markedly escalate their intake and show a persistent susceptibility to reinstatement only when cocaine is injected rapidly. *The Journal of neuroscience : the official journal of the Society for Neuroscience* 2010, 30 (34): 11346-11355.

[14]   Klein JS, Gnanapragasam PN, Galimidi RP, Foglesong CP, West AP, Jr., Bjorkman PJ: Examination of the contributions of size and avidity to the neutralization mechanisms of the anti-HIV antibodies b12 and 4E10. *Proceedings of the National Academy of Sciences of the United States of America* 2009, 106 (18): 7385-7390.

[15]   Wienken CJ, Baaske P, Rothbauer U, Braun D, Duhr S: Protein-binding assays in biological liquids using microscale thermophoresis. *Nature communications* 2010, 1: 100.

[16]   Edwards DJ, Bowles SK: Protein binding of cocaine in human serum. *Pharmaceutical research* 1988, 5 (7): 440-442.

[17]   Negrete JC: Cocaine problems in the coca-growing countries of South America. *Ciba Foundation symposium* 1992, 166:40-50; discussion 50-46.

[18] Jeri FR: Coca-paste smoking in some Latin American countries: a severe and unabated form of addiction. *Bulletin on narcotics* 1984, 36 (2): 15-31.

[19] Spielvogel H, Caceres E, Koubi H, Sempore B, Sauvain M, Favier R: Effects of coca chewing on metabolic and hormonal changes during graded incremental exercise to maximum. *J. Appl. Physiol.* 1996, 80 (2): 643-649.

[20] Phares TW, Kean RB, Mikheeva T, Hooper DC: Regional differences in blood-brain barrier permeability changes and inflammation in the apathogenic clearance of virus from the central nervous system. *J. Immunol.* 2006, 176 (12): 7666-7675.

[21] Lile JA, Babalonis S, Emurian C, Martin CA, Wermeling DP, Kelly TH: Comparison of the behavioral and cardiovascular effects of intranasal and oral d-amphetamine in healthy human subjects. *Journal of clinical pharmacology* 2011, 51 (6): 888-898.

[22] Hatsukami DK, Fischman MW: Crack cocaine and cocaine hydrochloride. Are the differences myth or reality? *JAMA : the journal of the American Medical Association* 1996, 276 (19): 1580-1588.

[23] Gao Y, Orson FM, Kinsey BM, Kosten TR, Brimijoin S: The concept of pharmacologic cocaine interception as a treatment for drug abuse. *Chemico-biological interactions* 2010, in press.

[24] Koob GF: Dynamics of neuronal circuits in addiction: reward, antireward, and emotional memory. *Pharmacopsychiatry* 2009, 42 Suppl 1: S32-41.

[25] Berkowitz B, Spector S: Evidence for active immunity to morphine in mice. *Science* 1972, 178 (67): 1290-1292.

[26] Kreek MJ, Borg L, Ducat E, Ray B: Pharmacotherapy in the treatment of addiction: methadone. *J. Addict. Dis.* 2010, 29 (2): 200-216.

[27] Heimer R, Barbour R, Shaboltas AV, Hoffman IF, Kozlov AP: Spatial distribution of HIV prevalence and incidence among injection drugs users in St Petersburg: implications for HIV transmission. *Aids* 2008, 22 (1): 123-130.

[28] Kermode M, Longleng V, Singh BC, Hocking J, Langkham B, Crofts N: My first time: initiation into injecting drug use in Manipur and Nagaland, north-east India. *Harm. Reduct. J.* 2007, 4 (1): 19.

[29] Liu ZM, Lu XX, Mu Y, Lian Z, Zhou WH: Epidemiological features of drug abusers in China. *Journal of Drug Abuse Prevention and Treatment* 2002, 8: 27-30.

[30] Inturrisi CE, Schultz M, Shin S, Umans JG, Angel L, Simon EJ: Evidence from opiate binding studies that heroin acts through its metabolites. *Life Sci.* 1983, 33 Suppl 1: 773-776.

[31] Wainer BH, Fitch FW, Fried J, Rothberg RM: A measurement of the specificities of antibodies to morphine-6-succinyl-BSA by competitive inhibition of 14 C-morphine binding. *J. Immunol.* 1973, 110 (3): 667-673.

[32] Anton B, Salazar A, Florez A, Matus M, Marin R, Hernandez JA, Leff P: Vaccines against morphine/heroin and its use as effective medication for preventing relapse to opiate addictive behaviors. *Human vaccines* 2009, 5 (4).

[33] Ahmed SH: The science of making drug-addicted animals. *Neuroscience* 2011.

[34] Bell J: The global diversion of pharmaceutical drugs: opiate treatment and the diversion of pharmaceutical opiates: a clinician's perspective. *Addiction* 2010, 105 (9): 1531-1537.

[35] Watkins D, Ashby R: *Gang Investigations: A street cop's guide.* . Sudbury, MA: Jones and Bartlett; 2007.

[36] Rash CJ, Alessi SM, Petry NM: Contingency management is efficacious for cocaine abusers with prior treatment attempts. *Experimental and clinical psychopharmacology* 2008, 16 (6): 547-554.

[37] Fox BS, Kantak KM, Edwards MA, Black KM, Bollinger BK, Botka AJ, French TL, Thompson TL, Schad VC, Greenstein JL *et al*: Efficacy of a therapeutic cocaine vaccine in rodent models. *Nat. Med.* 1996, 2 (10): 1129-1132.

[38] Jufer RA, Wstadik A, Walsh SL, Levine BS, Cone EJ: Elimination of cocaine and metabolites in plasma, saliva, and urine following repeated oral administration to human volunteers. *J Anal Toxicol* 2000, 24 (7): 467-477.

[39] Carrera MR, Ashley JA, Parsons LH, Wirsching P, Koob GF, Janda KD: Suppression of psychoactive effects of cocaine by active immunization. *Nature* 1995, 378 (6558): 727-730.

[40] Carrera MR, Ashley JA, Zhou B, Wirsching P, Koob GF, Janda KD: Cocaine vaccines: antibody protection against relapse in a rat model. *Proceedings of the National Academy of Sciences of the United States of America* 2000, 97 (11): 6202-6206.

[41] Kantak KM, Collins SL, Lipman EG, Bond J, Giovanoni K, Fox BS: Evaluation of anti-cocaine antibodies and a cocaine vaccine in a rat self-administration model. *Psychopharmacology* 2000, 148 (3): 251-262.

[42] Paula S, Tabet MR, Farr CD, Norman AB, Ball WJ, Jr.: Three-dimensional quantitative structure-activity relationship modeling of cocaine binding by a novel human monoclonal antibody. *Journal of medicinal chemistry* 2004, 47 (1): 133-142.

[43] Haney M, Gunderson EW, Jiang H, Collins ED, Foltin RW: Cocaine-specific antibodies blunt the subjective effects of smoked cocaine in humans. *Biol. Psychiatry* 2010, 67 (1): 59-65.

[44] Venneman S, Leuchter A, Bartzokis G, Beckson M, Simon SL, Schaefer M, Rawson R, Newton T, Cook IA, Uijtdehaage S *et al*: Variation in neurophysiological function and evidence of quantitative electroencephalogram discordance: predicting cocaine-dependent treatment attrition. *The Journal of neuropsychiatry and clinical neurosciences* 2006, 18 (2): 208-216.

[45] Byrnes-Blake KA, Carroll FI, Abraham P, Owens SM: Generation of anti-(+)methamphetamine antibodies is not impeded by (+)methamphetamine administration during active immunization of rats. *Int Immunopharmacol* 2001, 1 (2): 329-338.

[46] Results from the 2007 National Survey on Drug Use and Health: National Findings (NSDUH Series H-34, DHHS Publication No. SMA 08-4343). Rockville, MD. [http://oas.samhsa.gov.].

[47] McKetin R, Kozel N, Douglas J, Ali R, Vicknasingam B, Lund J, Li JH: The rise of methamphetamine in Southeast and East Asia. *Drug and alcohol review* 2008, 27 (3): 220-228.

[48] Hill KP, Weiss RD: Amphetamines and other Stimulants. In *Substance Abuse: A Comprehensive Textbook*. 5th edition. Edited by Ruiz P, Strain EC. Philadelphia: Wolters Kluwer; Lippincott Williams and Wilkins; 2011: 238-254.

[49] Gentry WB, Laurenzana EM, Williams DK, West JR, Berg RJ, Terlea T, Owens SM: Safety and efficiency of an anti-(+)-methamphetamine monoclonal antibody in the protection against cardiovascular and central nervous system effects of (+)-methamphetamine in rats. *Int Immunopharmacol* 2006, 6 (6): 968-977.

[50] Laurenzana EM, Byrnes-Blake KA, Milesi-Halle A, Gentry WB, Williams DK, Owens SM: Use of anti-(+)-methamphetamine monoclonal antibody to significantly alter (+)-methamphetamine and (+)-amphetamine disposition in rats. *Drug Metab. Dispos.* 2003, 31 (11): 1320-1326.

[51] Gentry WB, Ruedi-Bettschen D, Owens SM: Development of active and passive human vaccines to treat methamphetamine addiction. *Human vaccines* 2009, 5 (4).

[52] Scolnik PA: mAbs: a business perspective. *mAbs* 2009, 1 (2): 179-184.

[53] Duryee MJ, Bevins RA, Reichel CM, Murray JE, Dong Y, Thiele GM, Sanderson SD: Immune responses to methamphetamine by active immunization with peptide-based, molecular adjuvant-containing vaccines. *Vaccine* 2009, 27 (22): 2981-2988.

In: Emerging Targets for Drug Addiction Treatment
Editor: Juan Canales

ISBN 978-1-62081-913-5
©2012 Nova Science Publishers, Inc.

Chapter 4

DEVELOPMENTS IN OPTIMIZING TREATMENT OF OPIOID ADDICTION: A SHORT OVERVIEW

*Ambros A. Uchtenhagen**

Research Institute for Public Health and Addiction,
affiliated with Zurich University, Switzerland

ABSTRACT

The treatment of opioid dependence is one of the best researched in the addiction field, and an appropriate mix of therapeutic approaches, including substitution maintenance, is effective in reducing prevalence and the negative health and social consequences.

But severe deficiencies in quality and coverage are major causes for missing the full potential of these approaches. The extent of deficiencies and the main efforts how to improve quality and coverage of treatment are summarised in this chapter.

1. INTRODUCTION

Opioid dependence has a unique position among substance abuse disorders. Not only have opiates, especially if injected, one of the highest rates of morbidity and mortality. Historically and at present it is the only dependence for which replacement or substitution therapy has been vastly researched and implemented. Opioid substitution treatment (OST) became an indispensible element for the treatment system.

UN agencies consider OST to be one of the most effective instruments for the management of opioid dependence, for individuals as well as for populations in a Public Health perspective [1]. However, safety and efficacy of this treatment is bound to respecting good practice rules which are often neglected. This chapter tries to summarize the present deficiencies as well as efforts which have been made to improve outcomes. Two aspects are paramount here: quality and coverage.

---

* Email: ambros.uchtenhagen@isgf.uzh.ch

2. QUALITY

2.1. Deficiencies

Quality issues are indispensible for optimal results of treatment. There is no updated detailed research evidence about the status quo of treatment quality, but some studies have clearly indicated severe deficiences. Shocking findings from a prominent US example documented low professional status in a representative sample of addiction services and lack of competence due to high staff turnover [2]. A study on the management of high-risk opioid addicts in EU Member States documented a major need for improvements in all treatment centres, in spite of great differences between centres [3]. Guidelines for treatment are not always reliable guidance. A review of 28 national guidelines for OST documented a range of inappropriate restrictions without an evidence base, such as a minimal duration of dependence of 3 years before starting OST, a minimal age of >25 years, or excessive exclusion rules. The review found major dissent among guidelines concerning settings, indication rules, dosage schemes, controls, funding and quality management [4]. But which improvements should be implemented? And on which basis? One approach is to establish normative standards, based on evidence and on expert consensus. Another is to set up research-based best practice rules and guidelines. A third one focuses on the development of instruments how to assess the quality of a given treatment system or network, how to identify deficits and to prioritize improvements.

2.2. Normative Standards

A first European effort to collect systematic information and to establish *qualitative norms* for the care of drug abusers was focusing on professional standards, ethical standards, needs assessment, evaluation of effectiveness and economic evaluation [5]. It resulted in guidelines, assessment procedures and checklists in each one of those domains. A more recent European project collected relevant guidelines and other documents from all EU Member States and extracted from those a set of lists of *minimum quality standards* for interventions, services and treatment systems, separately for treatment and rehabilitation, and for harm reduction approaches. The lists were submitted in a comprehensive consensus building process, through on-line stakeholder surveys and a European stakeholder conference discussing the survey results, the implementation problems and some models of implementation strategies [6, 7]. Structural standards for services include the physical environment, staff composition and indication criteria; process standards for services and interventions include assessment procedures, treatment planning and informed consent, patient records and data protection, continued staff training and routine cooperation among services; outcome standards are monitoring and evaluation procedures. Similar standards are identified for harm reduction services and interventions. Political decisions on next steps to be taken are expected for 2012. There is an interest to adapt the minimum standards for international use, especially in medium and low resource countries.

Other normative efforts focus on the objectives of therapeutic interventions. Besides a reduction of addictive behaviour – ideally abstinence from problematic or any use of psychoactive drugs -, a range of intermediate and complimentary objectives, e.g. craving, are traditionally recommended to be applied in measuring effects in clinical trials. In contrast, new developments propose to reconsider what should be achieved in treatment [8, 9]. A recent attempt at defining recovery from addiction has not achieved a general consensus and leaves open many questions [10]. New efforts will be needed to clarify these issues.

2.3. Evidence Based Best Practice

Best practice rules and evidence-based therapeutic guidelines became a necessity, with the growing amount of research results and a need for a meta-evaluation and summary of such results for professionals working at the frontline. Examples are the NIDA principles of substance abuse treatment ~~By~~ by the US National Institute of Drug Abuse NIDA [11], the discussion paper on the principles of treatment by the United Nations Office on Drugs and Crime UNODC and World Health Organisation WHO [12], the UNODC treatment toolkit on contemporary drug abuse treatment [13]. A special effort was made by the European Monitoring Centre on Drugs and Drug Abuse EMCDDA, by implementing a best practice portal on their website with a growing amount of information on relevant research findings. Specific guidelines were published for drug policy makers and managers [14, 15]. Other guidelines covered the evidence-based state of the art for specific treatment approaches, mainly pharmacological treatments [16], but also for psychosocial interventions [17] and for residential rehabilitation centres [18]. The evidence for the feasibility, safety and outcomes of harm reduction approaches has been collected and published in a comprehensive EMCDDA monograph [19].

2.4. Assessment Instruments

A somehow different approach is chosen when checklists or questionnaires for quality assessment are proposed without providing standards. The main objective here is to allow a review of a given treatment system by use of a detailed catalogue of issues which have to be taken into consideration as key components of a treatment and care system. The instrument is designed in order to describe the system, to identify need for improvements and to document the achieved changes.

A prominent example of this approach is derived from an instrument in the mental health field: the international instrument for the assessment of prevention and treatment of substance use disorders, developed by WHO [20]. The functions of this instrument are the description, monitoring and evaluation of the relevant processes and of their impact. It allows an examination of all structural and functional aspects of the system. A range of 8 domains has to be looked at and covers issues such as: policy and legislation, epidemiology-based service needs, typology and mix of services provided, operational processes in and between services, availability of treatment modalities and harm reduction services, interventions in primary care settings, staff training, public education, monitoring and research. The feasibility and usefulness of the instrument has been tested in a few countries, and finalisation is intended, based on the results from field testing. Other instruments have been developed for the description of specific quality aspects, such as questionnaires on patient satisfaction, staff competence and satisfaction, quality of life. They all have the function of describing a status quo, to identify areas for improvement and to measure change over time. The European Monitoring Centre EMCDDA has set up an evaluation instrument bank EIB in order to facilitate their use [21].

3. COVERAGE IMPROVEMENT

It is not enough to have good quality services if they are unable to reach those in need of treatment. A WHO global survey of 147 countries documented a severe deficit in treatment coverage for drug users in need of treatment. The authors conclude that "coverage of the population in need with alcohol and drug use disorder treatment services seems to be low", and "in low-income countries the majority of persons with alcohol and drug use disorders are not covered by the respective treatment services" [22 p.XI]. Furthermore, the predominant therapeutic approach according to the survey is detoxification, with an average duration of two weeks [22]. As we know, detoxification alone is rarely sufficient to change addictive behaviour, and relapse rates are high, with fatal risks [23]. Not all opiate dependent persons must necessarily be on replacement therapy, but all should have access to it if they wish so and if there is no contra-indication. The WHO survey found that 41.6% of responding countries provided agonist substitution treatment with methadone and 27.7% with Buprenorphine. The highest proportions were reported from Europe (88.6% of countries providing methadone, 59.1% Buprenorphine) [22].

Another world wide survey found OST in 26 countries, no OST in 66 countries [24]. A recent overview of estimated OST coverage provides rates of 55% (USA), 53% (Europe), 48% Australia), 28% (Canada), 10% (China) and 0% (Russia) [25]. Also, there are major differences in coverage. Europe, a region with an estimated number of problem opioid users of 1.1 Million [25], has a comparatively high rate in treatment and especially in substitution treatment, but the national coverage of OST varies between around 6 and 65% in the community, 0 and 55% in prison populations [26]. An indirect indicator of coverage is waiting time for treatment. While waiting time for detoxification is rarely more than one month in Europe, addicts have to wait longer for psychosocial outpatient treatment and in a number of countries even many months for OST, with important regional differences within countries [27]. What efforts are made to change this situation?

3.1. Integrative Approaches

Treatment of substance abuse must not be restricted to specialised services. A prominent example is the integration into primary health care, in hospitals, community health centres and in general practitioners offices where a large portion or majority of people with addiction problems are seen. In this model, addiction specialists can function as consultants, trainers or supervisors of non-specialists. 17 out of 28 member states of the European Union have introduced this model [27]. It allows an important expansion of coverage; the number of patients in OST increased from ca. 500'000 in 2003 to 700'000 in 2009 [24]. Diversion of addicts from the judiciary system to treatment is another way to increase coverage. There is evidence from a multi-country research project showing that treatment on court order as an option, with informed consent, has the same outcomes as formally voluntary patients [28]. Integrating treatment and self-help approaches also can contribute to more therapeutic capacity and increased sustainability of treatment effects [29]. In an integrative system of harm reduction approaches and treatment, the contact with users of harm reduction services including outreach teams has a proven potential to facilitate entry to structured treatment [19].

3.2. Coverage Improvement: Diversification

Adapting treatment services to the needs of specific target groups – adolescents, pregnant women, prisoners, dual diagnosis patients, addicts with blood borne infections – is an invitation to many addicts who otherwise would not be ready or eligible to enter treatment. In the case of OST, a diversification in regard to substitution medications – methadone, buprenorphine, retarded morphine, diamorphine – allows to attract additional addicts into treatment. The prescription of opium tincture to opium addicts intends to increase the capacity of methadone clinics for heroin addicts in Iran.

3.3. Coverage Improvement: Training Systems

Two examples are mentioned here. The *TREATNET* project of UNODC, in a first phase starting 2005, engaged staff from 20 resource centres in 19 countries in a comprehensive training programme and set up workgroups to produce best practice papers on specific issues. Packages with modules for training trainers were developed and supported the resource centres in their function as trainers for other services in their respective regions; the packages cover assessment, psychosocial treatments, pharmacological treatments and an administrative toolkit.

A second phase, based on the evaluation of the first one, is dedicated to a consolidation and an expansion to 36 resource centres and over 60 partner centres in 27 countries. The project combines advocacy, capacity building and service improvement [30]. Another example is the Middle East and North Africa Harm Reduction Network MENAHRA. Its objectives are to establish sustainable structures for capacity building activities, advocacy and model programs for feasible and effective harm reduction activities. Three sub-regional knowledge hubs developed in Lebanon, Iran and Morocco [31].

3.4. Coverage Improvement: Changing the Paradigm

Finally, it should be mentioned that in a few countries a major policy change has opened the road to better treatment coverage. Mainland China is moving from a re-education camp approach to substitution maintenance treatment for opioid addicts, and in Iran a similar process has replaced punishment of opioid use by harm reduction measures and substitution maintenance. Some other Asian countries however still follow a compulsory camp approach with high relapse rates, and in the Russian Federation OST is made illegal.

REFERENCES

[1]   UNODC/WHO/UNAIDS: *Substitution maintenance treatment in the management of opioid dependence and HIV/Aids prevention.* Position paper. World Health Organisation, United Nations Office for Drugs and Crime, UNAIDS (2004).

[2]   McLellan TA, Carise D, Kleber H. Can the National Addiction Treatment Infrastructure Support the Public's Demand for Quality Care? *J. Substance Abuse Treatment* 25:117-121 (2004).

[3]   Haasen Ch, Stallwitz A, Lachmann A, Prinzleve M, Güttinger F, Rehm J. *Management of high risk opiate addicts in Europe. Final research report to European Commission.* Centre for Interdisciplinary Addiction Research, University of Hamburg (2004).

[4]   Uchtenhagen A, Ladjevic T, Rehm J. *A systematic review of existing guidelines.* Working paper for World Health Organisation, Geneva (2005).

[5]   Uchtenhagen A, Guggenbühl L. *Adequacy in Drug Abuse Treatment and Care in Europe (ADAT). Ethical Aspects, Treatment and Support Needs, Professionalism, Effectiveness and Economic Evaluations: Reports, Guidelines, Instruments.* WHO Regional Office for Europe, Copenhagen, and Research Institute for Public Health and Addiction, Zurich (2000).

[6]   Commission of the European Union. *Study on the Development of an EU Framework for minimum quality standards and benchmarks in drug demand reduction (EQUS).* Final Project Report 2012 (http://www.suchtforschung.ch/index.php?id= 59&uid-=41&year=2011)

[7]   Commission of the European Union. *Building an EU consensus for minimum quality standards in the prevention, treatment and harm reduction of drugs.* Working paper for a European Conference, Brussels 22.06.2011 (http://ec.europa.eu/justice/newsroom/anti-drugs/events/110615_en.htm).

[8]   McLellan AT, McKay ER, Forman R, Cacciola J, Kemp J. Reconsidering the evaluation of addiction treatment : from retrospective follow-op to concurrent recovery monitoring. *Addiction* 100 :447-458 (2005).

[9]   Miller PG, Miller WR. What should we be aiming for in the treatment of addiction ? Editorial *Addiction* 104:685-686 (2009).

[10] White WL. Addiction recovery: its definition and conceptual boundaries. *J. Substance Abuse Treatment* 33:229-241 (2007).

[11] NIDA. *Principles of drug addiction treatment.* A research-based guide. 2nd ed. National Institute of Drug Abuse, Rockville MD (2009).

[12] UNODC/WHO. *Principles of drug dependence treatment.* A discussion paper. United Nations Office on Drugs and Crime, Vienna, and World Health Organisation, Geneva (2011).

[13] UNODC. *Contemporary drug abuse treatment.* A review of the evidence base. United Nations Office on Drugs and Crime, Vienna (2002).

[14] UNODC. *Investing in drug abuse treatment.* A discussion paper for policy makers. United Nations Office on Drugs and Crime, Vienna (2003).

[15] Stevens A, Halam Ch, Trace M. *Treatment for dependent drug use.* A guide for policy makers. The Beckley Foundation, London (2006).

[16] WHO. *International Guidelines for psychosocially assisted pharmacological treatment for opioid dependence.* World Health Organisation, Geneva (2009).

[17] *Drug and Alcohol Psychosocial Interventions Professional Practice Guidelines.* New South Wales Ministry of Health, Mental Health and Drug and Alcohol Office, Sydney (2008).

[18] Sha D, Paget S (Eds.) *Service Standards for Addiction Therapeutic Communities.* Community of Addiction Therapeutic Communities CATC (2007).

[19] Rhodes T, Hedrich D. *Harm reduction : evidence, impact and challenges.* European Monitoring Centre for Drugs and Drug Addiction, Lisbon (2010).

[20] *WHO Technical Consultation on the Assessment of Prevention and Treatment Systems for Substance Use Disorders.* Report. World Health Organisation, Geneva (2006).

[21] *Evaluation Instrument Bank EIB.* . European Monitoring Centre for Drugs and Drug Addiction, Lisbon (http://www.emcdda.europa.eu/eib).

[22] *WHO ATLAS on Substance Use. Resources for the prevention and treatment of substance use disorders.* World Health Organisation, Geneva (2010).

[23] Strang J, McCambridge J, Best D, Beswick T, Bearn J, Rees S, Gossop M. Loss of tolerance and overdose mortality after inpatient opiate detoxification: follow up study. *BMJ* 326:959-960 (2003).

[24] *Towards Universal Access. Scaling up priority HIV/Aids interventions in the health sector.* Progress report 2009. World Health Organisation, UNAIDS, UNICEF (2009).

[25] *EMCDDA. Annual Report 2011.* European Monitoring Centre for Drugs and Drug Addiction, Lisbon (2011). http://www.emcdda.europa.eu/online/annual-report/2011/.

[26] Stöver H, Hennebel LC, Casselmann J: *Substitution treatment in European prisons. A study of policies and practices of substitution treatment in prisons in 18 European countries.* London, European Network on Drug Services in Prison (2004).

[27] *EMCDDA. Annual Report 2010.* European Monitoring Centre for Drugs and Drug Addiction, Lisbon (2010). http://www.emcdda.europa.eu/online/annual-report/2010/.

[28] Uchtenhagen A, Stevens A, Berto D et al. Evaluation of therapeutic alternatives to imprisonment for drug dependent offenders. Experience from a comparative multi-country European study. *Heroin Addiction and Related Clinical Problems* 10:5-10 (2008).

[29] Timko C. Intensive referral to 12-step self-help groups and 6-month substance use disorder outcomes. *Addiction* 101:678-688 (2006).

[30] *Treatnet project.* United Nations Office on Drugs and Crime, Vienna (2011) www.unodc.org/docs/treatment.

[31] *Middle East and North Africa Harm Reduction Association MENAHRA*, Lebanon (2011) www.menahra.com.

In: Emerging Targets for Drug Addiction Treatment
Editor: Juan Canales

ISBN 978-1-62081-913-5
©2012 Nova Science Publishers, Inc.

Chapter 5

CANNABIS USE DISORDER: EPIDEMIOLOGY, MANAGEMENT AND FUTURE DIRECTIONS

Wendy Swift[1] *and Jan Copeland[1,2]*

[1]National Drug and Alcohol Research Centre,
University of New South Wales, Sydney, NSW, Australia
[2]National Cannabis Prevention and Information Centre,
University of New South Wales, Sydney, NSW, Australia

ABSTRACT

This chapter provides an overview of the epidemiology of cannabis use, cannabis use disorder and its treatment. Cannabis is the most commonly used illicit drug internationally, although global consumption patterns and trends are unevenly distributed. Early initiation and regular adolescent use have been identified as particular risk factors for later problematic cannabis (and other drug) use, impaired mental health, delinquency, lower educational achievement, risky sexual behaviour and criminal offending in a range of studies. It is estimated that approximately one in ten people who have ever used cannabis will become dependent with risk increasing markedly with frequency of use. While relatively few users who may potentially experience such problems seek professional assistance, there have been increases in demand for cannabis treatment services.

There are as yet no evidence-based pharmacotherapies available for the management of cannabis withdrawal and craving. Relatively brief cognitive behavioural therapy and contingency management have the strongest evidence of success, and structured, family-based interventions, provide potent treatment options for adolescents. Innovative models of intervention delivery, such as mail, telephone and web-based interventions, may be promising ways of reducing the barriers to cannabis treatment provision, With criminally involved young people and those with severe, persistent mental illness, longer and more intensive therapies provided by interdisciplinary teams may be required.

---

[*] Email: w.swift@unsw.edu.au

1. EPIDEMIOLOGY OF CANNABIS USE

Cannabis is the most widely produced and used illicit drug globally, with approximately three to five percent of the world's 15-64 year olds having used it in 2009. However, its consumption patterns are unevenly distributed, with the highest prevalence rates in Oceania (including Australia, New Zealand) and North America. Use trends also fluctuate; while use appears to be stable or in decline in Canada, western Europe and NZ after peaks in the 1990s, trends towards increased use are being reported in Africa, eastern Europe, South and Central America, Asia, and in very recent surveys, Australia and the USA [1-5].

After peaking in 1998, there had been a decline in the proportion of Australians aged 14 years or older reporting recent (past year) use of cannabis throughout the 2000s. 2010 data revealing a statistically significant increase in past year use across both genders represent a reversal of this trend, with 10.3% reporting recent use [1]. Likewise, 2008 and 2010 rates of current (past month) use among North Americans aged 12 years and older represent an increase from those earlier in the decade, with almost nine percent reporting current cannabis use [4]. In contrast, New Zealand national data from 2007/8 showing 14.6% of 16 to 64 year olds had engaged in past year use appears to represent a continuing downward trend in recent use throughout the past decade [6,7]. While an average of 6.7% of 15-64 year olds in the European Union report past year cannabis use, and there appears to be an overall trend towards stable or declining levels of use [3,8], this masks the tremendous range in national use patterns, from 0.4% reporting recent use in Romania and 14.3% in Italy [3].

In 2010, 23% of Australians who reported last year use reported at least weekly use of the drug and a further 13% reported daily use [1], with almost identical figures reported in New Zealand (25.6% at least weekly and 13.4% daily) [6]. Similarly, almost 16% of North Americans aged 12 years or older reporting use in the last year had used on a near daily to daily basis [4]. It is estimated that between 19% and 33% of past month users in the European Union are daily or near daily users [8].

Two consistent correlates of cannabis use are gender and age. Consumption, particularly regular or heavy, typically predominates among males. However, there is some evidence that gender differences may be diminishing among more recent cohorts of users [e.g., 2, 9]. Cannabis use is also typically most common among young adults. Thus, it predominates among Australians aged 18-29 years (21% reported past year use) [1], North Americans aged 18-25 years (19% reported past month use) [4] and 15-24 year olds in the European Union (an average of 15% reported last year use) [3]. Nevertheless, several age-related trends have become apparent which may have implications for the natural history of cannabis use, including a decrease in the age of initiation to cannabis use among younger age groups in some developed countries, and an apparent prolongation of risk of initiation to cannabis use beyond adolescence, in more recent cohorts of users [e.g., 2,10]. North American and Australian national data also indicate increases in recent cannabis use among 50-59 year olds, which may partially reflect the ageing of members of cohorts who commenced use when cannabis use became popular [1,4].

Indigenous communities in the US [11] and Australia [12] appear to have markedly higher levels of cannabis use, particularly daily use, than the non-indigenous members of their communities. In a New Zealand longitudinal birth cohort study there were consistent trends for cohort members reporting a Maori identity to have higher rates of cannabis use and dependence during adolescence and young adulthood. Among those reporting Maori identity, however, rates of cannabis use and dependence did not differ detectably between those reporting a sole Maori identity and those reporting a Maori/other identity [13]. The epidemiology of cannabis use amongst these groups is at an early stage of development and requires urgent attention as it is running contrary to wider community trends and raises important questions about the role of culture in the tailoring of intervention approaches.

2. NATURAL HISTORY OF CANNABIS USE

Cannabis use is typically initiated during adolescence but the incidence and intensity of use typically increases over the mid to late teens [e.g., 14-17], before a decline in use from the mid 20s which has been associated with the adoption of new, more normative roles and responsibilities [18-20]. For example, US data reveal that approximately one tenth to one third of those who used at least once a month at age 20 were doing so in their early 30s [18, 21]. Nevertheless, a minority of young people report use patterns that increase the likelihood of long-term use and dependence, regular use of other drugs, and exposure to cannabis-related harms.

While most cannabis use remains sporadic, of limited duration and without major consequences, entrenched users are at high risk of cannabis dependence and other related adverse outcomes. In particular, early initiation and regular adolescent use have been identified as risk factors for later problematic cannabis (and other drug) use, impaired mental health, delinquency, lower educational achievement, risky sexual behavior and criminal offending [e.g., 20, 22-26]. However, adolescents who initiate cannabis use early and use it regularly differ from their non-using and less entrenched peers in several ways, including their use of other drugs, having a history of antisocial and non-conformist behaviour, poor academic expectations and performance and affiliation with drug-using peers [27,28]. Thus, these associations may be at least partially reflect common or overlapping risk factors and life pathways among young people who may be predisposed to cannabis use and those at increased risks of these other outcomes [e.g., 29, 30].

3. CANNABIS USE DISORDERS

Despite a burgeoning literature, there remains considerable debate about cannabis-related harm, including its addictive potential. This partly stems from doubts about its ability to produce tolerance to its effects or the existence of a cannabis withdrawal syndrome, often considered the hallmarks of dependence on other drugs. However, advances in our understanding of the action of cannabis on the body have enabled research which has clearly identified that these phenomena can be a feature of cannabis use [e.g., 31]. Contemporary concepts of problematic drug use typically reflect the drug dependence syndrome, a cluster of physical, behavioural and psychological elements, which together define a pattern in which drug use is given priority over previously more highly valued behaviours. Cannabis use disorders (comprising dependence and the related concepts of cannabis abuse and harmful use) are evaluated using instruments that operationalise standard psychiatric nomenclatures ([see [32] for review)]. Proposed changes to the North American nomenclature, as represented in the upcoming fifth version of the Diagnostic and Statistical Manual of Mental Disorders (DSM-V), will see the abolition of the "abuse" category, due to a lack of data supporting an intermediate stage between drug use and disorder. In addition, the word drug use disorder will replace the dichotomy between abuse and dependence, as a means of reflecting an underlying continuum of severity of drug-related problems [33, 34]. However, there is ongoing debate about the nature of drug-related problems and the way in which they are classified (see commentaries to [34]), which has implications for screening, diagnosis and treatment.

Despite the widespread global prevalence of cannabis use, relatively few countries have produced population-based cannabis dependence estimates [35]. Nationally based data from the Epidemiologic Catchment Area Study and the National Comorbidity Survey have indicated that approximately 3 to 4% of North American adults met criteria for a lifetime diagnosis of DSM-III or DSM-III-R cannabis dependence [36-38], although more recent data from the National Epidemiologic Survey on Alcohol and Related Conditions (NESARC) study reports much lower rates, with the prevalence of 12-month and lifetime DSM-IV cannabis abuse (1.1% and 7.2%) exceeding the corresponding rates of cannabis dependence (0.3% and 1.3%) [39]. Similar past year cannabis use disorder rates (1.8%) have been reported from the US National Survey on Drug Use and Health, with rates remaining steady between 2002 and 2009 [4]. Using data from two large representative samples, Compton and colleagues [40] claim that despite the stability in the overall prevalence of cannabis use, the prevalence of cannabis use disorder in the US in 2001-2002 was greater than in 1991-1992 (representing an increase from 2.2 to 3 million people), most notably in young black men and women and young Hispanic men.

The 1997 National Survey of Mental Health and Wellbeing (NSMHWB) found approximately 2% of Australian adults were diagnosed with a past-year DSM-IV cannabis use disorder, largely cannabis dependence (1.5%) [41], which is similar to earlier US findings. The 2007 NSMHWB reports 1% of Australians aged 16 to 85 years had a past year ICD-10 (the European World Health Organization diagnostic nomenclature) cannabis disorder diagnosis [42]. While cannabis use disorders are typically second only to alcohol and tobacco in absolute terms, this is not necessarily so for conditional prevalence (i.e., disorders among current users). For example, the *conditional* lifetime prevalence of cannabis dependence (9.1%) in the National Comorbidity Study was exceeded by nicotine (32%), heroin (23%), cocaine (17%), alcohol (15%) and stimulant (11%) dependence [37], while in the 1997 Australian NSMHWB the conditional prevalence of cannabis use disorders (31.7% of cannabis users) was exceeded by stimulant use disorders (36.4% of stimulant users) [41].

There is evidence of substantial heritability in risk for cannabis use and disorders, and the likelihood of common genetic and environmental influences on liability to cannabis and other drug involvement [43]. Cannabis affects dopaminergic reward systems implicated in the rewarding and reinforcing properties of several drugs, including alcohol, opioids and MDMA [44-47]. Recent evidence suggests that both repeated administration of THC and cannabis withdrawal may exert long-lasting functional and structural changes to this system [48, 49]. Rates of dependence tend to be higher among young people [39-41], who may be significantly more likely to develop cannabis dependence for a given dose than adults; early initiators may be particularly at risk. It has been estimated that among young people who have used cannabis one in six or seven will become dependent [50]. A ten year prospective population study of Australian adolescents found that 43% of weekly or more frequent adolescent cannabis users (two thirds of whom commenced use early, i.e., before age 16) were using regularly (weekly+) at age 24 and 29% were dependent. Daily adolescent users had almost a four times elevated risk of young adult dependence than occasional adolescent users [25]. This study has also examined a distinct group of cannabis users who reported some symptoms of cannabis use disorder in young adulthood but did not meet full diagnostic criteria. A four year follow-up of these "diagnostic orphans" found they were less likely to be daily or dependent users at age 24 than those who were dependent at age 20, but were at greater risk than non-problem users for developing dependent and daily cannabis use, suggesting that a strict focus on dependence may exclude important prognostic clinical information on some cannabis users [51].

Relatively little is known about the natural history of cannabis dependence. The onset of dependence most commonly occurs in adolescence or young adulthood, within 10 years of initiation [38,50]. Some research has documented the onset of clinical symptoms, commencing with loss of control and continued use despite harm, with withdrawal experienced at a later age by relatively fewer users [52]. However, recent age-related trends concerning age of initiation and a prolongation of the risk period for initiation among more recent cohorts (above) may have implications for the natural history of this syndrome and prevention and intervention strategies.

4. TREATMENT SEEKING

While there is insufficient epidemiological evidence to assess whether the all-cause mortality rate is elevated among cannabis users, case-control data suggest that rates of respiratory and brain cancers and fatal motor vehicle accidents may be elevated among heavy users [53]. In Australia, the occurrence of population indicators of cannabis-related harm, such as hospital separations for cannabis-induced psychosis and cannabis-related problems such as dependence, increased over the 2000s, particularly among older age groups [54]. While most cannabis users will not require treatment, cannabis is a public health issue due to the large numbers of people who use the drug and become dependent. Dependence can be distressing and its chronic, relapsing nature increases the risk of users' long-term exposure to any adverse effects of cannabis. Adult cannabis users who seek professional help typically report numerous cannabis-related problems, some clearly related to core dependence criteria, such as an inability to stop or cut down and withdrawal symptoms, and others such as relationship, family and financial difficulties, health concerns and poor life satisfaction [e.g., 55, 56]. Many will have been using regularly for several years and have made previous unsuccessful attempts at moderating their use over this time, prior to entering treatment.

Nevertheless, relatively few users who may potentially experience such problems seek professional assistance [57]. In 2008, only 2.4% of past-year cannabis users in New Zealand had received help to reduce their level of cannabis use, yet 13% of recent users reported daily consumption [6]. Stinson and colleagues [38] reported low rates of drug treatment among those with lifetime cannabis abuse (9·8%) and dependence (34·7%) in the US NESARC, while corresponding figures for those with diagnoses in the last 12 months (6·4% and 18·1%) were even lower. This phenomenon is not unique to cannabis users, with similar low rates of help-seeking among those diagnosed with alcohol use disorders [39]. Recent research examining barriers to cannabis treatment reported that in addition to barriers associated with a perceived or actual lack of treatment services and difficulties in accessing them, the most commonly identified barrier was the belief that treatment was not necessary for reducing use [57]. Australian research on two samples of long-term urban and rural cannabis users found that while more than a half of each group met lifetime criteria for cannabis dependence fewer than one in ten had ever sought professional assistance, with participants much more likely to have made their own attempts at use moderation. Importantly, only one quarter to one third believed their use was a *problem* [58, 59].

Despite this disparity, there have been increases in demand for cannabis treatment services. Cannabis ranks closely second to opiates in overall illicit drug admissions in the US, with an increase in such admissions from 13% in 1999 to 18% in 2009 [60]. The majority (86%) of treatment admissions among 12-17 year olds involved cannabis as the primary or secondary drug of concern. Most treatment seekers received ambulatory treatment for their cannabis problem [60]. Among those in the NESARC with cannabis abuse or dependence, the most commonly accessed forms of treatment were 12-step programs, physicians, rehabilitation programs and detoxification services, with inpatient and outpatient services equally accessed (each approximately 10%) [39]. In the EU, approximately 23% of all admissions in 2009 had primary cannabis problems, second only to heroin. Between 2004 and 2009 there was a 40% increase in the proportion of first time entrants to treatment who were primary cannabis users. Primary cannabis clients tend to be one of the youngest client groups entering treatment with a mean age of 25 years [3]. In Australia between 2009 and 2010, cannabis was the second most common principal drug of concern for which treatment was sought after alcohol, accounting for 23% of closed treatment episodes; this has remained fairly stable over the last decade. Among 10-19 year old clients, cannabis represented one half of episodes compared to a third for alcohol [61]. Some of the increases observed in certain countries, especially the US, are likely to be due to increases in judicial mandating of (particularly young) cannabis users to treatment. For example, 49% of TEDS referrals aged 12-17 years came from the criminal justice system [60]. Of the 600 participants in the US Cannabis Youth Treatment Study, a large scale examination of a variety of treatment modalities, 62% were involved in the criminal justice system, and while 96% met abuse or dependence criteria only 20% believed they had a problem [62].

5. INTERVENTIONS FOR CANNABIS USE DISORDER

While there is an extensive literature on the epidemiology of cannabis use, the evidence-base on the management of cannabis use disorder is embryonic compared with that for nicotine, alcohol and opioids. There have been so few randomised controlled trials (RCTs) that no meta-analyses have been conducted on the question. A recent study comparing characteristics of successful and unsuccessful quitters reported that unsuccessful quitters focus on the desire to quit, but do not sufficiently plan strategies for coping. Unsuccessful quitters also had significantly more symptoms of depression and stress; less education; lower exposure to formal treatment; higher day-to-day exposure to other cannabis users; and higher cannabis dependence scores [63].

5.1. Evidence for Cannabis Treatment among Adults

Despite high rates of cannabis use in the general population, and rising rates of treatment seeking for cannabis use disorders it has only been in the last 15 years that rigorous controlled studies of interventions for cannabis use disorders have appeared in the literature [cf. 64, 65]. Adults seeking treatment for cannabis use disorders have typically used cannabis near-daily for more than a decade and have made more than six serious attempts to reduce or stop.

5.2. Psychological Interventions

Most interventions used for cannabis dependence have been adaptations of alcohol interventions. A recent review of relapse reported that cannabis-dependent outpatients have similar problems initiating and maintaining abstinence as do those dependent on other illicit drugs [66, 67]. In the past 15 years, a handful of RCTs of motivational enhancement therapy (MET) and cognitive-behavioural therapy (CBT) for cannabis dependence, in which outcomes are confirmed by urinalysis for cannabinoids or collateral validation, have been performed in the USA [68, 69] and Australia [70]. Motivational enhancement therapy addresses ambivalence about quitting and seeks to strengthen motivation to change. The key clinical skills are using a non-confrontational, non-judgemental approach to guide the person towards awareness, commitment and action. Cognitive behavioural therapy teaches skills relevant to reducing or quitting cannabis use and managing other psychosocial or health problems that impact on treatment outcome.

The largest and most comprehensive published trial of interventions for cannabis dependence was a multi-site RCT of 450 adults [69]. The participants were randomised to either two sessions of MET or nine sessions that included MET, CBT and case management or a Delayed Treatment Control (DTC). At 4 months follow-up, the nine-session treatment reduced cannabis smoking and associated consequences, such as dependence symptoms, significantly more than the two-session treatment, which significantly reduced cannabis use relative to the DTC condition. At 15-month follow-up, the superior outcome for the more intensive intervention had dissipated; however, significant improvement from baseline was maintained. There were no sex or ethnic differences in treatment outcome. The most recent trial of 122 participants aged 16-44 years, who met criteria for DSM-IV cannabis dependence, was conducted in Germany [71]. Participants were randomly assigned to 10 sessions of manualised CBT versus delayed treatment control. At end of treatment, this younger than average cohort reported promising past 7 days abstinence rates (49% versus 13%) with program effects on quantity and frequency of cannabis use maintained over 3 and 6 months follow-up.

A very promising adjunct to MET and CBT interventions is contingency management (CM) [72-74]. Across three trials, CM programs that provided monetary-based reinforcement contingent on documented cannabis abstinence improved abstinence outcomes both during and post treatment when combined with MET/CBT. Whereas contingency management has not always been seen as a practical strategy for many clinicians, as the weight of evidence increases in its ability to support long-term change in combination with MET-CBT, its acceptance should increase.

In conclusion, while many cannabis-dependent adults respond well to MET, CBT and CM, continuous abstinence is a less common outcome than reduced cannabis use. Note however, that as with other types of substance disorders, complete abstinence is not necessary to achieve clinically meaningful improvement and reductions in cannabis-related problems [66, 69, 70]. These studies demonstrate that cannabis use and dependence is amenable to treatment in adults, and also made it clear that specialist cannabis treatment services can attract people who are looking for assistance with their cannabis use issues, but may be less willing to engage with generalist drug and alcohol services. There is much yet to be known about how it is that interventions exert an effect.

One of the promising new areas of intervention research are innovative models of intervention delivery to reduce the barriers to cannabis treatment provision, A pilot study of mail-based cognitive behavioural therapy for cannabis use disorder has shown promising findings on abstinence rates [75]. Studies are also soon to be published on telephone and true web-based intervention delivery models. The capacity to monitor progress and manage contingencies is a very promising innovation that will become increasingly feasible as technologies decrease in size and cost and increase in community accessibility. These open up a whole new frontier of real-time data collection and opportunities for cost-effective, easily accessible interventions for cannabis use and related disorders [76].

5.3. Pharmacotherapy for Cannabis Use Disorders

There is ample evidence that THC is the primary component underlying the reinforcing effect of cannabis in humans, and the CB1 receptor is clearly implicated in the development of cannabis dependence and withdrawal [77]. In addition, cannabis shares neurobiological features associated with dependence on other drugs [78], with commonalities in the dopaminergic reward systems implicated in the rewarding and reinforcing properties of several drugs, including cannabis, alcohol, opioids and MDMA [44-47]. Despite these advances in our understanding of the mechanisms underlying the reinforcing effects of cannabis, there is currently little evidence for effective pharmacotherapies for the treatment of cannabis dependence in humans [79-81]. Studies on medications for treating cannabis use disorders have been sparse and have largely focused on withdrawal management. They have typically focussed on small scale laboratory studies or open-label trials examining the potential of various medications, with few controlled clinical trials conducted among treatment seekers. One of the limitations of this research is the difficulty experienced in extending relevant animal models to humans. For example, research on the role of the opioid system in the reinforcing actions of cannabis shows that naloxone, an opioid antagonist, blocks cannabis-mediated reward in rodents, but this has been difficult to demonstrate in humans, with evidence that the opioid antagonist naltrexone not only fails to precipitate withdrawal in cannabis smokers but may increase the intoxicating effects of cannabis in non-treatment seekers [82].

To date, the most promising findings have been with an agonist medication, oral THC (dronabinol) [78]. Agonist substitution, in combination with psychosocial interventions, is a plank of pharmacological approaches for substance dependence on other drugs such as nicotine (nicotine replacement therapy) and heroin (methadone maintenance treatment). Both inpatient and outpatient laboratory studies have shown that oral THC dose-dependently reduces or suppresses cannabis withdrawal symptoms [83, 84]. Recently, Levin and colleagues [79] conducted a randomised, double blind, placebo-controlled trial comparing oral THC to placebo, among cannabis-dependent adults. They found dronabinol superior to placebo in retention to treatment and reducing withdrawal symptoms, but conferred no advantage over placebo in terms of achieving abstinence or in reducing use. They concluded that dronabinol was a promising intervention as it was well accepted, promoted good adherence and produced few adverse events, and that its potential could be improved through higher doses, and combinations with other medications and/or potent behavioural interventions.

Another approach to attenuating the reinforcing effects of cannabis is through the use of a cannabinoid antagonist. SR141716, or rimonabant, a CB1 selective antagonist, has been found to precipitate withdrawal in rodents [77], but this effect has been more difficult to reproduce in humans. One study with rimonabant demonstrated that it successfully blocks the acute psychological and physiological effects of smoked cannabis and is well tolerated [85]. Unfortunately research on the potential of rimonabant has currently been stalled. The first human study of rimonabant-elicited withdrawal recently found that 20mg of the drug produced only weak evidence of cannabis withdrawal symptoms. Evaluation of higher doses was not possible as rimonabant was withdrawn from global clinical development and the study was prematurely terminated [86].

Additional agents that have been tested in lab studies or open-label trials include atomoxetine [87], nefazadone, buspirone, divalproex [cf., 88], lithium carbonate [89] and the combination of oral THC and lofexedine [90]. Of these studies, only the findings from the THC and lofexidine combination study showed substantial promise. Two recent studies have explored adjunct medications for the management of cannabis withdrawal. Sugarman and colleagues [80] have examined a novel strategy of using cognitive-enhancing medications to target cognitive impairment associated with chronic use. They conducted a double-blind, placebo controlled, crossover study of modafinil, a wakefulness-promoting medication approved for sleep apnoea and which has also been trialled for cocaine and methamphetamine dependence. They hypothesised that modafinil may alleviate cognitive deficits and withdrawal symptoms of depressed mood, irritability, anxiety and anger, and administered it in conjunction with oral THC. The two medications appeared to provide a safe combination. While modafinil alone had some impact on mood states, increasing tension and vigour and decreasing ratings of depressed mood, it had no impact on cognition. The authors suggested future studies should examine the potential utility of a range of dose combinations of modafinil and oral THC. In the second study, extended-release zolpidem, a non-benzodiazepine $GABA_A$ receptor agonist [81] aimed at reducing sleep disturbance in cannabis withdrawal, was found to attenuate the effects of withdrawal on sleep, but did not reduce overall withdrawal severity or craving. Thus, it is currently unclear how these findings translate to better clinical outcomes with regard to reduced use.

Despite the limited research evidence to date, there are a number of promising avenues for future research involving cannabis pharmacotherapies. These include further developing current approaches involving activation or deactivation of CB1 receptors for managing withdrawal and abstinence, by investigating combinations of existing medications at different dosages, and medications with existing effective psychosocial interventions. However, concerns over the potential for abuse liability and adverse side effects from these medications [78] have prompted calls for the development of other pharmacotherapies. These include second generation cannabinoid antagonists [78], alternative high affinity CB1 receptor partial agonists [79] and agents that enhance endogenous cannabinoid signalling, which has been shown to potentiate stress-coping behaviours in animals and may assist in blunting negative affect and stress in humans during withdrawal [91]. Finally, Russo [92] has suggested harnessing the cannabinoid profile of cannabis by using selective cross-breeding to modulate the reinforcing properties of the drug (e.g., through manipulation of cannabinoids such as THC, cannabidiol and plant terpenoids).

Consistent with this approach an in-patient trial is currently underway in Australia to test the efficacy of Sativex in the management of cannabis withdrawal. Sativex differs from all other cannabinoid based medications on the market in that it is the world's first derived from botanical material. Sativex is a regulated pharmaceutical product, standardized in formulation, composition and dose. The spray contains equal proportions Δ-9-THC and cannabidiol (CBD), with one spray delivering a fixed dose of 2.7mg THC and 2.5mg CBD. Cannabidiol can comprise up to 40% of the active ingredients of the cannabis plant and acts to counteract the intoxicating effects of Δ-9-THC in smoked cannabis [93]. It has also been reported to relieve anxiety and nausea. The combination of CBD and Δ-9-THC means that Sativex will more fully activate the endogenous receptor system upon which smoked cannabis acts, relative to Δ-9-THC alone [94].

5.4. Treatments for Special Populations

There are two population groups for whom the issue of interventions for cannabis use disorder are especially problematic. Cannabis use is most commonly initiated in adolescence, when heavy, regular use is of concern, and voluntary treatment seeking is rare. Second, those with psychotic disorders are also particularly vulnerable to the effects of cannabis and are difficult to engage, retain and successfully treat for cannabis dependence.

5.4.1. Adolescents

The literature regarding interventions for cannabis use in adolescents is sparse. In recent years there has been increased attention given to developing general substance use treatment models that take cognizance of the issues and developmental stage of young people, rather than simply generalising (potentially age-inappropriate) adult programs to this group [95]. Manualised therapies have become available for dissemination to the field, and evidence is emerging for the efficacy of a number of treatment models including structured, family-based therapies, and motivational enhancement and cognitive behavioural interventions [cf. 96]. The largest randomised trial for adolescent cannabis use, the Cannabis Youth Treatment (CYT) study, was a multi-site intervention study of 600 young cannabis users aged between 12 and 18 years who reported one or more DSM-IV cannabis abuse or dependence criteria [97]. Participants received one of five outpatient interventions of various types, ranging from a relatively brief 5 sessions (MET/CBT) to up to 22 sessions of Family Support Network therapy that included aspects of CBT, family therapy, and additional case management contact. Overall, the clinical outcomes were similar across conditions. All five CYT interventions showed significant pre-post treatment effects; compared with baseline, at 12 months there was an increase in reported abstinence, and decreases in symptoms of cannabis abuse and dependence. As with adult interventions, researchers are also investigating the use of CM in combination with MET-CBT for adolescents with cannabis related problems [98]. A RCT of 69 adolescents aged 14-18 years with cannabis related problems suggested that the MET/CBT+CM improved cannabis abstinence rates post treatment compared with MET/CBT combined with weekly parental psychoeducation [99]. This supports the findings of other studies reporting positive outcomes for CM incorporated in multisystemic therapy or MET/CBT among juvenile offenders [100-102].

The studies above relate to adolescents or young adults who present for treatment. This population represents a very small percentage of young people who use substances [103], and may constitute a more troubled population. There is a need for active secondary prevention efforts targeting young people at an early stage of their cannabis using career in an effort to minimise problematic use, promote problem recognition, and facilitate informed choice regarding cannabis use and its potential consequences.

There have been a number of studies exploring brief, opportunistic, motivational interventions among UK college students. While initially encouraging these non-cannabis specific interventions did not maintain an effect over time [104]. In the US and Australia, studies of brief (2-3 session) MET interventions, the Teen Marijuana Check-up [105] and the Adolescent Cannabis Check-up [106, 107] have been reported. The school-based Teen Marijuana Check-up [105] was compared with a three month assessment only waitlist control, and showed reductions in cannabis use, but no significant differences between groups. The Adolescent Cannabis Check-up (ACCU) recruited from the general community and compared it with a three month waitlist control group. At the three month follow-up, significant between group differences in levels of cannabis use and dependence favoured the ACCU group. Current evidence supports the use of MET and CBT approaches in addition to a range of systemic family therapy approaches and CM. A limitation of the current brief intervention literature is that follow-up periods have been relatively short and it remains unclear whether multiple iterations of the intervention over a relatively long period would aid to entrench or support the short term gains observed. While the findings of adolescent interventions are encouraging, as with adults, continuous abstinence rates are low. There is much yet to be learned about effective and sustainable interventions for adolescents with cannabis related problems and dependence.

5.4.2. What is Available for Those with Serious Mental Health Problems?

One of the most challenging clinical issues is the management of comorbid schizophrenia and cannabis dependence [108]. There have been few studies of interventions among this challenging group. A small, retrospective study of the effects of clozapine versus resperidone on cannabis use in schizophrenia reported that those patients treated with clozapine were significantly more likely to abstain from cannabis and alcohol than those treated with resperidone [109].

With little evidence-based pharmacotherapy for comorbid schizophrenia and cannabis dependence, the use of psychological interventions and shared care with mental health and substance use disorder treatment services is central to their optimal management [110]. There are no published RCTs of CBT among psychiatric populations specifically directed at cannabis use and related problems. A study of patients with first episode schizophrenia randomised participants to either a cannabis focussed intervention using a combined cannabis and psychosis therapy (CAP) or a clinical control condition of psycho-education (PE). There were no significant differences between the CAP and PE groups on cannabis use at end of treatment and 6 months post-intervention. Similarly, there were no significant group differences on psychopathology and functional ratings at follow-up [111].

A more recent study exploring the use of motivational interviewing with parents of young adults with recent onset schizophrenia found that compared with routine family support there was a reduction in frequency, quantity and craving for cannabis use at 3 months follow-up [112]. It appears, therefore, that this is an especially challenging group to engage and retain in treatment but intervention with parents in recent onset schizophrenia is showing some promise. In conclusion, clinician's recommendations for the management of substance use in the context of severe and persistent mental illness rests with integrated shared care or dual diagnosis services, in which the critical components are staffed interventions, assertive outreach, motivational interventions, counselling, social support interventions, a comprehensive and long-term perspective and cultural sensitivity and competence [113].

CONCLUSION

There is a growing demand for the treatment of cannabis use disorders and a paucity of evidence on best practice interventions. The targeted screening of high-risk individuals such as clients of mental health services, patients presenting with respiratory and other smoking-related complaints to general medical practices, juvenile justice populations and those with other substance use disorders would be useful places to identify those with earlier stage cannabis use problems for motivational and brief cognitive behavioural interventions.

Clinicians are sometimes reluctant to intervene with cannabis use disorders. A recent small study in the UK [114] designed to stimulate general practitioners' incorporation of cannabis-related clinical enquiry in their practice, found that a brief motivational interview led to more positive attitudes and greater clinical activity up to 3 months later.

For those seeking treatment, relatively brief CBT and CM have strong evidence of success for adults and adolescents, and structured, family-based interventions may increase the potency of these interventions for adolescents. Among those involved in the juvenile justice system and those with severe, persistent mental illness, longer and more intensive therapies provided by interdisciplinary teams may be required. Overall, there remains a strong need for the continued development of more effective interventions for prevention and treatment of cannabis use disorders and innovative models of their delivery to improve accessibility and reduce costs.

REFERENCES

[1]   Australian Institute of Health and Welfare, *2010 National Drug Strategy Household Survey report* (AIHW Cat. No. PHE 145), AIHW, Canberra (2011).

[2]   L. Degenhardt, W-T. Chiu, N. Sampson, R.C. Kessler, J.C. Anthony, M. Angermeyer, R. Bruffaerts , G. de Girolamo, O. Gureje, Y. Huang, A. Karam, S. Kostyuchenko, J.P. Lepine, M.E. Mora, Y. Neumark, J.H. Ormel, A. Pinto-Meza, J. Posada-Villa, D.J. Stein, T. Takeshima and J.E. Wells, Toward a global view of alcohol, tobacoo,

cannabis, and cocaine use: Findings from the WHO World Mental Health Survey. *PLoS Medicine*, 5, doi:10.1371/journal.pmed.0050141 (2008).

[3]   EMCDDA, *Annual report 2011: the state of the drugs problem in Europe*, Publications Office of the European Union, Luxembourg (2011).

[4]   SAMHSA, *Results from the 2010 National Survey on Drug Use and Health: Summary of national findings* (NSDUH series H-41; HHS Publication No. (SMA) 11-4658), SAMHSA, Rockville, MD, (2011).

[5]   UNODC, *2011 World Drug Report*, United Nations, Vienna (2011).

[6]   Ministry of Health, *Drug use in New Zealand: Key results of 2007/08 New Zealand Alcohol and Drug Use Survey*, Ministry of Health, Wellington (2010).

[7]   C. Wilkins and P. Sweetsur, *JNZMA*, 121, 61 (2008).

[8]   J. Vicente, D. Olszewski and J. Matias, in EMCDDA (Ed.), *A cannabis reader: global issues and local experiences* (Monograph Series 8, Volume 2; pp. 6-26), European Monitoring Centre for Drugs and Drug Addiction, Lisbon (2008).

[9]   K. Von Sydow, R. Lieb, H. Pfister, M. Höfler, H. Sonntag and H.U.Wittchen, *Drug Alcohol Depend*, 64, 347 (2001).

[10]   A. Agrawal, and M. Lynskey, *Drug Alcohol Depend*, 105, 71 (2009).

[11]   F. Beauvais, P. Jumper-Thurman, H. Helm, B. Plested and M. Burnside, *J. Adolescent Health*, 34, 393 (2004).

[12]   K. Lee, K.M. Conigrave, A.R. Clough, T.A. Dobbins, M.J. Jaraqba and G.C. Patton, *Drug Alcohol Rev.*, 28, 623 (2009).

[13]   M. Dannette, D.M. Fergusson and J.M. Boden, *ANZ J. Psychiatry*, 42, 780 (2008).

[14]   C. Coffey, M. Lynskey, R. Wolfe and G.C. Patton, *Addict*, 95, 1679 (2000).

[15]   L. Degenhardt, C. Coffey, J.B. Carlin, W. Swift, E. Moore and G.C. Patton, *Br. J. Psychiatry*, 196, 290 (2010).

[16]   A. Perkonnig, R. Lieb, M. Höfler, P. Schuster, H. Sonntag and H-U. Wittchen, *Addict*, 94, 1663 (1999).

[17]   R.G. Poulton, M. Brooke, T.E. Moffitt, W.R. Stanton and P.A. Silva, *N. Z. Med. J.*, 110, 68 (1997).

[18]   J. Bachman, P. O'Malley, J. Schulenberg, L. Johnston, A. Bryant and A Merline, *The decline of substance use in young adulthood: Changes in social activities, roles, and beliefs*, Lawrence Erlbaum Associates Publishers, Mahwah, New Jersey (2002).

[19]   K. Chen and D.B. Kandel, *Am. J. Public Health*, 85, 41 (1995).

[20]   K. Chen and D.B. Kandel, *Drug Alcohol Depend.*, 50, 109 (1998).

[21]   D.B. Kandel and M. Davies, In M. Glantz and R. Pickens (Eds.), *Vulnerability to drug abuse* (pp.211-242). American Psychological Association, Washington, DC (1992).

[22]   Global Cannabis Commission, *Cannabis policy: Moving beyond stalemate*, Oxford University Press and Beckley Foundation Press, Oxford (2010).

[23]   D.M. Fergusson and J.M. Boden, *Addict*, 103, 969 (2008).

[24]   J. Horwood, D.M. Fergusson, M. Hayatbakhsh, J. Najman, C. Coffey, G.C. Patton, Silins and D.M. Hutchinson, *Drug Alcohol Depend.*, 110, 247 (2010).

[25]   A. Perkonnig, R.D. Goodwin, A. Fiedler, S. Behrendt, K. Baesdo, R. Lieb and H.-U. Wittchen, *Addict*, 103, 439 (2008).

[26]   W. Swift, C. Coffey, J.B. Carlin, L. Degenhardt and G. Patton, *Addict*, 103, 1361 (2008).

[27]   W. Hall and L. Degenhardt, *Current Opinion Psychiatry*, 20, 393 (2007),

[28] D. Kandel and K. Chen, *J. Studies Alcohol,* May, 367 (2000).

[29] W. Hall, L. Johnston and N. Donnelly, In: H. Kalant, W.Corrigall, W. Hall and R. Smart (Eds.), *The health effects of cannabis* (pp.71-125), Centre for Addiction and Mental Health, Toronto (1999).

[30] M. Lynskey and W. Hall, *Addict,* 95, 1621 (2000).

[31] A.J. Budney, J.R. Hughes, B.A. Moore and R.G. Vandrey, *Am. J. Psychiatry,* 161, 1967 (2004).

[32] T.F. Babor, In R.A. Roffman and R.S. Stephens (Eds.), *Cannabis dependence: Its nature, consequences and treatment* (pp.21-36), Cambridge University Press, Cambridge (2006).

[33] D.S. Hasin, M.C. Fenton, C. Beseler, J.Y. Park and M.M. Wall, *Drug Alcohol Depend,* doi: 10.1016/j.drugalcdep.2011.09.005 (2011).

[34] C. O'Brien, *Addict,* 106, 866 (2011).

[35] L. Degenhardt, C. Bucello, B. Calabria, P. Nelson, A. Roberts, W. Hall, M. Lynskey, L. Wiessing and the GBD illicit drug use writing group (2011). *Drug Alcohol Depend.,* 117, 85 (2011).

[36] J.C. Anthony and J.E. Helzer, J.E, In L.N. Robins and D.A. Regier (Eds.), *Psychiatric disorders in America: the Epidemiologic Catchment Area study* (pp. 116-154), Free Press, MacMillan, New York (1991).

[37] J.C. Anthony, L.A. Warner and R.C. Kessler, *Exp. Clin. Psychopharm,* 2, 244 (1994).

[38] W. Hall, N. Solowij and J. Lemon, *The health and psychological consequences of cannabis use,* Australian Government Publishing Service, Canberra (1994).

[39] F.S. Stinson, W.J. Ruan, R. Pickering and B.F. Grant, *Psychol. Med.,* 36, 1447 (2006).

[40] W.M. Compton, B.F. Grant, J.D. Colliver, M.D. Glantz and F.S. Stinson, *JAMA,* 291, 2114 (2004).

[41] W. Swift, W. Hall and M Teesson, *Addict,* 96, 737 (2001).

[42] T. Slade, A. Johnston, M. Teesson, H. Whiteford, P. Burgess, J. Pirkis and S. Saw, *The mental health of Australians 2: Report on the 2007 National Survey of Mental Health and Wellbeing,* Department of Health and Ageing, Canberra (2009).

[43] A. Agrawal and M.T. Lynskey, *Addict,* 101, 801 (2006).

[44] D. Piomelli, *Nature Reviews Neuro Science,* 4, 873 (2003).

[45] P. Robledo, *Curr. Drug Targets,* 11, 429 (2010).

[46] J.A. López-Moreno, A, López-Jiménez, M.A. Gorriti and F.R. de Fonseca, *Curr. Drug Targets,* 11, 406 (2010).

[47] M.S. Spano, P. Fadda, W. Fratta and L. Frattore, *Curr. Drug Targets,* 11, 450 (2010).

[48] S. Spiga, A. Lintas, M. Migliore and M. Diana, *Addict Biology,* 15, 266 (2010).

[49] W. Shen, M. Flajolet, P. Greengard and D.J. Surmeier., *Science,* 321, 848 (2008).

[50] J. Anthony, In R.A. Roffman and R.S. Stephens (Eds.), *Cannabis dependence: Its nature, consequences and treatment* (pp.58-105), Cambridge University Press, Cambridge (2006).

[51] L. Degenhardt, C. Coffey, J.B. Carlin, W. Swift and G.C. Patton, *Drug Alcohol Depend.,* 92, 86 (2008).

[52] M.F. Rosenberg and J.C. Anthony, *Drug Alcohol Depend.,* 64, 123 (2001).

[53] B. Calabria, L. Degenhardt, W. Hall and M. Lynskey, *Drug Alcohol Rev.,* 29, 318 (2010).

[54] A. Roxburgh, W.D. Hall, L. Degenhardt, J. McLaren, E. Black, J. Copeland and R Mattick, *Addict,* 105, 1071 (2010).

[55] J. Copeland, W. Swift, R. Roffman and R. Stephens, *J. Substance Abuse Treat*, 21, 55 (2001).

[56] R.S. Stephens, R.A. Roffman and E.E. Simpson, *J. Consult. Clin. Psychol.*, 61, 1100 (1993).

[57] P. Gates, J. Copeland, W. Swift and G. Martin, *Drug Alcohol Rev*, 31, 311 (2011)

[58] W. Swift, J. Copeland and W. Hall, *Addict*, 93, 1681 (1998).

[59] W. Swift, W. Hall, P. Didcott and D. Reilly, *Addict*, 93, 1149 (1998).

[60] SAMHSA, *Treatment Episode Data Set (TEDS): 1999-2009. National admissions to substance abuse treatment services* (DASIS Series S-56; DHHS Publication No. (SMA) 11-4646), SAMHSA, Rockville, MD: (2011).

[61] Australian Institute of Health and Welfare, *Alcohol and other drug treatment services in Australia 2009-2010. Report on the National Minimum Data Set* (AIHW Cat. No. HSE 114). AIHW: Canberra (2011).

[62] G. Diamond, J. Leckrone, M.L. Dennis and S.H. Godley, In R.A. Roffman and R.S. Stephens (Eds.), *Cannabis dependence: Its nature, consequences and treatment* (pp.247-274), Cambridge University Press, Cambridge (2006).

[63] S. Rooke, M. Norberg and J. Copeland, *Subst. Abuse Treat Prev. Policy,* 6, 30 (2011).

[64] A.J. Budney, R. Roffman, R.A Stephens and D. Walker, *Addict Science Clin. Practice,* December, 4 (2007).

[65] J. Copeland, *Curr. Opinion Psychiatry*, 17, 2114 (2004).

[66] R.S. Stephens, R.A. Roffman, S.A Fearer, C. Williams, J.F. Picciano and R.S. Burke, *Addict*, 99, 1323 (2004).

[67] B. Moore and A. Budney, *J. Subst. Abuse Treat,* 25, 85 (2003).

[68] R.S. Stephens, R.A. Roffman and L. Curtin, *J. Consult. Clin. Psychol.*, 68, 898 (2000).

[69] MTPRG, *J Consult Clin Psychol*, 72, 455 (2004).

[70] J. Copeland, W. Swift, R. Roffman and R. Stephens, *J. Subst. Abuse Treat*, 21, 55 (2001).

[71] E Hoch, R. Noak, J. Henker, A. Pixa, M. Hofler, S. Behrendt, G. Buhringer and H-U. Wittchen, *Eur. Neuropsychpharm*, doi 10.1016 euroneuro 2011.07.014 (2011).

[72] A. Budney, S. Higgins, K. Radanovich and P. Novy, *J. Consult. Clin. Psychol.*, 68, 1051 (2000).

[73] A.J. Budney, B.A. Moore, H.L. Rocha and S.T Higgins, *J. Consult. Clin. Psychol.*, 74, 307 (2006).

[74] J.L. Kamon, A.J. Budney and C. Stanger, *J. Amer. Acad. Child Adol. Psychiatry*, 44, 513 (2005).

[75] M.M. Norberg, T. Wright, K. Hickey and J. Copeland, *Drug Alcohol Rev.* DOI: 10.1111/j.1465-3362.2011.00317.x (2011).

[76] J. Copeland, *J. Subst. Use Misuse,* 46, 112 (2011).

[77] Z.V. Cooper and M. Haney, *Int. Rev. Psychiatry,* 21, 104 (2009).

[78] R. Vandrey and M. Haney, *CNS Drugs*, 23, 543 (2009).

[79] F.R. Levin, J.J. Mariani, D.J. Brooks, M. Pavlicova, W. Cheng and E.V. Nunes, *Drug Alcohol Depend.*, 116, 142 (2011).

[80] Sugarman, D.E., Poling, J. and Sofuoglu, M. (2011). The safety of modafinil in in combination with oral Δ9-tetrahydrocannabinol in humans. *Pharmacology, Biochemistry and Behavior, 98*, 94-100.

[81] R. Vandrey, M.T. Smith, U.D. McCann, A.J. Budney and E.M. Curran, *Drug Alcohol Depend.*, 117, 38 (2011).

[82] Z.V. Cooper and M. Haney, *Psychopharm*, 211, 141(2010).

[83] A.J. Budney, J.R. Hughes, R.G. Vandrey, B.A. Moore, B.A and B. Bahrenburg, *Drug Alcohol Depend.,* 86, 22 (2007).

[84] M. Haney, C. Hart, S. Vosburg, J. Nasser, A. Bennett, C. Zuberin and R.W. Foltin, *Neuropsychopharm,* 29, 158 (2004).

[85] M. Huestis, D. Gorelick, S. Heishman, K.L. Preston, R.A. Nelson, E.T. Moolchan and R.A. Drank, *Arch. Gen. Psychiatry,* 58, 322 (2001).

[86] D.A. Gorelick, R.S. Goodwin, E. Schwile, D.M. Schwope, W.D. Darwin, D.L. Kelly, R.P. Mahon, F. Liu, C. Ortemann-Renon, D. Bonnet and M.A. Huestis, *J. Clin. Psychopharm,* 31, 603 (2011).

[87] A. Tirado, M. Goldman, K. Lynch, K. Kampman and C. O'Brien, *Drug Alcohol Depend., 94, 254 (2008).*

[88] C. Hart, *Drug Alcohol Depend., 80, 147* (2005).

[89] A.R. Winstock, T. Lea and J. Copeland, *J. Psychopharm*, 23, 84 (2009).

[90] M. Haney, C. Hart, S. Vosburg, S.D. Comer, S.C. Reed and R.W. Foltin, *Psychopharm, 197, 157* (2008).

[91] J.R. Clapper, R.A. Mangieri and D. Pomelli, *Neuropharm,* 56, 235 (2009).

[92] E. Russo, *Br. J. Pharmacol.*, 163, 1344 (2011).

[93] I.G. Karniol and E. A. Carlini, *Psychopharmacologia,* 33, 53 (1973).

[94] E. Russo and G. W. Guy, *Med. Hypotheses,* 66, 234 (2006).

[95] A.J. Pumariega, L. Rodriguez and M.D. Kilgus, *Addict Disorders Treat,* 3, 145 (2004).

[96] H.B. Waldron and C.W. Turner, *J. Clin. Child Adolescent Psychol.,* 37, 238 (2008).

[97] M. Dennis, S.H. Godley, G. Diamond, F.M. Tims, T. Babor, J. Donaldson, H. Liddle, J.C. Titus, Y. Kaminer, C. Webb, N. Hamilton and R. Funk, *J. Subst. Abuse Treat,* 27, 197 (2004).

[98] J.L. Kamon, A.J. Budney and C. Stanger, *J. Am. Academy Child Adolescent Psychiatry,* 44, 513 (2005).

[99] C. Stanger, A. Budney, J. Kamon and J. Thostensen, *Drug Alcohol Depend,* 10, 240 (2009).

[100] S.W. Henggeler, C.A. Halliday-Boykins, P.B. Cunningham, J. Randall, S.B. Shapiro and J.E. Chapman, *J. Consult. Clin. Psychol.,* 74, 42 (2006).

[101] K.M. Carroll, C.J. Easton, C. Nich, K.A. Hunkele, T.M. Neavins, R. Sinha, H. L. Ford, S.A. Vitolo, C.A. Doebrick and B.J. Rounsaville, *J. Consult. Clin. Psychol.*, 74, 955 (2006).

[102] R. Sinha, C. Easton, R. Renee-Aubin and K.M. Carroll, *Amer. J. Addict*, 12, 314 (2003).

[103] F.M. Tims, M.L. Dennis, N. Hamilton, B.J. Buchan, G. Diamond, R. Funk and L.B. Brantley, *Addict,* 97 (Suppl. 1), 46 (2002).

[104] J. McCambridge, R.L. Slym and J. Strang, *Addict,* 103, 1809 (2008).

[105] D.D. Walker, R.A. Roffman, R.S. Stephens, K. Wakana, J. Berghuis and W. Kim, *J. Consult. Clin. Psychol.*, 74, 628 (2006).

[106] G. Martin and J. Copeland, *J. Subst. Use Treat,* 34, 407 (2008).

[107] G. Martin, J. Copeland and W. Swift, *J. Subst. Use Treat,* 29, 207 (2005).

[108] R. Drake R and K. Muesner, *Curr. Psychiatric Reports,* 3, 418 (2001).

[109] A. Green, E. Burgess, R. Dawson, S.V. Zimmet and R.D. Strous, *Schiz Res.,* 60, 81 (2003).

[110] R. Drake, S. Essock and A. Shaner, *Psychiatric Services,* 52, 469 (2001).

[111] J. Edwards, K. Elkins, M. Hinton, S.M. Harriganm K. Donovan, O. Athanasopoulis and P.D. McGorry, *Acta. Psychiatr. Scand.,* 114, 109 (2006).

[112] M. Smerdijk, R. Keet, N. Dekker, M. Van Raaij, M. Koeter, N. de Haan, C. Barraclough, G. Shippers and D. Linzen, *Psychol. Med.,* Dec 8, 1 (2011).

[113] K. Carey, D. Purnine, S. Maisto and J.S. Simons, *J. Subst. Abuse Treat,* 19. 189 (2000).

[114] J. McCambridge, J. Strang, S. Platts and J. Witton, *Br. J. Gen. Practice,* 53, 637 (2003).

In: Emerging Targets for Drug Addiction Treatment
Editor: Juan Canales

ISBN 978-1-62081-913-5
©2012 Nova Science Publishers, Inc.

Chapter 6

PSYCHOSOCIAL AND PHARMACOLOGICAL TREATMENTS FOR BEHAVIORAL ADDICTIONS

David M. Ledgerwood[*1] *and Megha D. Patel*[2]

[1]Department of Psychiatry and Behavioral Neurosciences,
Wayne State University School of Medicine, Detroit, Michigan, US
[2]Lyman Briggs College, Michigan State University, East Lansing, Michigan, US

ABSTRACT

Recent research evidence reveals that some behaviors often considered to be impulse control problems share several of the same underlying mechanisms as drug and alcohol use disorders. These non-substance or behavioral addictions have become the focus of an increasing amount of scientific study in recent years, and one disorder, pathological gambling, is being considered for inclusion as an addictive disorder in the upcoming 5th edition of the Diagnostic and Statistical Manual of Mental Disorders. In this chapter, the authors provide an overview of research covering four behavioral addictions – pathological gambling, compulsive shopping/buying, sexual addiction and computer/internet addiction. They then provide a review of the scientific literature on the effectiveness of pharmacological and psychological treatments for each of these disorders. It is concluded that the treatment literature for several behavioral addictions is in its infancy, and a number of strategies are suggested for advancing the field of knowledge.

1. INTRODUCTION

In psychiatry, substance use disorders alone have traditionally been viewed as *bona fide* addictions. This view, however, has changed substantially in the past decade with new findings that suggest substantial similarities between substance and non-substance addictions [1, 2]. Behavioral or non-substance addictions have been defined as "…syndromes analogous

---

* Email: dledgerw@med.wayne.edu

to substance addiction, but with a behavioral focus other than ingestion of a psychoactive substance" [3].

While some early theorists suggested that substance use disorders are actually better thought of as impulse control disorders (e.g., [4]), more recently the reverse has been true; that is, impulse control disorders are better conceptualized as addictive disorders (see McElroy et al. [5] for review). Indeed, there is emerging evidence that there may be common molecular and neurobiological pathways of addiction that may also include behavioral addictions [1, 5, 6]. Some disorders that are considered as behavioral addictions (e.g., pathological gambling, kleptomania) have been included as impulse control disorders in the DSM-IV [7], while many others (e.g., compulsive buying, sexual addiction, computer/internet addiction, food addiction) do not have official psychiatric disorder status. Nevertheless, behavioral addictions have received an increasing amount of attention in the research literature in the past decade, including several review articles (e.g., Grant et al. [1, 3]) and journal special issues (e.g., American Journal of Drug and Alcohol Abuse, vol. 36). Indeed, for the first time, a behavioral addiction (pathological gambling) is being considered for inclusion into a Substance-Related Disorders (possibly to be renamed Addiction and Related Disorders) category of the Diagnostic and Statistical Manual for Mental Disorders, 5th edition (DSM 5; American Psychiatric Association), along with drug and alcohol use disorders.

Nonetheless, the inclusion of behavioral addictions along with substance use disorders is controversial [8-10]. Some have noted, for example, that behavioral addictions are qualitatively different from substance use disorders in their lack of ingestion of a brain-altering substance, differing consequences of the behavior, and dissimilarity between diagnostic criteria [9]. Others have noted that there are significant gaps in the research literature which may preclude a definitive linking of behavioral addictions with substance use disorders [10].

Yet others have decried the pathologizing of otherwise normative behaviors that are engaged in excessively [11]. Controversy notwithstanding, enough research has been conducted to demonstrate that several behavioral addictions resemble substance use disorders in many ways. In this chapter, we focus on pharmacological and psychological treatments for four of the more frequently studied behavioral addictions (pathological gambling, compulsive shopping, sexual addiction, and computer/internet addiction). Although the list of potential behavioral addictions is long (e.g., kleptomania, food addiction, excessive tanning, skin picking and several others have been suggested), we focus here on four behavioral addictions because many other potential behavioral addictions have few if any controlled trials documenting the efficacy of treatment approaches. The four behavioral addictions addressed in this chapter may represent exemplars for other behavioral addictions for which there is less research.

First, we briefly describe the current state of the literature for each disorder, including the clinical characteristics, epidemiology, etiology and neurobiology. This section is meant as a brief overview, and the reader is referred elsewhere for full literature reviews of individual behavioral addictions (e.g., the special issue cited above). We then review our current knowledge of the efficacy of pharmacological and psychological treatments for this class of disorders. Our focus is primarily on clinical trials published in peer review journals. Finally, we provide some directions for future research.

2. SPECIFIC BEHAVIORAL ADDICTIONS

2.1. Pathological Gambling

Pathological gambling is the most studied of the behavioral addictions to date. Listed as an impulse control disorder in the DSM-IV, pathological gambling is being considered for inclusion into a new Addiction and Related Disorders category in DSM 5. Although the study of pathological gambling lags behind that of substance use disorders, there is a fairly large body of research relevant to the question of whether pathological gambling is similar to substance use disorders in terms of etiology, clinical characteristics, course and treatments.

Pathological gambling has been described as "...persistent and recurrent maladaptive gambling behavior that disrupts personal, family, or vocational pursuits" [7]. Adult prevalence estimates for pathological gambling vary between about 0.4% and 4.0% depending on the survey methods employed [12-14]. The etiology of pathological gambling is not completely known, but several studies have been conducted that identify demographic factors (e.g., younger age, ethnic minority status), co-occurring disorders (e.g., depression, substance abuse) and neurobiological vulnerabilities (e.g., genetic influence, increased activation and arousal, abnormal neurotransmitter function) may all contribute to increase one's vulnerability to developing a gambling disorder (see Petry [15] for review). Pathological gambling is associated with several psychosocial difficulties including serious financial issues, legal and vocational problems, and interpersonal conflict [16]. It is also associated with many other psychiatric problems. Individuals with pathological gambling, for example are significantly more likely than non-problem gamblers to experience clinical depression, anxiety disorders and personality disorders [12]. Pathological gamblers are more likely to experience suicidal ideation and more likely to attempt suicide than are non-problem gamblers [17]. Finally, a recent population-based study in the U.S. found that over 70% of pathological gamblers have a history of alcohol abuse and/or dependence, over 38% have had other substance use disorders and as many as 60% are nicotine dependent [12].

Neurobiology studies have found important similarities between pathological gambling and substance use disorders. Addiction research evidence suggests that substance-abusing individuals show deficits in activation of the orbitofrontal cortex and dorsolateral prefrontal cortex compared with normal controls [18]. Similar results have been found with pathological gamblers. For example, impaired decision-making – which partly depends on the orbitofrontal cortex – appears to be a risk factor for relapse in treatment-seeking pathological gamblers [19]. A recent study found that Parkinson's patients who developed compulsive gambling behaviors subsequent to initiating dopamine replacement therapy experienced poorer functioning on the Iowa Gambling Task than Parkinson's patients without gambling problems [20]. We recently found similar deficits in decision-making among pathological gamblers compared with healthy controls [21]. Goudriaan et al. [22] noted an absence of increased heart rate in pathological gamblers (not found in controls) after wins on the Iowa Gambling Task, and suggested that this absence may be indicative of decreased reward sensitivity in pathological gamblers. Consistent with these findings, data from recent functional magnetic resonance imaging (fMRI) studies suggest that compared to controls pathological gamblers experience deficits in functioning in frontal areas of the brain associated with executive function and decision-making (e.g., orbitofrontal cortex, caudate/basal ganglia, thalamus, ventromedial prefrontal cortex, ventral striatum; e.g., Potenza et al. [23, 24). Crockford et al., [25] for example, found that male pathological gamblers experienced increased activity in the dorsolateral prefrontal cortex than male control participants while exposed to gambling cues. Tanabe et al. [26] found that substance dependent individuals with co-occurring gambling problems showed reduced activity in the ventromedial frontal, right frontopolar and superior frontal cortex while completing the Iowa Gambling Task. Other studies have also found significant differences between pathological gamblers and controls in function in the ventral striatum and other limbic system structures [27, 28]. Reuter and colleagues [28] found that pathological gamblers exhibited reduced activation of the mesolimbic reward pathways (specifically the ventral striatum and ventromedial prefrontal cortex), suggesting hypoactivation of this system relative to non-problem gambling controls.

2.2. Compulsive Shopping/Buying

Initially termed oniomania by early psychiatrists [29, 30], compulsive buying (also referred to as compulsive shopping) is characterized by an intense urge to purchase accompanied by pleasure when buying items [31]. Although not included in the DSM-IV, several specific diagnostic features have been proposed including: irresistible, intrusive or senseless preoccupation with or impulses to buy; frequent buying of items that are not needed or that one cannot afford or shopping for prolonged periods of time; buying preoccupations, impulses or behaviors cause marked distress, consume a lot of time, interfere with social/occupational functioning or result in financial problems; and excessive buying that does not only occur during a manic or hypomanic episode [32].

It is estimated that anywhere from 1.8% to 5.8% of North Americans may meet diagnostic criteria for compulsive buying [33, 34], with some studies showing that women are substantially more likely than men to have this problem [33]. However, gender differences are not universally found [34]. Relatively few epidemiological studies have been conducted to date, and not all have consistently found gender differences in prevalence (See Black [35] for review). Several features and consequences of compulsive buying have been noted in the literature. In most cases, individuals with compulsive buying focus on the act of shopping and spending, and purchases are often discarded, given away or sold. Indeed, Black [35] notes four distinct phases of compulsive buying behavior: 1) anticipation of buying (development of thoughts, preoccupations, urges to shop); 2) preparation to purchase (decisions on where to shop, research into sales/specials, what accounts to use); 3) shopping (experienced as intensely exciting); and 4) spending (which is often followed by disappointment). Compulsive buying is associated with significant financial difficulties including trouble paying bills, debt and bankruptcy [36, 37]. Individuals with compulsive buying experience guilt, shame and marital conflict around their shopping, and compulsive shopping is often associated with other co-occurring disorders including depression, bipolar disorder, substance abuse/dependence, anxiety disorders, eating disorders, obsessive-compulsive, borderline, narcissistic, histrionic and avoidant personality disorders, and other impulse control disorders [37, 38]. Very little research has been conducted to examine the underlying neurobiology of compulsive buying. To date, there are no fMRI studies on compulsive buying published in peer review journals. However, research has been conducted on brain processes that occur when people make decisions about purchases including activation of the nucleus accumbens in situations where a positive gain was anticipated, and activation of the insula and deactivation of the mesial prefrontal cortex in response to excessive prices presented prior to a purchase decision [39]. Thus, limbic system structures associated with reward processing are active when people evaluate purchases, and these are some of the same processes that appear to be at play in substance use disorders [40].

2.3. Sexual Addiction

As with compulsive buying, sexual addiction is not listed as a disorder in the DSM-IV. However, compulsive sexual behaviors may be diagnosed under the category Sexual Disorders Not Otherwise Specified. Sexual addiction has gone by many other terms such as sexual compulsion, excessive non-paraphillic sexual behavior, paraphilia-related disorder, nymphomania, Don Juanism, and hypersexuality. In this chapter we use these terms interchangeably, but primarily the term "sexual addiction" is used. Sexual addiction is characterized by "…intensely sexually arousing fantasies, urges, and sexual activities that are culturally sanctioned aspects of normative sexual arousal and behavior" [41]. Specific types of sexual addictions include consensual sex with another adult (both heterosexual and homosexual), excessive masturbation, pornography use, cybersex, telephone sex, attending strip clubs or other non-paraphilic sexual activities [41-45]. Compulsive sexual behaviors are distinguished from normative sexuality by an increase in frequency and/or intensity (for six months duration) leading to significant distress or social impairment, and in many cases a lowered capacity to have reciprocal affectionate relationships with others [41]. Recent proposals have been made to introduce "hypersexual disorder" into the DSM 5 [43]. Kafka [43] proposed criteria for hypersexual disorder include recurrent and intense sexual fantasies, urges or behaviors lasting six months or more, and three or more of the following: time consumed by sexual fantasies, urges or behaviors interferes with other important goals, activities or obligations; repetitive engagement in sexual fantasies, urges or behaviors to cope with dysphoric mood states; repetitive engaging in sexual fantasies, urges or behavior in response to stressful events; repetitive and/or unsuccessful attempts to cut down or control sexual urges and/or behaviors; and repetitive engaging in sexual behaviors despite potential risk of harm (physical or emotional) to others [43]. Additionally, there must be clinically significant distress or impairment in social, occupational and/or other areas of functioning, and the fantasies, urges and behaviors cannot be due to the direct physiological effect of a substance or medication. These diagnostic criteria are reminiscent of substance use disorders. Indeed, others have also suggested additional diagnostic criteria that are more consistent with an addiction model, including tolerance (a need to increase the intensity or frequency of the sexual behavior to reach the same level of stimulation), and withdrawal (restlessness or irritability when unable to engage in sexual behavior) [46].

Sexual addiction is generally distinguished from paraphilias; paraphilias are typically characterized by intense and deviant arousal and sexuality arising from non-normative stimuli, while sexual addiction is often (although not always) characterized by excessive but normophilic sexual behaviors [41, 47]. Paraphilic sexual behaviors include exhibitionism, pedophila, voyerism, sadism, masochism, frotteurism and other behaviors and are not generally accepted as normative sexual behaviors. There is substantial overlap, however, among paraphilias and non-paraphelic behaviors. Kafka and Hennen [44] for example, found that 86% of patients with paraphilias also engage in excessive non-paraphilic sexual behaviors. In this chapter, treatments for non-paraphillic sexual behaviors are the focus. Garcia and Thibaut [47] noted that no epidemiological studies have been conducted using proposed diagnostic criteria, but cited studies that estimate 3 to 6% of the general population experiences sexual addiction. A majority of individuals identified in the sexual addiction literature are men, with a ratio of about 5:1 men to women [47]. As with other behavioral addictions, there is substantial psychiatric comorbidity with sexual addictions. Mood disorders, anxiety disorders, alcohol and other substance use disorders, impulse control and personality disorders frequently co-occur with sexual addictions [48, 49]. One study of individuals with "compulsive sexual behavior" recruited from the community revealed that 100% endorsed at least one lifetime Axis I diagnosis and 88% met current diagnostic criteria for an Axis I disorder [49]. Individuals with sexual addictions also endorse higher levels of impulsivity than the general population [49]. Further, dissociation during sexual activity appears to be frequently reported among some samples [50].

Neurobiological studies have found dopamine (e.g., projected from the incerto-hypothalamic area to the hypothalamus and from the substantia nigra to the striatum) plays a substantial role in facilitation of normative sexual behavior in men [51]. An fMRI study of the effect of erotic visual stimuli on males revealed that a close connection exists between hypothalamus activation, sexual arousal, and individual deep sexual identity differences in sexual behavior [52]. Hamann et al. [53] also suggested a distinct role for the amygdala in male appetitive versus consummatory sexual responses based on previous animal studies. They proposed that viewing sexual stimuli correlates with increased amygdala activation, whereas decreased amygdala activity can be associated with consummatory sexual behaviour (e.g. erection and orgasm). For the most part, however, studies examining the differential functioning of the brains of individuals with and without sexual addictions have not been conducted.

2.4. Computer/Internet Addiction

Computer technology has become nearly ubiquitous in the daily lives of most people in the industrialized world. It is estimated that nearly two billion people world-wide are connected to the internet [54]. This development is remarkable given that a generation ago very few people were connected to the world-wide web. Computer/internet addictions can be defined as excessive computer, video game and/or internet use that is characterized by: preoccupation with computer use; urges to use, and computer use behaviors that are distressing or lead to impairment of daily life; and not occurring exclusively during manic or hypomanic episodes, and not better accounted for by other Axis I disorders [55]. Others have also incorporated criteria similar to substance and behavioral addictions, including: preoccupation with computer/internet use; a need to use the internet/computers in increasing amounts to achieve satisfaction; unsuccessful attempts to control, cutback or stop use; restlessness, moodiness, depression or irritability when cutting back use; online use longer than originally intended; risking a significant relationship, job, educational or career opportunity because of internet/computer use; lying to others (family, friends, therapist) to hide the extent of one's computing/internet involvement; and using computer/internet as a way of escaping problems or alleviating dysphoric mood [56]. In part because of such great proliferation of technology and the internet, computer-related addictions such as internet addiction, video game addiction, and internet pornography addiction are sometimes difficult to classify because in some cases the behaviors may be considered distinct (e.g., excessive internet use vs. excessive gaming), and in others there may be significant overlap with other types of behavioral addictions (e.g., internet pornography and sexual addictions).

Indeed, Block [57] recently noted that internet addiction may consist of three different subtypes, excessive gaming, sexual preoccupations, and e-mail/text messaging. These subtypes do not include individuals who spend excessive amounts of time "surfing" the web, spending time in chat rooms, shopping/auctioning, or several other online pursuits. In this chapter, we use the term computer/internet addiction to refer to excessive gaming and/or internet use, and discuss internet pornography within the context of sexual addictions.

One large U.S. based survey of 17,251 individuals conducted as a part of a larger ABC-News.com investigation found that 6% of the respondents met criteria for internet addiction [58]. Several other countries are estimated to have prevalence rates between 2-11% for adolescents [59-63]. However, these surveys are plagued by inconsistent and at times vague assessment techniques, and sampling biases that make accurate prevalence estimates elusive [64]. Computer and video gaming addiction prevalence is similarly elusive due to measurement inconsistencies. One recent review of prevalence studies from several countries found that between < 3% and 20% of youth video gamers are video computer game addicted [65]. Estimates varied widely by country, age of participants and assessment methods.

Psychosocial consequences of excessive computer/internet use include academic impairment, relationship problems, financial problems, occupational impairment (particularly in the case of using internet excessively at work) and sleep problems [66]. One early study that surveyed internet users by telephone and electronic questionnaire, and assessed internet addiction using a modified version of the DSM-IV criteria for pathological gambling found that those who met criteria for internet addiction spend 38.5 hours per week on-line, compared with 4.9 hours per week for non-addicted users [66]. As with other behavioral addictions, computer/internet addictions are associated with significant psychiatric comorbidity. One study of 20 individuals with problematic internet use found that all had at least one Axis I psychiatric disorder as assessing using the Structured Clinical Interview for the DSM-IV [67]. The most frequent diagnoses in this sample included bipolar I (60%), alcohol abuse and/or dependence (45%), other substance abuse and/or dependence (45%), social phobia (45%) and specific phobia (35%). Several other disorders were endorsed in a number of categories including mood disorders, anxiety disorders, eating disorders, impulse control disorders, paraphilias and psychotic disorders. Depression appears to be frequently reported among individuals with computer/internet addition [68].

Black, Belsare, and Schlosser [69] found lifetime mood disorder, substance use disorder, anxiety disorder, personality disorder, (most frequently borderline, antisocial, and narcissistic) and impulse-control disorders (most frequently compulsive buying) to be reported frequently among a sample of 21 individuals with compulsive computer use. Others have noted that loneliness, depressive moods and compulsive traits are higher among internet addicted individuals [70]. As with other addictive behaviors, computer/internet addicted individuals appear to gravitate to excessive use to escape from stressful situations or depressive affect [70].

Neurobiological studies of computer/internet addiction are only recently emerging. In one fMRI study, participants meeting criteria for internet gaming addiction (n = 11) experienced greater responses to computer gaming cues than healthy control participants (n = 8) in several brain areas including the left occipital lobe buneus, left dorsolateral prefrontal cortex, and left parahippocampal gyrus [71]. Following six weeks of treatment with bupropion (a norepinepherine and dopamine reuptake inhibitor), participants with internet gaming addictions experienced decreased activity in the dorsolateral prefrontal cortex compared with baseline, as well as reduced cravings to play and reduced total game time. Another study comparing college-aged Chinese participants meeting internet addiction criteria (n = 19) with controls (n = 19) found abnormalities in reward system areas of the brains (e.g., limbic system and frontal lobe) of internet addicted participants [72]. Finally, Ko et al., [73] studied blood-oxygen-level dependent (BOLD) signals of (n = 10) participant with online gaming addiction and (n = 10) controls presented with gaming and non-gaming pictures while in the MRI scanner. They found that individuals with gaming addictions experienced greater activation of the right orbitofrontal cortex, bilateral anterior cingulated and medial frontal cortex, right dorsal lateral prefrontal cortex, right nucleus accumbens, and right caudate nucleus in response to gaming pictures than control participants, and no differences in response to neutral pictures. Taken together, these studies show remarkable consistency with those of substance abuse and other behavioral addictions, particularly findings that suggest addictions are associated with the mesolimbic reward pathways of the brain.

3. TREATMENTS FOR BEHAVIORAL ADDICTIONS

Aside from a small number of behavioral addictions that have relatively extensive research literature (e.g., pathological gambling), the study of treatment efficacy for behavioral addictions is at an embryonic stage. Below, we first describe studies examining the efficacy of pharmacological treatments for four behavioral addictions. We then go on to provide a review of research on behavioral treatments.

3.1. Pharmacological Treatments

Pharmacological treatments may be selected either to treat a behavioral addiction directly (e.g., to reduce urges to engage in the behavior) or to reduce co-occurring psychopathology that may be contributing to the behaviors (e.g., selective serotonin reuptake inhibitors [SSRIs] for depression). To date, there have been relatively few medication trials for most behavioral addictions, and even fewer tightly controlled, double-blind trials. Below, the medication treatment research is summarized for each behavioral addiction.

Pathological Gambling. Pathological gambling has the most research evidence for the efficacy of pharmacological interventions. Pharmacological treatments used for pathological gambling have primarily been one of three categories: 1) opioid antagonists; 2) antidepressants; and 3) mood stabilizers. However, recently other medications have also been explored. Importantly, although there are several medications that appear to effectively reduce pathological gambling symptoms, no medication has received Food and Drug Administration approval for treatment of this disorder to date.

Addictive behaviors are thought to be associated with dysregulation of mesolimbic dopamine system. Other neurotransmitters are thought to modulate dopamine. For example, endogenous opioid systems may regulate the release of dopamine from the nucleus accumbens [74]. Opioid antagonist medications, typically used to treat dependence on opioids (like heroin) and alcohol, are proposed to regulate dopamine neurons in certain areas of the brain, possibly reducing urges and excitement associated with gambling [75] or other addictive behaviors. Naltrexone and nalmefene hydrochloride are two opioid antagonist medications that have been studied in problem gamblers. Naltrexone in particular has demonstrated efficacy in reducing gambling symptoms in clinical trials, case reports and chart review studies [75-79]. In one study, pathological gamblers (N = 83) were assigned to receive naltrexone (up to 250mg) or placebo in perhaps the largest double-blind study to date. Data from participants who remained in the study past week six and achieved naltrexone doses of 100 mg/day or more for two weeks or longer (n = 45) were analyzed. In total, 75% of those who received naltrexone were either "much improved" or "very much improved", compared with 24% of placebo-treated participants [75]. In another double-blind, controlled study, Grant, Kim and Hartman [80] randomly assigned pathological gamblers (N = 77) to placebo or one of three doses of naltrexone (50mg, 100mg, or 150mg). Participants receiving naltrexone experienced significant reductions in gambling symptoms, urges and behaviors relative to the placebo condition, and there were no significant differences between medication doses. At these doses, naltrexone was well tolerated relative to placebo.

In a rare double-blind direct comparison between two active medications, pathological gamblers were randomly assigned to receive naltrexone (n = 19) or bupropion (n = 17), a dopamine and norepinepherine re-uptake inhibitor that is often used to treat depression and nicotine dependence [77]. At the end of 12 weeks, 75% of treatment completers from the bupropion group (n = 12) abstained from gambling compared with a similar 76% of the completers from the naltrexone group (n = 13). Thus, both medications appeared to effectively reduce gambling problems. Another opioid antagonist, nalmefene, has also been studied as a treatment for pathological gambling in a large 16-week, double-blind, placebo controlled study [81]. Patients (N = 207) were randomly assigned to placebo, or 25 mg, 50 mg or 100 mg of nalmefene daily. Nalmefene resulted in significantly greater decreases in gambling disorder symptoms and gambling urges compared with placebo. Overall treatment response was most pronounced for patients who received 25 mg doses (59% were "much improved" or "very much improved", compared with 34% of those in the placebo group). Patients receiving 50 mg (48%) and 100 mg (42%) doses were not significantly improved compared with placebo patients. Nalmefene does not appear to elevate liver enzymes as frequently occurs with naltrexone.

Antidepressant medications, including selective serotonin reuptake inhibitors (SSRIs)[82] and norepinephrine/dopamine agonists [77,83] have been studied as potential treatment of pathological gambling in part because of the high rate of co-occurrence between pathological gambling and depression. Black [83] conducted an open-label study of bupropion (titrated to 200mg) and found patients significantly reduced their problem gambling symptoms at the end of eight weeks. A recent 10-week open label study of escitalopram also reported significantly reduced problem gambling symptoms, with 73.7% of participants considered "much" or "very much" improved [84]. However, in a chart review study only 45.5% of pathological gamblers treated with SSRIs responded to treatment, compared with 90.5% of patients who received naltrexone [78].

Several double-blind, placebo-controlled studies have also been conducted to evaluate the efficacy of SSRI's, but results have been mixed [85-88]. In one double-blind, placebo controlled study of the efficacy of paroxetine, 45 pathological gamblers participated in a one-week placebo lead-in phase followed by randomization to eight weeks of medication (titrated up to a maximum dose of 60 mg/daily) or placebo [86]. Paroxetine treated patients reported greater reductions in gambling disorder severity and gambling urges than patients in the placebo condition. Approximately 48% of patients in the paroxetine condition were rated as "very much improved", compared with about 5% of the placebo patients. In another double-blind, placebo controlled study of fluvoxamine, 32 pathological gamblers were randomly assigned to receive up to 200 mg/day of fluvoxamine or placebo for a 6-month treatment duration [85]. Fluvoxamine did not result in overall significant benefits over placebo, but men and younger patients taking fluvoxamine reported greater improvement in gambling symptoms. In another 16-week, double-blind, placebo-controlled crossover trial, however, fluvoxamine was associated with significantly greater overall improvement in problem gambling severity [89]. A single-blind study by the same group also found benefits of fluvoxamine treatment [90].

As noted above, initial evidence from an open-label study of the norepinepherine-/dopamine reuptake inhibitor bupropion appeared to support its efficacy for reducing problem gambling symptoms. A recent placebo-controlled, double blind study of bupropion was conducted with 39 pathological gamblers [91]. Bupropion treated participants were no more likely to be "much" or "very much" improved (35.7% of participants with at least one post-randomization visit) than were placebo patients (47.1%). The authors noted that high study non-completion rates may have complicated the treatment outcomes.

Mood stabilizers have been investigated as treatments for pathological gambling that occurs in individuals who have concurrent bipolar disorder. In one placebo controlled, double-blind study of 40 pathological gamblers with bipolar spectrum disorder (bipolar II, bipolar NOS, cyclothymia), those randomized to receive sustained-release lithium carbonate (10 week treatment, lithium dose titrated up to 300 mg/morning and 600 mg/evening dose) reduced their gambling symptoms, thoughts and urges to a significantly greater degree than did participants who received placebo.

Recently researchers have been targeting other neurotransmitters that may play salient roles in reward processes that affect addictions. An imbalance of glutamate homeostasis causes changes in neuroplasticity in the corticostriatal brain circiuitry and impairs communication between the nucleus accumbens and prefrontal cortex in individuals with drug and behavioral addictions [92,93]. In one eight-week, open-label pilot study, 27 pathological gamblers were treated with n-acetyl cysteine (NAC), an amino acid that appears to enhance extracellular glutamate levels in the nucleus accumbens [94]. Problem gambling symptoms were significantly reduced, and nearly 60% of participants were categorized as treatment responders. Placebo controlled trials are needed to further examine the efficacy of NAC for pathological gambling.

Compulsive Buying. Several studies have been conducted to examine the efficacy of antidepressant medications for treating compulsive buying. These studies have yielded primarily mixed results. For example, an open label trial [95] found that nine out of 10 non-depressed individuals meeting compulsive buying criteria who were treated with up to 300mg of fluvoxamine for nine weeks experienced symptom improvement, including being less preoccupied with shopping, spending less time shopping and reporting less money spent. However, a subsequent double blind comparison of fluvoxamine versus placebo conducted by the same research group found that fluvoxamine was statistically similar to placebo for most treatment outcomes [96]. An additional double blind controlled trial of fluvoxamine similarly revealed no significant benefits over placebo when applied to 37 randomized patients who met criteria for compulsive buying [97]. Both of the controlled trials also revealed robust placebo effects. Some authors argue that behavioral components of the treatment (e.g., spending logs) may have contributed to a reduction of compulsive buying behavior, thereby masking the effects of fluvoxamine [97].

Koran and colleagues conducted two studies of the SSRI citalopram for treating compulsive buying [98, 99]. In one 12-week open label trial that included 24 participants (22 women), overall response rate to treatment was high in those who completed the study (n = 20) [98]. The intent-to-treat sample improvement rate was 71%, with 17% percent being "much improved" and 54% being "very much improved". Mean endpoint citalopram dose was 35.4mg ($\pm$21.4). In the second study, participants from the first citalopram trial participated in an open label study followed by a double-blind, randomized discontinuation [99]. Thus, 24 patients were enrolled in the seven-week open-label citalopram lead in, and 15 patients (citalopram treatment responders) were randomly assigned to receive citalopram at the same dose as the open label lead in, or placebo, for nine weeks of treatment. All of those who received citalopram showed improvement, while five out of the eight placebo patients relapsed during treatment. The authors were careful to exclude behavioral intervention components that could account for symptom improvements.

Other medications have also been studied mainly in case reports. Guzman et al. [100] describe a case report of a 37 year old female patient who experienced a reduction in her excessive buying behaviors and depression symptoms within a month of beginning topiramte, a medication that is primarily an anticonvulsant and has also been used to treat migraines, bipolar disorder and binge eating disorder. Grant [101] described three cases of compulsive buying treated with naltrexone; high doses (100-200 mg/day) appeared to decrease both urges to buy and buying behavior in all three cases. Discontinuation and re-administration of naltrexone appeared to provide further evidence that the changes in buying were due to the medication. Yet another case study found that quetiapine, a second generation antipsychotic, was associated with reductions in compulsive buying behaviors in a male patient with co-occurring bipolar disorder [102]. No large scale studies have been conducted to examine the efficacy of these medications for compulsive buying.

Sexual Addiction. Pharmacological research on sexual addictions has some cross over between non-paraphilic sexual addictions and paraphilias, which have been studied extensively over the past several decades in the forensic literature. In this chapter, we mainly describe studies that focus on non-paraphilic sexual addictions. However, it is important to acknowledge that treatments for paraphilic and non-paraphilic sexual disorders overlap substantially. Comprehensive reviews on medication treatments for paraphilias are available [103]. Antiandrogen medications (e.g., cyproterone acetate and medroxyprogesterone acetate) are designed to depress sexual libido through reductions in male hormones. These medications have demonstrated some benefits in reducing sexual behaviors and fantasies in patients with paraphilic behaviors [104]. However, few studies have explored the effectiveness of these medications in individuals with non-paraphillic sexual addictions. One placebo-controlled study (N = 9) found that cyproterone acetate reduced spontaneous daytime erections, spontaneous sexual outlets, sexual interest and sexual arousal during masturbation among adjudicated outpatients who committed crimes related to their sexual addictions [105]. A few small scale and case studies have demonstrated effectiveness of antiandrogen medications for compulsive sexual behavior among individuals with concurrent medical conditions that contribute to the behaviors, including traumatic brain injury [106], dementia [107,108], and AIDS dementia [109]. No other controlled trials have examined the use of these medications in sexual addictions.

Antidepressant medications have been studied most frequently in individuals with sexual addictions. One retrospective chart review study examined the effectiveness of nefazodone, a noradrenergic/serotonergic reuptake inhibitor, for reducing compulsive sexual behavior [110]. Of the 14 (all male) patients treated with nefazodone, 11 responded well to the medication with six individuals experiencing improved control of recurrent, intrusive sexual thoughts, and five individuals indicating total remission of intrusive sexual thoughts. Placebo-controlled studies of antidepressants for sexual addiction are rare. In one 12-week, double-blind, placebo controlled study examining the efficacy of a flexible dose of citalopram (20 – 60 mg/day) for compulsive sexual behaviors in 28 gay and bisexual men, both treatment and placebo groups experienced significant reductions in sexual addiction symptoms, and citalopram-treated patients experienced significant decreases in sexual drive, frequency of masturbation, and hours of pornography use relative to placebo patients [111].

Naltrexone has been studied much less frequently than antidepressants. It has been shown to have some benefits in adolescent sexual offenders [112]. Case studies have also reported anecdotal positive effects of naltrexone [113,114]. In a retrospective case series study of 19 patients with compulsive sexual behavior treated with naltrexone (treated for periods ranging from two months to 2.3 years; mean effective dose 104 mg/day), 89% experienced significant reduction in compulsive sexual behavior symptoms [115]. This finding is particularly salient as most of the patients had received treatment for their compulsive sexual behaviors for several months to several years prior to beginning naltrexone. Nevertheless, controlled clinical trials are needed to further determine the efficacy of naltrexone for sexual addictions.

In a few cases, combinations of medications have also been tried. In one open label trial [116], 26 (N = 21 treatment completers) outpatients with either paraphilias (n = 14) or non-paraphilic sexual addictions (n = 12) who were already being treated with SSRIs were also given sustained release methylphenidate (40mg/day average dose) to determine whether this medication would augment treatment. Participants reported significant reductions in amount of time spent in paraphilia/compulsive sexual activities, and in a measure of total sexual outlet (defined as total number of sexual behaviors resulting in orgasm) during an initial period (average 8.8 months) maintained on SSRIs, and further significant reductions during the stimulant augmentation period (which lasted an additional average 9.6 months).

Computer/Internet Addiction. Relatively few studies have examined the efficacy of medications for computer/internet addictions. Han et al. [117] examined the efficacy of methylphenidate for reducing internet video game play in children (N = 62) with co-occurring attention deficit-hyperactivity disorder (ADHD) and internet video game addiction. Over the course of this eight-week, open-label trial, significant reductions in internet usage were noted, and these reductions were associated with improvements in ADHD inattention symptoms. Han et al. suggested that excessive computer/internet use among children may serve to self-medicate symptoms of ADHD, and thus methylphenidate may provide an efficacious treatment of internet addiction. One additional study examined the efficacy of treating internet addiction with the SSRI escitalopram in a 10-week open-label trial followed by a nine-week, double-blind, placebo-controlled discontinuation phase in 19 (12 men) adults with internet addiction [118]. The 14 treatment completers demonstrated significant reduction in amount of time spent on the internet at the end of the open-label period, and these benefits were maintained throughout the discontinuation phase for both escitalopram and placebo treated participants. No significant differences were noted between the placebo and escitalopram conditions.

3.2. Psychological Treatments

Many different psychological treatments have been adapted for behavioral addictions, but with the exception of pathological gambling, there are few well controlled trials that address the efficacy of these interventions. Below, we review research that describes the efficacy of these behavioral treatments.

Pathological Gambling. As with pharmacological treatments, behavioral treatments for pathological gambling have been more extensively studied than other behavioral addictions. As with alcohol dependence, 12-step mutual-help approaches are frequently utilized by pathological gamblers. Gamblers Anonymous (GA), which is based on principles similar to Alcoholics Anonymous, has groups in 57 countries and groups operate in many North American cities. GA is a recovery oriented fellowship of individuals who engage in recovery from problem gambling through sharing experience and support, and by working through 12 steps of recovery (e.g., admitting powerlessness over gambling). Because of its anonymous nature, GA (and other 12-step organizations) is not well suited to controlled efficacy trials. Nevertheless, a small number of studies have examined characteristics of individuals who attend GA. These studies have provided mixed results. In one study, people who attended an initial GA meeting (N = 232) were followed through their time with the organization. A year after their first GA meeting, only 8% of individuals maintained abstinence from gambling [119]. Seven percent maintained abstinence after two years. Twenty-two percent attended only one initial meeting, and 70% had stopped attending GA by their 10th meeting. In another study, pathological gamblers who attended GA while also in structured treatment (n = 184) were compared to individuals who attended no GA meetings during treatment (n = 158) [120]. Those who attended GA were more likely to abstain from gambling after 2 months of treatment (48%), compared with gamblers who did not attend GA (36%). Finally, a study examining predictors of outcome among GA members found that group attendance and participation, and available social support were the most robust factors associated with prevention of relapse to gambling [121]. Thus, individuals who engage in GA and who attend meetings more frequently appear to have better outcomes than individuals who do not engage or even initiate attendance in GA.

Most of the randomized clinical trials of psychological treatments for PG have focused on cognitive, cognitive behavioral or motivational interviewing approaches. Cognitive and cognitive behavioral (CBT) treatment approaches are associated with the greatest empirical support for efficacy. Cognitive and CBT approaches vary in the extent to which the interventions deal primarily with gambling-related cognitive distortions (e.g., biased memories about wins/losses, illusions of control), and more behavioral interventions such as reinforcement of non-gambling behaviors, encouragement of problem solving, social skills building and relapse prevention. However, for the purposes of the present chapter, we use "CBT" to reflect cognitive and CBT approaches. Ladouceur and colleagues conducted a series of studies examining the efficacy of CBT for pathological gambling in individual [122,123] and group [124] modalities. In one study, pathological gamblers (N = 40) were randomly assigned to twice-weekly (total 30 hours) CBT or placed on a waitlist [123]. Although the study experienced lowered retention (n = 29 were assisted at follow-up), eight of 14 gamblers who participated in CBT experienced significant improvement in gambling severity compared with one of 15 participants in the control condition. In a follow-up study that examined 20 sessions of individual CBT (N = 88; n = 64 in the follow-up sample), 19 of 35 participants randomly assigned to CBT demonstrated significant improvement compared with two of 29 participants in the control group. When carried out in a group therapy modality, participants randomly assigned to 10 weekly CBT groups similarly demonstrated greater improvements in problem gambling severity compared with participants assigned to the waitlist control condition [124].

Several other researchers have also examined the efficacy of CBT approaches. For example, Petry et al. [125] assigned 231 pathological gamblers to one of three treatment groups - referral to GA, GA referral plus a self-directed CBT manual, or GA referral plus eight sessions of individual CBT. Participants in the individual CBT condition experienced greater improvement than participants in the GA referral condition on all of the primary outcome measures (which included measures of problem gambling severity, frequency of gambling and amount of money gambled). Echeburua et al. [126] found significant benefits of individual CBT among pathological gamblers (N = 64; follow-up n = 50) randomly assigned to one of four groups: individual CBT, group cognitive therapy, combined individual and group or waitlist. Benefits of individual CBT were apparent at six- and 12-month follow-up. One study, comparing participants (N = 126) randomly assigned to CBT to those assigned to GA referral found no differences between groups on problem gambling severity measures at 12-months post treatment [127]. However, therapy session attendance and selection of an abstinence (rather than controlled gambling) goal predicted better outcomes.

Women have traditionally been understudied in the pathological gambling literature. Two studies examined the efficacy of CBT treatment specifically for female pathological gamblers [128,129]. In one, female pathological gamblers (N = 19) were randomly assigned to a 12-week (1.5 hour sessions) CBT treatment condition or a waitlist control group [128]. Compared to the waitlisted participants, those receiving CBT reported significant improvement on all aspects of problem gambling (e.g.,frequency, duration, amount of money wagered) and psychological (e.g., depression, anxiety) severity at post treatment. Gains in these areas were maintained at six-month follow-up. Indeed, 89% of participants no longer met diagnostic criteria for pathological gambling at 6-months. In a subsequent study, these investigators randomly assigned female pathological gamblers (N = 56) to 12 sessions of individual CBT, group CBT or a waitlist condition [129]. Both individual and group treatment approaches improved problem gambling outcomes relative to the waitlist control group. Individual and group treatment both improved psychological functioning outcomes (e.g., depression, anxiety). However, group therapy did not perform as well as individual therapy in reducing state anxiety and elevating self-esteem. Further, at six-month follow-up,

92% of individually treated gamblers no longer met diagnostic criteria for pathological gambling compared with 60% of the group-treated participants.

Some studies have examined the effectiveness of CBT approaches when combined with motivational interviewing (MI), a therapeutic approach that is focused on assessing and enhancing one's intrinsic motivation for changing addictive behaviors [130]. In one pilot study of combined CBT/MI, nine severe pathological gamblers were followed for 12-months, and comparison data were obtained for 12 male PGs receiving treatment as usual (TAU) at a community treatment center [131]. Treatment retention was significantly higher in the CBT/MI condition than among TAU participants. Further, among the gamblers who received CBT/MI, six maintained total abstinence during the 12-month follow-up period, two were significantly improved, and one remained unimproved. Another study examined the differences between individual and group forms of CBT plus MI [132]. Pathological gamblers (N = 102) were also randomly assigned to begin treatment immediately or after a six-week delay. Overall, participants who received treatment (regardless of modality) evidenced significant reductions in all problem gambling severity variables assessed, while waitlist participants did not. Therapeutic gains were maintained at six-month follow-up. A third study combined MI with CBT, and randomly assigned participants (N = 68) to six-sessions of treatment or referral to GA [133]. MI/CBT participants experienced significant reductions of their problem gambling severity during treatment compared with GA referred individuals. Very few studies have directly compared different active psychotherapies for pathological gambling.

An early study compared CBT to an aversion (electric shock paired with gambling stimuli) therapy in a five-day inpatient treatment study found that up to 79% of those who receive CBT reported abstinence or controlled gambling at follow-up compared to 53% of those who received the behavioral treatment [134]. In a more recent investigation, problem gamblers (N = 150) were randomly assigned to four sessions of individual MI, eight sessions of group CBT or a waitlist group [135]. Treatment (either MI or CBT) significantly reduced problem gambling disorder severity and depression severity. However, there were no significant differences between the two active treatment conditions, suggesting that individual MI and group CBT are comparable.

Finally, brief and self-guided interventions for reducing the impact of problem gambling that are often based on MI and CBT approaches have also been tested. Brief and self-guided interventions are frequently used with problem gamblers who have relatively less severe gambling problems, or who are not interested in full-scale treatment. In one study, for example, problem gamblers (N = 102) were randomly assigned to receive a self-help workbook alone, a self-help workbook plus one motivational interview, or placement on a waiting list [136]. Assignment to the workbook plus motivational interview resulted in the greatest reductions in gambling symptoms, and self-help workbook alone did not produce greater reductions in gambling symptoms relative to the waitlist condition. Another study similarly revealed that a brief intervention resulted in greater short-term reductions in gambling compared with no in-person contact [137]. More recently, 314 problem gamblers were randomized to either a group that received a brief telephone motivational interview plus a self-help workbook, a group that received the same treatment as the first plus six booster telephone calls over a nine-month period, a group (control) that received a workbook only, or a group that received a waitlist (another control group) [138]. The first two aforementioned groups reported less gambling at six-weeks and six-months than those assigned to the control groups. Contrary to the hypotheses, however, there were no differences between the first two groups with respect to showing greater improvement on the primary outcomes throughout the 12-month follow-up.

Two other recently published studies compared very brief (one to four sessions) face-to-face counseling for problem gambling. In one, non-treatment-seeking problem gamblers recruited from the community (N=180) were randomly assigned to one of four brief intervention groups: 1) assessment only control; 2) 10 minutes of brief advice (to reduce gambling); 3) one 50-minute session of motivational enhancement therapy (MET; based on the principles of MI); or 4) one 50-minute session of MET and three sessions of CBT [139]. Brief advice resulted in significant reductions in gambling at the six-week point and at nine-months. MET+CBT significantly reduced gambling severity on one outcome measure between the six-week and nine-month follow-up assessments, but MET alone did not result in significant changes compared with assessment only. A second study examining problem gambling college students (N = 117) and using the same four treatments found that relative to those assigned to the assessment-only condition, those assigned to the MET condition showed significant decreases in problem gambling severity over time [140]. The MET condition also significantly increased the odds of a clinically significant reduction in gambling at the nine-month follow-up, even after controlling for baseline indices that could impact outcomes. The brief advice and MET+CBT conditions also had benefits on some indices of gambling. Finally, Carlbring and Smit [141] conducted a study of brief internet-based counseling for problem gamblers compared to a waitlist control group (total N = 66). The intervention resulted in significant improvements in gambling, anxiety and depression symptoms, and quality of life. Several benefits were still evident at 36-month follow-up. Taken together, these studies show that there is substantial research evidence for the efficacy of CBT for pathological gambling. Further, there is also important evidence for the usefulness of motivational approaches (MI). These approaches have demonstrated efficacy in nearly every published study, in both individual and group modalities, and in both longer and brief therapy formats.

Compulsive Buying. Few psychological intervention studies for compulsive buying have been conducted to date. Mitchell et al. [142] (non-randomly) assigned 28 female compulsive buyers to CBT group therapy, and 11 participants to a waitlist control condition. Group CBT involved 12, 1.5 hour sessions over a period of 10 weeks. Participants who received CBT showed significant reduction in number of compulsive buying episodes, time spent buying and indicators of compulsive buying severity that were maintained at six-month follow-up. A second trial examined 60 participants randomly assigned to a 12-session, 12-week group CBT intervention or to waitlist control condition [143]. Compared to waitlist, CBT resulted in significant reductions in compulsive buying behavior and related symptoms with effect sizes in the moderate to large range (Cohen's d scores ranged from .56 to .88 for primary outcomes), and benefits were evident at six month follow-up. Pre-treatment hoarding and poor therapy attendance were predictors of worse treatment outcomes. No other clinical trials have been published in peer review journals, and neither of these studies compared CBT to another active treatment, limiting the conclusions that can be made about the efficacy of treatments for compulsive buying.

Sexual Addictions. Several treatments have been recommended for the treatment of sexual addictions, including 12-step approaches and group therapy (e.g., see Gold and Heffner [144] for review). However, very few studies have been conducted examining the efficacy of behavioral treatments for sexual addictions. One early study examined the efficacy of group-based psychotherapy for gay and bisexual men reporting compulsive sexual behaviors (n = 30) compared to a matched no-treatment control group (n = 24) [145]. Six-month follow up data for retained participants (n = 15 treated and n = 14 controls) revealed that treated participants reported reduced frequency of sexual behaviors with different partners, and reduced drug and alcohol use during sexual encounters. While the findings are promising, this study was significantly hampered by study drop-out. A more recent study examined the effectiveness of a 16-week group therapy for internet sexual addiction in men that combined CBT, MI and peer-support elements [146]. Participants (N = 35) were assessed at baseline, mid-treatment and post-treatment, and the data revealed significant improvements in quality of life and depression symptoms, but improvements in time spent engaging in inappropriate internet use, while trending toward improvement, did not meet statistical significance. Participants who were characterized as "anxious" showed the greatest improvement, those with "mood" issues showed moderate improvement, and individuals with ADHD symptoms did not demonstrate improvement.

Computer/Internet Addiction. The treatment literature on computer and internet addiction is similarly as a nascent stage. Recent reviews have identified clinical trials for the efficacy of various psychological treatments for internet addiction, including CBT, MI, group therapy, family therapy and multimodal approaches [147]. One recent, well-controlled study included adolescents (N = 56) meeting criteria for internet addiction who were randomly assigned to eight sessions of group CBT or a control condition [148]. The study revealed that internet use decreased in both treatment conditions by post-treatment, but those in the CBT group experienced greater relative improvements in time management, and in emotional, cognitive and behavioral symptoms. Improvements were maintained at the six-month follow-up assessment. Another study examined the treatment efficacy of a CBT approach called reality therapy that places an emphasis on problem solving, and having responsibility for all behavior change reside with the client [149]. In total, 25 internet-addicted university students (20 males) were randomly assigned to a 10 session, group-based reality therapy or a control condition. Participants in the treatment condition experienced significant improvements in internet addiction problem severity and significant increases in self-esteem relative to control participants at post-treatment. No follow-up assessments were reported.

Most other studies include only a treatment group (i.e., no control group) and use a pre-/post-test design. For example, an examination of 59 participants (primarily adolescents; all male but one) in a MI-based multi-modal (individual, family and group-based) treatment program revealed that participants experienced significant reductions in internet addiction symptoms and greater parental knowledge about adolescent activities, but few differences on other indices related to beliefs about the internet and psychological well-being [150]. A study of 114 adult (58% male) outpatients who received CBT for internet addiction revealed positive changes that lasted to the six-month follow-up in several domains including motivation to change, time management, relationship function, sexual function, engagement in offline activities and abstinence from problematic internet use [151]. However, inferential statistics were not reported, making the pre- to post-treatment changes difficult to interpret. A further study examining a combined MI, CBT and peer-support group therapy for adults with internet sexual addiction is described above [146].

CONCLUSION AND RECOMMENDATIONS

The state of research for behavioral addictions is in a very early stage. Some disorders such as pathological gambling have a fast growing body of treatment literature, both with regard to pharmacological and psychological treatments. Most other behavioral addictions do not have a large number of studies examining treatment efficacy. Most are also not classified as psychiatric disorders in the DSM-IV. Furthermore, the available treatment studies often have methodological limitations, such as lack of blind control procedures, high study attrition, small samples, no follow-up and other problems. One recent review of treatments for internet addiction, for example, noted that the published literature was hampered significantly by inconsistent definition of internet addiction, lack of randomization, lack of adequate control/comparison groups and insufficient information about important study characteristics (e.g., sample characteristics, effect sizes) [147].

Some fields of behavioral addiction have begun to overcome these methodological limitations. To date, pathological gambling research appears to be the one field that has begun to amass a body of literature that meets stringent criteria for establishing treatment efficacy. Pathological gambling is also the only behavioral addiction currently being considered for incorporation into the Addictive Disorders section of the DSM5. As such, pathological gambling may provide an important exemplar for modeling treatment research studies for other behavioral addictions. Efficacy studies for other behavioral addictions, such as those presented in this chapter, while limited in number and scope, are beginning to show signs of proliferation. Future studies will likely remedy the methodological limitations that seem pervasive in the current literature.

Limitations notwithstanding, the psychosocial and pharmacological treatments described above have led to some promising treatment outcomes. With regard to pharmacological interventions, there appears to be some consistency in treatments across addictive disorders. Antidepressant medications (SSRIs and norepinepherine/dopamine reuptake inhibitors) seem to have some effect at reducing addictive behaviors, but the findings to date have been inconsistent. It is possible that antidepressant medications may have a greater effect among individuals with particular profiles of co-occurring disorders (e.g., anxiety and depression), but more research is needed to establish with whom these medications work best. Opioid antagonists, although studied almost exclusively for pathological gambling, may be very good candidates for treatment of other behavioral addictions given their consistently demonstrated efficacy reducing problem gambling symptoms. Other medications, such as NAC and mood stabilizers, may have some benefits for behavioral addictions other than pathological gambling, but to date these medications remain unstudied with other behavioral addictions. Other medications, such as anti-androgen medications for sexual addictions, and methylphenidate to treat co-occurring ADHD symptoms among adolescents with computer addictions may have more circumscribed uses, but deserve further study. Thus, future research should further address the efficacy of medications for behavioral addictions using rigorous standards that include random assignment and double blind methods. It is also important to establish standard of care guidelines for prescribers so that they may use effective medications to treat behavioral addictions.

With regard to behavioral interventions, CBT approaches are the most frequently studied and have demonstrated the most evidence for efficacy across the behavioral addictions reviewed here. CBT approaches seem to be successful in addressing behavioral addiction symptoms and concurrent problems in many cases regardless of the modality of treatment delivery (i.e., individual or group). Other approaches rooted in motivational interviewing have also demonstrated some efficacy, although aside from pathological gambling, this approach has not been widely studied. Regardless of the approach, it would seem that new studies should address the relative efficacy of different psychological (and pharmacological) treatments and the additive efficacy of combined treatments. Furthermore, while several efficacy studies have been conducted to date, very few effectiveness trials have been carried out; that is, although we know what treatments work in tightly controlled clinical trials carried out by research teams closely affiliated with academic settings, very few studies have examined whether these treatments can be transferred to community-based clinics and providers who treat a more broad clientele. Together the research presented in this chapter provides a basic foundation upon which to build a more solid body of research on treatment efficacy and effectiveness. Future studies should be more systematic in the use of research methods that ensure their internal and external validity. With such a focus as well as a more firm understanding of where behavioral addictions fall within the psychiatric lexicon, researchers and treatment providers will have a solid understanding of what works for treating these disorders.

REFERENCES

[1]   Grant JE, Brewer JA, Potenza MN. The neurobiology of substance and behavioral addictions. *CNS Spectr.*, 2006, 11, 924-30.

[2]   Holden C. 'Behavioral' addictions: Do they exist? *Science,* 2001, 294, 980-2.

[3]   Grant JE, Potenza MN, Weinstein A, Gorelick DA. Introduction to behavioral addictions. *Am. J. Drug Alcohol Ab.,* 2010, 36, 233-41.

[4]   Frosch J, Wortis SB. A contribution to the nosology of the impulse disorders. *Am. J. Psychiatry,* 1954, 111, 132-8.

[5]   McElroy SL, Soutullo CA, Goldsmith RJ. Other impulse control disorders, In A.W. Graham, and T.K. Schultz (Eds.), *Principles of Addiction Medicine (2nd ed.).* Chevy Chase, MD: American Society of Addiction Medicine, 1998.

[6]   Nestler EJ. Is there a common molecular pathway for addiction? *Nat. Neurosci.*, 2005, 8, 1445-9.

[7]   American Psychiatric Association. *Diagnostic and Statistical Manual of Mental Disorders, 4th ed.* Washington, DC: American Psychiatric Association, 1994.

[8]   Martin PR, Petry NM. Are non-substance-related addictions really addictions? *Am. J. Addictions,* 2005, 14, 1-7.

[9]   Petry NM. Should the scope of addictive behaviors be broadened to include pathological gambling? *Addiction,* 2006, 101, s152-60.

[10]   Potenza MN. Should addictive disorders include non-substance-related conditions? *Addiction,* 2006,101, s142-51.

[11]   Levine MP, Troiden RR. The myth of sexual compulsivity. *J. Sex Res.,* 1988, 25, 347-63.

[12] Petry NM, Stinson FS, Grant BF. Comorbidity of DSM-IV pathological gambling and other psychiatric disorders: Results from the National Epidemiological Survey on Alcohol Related Conditions. *J. Clin. Psychiat.*, 2005, 66, 564-74.

[13] Shaffer HJ, Hall MN, Vander Bilt J. Estimating the prevalence of disordered gambling behavior in the United States and Canada: A research synthesis. *Am. J. Public Health*, 1999, 89, 1369-76.

[14] Welte J, Barnes GM, Wieczorek W, Tidwell MC, Parker J. Alcohol and gambling pathology among U.S. adults: Prevalence, demographic patterns and comorbidity. *J. Stud. Alcohol*, 2001, 62, 706-12.

[15] Petry NM. *Pathological gambling: Etiology, comorbidity, and treatment.* Washington DC: American Psychological Association, 2005.

[16] Petry NM, Armentano C. Prevalence, assessment, and treatment of pathological gambling: A review. *Psychiatr. Serv.*, 1999, 50, 1021-27.

[17] Kausch O. Suicide attempts among veterans seeking treatment for pathological gambling. *J. Clin. Psychiat.*, 2003, 64, 1031–8.

[18] Bolla KI, Eldreth DA, Matochik JA, Cadet JL. Neural substrates of faulty decision-making in abstinent marijuana users. *Neuroimage*, 2005, 26, 480-92.

[19] Goudriaan AE, Oosterlaan J, DeBeurs E, Van Den Brink W. The role of self-reported impulsivity and reward sensitivity versus neurocognitive measures of disinhibition and decision-making in the prediction of relapse in pathological gambling. *Psychol. Med.*, 2007, 38, 41-50.

[20] Rossi M, Gerschcovich ER, de Achaval D, Perez-Lioret S, Cerquetti D, Cammorota A, Ines Nouzeilles M, Fahrer R, Merello M, Leiguarda R. Decision-making in Parkinson's disease patients with and without pathological gambling. *Eur. J. Neuro.*, 2009, 17, 97-102.

[21] Ledgerwood DM, Kaploun K, Milosevic A, Orr E, Frisch GR, Rupcich N, Lundahl LH. Executive function deficits in pathological gamblers compared with healthy non-problem gambling controls. *J. Gamb. Stud.*, 2012, 28, 89-103.

[22] Goudriaan AE, Oosterlaan J, DeBeurs E, Van Den Brink W. Psychophysiological determinants and concomitants of deficient decision making in pathological gamblers. *Drug Alcohol Dep.*, 2006, 84, 231-9.

[23] Potenza MN, Leung H-C, Blumberg HP, Peterson BS, Fulbright RK, Lacadie CM, Skudlarski P, Gore JC. An fMRI Stroop task study of ventromedial prefrontal cortical function in pathological gamblers. *Am. J. Psychiatry*, 2003a, 160, 1990-4.

[24] Potenza MN, Steinberg MA, Skudlarski P, Fulbright RK, Lacadie CM, Wilber MK, Rounsaville BJ, Gore JC, Wexler BE. Gambling urges in pathological gambling. *Am. J. Psychiatry*, 2003b, 160, 828-36.

[25] Crockford DN, Goodyear B, Edwards J, Quickfall J, el-Guebaly N. Cue-induced brain activity in pathological gamblers. *Biol. Psychiatry*, 2005, 58, 787-95.

[26] Tanabe J, Thompson L, Claus E, Dalwani M, Hutchinson K, Banich MT. Prefrontal cortex activity is reduced in gambling and nongambling substance users during decision-making. *Hum. Brain Mapp*, 2007, 28, 1276-86.

[27] Miedl SF, Fehr T, Meyer G, Herrmann M. Neuroiological correlates of problem gambling in a quasi-realistic blackjack scenario as revealed by fMRI. *Psychiat. Res. Neuroimaging*, 2010, 181, 165-73.

[28] Reuter J, Raedler T, Rose M, Hand I, Gläscher J, Büchel C. Pathological gambling is linked to reduced activation of the mesolimbic reward system. *Nat. Neurosci.*, 2005, 8, 147-8.

[29] Bleuler E. *Textbook of Psychiatry*. New York: MacMillan, 1924.

[30] Kraepelin E. *Psychiatric (8ᵗʰ ed.)*. Leipzig, Verlag Von Johann Ambrosius Barth, 1915.

[31] Lejoyeux M, Weinstein A. Compulsive buying. *Am. J. Drug Alcohol Ab.*, 2010, 36, 248-53.

[32] McElroy SL, Keck PE, Pope HG, Smith JMR., Strakowski SM. Compulsive buying: A report of 20 cases. *J. Clin. Psychiat.*, 1994, 55, 242-8.

[33] Faber RJ, O'Guinn TC. A clinical screener for compulsive buying. *J Consum Res*, 1992, 19, 459-69.

[34] Koran LM, Faber RJ, Aboujaoude E, Large MD, Serpe MT. Estimated prevalence of compulsive buying behavior in the United States. *Am. J. Psychiatry*, 2006, 163, 1806-12.

[35] Black DW. A review of compulsive buying disorder. *World Psychiatry*, 2007, 6, 14-8.

[36] Miltenberger RG, Redlin J, Crosby R, Stickney M, Mitchell J, Wonderlich S, Faber R, Smyth J. Direct and retrospective assessment of factors contributing to compulsive buying. *J. Beh. Ther. Exp. Psychiatry*, 2003, 34, 1-9.

[37] Schlosser S, Black DW, Repertinger S, Freet D. Compusive buying: Demography, phenomenology, and comorbidity in 46 subjects. *Gen. Hosp. Psych.*, 1994, 16, 205-12.

[38] Lejoyeux M, Ades J, Tassain V, Solomon J. Phenomenology and psychopathology of uncontrolled buying. *Am. J. Psychiatry*, 1996, 153, 1524-9.

[39] Knutson B, Rick S, Wimmer GE, Prelec D, Loewenstein G. Neural predictors of purchases. *Neuron*, 2007, 53, 147-56.

[40] Koob GF, LeMoal M. Addiction and the brain antireward system. *Annu. Rev. Psychol.*, 2008, 59, 29-53.

[41] Kafka MP. Hypersexual desire in males: An operational definition and clinical implications for males with paraphilias and paraphilia-related disorders. *Arch. Sex Behav.*, 1997, 26, 505-26.

[42] Griffiths M. Sex on the internet: Observations and implications for internet sex addiction. *J. Sex. Res.*, 2001, 38, 333-42.

[43] Kafka MP. Hypersexual disorder: A proposed diagnosis for DSM-V. *Arch Sex Behav*, 2010, 39, 377-400.

[44] Kafka MP, Hennen J. The paraphilia-related disorders: An empirical investigation of nonparaphilic hypersexuality disorders in outpatient males. *J. Sex. Marital Ther.*, 1999, 25, 305-19.

[45] Kuss DJ, Griffiths MD. Internet sex addiction: A review of empirical research. *Addiction Res. Theory*, in press.

[46] Goodman A. Sexual addiction: Designation and treatment. *J. Sex Marital Ther.*, 1992, 18, 303-14.

[47] Garcia FD, Thibaut F. Sexual Addictions. *Am. J. Drug Alcohol Ab.*, 2010, 36, 254-60.

[48] Black DW, Kehrberg LLD, Flumerfelt DL, Schlosser SS. Characteristics of 36 subjects reporting compulsive sexual behavior. *Am. J. Psychiatry*, 1997, 154, 243-9.

[49] Raymond NC, Coleman E, Milner MH. Psychiatric comorbidity andcompulsive/impulsive traits in compulsive sexual behavior. *Compr. Psychiat.*, 2003, 44, 370-80.

[50] Bancroft J, Vukadinovic Z. Sexual addiction, sexual compulsivity, sexual impulsivity, or what? Toward a theoretical model. *J. Sex Res.*, 2004, 41, 225-34.

[51] Arnow BA, Desmond JE, Banner LL, Glover GH, Solomon A, Polan ML, Lue TF, Atlas SW. Brain activation and sexual arousal in healthy, heterosexual males. *Brain*, 2002, 125, 1014-23.

[52] Brunetti M, Babiloni C, Ferretti A, Del Gratta C, Merla A, Olivetti Belardinelli M, Romani GL. Hypothalamus, sexual arousal and psychosexual identity in human males: a functional magnetic resonance imaging study. *European Journal of Neuroscience*, 2008, 27, 2922–7.

[53] Hamann S, Herman RA, Nolan CL, Wallen K. Men and women differ in amygdala response to visual sexual stimuli. *Nat. Neurosci.*, 2004, 7, 411–6.

[54] CIA. *CIA World Factbook.* Data retrieved (11/4/11) from: https://www.cia.gov/library/publications/the-world-factbook/rankorder/2153rank.html.

[55] Shapira NA, Lessing MC, Goldsmith TD, Szabo ST, Lazoritz M, Gold MS, Stein DJ. Problematic internet use: Proposed classification and diagnostic criteria. *Depress Anxiety*, 2003, 17, 207-16.

[56] Beard KW, Wolf EM. Modification in the proposed diagnostic criteria for internet addiction. *Cyber Psychol. Behav.*, 2001, 4, 377-83.

[57] Block JJ. Issues for DSM-V: Internet addiction. *Am. J. Psychiatry*, 2008, 306-7.

[58] Greenfield DN. Psychological characteristics of compulsive internet use: A preliminary analysis. *Cyber Psychol. Behav.*, 1999, 2, 403-12.

[59] Aboujaoude E, Koran LM, Gamel N, Large MD, Serpe RT. Potential markers for problematic internet use: a telephone survey of 2,513 adults. *CNS Spectr.*, 2006, 11, 750-5.

[60] Aboujaoude E. Problematic internet use: an overview. *World Psychiatry*, 2010, 9, 85-90.

[61] Cao F, Su L. Internet addiction among Chinese adolescents: prevalence and psychological features. *Child Care Health Development*, 2007, 33, 275-81.

[62] Johansson A, Götestam KG. Internet addiction: characteristics of a questionnaire and prevalence in Norwegian youth (12-18 years). *Scand. J. Psychol.*, 2004, 45, 223-9.

[63] Park SK, Kim JY, Cho CB. Prevalence of Internet addiction and correlations with family factors among South Korean adolescents. *Adolescence*, 2008, 43, 895-909.

[64] Weinstein A, Lejoyeux M. Internet addiction or excessive internet use. *Am. J. Drug Alcohol Ab.*, 2010, 36, 277-83.

[65] Weinstein AM. Computer and video game addiction – A comparison between game users and non-game users. *Am. J. Drug Alcohol Ab.*, 2010, 36, 268-76.

[66] Young KS. Internet addiction: The emergence of a new clinical disorder. *Cyber Psychol. Behav.*, 1998, 1, 237-44.

[67] Shapira NA, Goldsmith TD, Keck PE, Khosla UM, McElroy SL. Psychiatric features of individuals with problematic internet use. *J. Affect. Disord., 2000, 57*, 267-72.

[68] Young KS, Rodgers RC. The relationship between depression and internet addiction. *Cyber Psychol. Behav.*, 1998, 1, 25-8.

[69] Black DW, Belsare G, Schlosser S. Clinical features, psychiatric comorbidity, and health-related quality of life in persons reporting compulsive computer use behavior. *J. Clin. Psychiat.*, 1999, 60, 839-44.

[70]   Whang LS-M, Lee S, Chang G. Internet over-users' psychological profiles: A behavior sampling analysis on internet addiction. *Cyber Psychol. Behav.,* 2003, 6, 143-50.

[71]   Han DH, Hwang JW, Renshaw PF. Bupropion sustained release treatment decreases craving for video games and cue-induced brain activity in patients with internet video game addiction. *Exp. Clin. Psychopharm.,* 2010, 18, 297-304.

[72]   Liu J, Gao XP, Osunde I, Li X, Zhou SK, Zheng HR, Li LJ. Increased regional homogeneity in internet addiction disorder: A resting state functional magnetic resonance imaging study. *Chin. Med. J.,* 2010, 123, 1904-8.

[73]   Ko CH, Liu GC, Hsiao S, Yen JY, Yang MJ, Lin WC, Yen CF, Chen CS. Brain activities associated with gaming urge of online gaming addiction. *J. Psychiatr. Res.,* 2009, 43, 739-47.

[74]   Spanagel R, Herz A, Shippenberg TS. Opposing tonically active endogenous opioid systems modulate the mesolimbi dopaminergic pathway. *Proc. Natl. Acad. Sci. USA,* 1992, 89, 2046-50.

[75]   Kim SW, Grant JE, Adson DE, Shin YC. Double-blind naltrexone and placebo comparison study in the treatment of pathological gambling. *Biol. Psychiat.,* 2001, 49, 914-21.

[76]   Crockford DN, el-Guebaly N. Naltrexone in the treatment of pathological gambling and alcohol dependence. *Can. J. Psychiat.,* 1998, 43, 86.

[77]   Dannon PN, Lowengrub K, Musin E, Gonopolski Y, Kotler M. Sustained-release bupropion versus naltrexone in the treatment of pathological gambling: a preliminary blind-rater study. *J. Clin. Psychopharmacol.,* 2005b, 25, 593-6.

[78]   Grant JE, Kim SW. Effectiveness of pharmacotherapy for pathological gambling: A chart review. *Ann. Clin. Psychiatry,* 2002, 14, 155-61.

[79]   Kim SW, Grant JE. An open naltrexone treatment study in pathological gambling disorder. *Int. Clin. Psychopharm,* 2001, 16, 285-9.

[80]   Grant JE, Kim SW, Hartman BK. A double-blind, placebo-controlled study of the opiate antagonist naltrexone in the treatment of pathological gambling urges. *J. Clin. Psychiat.,* 2008, 69, 783-9.

[81]   Grant JE, Potenza MN, Hollander E, Cunningham-Williams R, Nurminen T, Smits G, Kallio A. Multicenter investigation of the opioid antagonist nalmefene in the treatment of pathological gambling. *Am. J. Psychiatry,* 2006, 163, 303-12.

[82]   Zimmerman M, Breen RB, Posternak MA. An open-label study of citalopram in the treatment of pathological gambling. *J. Clin. Psychiat.,* 2002, 63, 44-8.

[83]   Black DW. An open-label trial of bupropion in the treatment of pathologic gambling. *J. Clin. Psychopharmacol.,* 2004, 24, 108-10

[84]   Black DW. An open-label trial of escitalopram in the treatment of pathological gambling. *Clin. Neuropharmacol.,* 2007, 30, 206-12.

[85]   Blanco C, Petkova E, Ibanez A, Saiz-Ruiz J. A pilot placebo-controlled study of fluvoxamine for pathological gambling. *Ann. Clin. Psychiatry,* 2002, 14, 9-15.

[86]   Kim SW, Grant JE, Adson DE, Shin YC, Zaninelli R. A double-blind placebo-controlled study of the efficacy and safety of paroxetine in the treatment of pathological gambling. *J. Clin. Psychiat.,* 2002, 63, 501-7.

[87]   Dannon PN, Lowengrub K, Gonopolski Y, Musin E, Kotler M. Topiramate versus fluvoxamine in the treatment of pathological gambling: A randomized, blind-rater comparison study. *Clin. Neuropsychopharmacol.,* 2005, 28, 6-10.

[88] Saiz-Ruiz J, Blanco C, Ibanez A, Masramon X, Gomez MM, Madrigal M, Diez T. Sertraline treatment of pathological gambling: A pilot study. *J. Clin. Psychiat.*, 2005, 66, 28-33.

[89] Hollander E, DeCaria CM, Finkell JN, Begaz T, Wong CM, Cartwright C. A randomized double-blind fluvoxmine/placebo crossover trial in pathologic gambling. *Biol. Psychiatry,* 2000, 47, 813-7.

[90] Hollander E, DeCaria CM, Mari E, Wong CM, Mosovich S, Grossman R, Begaz T. Short-term single-blind fluvoxamine treatment of pathological gambling. *Am. J. Psychiatry,* 1998, 155, 1781-3.

[91] Black DW, Arndt S, Coryell WH, Argo T, Forbush KT, Shaw MC, Perry P, Allen J. Bupropion in treatment of pathological gambling: A randomized, double-blind, placebo-controlled, flexible-dose study. *J. Clin. Psychopharmacol.*, 2007, 143-50.

[92] Kalivas PW. The glutamate homeostasis hypothesis of addiction. *Nat Rev Neurosci,* 2009, 10, 561-72.

[93] Potenza MN, Sofuoglu M, Carroll KM, Rounsaville BJ. Neuroscience of behavioral and pharmacological treatments for addictions. *Neuron,* 2011, 69, 695-712.

[94] Grant JE, Kim SW, Odlaug BL. N-acetyl cycteine, a glutamate-modulating agent in the treatment of pathological gambling: A pilot study. *Biol. Psychiatry,* 2007, 62, 652-7.

[95] Black DW, Monahan P, Gabel J. Fluvoxamine in the treatment of compulsive buying. *J. Clin. Psychiat.*, 1997, 58, 159-63.

[96] Black DW, Gabel J, Hansen J, Schlosser S. A double-blind comparison of fluvoxamine versus placebo in the treatment of compulsive buying disorder. *Ann. Clin. Psychiatry,* 2000, 12, 205-11.

[97] Ninan PT, McElroy SL, Kane CP, Knight BT, Casuto LS, Rose SE, Marsteller FA, Nemeroff CB. Placebo-controlled study of fluvoxamine in the treatment of patients with compulsive buying. *J. Clin. Psychopharmacol.*, 2000, 20, 362-6.

[98] Koran LM, Bullock KD, Hartston HJ, Elliott MA, D'Andrea V. Citalopram treatment of compulsive shopping: An open-label study. *J. Clin. Psychiat.*, 2002, 63, 704-8.

[99] Koran LM, Chuong HW, Bullock KD, Smith SC. Citalopram for compulsive shopping disorder: An open-label study followed by double-blind discontinuation. *J. Clin. Psychiat.*, 2003, 64, 793-8.

[100] Guzman CS, Filomensky T, Tavares H. Compulsive buying treatment with topiramate, a case report. Rev. Brasi Psiquiatr., 2007, 29, 383-4.

[101] Grant JE. Three cases of compulsive buying treated with naltrexone. *Int J. Psychiatry Clin. Prac.,* 2003, 7, 223-5.

[102] Di Nicola M, Martinotti G, Mazza M, Tedeschi D, Pozzi G, Janiri L. Quetiapine as add-on treatment for bipolar I disorder with comorbid compulsive buying and physical exercise addiction. *Prog. Neuro-Psychoph.,* 2010, 34, 713-4.

[103] Guay DRP. Drug treatment of paraphilic and nonparaphilic sexual disorders. *Clin. Ther.,* 2009, 31, 1-31.

[104] Bradford JMW, Pawlak A. Double-blind placebo crossover study of cyproterone acetate in the treatment of paraphilias. *Arch. Sex Behavs,* 1993, 22, 383-402.

[105] Cooper AJ. A placebo-controlled trial of the antiandrogen cyproterone acetate in deviant hypersexuality. *Compr. Psychiat,* 1981, 22, 458-65.

[106] Britton KR. Medroxyprogesterone in the treatment of aggressive hypersexual behaviour in traumatic brain injury. *Brain Inj.,* 1998, 12, 703-7.

[107] Haussermann P, Goecker D, Beier K, Schroeder S. Low-dose cyproterone acetate treatment of sexual acting out in men with dementia. *Int. Psychogeriatr.*, 2003, 15, 181-6.

[108] Levitsky AM, Owens NJ. Pharmacologic treatment of hypersexuality and paraphilias in nursing home residents. *J. Am. Geriatr. Soc.*, 1999, 47, 231-4.

[109] Potocnik F. Successful treatment of hypersexuality in AIDS dementia with cyproterone-acetate. *S. Afr. Med. J.*, 1992, 81, 433-4.

[110] Coleman E, Gratzer T, Nesvacil L, Raymond NC. Nafazodone and the treatment of nonparaphilic compulsive sexual behavior: A retrospective study. *J. Clin. Psychiat.*, 2000, 61, 282-4.

[111] Wainberg ML, Muench F, Morgenstern J, Hollander E, Irwin TW, Parsons JT, Allen A, O'Learly A. A double-blind study of citalopram versus placebo in the treatment of compulsive sexual behaviors in gay and bisexual men. *J. Clin. Psychiat.*, 2006, 67, 1968-73.

[112] Ryback RS. Naltrexone in the treatment of adolescent sexual offenders. *J. Clin. Psychiat.*, 2004, 65, 982-6.

[113] Bostwick JM, Bucci JA. Internet sex addiction treated with naltrexone. *Mayo Clin. Proc.*, 2008, 83, 226-30.

[114] Raymond NC, Grant JE, Kim SW, Coleman E. Treatment of compulsive sexual behaviour with naltrexone and serotonin reuptake inhibitors: Two case studies. *Int. Clin. Psychopharm.*, 2002, 17, 201-5.

[115] Raymond NC, Grant JE, Coleman E. Augmentation with naltrexone to treat compulsive sexual behavior: A case series. *Ann. Clin. Psychiatry*, 2010, 22, 56-62.

[116] Kafka MP, Hennen J. Psychostimulant augmentation during treatment with selective serotonin reuptake inhibitors in men with paraphilias and paraphilia-related disorders: A case series. *J. Clin. Psychiat.*, 2000, 61, 664-70.

[117] Han DH, Lee YS, Na C, Ahn JY, Chung US, Daniels MA, Haws CA, Renshaw PF. The effect of methylphenidate on internet video game play in children with attention-deficit/hyperactivity disorder. *Compr. Psychiat.*, 2009, 50, 251-6.

[118] Dell'Osso B, Hadley SJ, Allen A, Baker B, Chaplin WF, Hollander E. Escitalopram in the treatment of impulsive-compulsive internet usage disorder: An open-label trial followed by a double-blind discontinuation phase. *J. Clin. Psychiat.*, 2008, 69, 452-6.

[119] Stewart RM, Brown RI. An outcome study of Gamblers Anonymous. *Br. J. Psychiatry.*, 1988, 152, 284-8.

[120] Petry NM. Patterns and correlates of gamblers anonymous attendance in pathological seeking professional treatment. *Addict. Behav.*, 2003, 28, 1049-62.

[121] Oei TPS, Gordon LM. Psychosocial factors related to gambling abstinence and relapse in members of Gamblers Anonymous. *J. Gamb. Stud.*, 2008, 24, 91-105.

[122] Ladouceur R, Sylvain C, Boutin C, Lachance S, Doucet C, Leblond J, Jacques C. Cognitive treatment of pathological gambling. *J. Nerv. Ment. Dis.*, 2001, 189, 774-80.

[123] Sylvain C, Ladouceur R, Boisvert J-M. Cognitive and behavioral treatment of pathological gambling: A controlled study. *J. Consult. Clin. Psychol.*, 1997, 65, 727-32.

[124] Ladouceur R, Sylvain C, Boutin C, Lachance S, Doucet C, Leblond J. Group therapy for pathological gamblers: A cognitive approach. *Behavr. Res. Ther.*, 2003, 41, 587-96.

[125] Petry NM, Ammerman Y, Bohl J, Doersch A, Gay H, Kadden R, Molina C, Steinberg K. Cognitive-behavioral therapy for pathological gamblers. *J. Consult. Clin. Psychol.,* 2006, 74, 555-67.

[126] Echeburua E, Baez C, Fernandez-Montalvo J. Comparative effectiveness of three therapeutic modalities in the psychological treatment of pathological gambling: Long-term outcome. *Behav. Cog. Psychother.,* 1996, 24, 51-72.

[127] Toneatto T, Dragonetti R. Effectiveness of community-based treatment for problem gambling: a quasi-experimental evaluation of cognitive-behavioral vs. twelve-step therapy. *Am. J. Addictions,* 2008, 17, 298-303.

[128] Dowling N, Smith D, Thomas T. Treatment of female pathological gambling: The efficacy of a cognitive-behavioural approach. *J. Gamb. Stud.,* 2006, 22, 355-72.

[129] Dowling N, Smith D, Thomas T. A comparison of individual and group cognitive-behavioural treatment for female pathological gambling. *Behav Res Ther*, 2007, 45, 2192-202.

[130] Miller WR, Rollnick S. *Motivational interviewing: Preparing people for change (2nd ed.).* New York: Guilford, 2002.

[131] Wulfert E, Blanchard EB, Freidenberg BM, Martell RS. Retaining pathological gamblers in cognitive behavior therapy through motivational enhancement: A pilot study. *Behav. Mod.,* 2006, 20, 315-40.

[132] Oei TPS, Raylu N, Casey LM. Effectiveness of group and individual formats of a combined motivational interviewing and cognitive behavioral treatment program for problem gambling: A randomized controlled trial. *Behav. Cog. Psychother.,* 2010, 38, 233-8.

[133] Grant JE, Donahue CB, Odlaug BL, Kim SW, Miller MJ, Petry NM. Imaginal desensitization plus motivational interviewing for pathological gambling: Randomised controlled trial. *Br. J. Psychiatry*, 2009, 195, 266-7.

[134] McConaghy N, Blaszczynski A, Frankova A. Comparison of imaginal desensitization with other behavioral treatments of pathological gambling: A two- to nine-year follow-up. *Br. J. Psychiatry,* 1991, 159, 390-3.

[135] Carlbring P, Jonsson J, Josephson H, Forsberg L. Motivational interviewing versus cognitive behavioral group threrapy in the treatment of problem and pathological gambling: A randomized controlled trial. *Cog. Behav. Ther.,* 2010, 39, 92-103.

[136] Hodgins DC, Currie S, el-Guebaly N. Motivational enhancement and self-help treatments for problem gambling. *J. Consult. Clin. Psychol.,* 2001, 69, 50-7.

[137] Dickerson M, Hinchy J, Legg-England S. Minimal treatments and problem gamblers: A preliminary investigation. *J. Gamb. Stud.,* 1990, 6, 87-102.

[138] Hodgins DC, Currie SR, Currie G, Fick GH. Randomized trial of brief motivational treatments for pathological gamblers: More is not necessarily better. *J. Consult. Clin. Psychol.,* 2009a, 77, 950-60.

[139] Petry NM, Weinstock J, Ledgerwood DM, Morasco B. Brief interventions for problem gamblers. Manuscript submitted for publication. *J. Consult. Clin. Psychol.,* 2008, 76, 318-28.

[140] Petry NM, Weinstock J, Morasco BM, Ledgerwood DM. A randomized trial of brief interventions for problem and pathological gambling college students. *Addiction*, 2009, 104, 1569-78.

[141] Carlbring P, Smit F. Randomized trial of internet-delivered self-help with telephone support for pathological gamblers. *J. Consult. Clin. Psychol.,* 2008, 76, 1090-4.

[142] Mitchell JE, Burgard M, Faber R, Crosby RD, de Zwaan M. Cognitive behavioral therapy for compulsive buying disorder. *Behav Res Ther,* 2006, 44, 1859-65.

[143] Mueller A, Mueller U, Silbermann A, Reinecker H, Bleich S, Mitchell JE, de Zwaan M. A randomized, controlled trial of group cognitive-behavioral therapy for compulsive buying disorder: Posttreatment and 6-month follow-up results. *J. Clin. Psychiat.,* 2008, 69, 1131-8.

[144] Gold SN, Heffner CL. Sexual addiction: Many conceptions, minimal data. *Clin. Psychol. Rev.,* 1998, 18, 367-81.

[145] Quadland MC. Compulsive sexual behavior: Definition of a problem and an approach to treatment. *J. Sex Marital Ther.,* 1985, 11, 121-32.

[146] Orzack MH, Voluse AC, Wolfe D, Hennen J. An ongoing study of group treatment for men involved in problematic internet-enabled sexual behavior. *Cyber Psychol. Behav.,* 2006, 9, 348-60.

[147] King DL, Delfabbro PH, Griffiths MD, Gradisar M. Assessing clinical trials of internet addiction treatment: A systematic review and CONSORT evaluation. *Clin. Psychol. Rev.,* 2011, 31, 1110-6.

[148] Du Y-S, Jian W, Vance A. Longer term effect of randomized, controlled group cognitive behavioural therapy for internet addiction in adolescent students in Shanghai. *Aust NZ J. Psychiat.,* 2010, 44, 129-34.

[149] Kim JU. The effect of a R/T group counseling program on the internet addiction level and self-esteem of internet addiction university students. *Int. J. Reality Therapy,* 2008, 27, 4-12.

[150] Shek DTL, Tang VMY, Lo CY. Evaluation of an internet addiction treatment program for Chinese adolescents in Hong Kong. *Adolescence,* 2009, 44, 359-73.

[151] Young KS. Cognitive behavior therapy with internet addicts: Treatment outcomes and implications. *Cyber Psychol. Behav,* 2007, 10, 671-9.

In: Emerging Targets for Drug Addiction Treatment
Editor: Juan Canales

ISBN 978-1-62081-913-5
©2012 Nova Science Publishers, Inc.

Chapter 7

ATYPICAL DOPAMINE TRANSPORTER INHIBITORS: CANDIDATES FOR THE TREATMENT OF PSYCHOSTIMULANT ADDICTION

*Clara Velázquez-Sánchez and Juan J. Canales**
Behavioural Neuroscience, Department of Psychology,
University of Canterbury, New Zealand

ABSTRACT

The use of psychoactive drugs, such as cocaine and amphetamine, remains at epidemic levels in several North American, European and Oceanic countries. Stimulant addiction is a chronic neuropsychiatric disorder with somatic, psychological, socio-economic and legal implications.

Currently we lack specific pharmacological therapies with recognized efficacy for the treatment of this disorder and, in fact, medications that are used to manage stimulant abuse are specific for other pathologies and provide, at best, symptomatic relief.

Recent advances in neurobiology and neuropharmacology have allowed the development of new agents and approaches, such us novel dopamine agonists, GABA-related agents and immunization strategies, which remain to be fully evaluated. This review focuses on the new generation of compounds derived from the benztropine molecule.

Research shows that such compounds are atypical dopamine transporter inhibitors with a slower onset and longer duration of action than cocaine, diminished cocaine-like effects and ability to specifically block the neurochemical and behavioural actions of cocaine and amphetamines. Here we will review evidence that supports further development of these agents as possible "agonist" replacement medications in stimulant addiction.

* Email: juan.canales@canterbury.ac.nz

1. INTRODUCTION

Dopamine (DA), one of the classical monoaminergic neurotransmitters, plays a critical role in a myriad of physiological functions in the central nervous system (CNS). DA neurotransmission is strongly regulated by processes that affect its synthesis, packaging into vesicles, release, reuptake and catabolism. Many factors can affect DA homeostasis and drugs of abuse are most notorious. Most addictive drugs, despite differences in their mechanisms of action, share the ability to activate mesolimbic DA neurons in the brain. This is especially true for psychomotor stimulants, such as cocaine and amphetamines, which target the DA system directly. Although cocaine acts in the CNS at several neurobiological targets, the main physiological substrate contributing to its reinforcing effects and consequent abuse liability is its affinity for the monoamine transporters [1]. Albeit cocaine inhibits the transport of DA, serotonin and norepinephrine, it appears that blockade of the DA transporter (DAT) is the most important mechanism through which cocaine exerts its behavioural and reinforcing properties [2, 3]. The inhibition of the DAT results in an increase in the DA levels in the nucleus accumbens (NAc), which supports self-administration behaviour in animals and in humans. Natural reinforcers such as food and sex also activate DA transmission in the NAc, but generally do not lead to addiction partly because the elevations in DA levels are substantially lower than those produced by addictive drugs, including cocaine [4]. It has been hypothesized that drugs blocking the DAT may have reinforcing effects similar to those observed for cocaine [2]. However, some of the DAT inhibitors developed in the last 20 years display a different behavioral profile [5]. Some of these atypical DA uptake blockers do not produce cocaine-like effects, thus these compounds are candidate pharmacotherapies in the treatment of cocaine addiction.

The modest success of methadone in the treatment of opiate abuse and the nicotine patches for smoking cessation has stimulated the hypothesis that agonist substitution therapy may also be effective for psychostimulant dependence. The speed with which an addictive drug crosses the blood brain barrier and elevates DA levels within the NAc correlates positively with its ability to produce addiction [6, 7]. This correlation indicates that slow-onset, long-acting compounds may have less abuse potential and may substitute for one with higher potential, thereby diminishing the use of the addictive drug. Those long-term increases in NAc DA levels may ameliorate the hypodoparminergic dysfunction observed in cocaine addicts, decreasing drug craving and the likelihood of relapse [8-10]. To achieve DA agonist effects, research on new medications has focused for more than a decade on the development of DA reuptake or DA transporter inhibitors rather than direct DA agonists [11, 12]. A large number of chemical molecules with such desirable features, including benztropines, tropanes and substituted piperazines, have been synthesized. GBR 12909 (vanoxerine®), a phenyl-substituted piperazine derivative, is one of the most extensively studied DAT inhibitors. GBR 12909 binds to the DAT with high affinity and selectively inhibits DA reuptake, having a slower onset and longer duration of action than cocaine [13, 14]. In vivo microdialysis experiments performed in rats demonstrated that the administration of GBR 12909 produced only a mild increase in extracellular levels of striatal DA and was also able to compete with other psychostimulants at the DAT site, blocking the increase in DA levels induced by cocaine or amphetamine [13, 15]. Self-administration studies in rats and rhesus monkeys revealed that GBR 12909 administered as a pretreatment produced a dose-dependent reduction in the intake of cocaine, having a weak or no effect on food intake [16-19]. However, studies with other GBR 12909-like molecules demonstrated that not all DA uptake inhibitors had identical neurochemical and behavioural properties. For instance, GBR 12935 does not have the ability to decrease the response maintained by cocaine without affecting food-maintained responding [20]. Further studies with GBR 12909 showed that this inhibitor is self-administered and triggers relapse of drug seeking behaviour after extinction in both rats and nonhuman primates [21-23]. Studies performed in humans did not confirm this abuse potential [24, 25], however, and clinical trials were initiated in cocaine dependent patients. Unfortunately, GBR 12909 was shown to prolong the rate rate-dependent cardiac QTc interval, prompting the discontinuation of the phase I clinical trial [26]. Benztropine (Cogentin®) is an anticholinergic and antihistaminic molecule used in the treatment of the early-stage symptoms associated with Parkinson's disease [27]. It is also a dopamine uptake inhibitor [28] with potency similar to that of cocaine and exhibits stimulant activity in animal models [29, 30]. The combination of a tropane ring, which is present in the cocaine molecule, with the diphenyl ether function, found in the GBR molecules such as GBR 12909, suggested that the benztropine (BZT) molecule may serve as interesting template for the design of a new generation of dopamine uptake inhibitors. In the past 15 years many compounds derived from the BZT molecule have been developed (Table 1) and extensively evaluated [31-36]. One of the most relevant features revealed by these studies was that these BZT analogs had very high affinity for the DAT and strongly inhibited DA reuptake, inhibition that was positively correlated with DAT binding affinities [33].

Table 1. Molecular structure of cocaine, GBR 12909 and BZT molecules showing their structural similarities. In vitro affinity for the DAT, SERT, NET, M1 and H1 receptor is shown for these agents as well as for some BZT derivatives

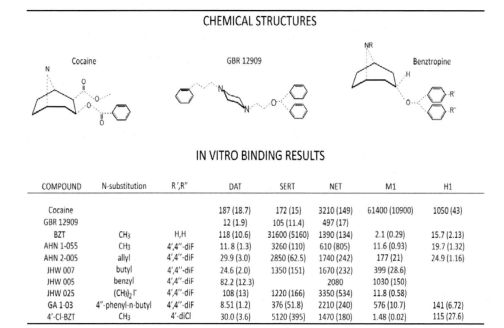

CHEMICAL STRUCTURES

Cocaine   GBR 12909   Benztropine

IN VITRO BINDING RESULTS

COMPOUND	N-substitution	R',R''	DAT	SERT	NET	M1	H1
Cocaine			187 (18.7)	172 (15)	3210 (149)	61400 (10900)	1050 (43)
GBR 12909			12 (1.9)	105 (11.4)	497 (17)		
BZT	CH₃	H,H	118 (10.6)	31600 (5160)	1390 (134)	2.1 (0.29)	15.7 (2.13)
AHN 1-055	CH₃	4',4''-diF	11.8 (1.3)	3260 (110)	610 (805)	11.6 (0.93)	19.7 (1.32)
AHN 2-005	allyl	4',4''-diF	29.9 (3.0)	2850 (62.5)	1740 (242)	177 (21)	24.9 (1.16)
JHW 007	butyl	4',4''-diF	24.6 (2.0)	1350 (151)	1670 (232)	399 (28.6)	
JHW 005	benzyl	4',4''-diF	82.2 (12.3)		2080	1030 (150)	
JHW 025	(CH₃)₂ I⁻	4',4''-diF	108 (13)	1220 (166)	3350 (534)	11.8 (0.58)	
GA 1-03	4''-phenyl-n-butyl	4',4''-diF	8.51 (1.2)	376 (51.8)	2210 (240)	576 (10.7)	141 (6.72)
4'-Cl-BZT	CH₃	4'-diCl	30.0 (3.6)	5120 (395)	1470 (180)	1.48 (0.02)	115 (27.6)

In vitro studies combining molecular structure and activity, demonstrated that modifications and chemical substitutions in different sites of the original BZT molecule, produced changes in the affinity for the DAT and enhanced the potency of DA inhibition. For example, α-configuration of the diphenyl ether at the position 3 of the tropane ring [37] and substitution of the β benzoil group with some substituted phenyl rings, significantly modified the affinity for the DAT [38].

Specifically, para or meta-substitution with chloro or fluoro on the phenyl rings altered affinity for the DAT, with the analog 4'-4''-diF (AHN 1-055) displaying the highest affinity of all. Neurochemical studies revealed that the affinity of most of these analogs for other transporters, including the serotonin transporter (SERT) and the norepinephrine transporter (NERT) was low, although a moderate-to-high affinity for muscarinic and histaminic 1 receptors (M1 and H1) was apparent [38-40] (Table 1). Further studies demonstrated that cocaine, GBR 12909 and BZT analogs all displaced a high selective DA uptake inhibitor, $[I]^{125}$ RTI-121, and increased locomotor activity in a dose and time dependent manner, in a way such that a positive correlation between the affinity for the DAT and the behavioral responses was observed [32, 41]. Such relationship was lacking when H1 and M1 receptors were considered [42, 43].

In spite of the similarities in chemical structure between BZT, analogs of BZT and cocaine, there is evidence to suggest that the manner in which these compounds interact with the DAT is different. Studies with a mutated DAT in which the aspartate amino acid at position 79 was substituted for glutamate showed an increase in the potency of the BZT and its analogs in the inhibition of DA reuptake, whereas the potency for cocaine and other classical DAT blockers did not change [36]. Additional studies reported evidence suggesting that BZT and cocaine analogs bind to different domains within the DAT [44]. The binding site for cocaine and its analogs is deeply buried between transmembrane regions 1, 3, 6 and 8 and overlaps with the binding sites for the substrates DA and amphetamine [45, 46] as well as the for the BZT analogs [45, 47].

These differing molecular interactions may explain the different effects obtained in microdialisys studies. For example, it has been shown that in contrast with cocaine, which induces a pronounced and rapid elevation of DA in the NAc, BZT analogs produce a more gradual increment spanning over a prolonged period of time [48]. In a study comparing the effects of one of the BZT analogs, 4'-Cl-BZT, with those of cocaine on DA levels in specific DA terminal areas including NAc core and shell, dorsal caudate and medial prefrontal cortex (mPFC), data indicated that both compounds dose-dependently increased DA levels in all the brain regions analyzed. However, the effects of the BZT analog were weaker, except in the mPFC [49]. This different pattern of DA activation may be linked with the behavioural differences observed between these analogs and cocaine.

A recent study compared in mice the effects produced by cocaine, the phenyltropane WIN 35,428, and the BZT analog JHW 007 on DA levels in the shell of NAc. The results revealed that all the compounds tested alone increased the DA levels in a dose-dependent manner, although JHW 007 was less effective than the other molecules and had a slower onset of increase, reaching the maximum level 4-5 h after administration. Combinations of cocaine and WIN 35,428 had greater effects than those expected due to an additive effect and by contrast the effect of the combination of cocaine and JHW 007 was less than predicted [50].

Although BZT itself did not change the effects induced by cocaine in a clinical trial performed with recreational users [51], the neurochemical differences mentioned above between cocaine and the structurally modified BZT derivatives support the hypothesis that the new analogs may be useful pharmacotherapies in the treatment of cocaine dependence. Below we summarize recent studies using animal models of drug addiction that provide further evidence to support this claim.

2. PRECLINICAL EVIDENCE

2.1. Locomotor Activity

Addictive drugs exert reinforcing properties through activation of brain circuits recruited by normal behaviors, such as exploration and locomotor activity. These effects are linked with their ability to interact with the DA system in specific regions of the brain. Given that locomotor activity is a variable that is relatively easy to quantify, this test is frequently used to investigate the stimulant-like effects of different compounds. However, this measure is not directly correlated with the reinforcing effects of stimulant drugs.

It has been extensively demonstrated that DAT inhibitors such as cocaine, methyl-phenidate, mazindol and nomifensine have dose-dependent effects on motor activity. Low and intermediate doses produce an increase in activity, while higher doses produce a decrease as a result of the induction of perseverative motor behaviors (i.e., stereotypies), which compete with the expression of locomotor behavior [52-54].

Assays performed in rodents comparing the locomotor activity induced by BZT analogs and cocaine, revealed that these analogs produced, compared with saline treatment, mild stimulation that was in all cases lower than that evoked by cocaine [39-42, 48, 55-60] (Figure 1A, 1B).

Time course studies revealed that such moderate increase in locomotion has a slow onset and long duration compared with the fast and short effect elicited by cocaine [42, 48]. It is important to mention that BZT analogs with a fluoro substitution in the phenyl ring generally have greater effects on locomotor activity than those with a chloro substitution, despite having similar binding affinities [42].

Most interaction studies in rats and mice demonstrated that when administered as a pretreatment before cocaine, BZT analogs such as AHN 1-055, JHW 007, and AHN 2-005, are able to attenuate or completely block the effects induced by the stimulant on locomotor activity without producing abnormal behaviors, such as stereotypy [41, 59, 60] (Figure 1A, 1B). Contrary to pre-treatment with the analog AHN 1-055, administration of amphetamine prior to cocaine produced in mice a robust increase in both locomotion and stereotyped behavior. Significantly, combined with other DA reuptake inhibitor, nomifensine, cocaine-induced locomotion was attenuated but intense stereotypies were observed after repeated administration.

AHN 1-055 blocked cocaine-induced locomotor activity without increasing stereotyped behavior. Therefore, these interaction assays evidenced that AHN 1-055 differs from a classical psychostimulant drug, such as amphetamine, and from another DAT inhibitor, such as nomifensine [59].

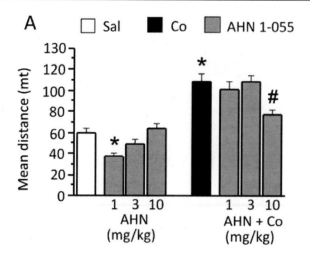

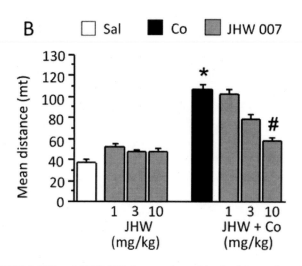

Figure 1. Effects of AHN 1-055 and JHW 007 alone and combined with cocaine after four days of treatments in mice. Both analogs given alone had not stimulant effects at any dose tested (A, B), In fact, low doses of AHN 1-055 induced an attenuation locomotor activity compared with saline treatment (A). Given as pre-treatment both compounds significantly reduced cocaine-induced hyperlocomotion (A, B).

2.2. Sensitization

Behavioural sensitization, or reversed tolerance, is a process characterized by a progressive increase in the psychomotor effects of a drug when it is administered repeatedly [61, 62]. This hypersensitivity to the psychomotor effects of the drug is mediated by molecular and physiological adaptations in the NAc and associated anatomical regions, such as the ventral tegmental area (VTA) [63,64], and may persist for months, years or even a lifetime after the withdrawal [65-67]. Such persistence of behavioral changes has been linked to structural modifications in the neural circuits, especially changes in synaptic plasticity [61, 67-69].

It has been extensively demonstrated that classical psychostimulant drugs produce a form of behavioral sensitization which results in an augmented locomotor response after chronic exposure and challenge administration [65, 70-72]. Again, the BZT analogs differ from classical psychomotor stimulants in this regard. Data accumulated in mice revealed that subchronic administration of cocaine produced locomotor sensitization manifested as a boost of locomotor behavior observed immediately after cocaine challenge. However, JHW 007 produced only a weak increase in locomotion, and no evidence of sensitization. Given as a pre-treatment, JHW 007 did not prevent the locomotor effects induced by repeated treatment with cocaine, but it blocked the locomotor boost observed in sensitized animals [60].

2.3. Conditioned Place Preference

Conditioned place preference (CPP) continues to be one of the most widely used models to assess the rewarding effects induced by different drugs. Essentially, in the CPP paradigm, the physiological and interoceptive effects of a given drug act as the unconditioned stimulus (UCS), which is repeatedly paired with a set of environmental cues (i.e., the place) that act as conditioned stimuli (CS). CPP is carried out in an apparatus that is typically made of two clearly distinguishable compartments, one being the drug-paired compartment and the other the vehicle-paired compartment. The procedure consists of placing the subject in the drug-paired and vehicle-paired compartments in different sessions after administration of the appropriate treatment. Given the slow onset of effects induced by BZT analog treatment, time is an important variable to control for during conditioning. For example, AHN 2-005 at dose of 1 mg/kg and JHW 007 at dose of 10 mg/kg administered 45 minutes before the start of the conditioning sessions produced significant CPP, but not at other doses or times [73]. On the contrary, neither JHW 007 nor AHN 1-055 produced CPP at any of the doses tested when administered 1h before conditioning. What is most remarkable, however, is that BZT derivatives interfere with cocaine- and amphetamine-induced CPP. Interaction experiments revealed that administered as pre-treatments 1h before the drug, BZT analogs were able to block the CPP induced by cocaine [59, 60] (Figure 2A, 2B). These data suggest that BZT derivatives reduce cocaine-induced reward.

2.4. Cocaine Discrimination

Drug discrimination (DD) is a useful method to study the behavioural and neuropharmacological effects of the drugs. The four basic variables for this type of study are the subject, the dose of the drug, the response and the reinforcement. In these studies, the effect of the drug serves as discriminative stimulus. The subjects learn to distinguish between the administration of a drug or vehicle and respond according to the interoceptive state produced by the treatments. After drug injection, responses on only one lever are reinforced; after vehicle injection, responses on the other lever are reinforced. The assignment of drug- and vehicle-appropriate levers is generally counterbalanced across rats. Once discrimination training has been completed, the method can be used to determine whether the substance being tested (e.g., a possible substitute) is identified as similar or dissimilar with the drug used during the training. Stimulants such as caffeine, amphetamine, methamphetamine and cocaine have been extensively used as discriminative stimulus in the DD paradigm [74-80]. It has been demonstrated that the ability of most monoamine uptake inhibitors to substitute for cocaine is related to their specific affinity for the DAT [81, 82] and that compounds with high affinity for either the SERT or the NET do not fully substitute for cocaine [81, 83]. Compounds including mazindol, nomifensine, GBR 12909 or bupropion, which are primarily DA uptake inhibitors, fully substitute for cocaine [81]. By contrast, BZT analogs, being also DA uptake blockers, vary significantly in their capacity to substitute for cocaine, and most of them do not fully. A comparative study between fluoro-, chloro-, bromo- and methoxy substitutions indicated that the most efficacious BZT analogs at stimulating locomotor activity in mice were those with a fluoro-substituent in at least one of the phenyl rings of the structure [42].

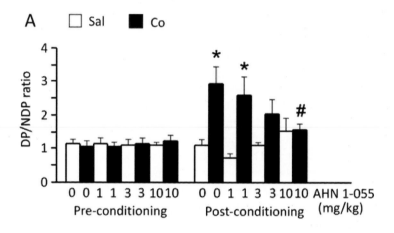

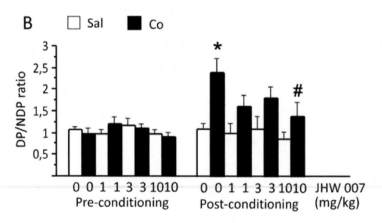

Figure 2. Effects of AHN-1055 and JHW 007 on conditioned place preference (CPP) and interactions with cocaine. Cocaine exposure produced a significant CPP while neither AHN 1-055 nor JHW 007 elicited CPP or place aversion at any dose (A, B, pre-conditioning). When given before cocaine challenge, both AHN 1-055 and JHW 007 significantly blocked cocaine-induced CPP (A, B, post-conditioning).

In DD assays only the 4',4"-difluoro-substituted analog produced effects similar to those of cocaine. Interaction experiments in which JHW 007 was administered as a pre-treatment before cocaine, demonstrated that the cocaine-dose effect curve shifted to the right, suggesting a competitive antagonism [41]. Taken together, DD experiments indicate that BZT analogs do not fully substitute for cocaine, on the one hand, and modify the discriminative stimulus properties of cocaine, on the other, which supports their candidacy as replacement medications in stimulant abuse.

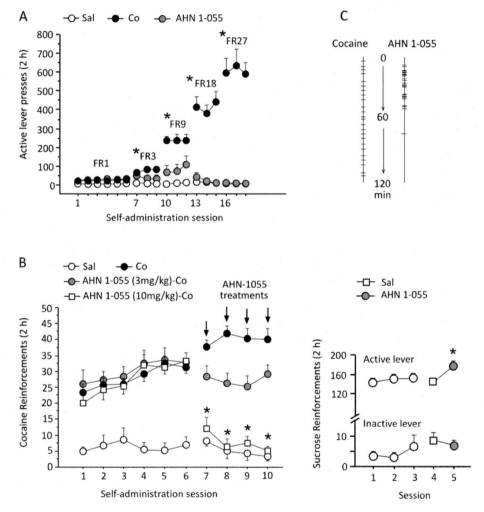

Figure 3. Effects of cocaine and AHN 1-055 in a progressive ratio-like schedule of reinforcement and effects on cocaine intake. Under FR1, rats trained to self-administer cocaine or the analog behaved similarly, obtaining similar number of reinforcements. As the task requirement was increased, rats responding for cocaine adjusted their responses according to the demand, whereas rats responding for the analog began to decrease responding under FR3, extinguishing thereafter (A). Given as pre-treatment, AHN 1-055 dose-dependently suppressed the response maintained by cocaine (B, left) while the response maintained by sucrose was increased (B, right). The pattern of self-administration differs between cocaine and the analog. Typically, rats responding for AHN 1-055 accumulated their responses in the first part of the session whereas rats responding for cocaine showed the cyclic regularity observed in (C).

2.5. Self-Administration

Self-administration (SA) is an animal model of drug addiction that provides information about the reinforcing efficacy of a drug. In general, drugs that are self-administered by the animals are those that have high potential of abuse in humans [84]. In intravenous SA assays, the animal receives an intravenous drug infusion when it executes a discrete response, generally pressing a lever. The frequency with which the animal performs the response, which therefore determines the intake, is indicative of how reinforcing the self-administered substance is. Motivation can be measured in progressive ratio schedules of reinforcement, in which the experimenter can change the demand on the task (i.e., the number of responses needed to obtain one infusion). Psychostimulant drugs such as cocaine, amphetamine or methylphenidate are self-administered by the animals indicating reinforcing effects [85-88].

The rate of SA maintained by the BZT analogs is lower than the rate maintained by cocaine, suggesting that these compounds have a weak reinforcing efficacy [89, 90]. In a recent study, Ferragud et al. (2009) compared the self-administration of cocaine and AHN 1-055 [91] (Figure 3A). The analog was only self-administered by a subset of rats (ca. one in three rats). Once the groups self-administering cocaine and AHN 1-055 were matched in terms of number of responses under an FR1 schedule of reinforcement, task requirement was progressively increased using a between-sessions pseudo-progressive ratio schedule. Rats responding for cocaine adjusted their response to obtain similar intake per session, even under FR27, whereas rats responding for the analog began to decrease responding as soon as demand increased under an FR3 schedule. These data clearly indicated that the BZT analog has less reinforcing efficacy than cocaine and possesses less incentive motivational properties. Given as pre-treatment, the analogs AHN 2-005, JHW 007 and AHN 1-055 all suppressed cocaine intake in a dose-dependent manner without affecting the response for food or sucrose [90,91] (Figure 3B). It is also interesting to note the different pattern of SA for cocaine and AHN 1-055. Typically, rats receiving cocaine infusions exhibited responses that were spaced cyclically throughout the session, whereas rats self-administering the analog accumulated most of the infusions in the first half of the session (loading phase) (Figure 3C).

2.6. Relapse

Relapse is defined by renewed desire to take the drug once abused and by the sequence of behaviors aimed at procuring and taking it. Relapse can occur after long periods of withdrawal. Despite significant advances in the treatment of the physical symptoms induced by abstinence of opiates, nicotine and alcohol, relapse is still considered one of the most challenging aspects in the treatment of drug addiction [92]. Relapse can be modeled in laboratories using the reinstatement paradigm. One of the most commonly used and predictive animal models to study relapse is the self-administration model followed by extinction-reinstatement of drug seeking. After extinction, drug seeking can be reinstated by different trigger factors such as stress [93, 94], re-exposure to the environment or cues previously associated with the drug [95] and administration of a priming injection with a small dose of the drug [96]. The number of studies and compounds tested to evaluate their potential as medications to prevent relapse has grown considerably in the past few years. Thus far, studies have assessed monoaminergic drugs with primary selectivity for DA, serotonin and/or norepinephrine receptors. The BZT analogs, and specifically the AHN 1-055, are the first DA uptake blockers tested in extinction-reinstatement experiments of cocaine-seeking. The results that we have obtained in these tests are very promising.

First, after 2 weeks of abstinence, rats that self-administered cocaine exhibited high rates of relapse following reexposure to the self-administration context, whereas rats trained to self-administered AHN 1-055 did not show evidence of relapse to drug seeking [91]. Second, we have recently examined the possibility of using AHN 1-055 as a substitute for cocaine in a cocaine-induced model of reinstatement (unpublished observations). Rats with a stable history of cocaine intake underwent extinction when the drug was substituted by saline or AHN 1-055. Rats, however, did not extinguish responding when the substitute was amphetamine. Following extinction, responding was reinstated by cocaine priming. After 18 days of substitution treatment, drug challenge produced weak cocaine-induced reinstatement in the animals that received AHN-1-055 substitution, by contrast with the strong reinstatement observed in the animals that received saline substitution. The reduced cocaine-induced reinstatement of drug seeking observed in rats receiving BZT analog therapy may have resulted from purely pharmacological effects rather than by active learning, because yoked rats receiving AHN 1-055 passively also showed diminished cocaine-induced reinstatement. The expression of certain proteins in the mPFC has been linked with reinstatement of cocaine seeking [97, 98]. We have studied the expression of c-Fos, brain derived neurotrophic factor (BDNF) and Fas-associated death domain (FADD) in relapsing rats receiving substitution treatments. Reductions in drug seeking during reinstatement were matched by downward shifts in the contents of BDNF, c-Fos and FADD proteins in the mPFC, which were elevated in relapsing rats. These findings support the idea that the susbtitution with AHN 1-055, and possibly with structurally and functionally related agents, could reduce craving and vulnerability to relapse after stimulant self-administration.

CONCLUSION

The search for efficacious medications for stimulant addiction has long focused on the design of drugs that (1) act as a substitute for the stimulant drug by inducing similar effects on dopamine neurotransmission or (2) exert antagonistic actions by preventing the binding of the stimulant to the DAT. Most efforts have concentrated on the identification of molecules that mimic the DAT-binding properties of a stimulant, such as cocaine, but are less stimulating and act with a slower receptor onset and offset than cocaine. Recent research has shown that binding to the DAT and subsequent transport inhibition does not invariably produce stimulant-like effects.

This means that the design of DAT inhibitors with low abuse profile to efficaciously treat stimulant addiction remains possible, even if those molecules impede dopamine transport. The rationale for targeting the DAT in stimulant abuse is fuelled by the existence of slow-onset, long-acting DAT inhibitors with weak stimulant and reinforcing effects, which can be used as a "substitute". The substitute medication approach is currently the treatment of choice for opiate addiction. The recently designed generation of benztropine (BZT) derivatives includes compounds with both high affinity for the dopamine transporter, the main target of psychostimulants in the brain, and markedly low abuse liability. Evidence we and others have accumulated in recent years demonstrates that BZT analogs show psychopharmacological features consistent with those of an ideal replacement or "substitute" treatment. BZT analogues, such as AHN-1055 and JHW 007, block cocaine- and amphetamine-induced locomotor stimulation, sensitization, reward and reinforcement. Our data further indicates that the analogs are effective in models of relapse, thus strongly supporting the rationale for further studies including both preclinical assays and clinical trials.

REFERENCES

[1]   Carroll FI, Howell LL, Kuhar MJ. Pharmacotherapies for treatment of cocaine abuse: preclinical aspects. *J. Med. Chem.,* 1999, 42, 2721-36.

[2]   Kuhar MJ, Ritz MC, Boja JW. The dopamine hypothesis of the reinforcing properties of cocaine. *Trends. Neurosci.,* 1991, 14, 299-302.

[3]   Ritz MC, Boja JW, George FR, Kuhar MJ. Cocaine binding sites related to drug self-administration. *NIDA Res. Monogr.,* 1989, 95, 239-46.

[4]   Volkow ND, Li TK. Drug addiction: the neurobiology of behaviour gone awry. *Nat. Rev. Neurosci.,* 2004, 5, 963-70.

[5]   Newman AH, Kulkarni S. Probes for the dopamine transporter: new leads toward a cocaine-abuse therapeutic--A focus on analogues of benztropine and rimcazole. *Med. Res. Rev.,* 2002, 22, 429-64.

[6]   Volkow ND, Ding YS, Fowler JS, Wang GJ, Logan J, Gatley JS, et al. Is methylphenidate like cocaine? Studies on their pharmacokinetics and distribution in the human brain. *Arch. Gen. Psychiatry,* 1995, 52, 456-63.

[7]   Kimmel HL, O'Connor JA, Carroll FI, Howell LL. Faster onset and dopamine transporter selectivity predict stimulant and reinforcing effects of cocaine analogs in squirrel monkeys. *Pharmacol. Biochem. Behav.,* 2007, 86, 45-54.

[8]   Gardner EL. What we have learned about addiction from animal models of drug self-administration. *Am. J. Addict.,* 2000, 9, 285-313.

[9]   Volkow ND, Fowler JS, Wang GJ. Imaging studies on the role of dopamine in cocaine reinforcement and addiction in humans. *J. Psychopharmacol.,* 1999, 13, 337-45.

[10]   Volkow ND, Wang GJ, Telang F, Fowler JS, Logan J, Childress AR, et al. Cocaine cues and dopamine in dorsal striatum: mechanism of craving in cocaine addiction. *J. Neurosci.,* 2006, 26, 6583-8.

[11]   Howell LL, Kimmel HL. Monoamine transporters and psychostimulant addiction. *Biochem. Pharmacol.,* 2008, 75, 196-217.

[12]   Wise RA, Gardner EL. *Neurobiology of mental illness.* London: Oxford University; 2004.

[13]   Rothman RB, Mele A, Reid AA, Akunne HC, Greig N, Thurkauf A, et al. GBR12909 antagonizes the ability of cocaine to elevate extracellular levels of dopamine. *Pharmacol. Biochem. Behav.,* 1991, 40, 387-97.

[14]   Rothman RB, Grieg N, Kim A, de Costa BR, Rice KC, Carroll FI, et al. Cocaine and GBR12909 produce equivalent motoric responses at different occupancy of the dopamine transporter. *Pharmacol. Biochem. Behav.,* 1992, 43, 1135-42.

[15] Baumann MH, Char GU, de Costa BR, Rice KC, Rothman RB. GBR12909 attenuates cocaine-induced activation of mesolimbic dopamine neurons in the rat. *J. Pharmacol. Exp. Ther.,* 1994, 271, 1216-22.

[16] Tella SR. Effects of monoamine reuptake inhibitors on cocaine self-administration in rats. *Pharmacol. Biochem. Behav.,* 1995, 51, 687-92.

[17] Schenk S. Effects of GBR 12909, WIN 35,428 and indatraline on cocaine self-administration and cocaine seeking in rats. *Psychopharmacology (Berl),* 2002, 160, 263-70.

[18] Glowa JR, Wojnicki F, Matecka D, Bacher JD, Mansbach RS, Balster RL, et al. Effects of dopamine reuptake inhibitors on food- and cocaine-maintained responding: I. Dependence on unit dose of cocaine. *Experimental and Clinical Psychopharmacology,* 1995, 3, 219-31.

[19] Stafford D, LeSage MG, Rice KC, Glowa JR. A comparison of cocaine, GBR 12909, and phentermine self-administration by rhesus monkeys on a progressive-ratio schedule. *Drug Alcohol. Depend.,* 2001, 62, 41-7.

[20] Glowa JR, Wojnicki FHE, Matecka D, Rice KC. Effects of dopamine reuptake inhibitors on food- and cocaine-maintained responding: II. Comparisons with other drugs and repeated administrations. *Experimental and Clinical Psychopharmacology,* 1995, 3, 232-9.

[21] Roberts DC. Self-administration of GBR 12909 on a fixed ratio and progressive ratio schedule in rats. *Psychopharmacology (Berl),* 1993, 111, 202-6.

[22] Woolverton WL, Hecht GS, Agoston GE, Katz JL, Newman AH. Further studies of the reinforcing effects of benztropine analogs in rhesus monkeys. *Psychopharmacology (Berl),* 2001, 154, 375-82.

[23] De Vries TJ, Schoffelmeer AN, Binnekade R, Vanderschuren LJ. Dopaminergic mechanisms mediating the incentive to seek cocaine and heroin following long-term withdrawal of IV drug self-administration. *Psychopharmacology (Berl),* 1999, 143, 254-60.

[24] Sogaard U, Michalow J, Butler B, Lund LA, Ingersen SH, Skrumsager BK, et al. A tolerance study of single and multiple dosing of the selective dopamine uptake inhibitor GBR 12909 in healthy subjects. *Int Clin. Psychopharmacol.,* 1990, 5, 237-51.

[25] Preti A. Vanoxerine National Institute on Drug Abuse. *Curr. Opin. Investig. Drugs,* 2000, 1, 241-51.

[26] Vocci FJ, Acri J, Elkashef A. Medication development for addictive disorders: the state of the science. *Am. J. Psychiatry,* 2005, 162, 1432-40.

[27] Grace RF. Benztropine abuse and overdose--case report and review. *Adverse Drug React. Toxicol. Rev.,* 1997, 16, 103-12.

[28] Coyle JT, Snyder SH. Antiparkinsonian drugs: inhibition of dopamine uptake in the corpus striatum as a possible mechanism of action. *Science,* 1969, 166, 899-901.

[29] McKearney JW. Effects of dopamine uptake inhibitors on schedule-controlled behaviour in the squirrel monkey. *Psychopharmacology (Berl),* 1982, 78, 377-9.

[30] Acri J, Seidleck B, Witkin JM. *NIDA Monograph*; 1993.

[31] Dar DE, Mayo C, Uhl GR. The interaction of methylphenidate and benztropine with the dopamine transporter is different than other substrates and ligands. *Biochem. Pharmacol.,* 2005, 70, 461-9.

[32] Desai RI, Kopajtic TA, French D, Newman AH, Katz JL. Relationship between in vivo
      occupancy at the dopamine transporter and behavioural effects of cocaine, GBR 12909
      [1-{2-[bis-(4-fluorophenyl)methoxy]ethyl}-4-(3-phenylpropyl)piperazine],   and
      benztropine analogs. *J. Pharmacol. Exp. Ther.*, 2005, 315, 397-404.

[33] Kulkarni SS, Grundt P, Kopajtic T, Katz JL, Newman AH. Structure-activity
      relationships at monoamine transporters for a series of N-substituted 3alpha-(bis[4-
      fluorophenyl]methoxy)tropanes: comparative molecular field analysis, synthesis, and
      pharmacological evaluation. *J. Med. Chem.*, 2004, 47, 3388-98.

[34] Kulkarni SS, Kopajtic TA, Katz JL, Newman AH. Comparative structure-activity
      relationships of benztropine analogues at the dopamine transporter and histamine H(1)
      receptors. *Bioorg. Med. Chem.*, 2006, 14, 3625-34.

[35] Reith ME, Berfield JL, Wang LC, Ferrer JV, Javitch JA. The uptake inhibitors cocaine
      and benztropine differentially alter the conformation of the human dopamine
      transporter. *J. Biol. Chem.*, 2001, 276, 29012-8.

[36] Ukairo OT, Bondi CD, Newman AH, Kulkarni SS, Kozikowski AP, Pan S, et al.
      Recognition of benztropine by the dopamine transporter (DAT) differs from that of the
      classical dopamine uptake inhibitors cocaine, methylphenidate, and mazindol as a
      function of a DAT transmembrane 1 aspartic acid residue. *J. Pharmacol. Exp. Ther.*,
      2005, 314, 575-83.

[37] Carroll FI. 2002 Medicinal Chemistry Division Award address: monoamine
      transporters and opioid receptors. Targets for addiction therapy. *J. Med. Chem.*, 2003,
      46, 1775-94.

[38] Rothman RB, Baumann MH, Prisinzano TE, Newman AH. Dopamine transport
      inhibitors based on GBR12909 and benztropine as potential medications to treat
      cocaine addiction. *Biochem. Pharmacol.*, 2008, 75, 2-16.

[39] Newman AH, Allen AC, Izenwasser S, Katz JL. Novel 3 alpha-(diphenyl-
      methoxy)tropane analogs: potent dopamine uptake inhibitors without cocaine-like
      behavioural profiles. *J. Med. Chem.*, 1994, 37, 2258-61.

[40] Agoston GE, Wu JH, Izenwasser S, George C, Katz J, Kline RH, et al. Novel N-
      substituted 3 alpha-[bis(4'-fluorophenyl)methoxy]tropane analogues: selective ligands
      for the dopamine transporter. *J. Med. Chem.*, 1997, 40, 4329-39.

[41] Desai RI, Kopajtic TA, Koffarnus M, Newman AH, Katz JL. Identification of a
      dopamine transporter ligand that blocks the stimulant effects of cocaine. *J. Neurosci.*,
      2005, 25, 1889-93.

[42] Katz JL, Izenwasser S, Kline RH, Allen AC, Newman AH. Novel 3alpha-
      diphenylmethoxytropane analogs: selective dopamine uptake inhibitors with
      behavioural effects distinct from those of cocaine. *J. Pharmacol. Exp. Ther.*, 1999, 288,
      302-15.

[43] Tanda G, Ebbs AL, Kopajtic TA, Elias LM, Campbell BL, Newman AH, et al. Effects
      of muscarinic M1 receptor blockade on cocaine-induced elevations of brain dopamine
      levels and locomotor behaviour in rats. *J. Pharmacol. Exp. Ther.*, 2007, 321, 334-44.

[44] Vaughan RA, Agoston GE, Lever JR, Newman AH. Differential binding of tropane-
      based photoaffinity ligands on the dopamine transporter. *J. Neurosci.*, 1999, 19, 630-6.

[45] Beuming T, Kniazeff J, Bergmann ML, Shi L, Gracia L, Raniszewska K, et al. The
      binding sites for cocaine and dopamine in the dopamine transporter overlap. *Nat.
      Neurosci.*, 2008, 11, 780-9.

[46] Indarte M, Madura JD, Surratt CK. Dopamine transporter comparative molecular modeling and binding site prediction using the LeuT(Aa) leucine transporter as a template. *Proteins,* 2008, 70, 1033-46.

[47] Bisgaard H, Larsen MA, Mazier S, Beuming T, Newman AH, Weinstein H, et al. The binding sites for benztropines and dopamine in the dopamine transporter overlap. *Neuropharmacology,* 2011, 60, 182-90.

[48] Tolliver BK, Newman AH, Katz JL, Ho LB, Fox LM, Hsu K, Jr., et al. Behavioural and neurochemical effects of the dopamine transporter ligand 4-chlorobenztropine alone and in combination with cocaine in vivo. *J. Pharmacol. Exp. Ther.,* 1999, 289, 110-22.

[49] Tanda G, Ebbs A, Newman AH, Katz JL. Effects of 4'-chloro-3 alpha-(diphenylmethoxy)-tropane on mesostriatal, mesocortical, and mesolimbic dopamine transmission: comparison with effects of cocaine. *J. Pharmacol. Exp. Ther.,* 2005, 313, 613-20.

[50] Tanda G, Newman AH, Ebbs AL, Tronci V, Green JL, Tallarida RJ, et al. Combinations of cocaine with other dopamine uptake inhibitors: assessment of additivity. *J. Pharmacol. Exp. Ther.,* 2009, 330, 802-9.

[51] Penetar DM, Looby AR, Su Z, Lundahl LH, Eros-Sarnyai M, McNeil JF, et al. Benztropine pretreatment does not affect responses to acute cocaine administration in human volunteers. *Hum. Psychopharmacol.,* 2006, 21, 549-59.

[52] Roy SN, Bhattacharyya AK, Pradhan S, Pradhan SN. Behavioural and neurochemical effects of repeated administration of cocaine in rats. *Neuropharmacology,* 1978, 17, 559-64.

[53] Bhattacharyya AK, Pradhan SN. Behavioural interactions in cocaine-treated rats. *Life Sci.,* 1979, 24, 1855-60.

[54] Zubrycki EM, Giordano M, Sanberg PR. The effects of cocaine on multivariate locomotor behaviour and defecation. *Behav. Brain Res.,* 1990, 36, 155-9.

[55] Kline RH, Izenwasser S, Katz JL, Joseph DB, Bowen WD, Newman AH. 3'-Chloro-3 alpha-(diphenylmethoxy)tropane but not 4'-chloro-3 alpha-(diphenylmethoxy)tropane produces a cocaine-like behavioural profile. *J. Med. Chem.,* 1997, 40, 851-7.

[56] Katz JL, Newman AH, Izenwasser S. Relations between heterogeneity of dopamine transporter binding and function and the behavioural pharmacology of cocaine. *Pharmacol. Biochem. Behav.,* 1997, 57, 505-12.

[57] Katz JL, Agoston GE, Alling KL, Kline RH, Forster MJ, Woolverton WL, et al. Dopamine transporter binding without cocaine-like behavioural effects: synthesis and evaluation of benztropine analogs alone and in combination with cocaine in rodents. *Psychopharmacology (Berl),* 2001, 154, 362-74.

[58] Katz JL, Kopajtic TA, Agoston GE, Newman AH. Effects of N-substituted analogs of benztropine: diminished cocaine-like effects in dopamine transporter ligands. *J. Pharmacol. Exp. Ther.,* 2004, 309, 650-60.

[59] Velazquez-Sanchez C, Ferragud A, Hernandez-Rabaza V, Nacher A, Merino V, Carda M, et al. The dopamine uptake inhibitor 3 alpha-[bis(4'-fluorophenyl)metoxy]-tropane reduces cocaine-induced early-gene expression, locomotor activity, and conditioned reward. *Neuropsychopharmacology,* 2009, 34, 2497-507.

[60] Velazquez-Sanchez C, Ferragud A, Murga J, Carda M, Canales JJ. The high affinity dopamine uptake inhibitor, JHW 007, blocks cocaine-induced reward, locomotor stimulation and sensitization. *Eur. Neuropsychopharmacol.,* 2010, 20, 501-8.

[61] Robinson TE, Becker JB. Enduring changes in brain and behaviour produced by chronic amphetamine administration: a review and evaluation of animal models of amphetamine psychosis. *Brain Res.,* 1986, 396, 157-98.

[62] Robinson TE, Berridge KC. The neural basis of drug craving: an incentive-sensitization theory of addiction. *Brain Res. Brain Res. Rev.,* 1993, 18, 247-91.

[63] Wise RA, Bozarth MA. A psychomotor stimulant theory of addiction. *Psychol. Rev.,* 1987, 94, 469-92.

[64] Koob GF, Bloom FE. Cellular and molecular mechanisms of drug dependence. *Science,* 1988, 242, 715-23.

[65] Paulson PE, Camp DM, Robinson TE. Time course of transient behavioural depression and persistent behavioural sensitization in relation to regional brain monoamine concentrations during amphetamine withdrawal in rats. *Psychopharmacology (Berl),* 1991, 103, 480-92.

[66] Kalivas PW, Stewart J. Dopamine transmission in the initiation and expression of drug- and stress-induced sensitization of motor activity. *Brain Res. Brain Res. Rev.,* 1991, 16, 223-44.

[67] Stewart J, Badiani A. Tolerance and sensitization to the behavioural effects of drugs. *Behav. Pharmacol.,* 1993, 4, 289-312.

[68] Pierce RC, Kalivas PW. A circuitry model of the expression of behavioural sensitization to amphetamine-like psychostimulants. *Brain Res. Brain Res. Rev.,* 1997, 25, 192-216.

[69] Wolf ME. The role of excitatory amino acids in behavioural sensitization to psychomotor stimulants. *Prog. Neurobiol.,* 1998, 54, 679-720.

[70] Martin-Iverson MT, Burger LY. Behavioural sensitization and tolerance to cocaine and the occupation of dopamine receptors by dopamine. *Mol. Neurobiol.,* 1995, 11, 31-46.

[71] Li Y, White FJ, Wolf ME. Pharmacological reversal of behavioural and cellular indices of cocaine sensitization in the rat. *Psychopharmacology (Berl),* 2000, 151, 175-83.

[72] Robinson TE, Camp DM. Long-lasting effects of escalating doses of d-amphetamine on brain monoamines, amphetamine-induced stereotyped behaviour and spontaneous nocturnal locomotion. *Pharmacol. Biochem. Behav.,* 1987, 26, 821-7.

[73] Li SM, Newman AH, Katz JL. Place conditioning and locomotor effects of N-substituted, 4',4"-difluorobenztropine analogs in rats. *J. Pharmacol. Exp. Ther.,* 2005, 313, 1223-30.

[74] Gatch MB, Youngblood BD, Forster MJ. Effects of ethanol on cocaine discrimination in rats. *Pharmacol Biochem Behav,* 2003, 75, 837-44.

[75] Harland RD, Gauvin DV, Michaelis RC, Carney JM, Seale TW, Holloway FA. Behavioural interaction between cocaine and caffeine: a drug discrimination analysis in rats. *Pharmacol. Biochem. Behav.,* 1989, 32, 1017-23.

[76] Mumfrd GK, Holtzman SG. Qualitative differences in the discriminative stimulus effects of low and high doses of caffeine in the rat. *J. Pharmacol. Exp. Ther.,* 1991, 258, 857-65.

[77] Filip M, Przegalinski E. The role of dopamine receptor subtypes in the discriminative stimulus effects of amphetamine and cocaine in rats. *Pol. J. Pharmacol.,* 1997, 49, 21-30.

[78] Suzuki T, Fukuoka Y, Mori T, Miyatake M, Narita M. Behavioural sensitization to the discriminative stimulus effects of methamphetamine in rats. *Eur. J. Pharmacol.*, 2004, 498, 157-61.

[79] Woolverton WL. Discriminative stimulus effects of cocaine. *NIDA Res. Monogr.*, 1991, 61-74.

[80] Kleven MS, Koek W. Discriminative stimulus properties of cocaine: enhancement by monoamine reuptake blockers. *J. Pharmacol. Exp. Ther.*, 1998, 284, 1015-25.

[81] Baker LE, Riddle EE, Saunders RB, Appel JB. The role of monoamine uptake in the discriminative stimulus effects of cocaine and related compounds. *Behav. Pharmacol.*, 1993, 4, 69-79.

[82] Katz JL, Izenwasser S, Terry P. Relationships among dopamine transporter affinities and cocaine-like discriminative-stimulus effects. *Psychopharmacology (Berl)*, 2000, 148, 90-8.

[83] Kleven MS, Anthony EW, Woolverton WL. Pharmacological characterization of the discriminative stimulus effects of cocaine in rhesus monkeys. *J. Pharmacol. Exp. Ther.*, 1990, 254, 312-7.

[84] Shippenberg T.S., Koob GF. *Psychopharmacology: the fifth generation of progress.* New York: 2011.

[85] Johanson CE, Balster RL, Bonese K. Self-administration of psychomotor stimulant drugs: the effects of unlimited access. *Pharmacol. Biochem. Behav.*, 1976, 4, 45-51.

[86] Gonzalez FA, Goldberg SR. Effects of cocaine and d-amphetamine on behaviour maintained under various schedules of food presentation in squirrel monkeys. *J. Pharmacol. Exp. Ther.*, 1977, 201, 33-43.

[87] Herling S, Downs DA, Woods JH. Cocaine, d-amphetamine, and pentobarbital effects on responding maintained by food or cocaine in rhesus monkeys. *Psychopharmacology (Berl)*, 1979, 64, 261-9.

[88] Carney JM, Landrum RW, Cheng MS, Seale TW. Establishment of chronic intravenous drug self-administration in the C57BL/6J mouse. *Neuroreport*, 1991, 2, 477-80.

[89] Woolverton WL, Rowlett JK, Wilcox KM, Paul IA, Kline RH, Newman AH, et al. 3'- and 4'-chloro-substituted analogs of benztropine: intravenous self-administration and in vitro radioligand binding studies in rhesus monkeys. *Psychopharmacology (Berl)*, 2000, 147, 426-35.

[90] Hiranita T, Soto PL, Newman AH, Katz JL. Assessment of reinforcing effects of benztropine analogs and their effects on cocaine self-administration in rats: comparisons with monoamine uptake inhibitors. *J. Pharmacol. Exp. Ther.*, 2009, 329, 677-86.

[91] Ferragud A, Velazquez-Sanchez C, Hernandez-Rabaza V, Nacher A, Merino V, Carda M, et al. A dopamine transport inhibitor with markedly low abuse liability suppresses cocaine self-administration in the rat. *Psychopharmacology (Berl)*, 2009, 207, 281-9.

[92] O'Brien C. *Goodman and Gilman's The Pharmacological Basis of Therapeutics.* 11th ed. ed. New York: McGraw-Hill; 2006.

[93] McFarland K, Davidge SB, Lapish CC, Kalivas PW. Limbic and motor circuitry underlying footshock-induced reinstatement of cocaine-seeking behaviour. *J. Neurosci.*, 2004, 24, 1551-60.

[94] Shepard JD, Bossert JM, Liu SY, Shaham Y. The anxiogenic drug yohimbine reinstates methamphetamine seeking in a rat model of drug relapse. *Biol. Psychiatry,* 2004, 55, 1082-9.

[95] See RE. Neural substrates of conditioned-cued relapse to drug-seeking behaviour. *Pharmacol. Biochem. Behav.,* 2002, 71, 517-29.

[96] De WH, Stewart J. Reinstatement of cocaine-reinforced responding in the rat. *Psychopharmacology (Berl),* 1981, 75, 134-43.

[97] Kalivas PW. Addiction as a pathology in prefrontal cortical regulation of corticostriatal habit circuitry. *Neurotox. Res.,* 2008, 14, 185-9.

[98] Shaham Y, Shalev U, Lu L, De WH, Stewart J. The reinstatement model of drug relapse: history, methodology and major findings. *Psychopharmacology (Berl),* 2003, 168, 3-20.

In: Emerging Targets for Drug Addiction Treatment
Editor: Juan Canales

ISBN 978-1-62081-913-5
©2012 Nova Science Publishers, Inc.

Chapter 8

LOOKING FOR CANNABINOID-BASED THERAPIES FOR DRUG ADDICTION

Jose Antonio López-Moreno and Kora-Mareen Bühler*

Department of Psychobiology, Faculty of Psychology,
Campus de Somosaguas, Complutense University, Madrid, Spain

ABSTRACT

The endocannabinoid system is distributed throughout the whole body, being the CB1 receptor most highly expressed in the brain. The main function of the endocannabinoid system is the control of other neurotransmitter systems. Its relatively recent discovery has led the major pharmacological companies of the world to search for pharmacological treatments based on this system for many different diseases. One of the most dominant strategies has been the blockade or inverse agonism of the CB1 receptor (e.g., via the drug rimonabant) for the treatment of obesity-related disorders and drug addiction. Many clinical trials were performed in Europe and America, but psychiatric side-effects, mainly anxiety and depression, caused the withdrawal of rimonabant from the market, and several Phase II-III trials testing similar molecules were also stopped. In most cases, stimulation of the cannabinoid receptors is followed by psychoactive effects; these side effects are a major concern regarding the potential therapeutic use of cannabinoid receptor activators. Despite these current issues, a deeper knowledge of the biochemistry of the entire endocannabinoid system, as well as the use of genetic biomarkers in personalised and preventive medicine (pharmacogenetics), could permit the full exploitation of the endocannabinoid system as a pharmacological target for drug addiction. In the present chapter, readers will find an overview of the endocannabinoid system, a summary of some clinical trials focused on the cannabinoid system and drug addiction, a brief description of the rise and fall of rimonabant, and finally, an introduction to the pharmacogenetics of the endocannabinoid system. As a conclusion, we speculate that it is not credible that one of the major regulators of brain neurotransmitters cannot be a pharmacological target for mood disorders and other psychiatric conditions, such as drug addiction.

---

* E-mail: jalopezm@psi.ucm.es

1. INTRODUCTION

The aims of this chapter are threefold: (a) to give the reader an overview of the endocannabinoid system, describing its receptors, its exogenous and endogenous ligands and its enzymes; (b) to provide a summary of the clinical trials that have examined the effectiveness of blockade/stimulation of the endocannabinoid system as a pharmacological target for drug addiction, including a brief description of the first worldwide-marketed molecule based on the antagonism of CB1 receptors (rimonabant); and (c) to introduce the pharmacogenetics of the endocannabinoid system, its two main genes, *CNR1* and *FAAH*, its main transcripts and polymorphisms, and the expected role of the development of personalised and preventive medicine using genetic biomarkers.

2. THE ENDOCANNABINOID SYSTEM

The endocannabinoid system (ECS) is a signalling system distributed throughout the body. It is composed of at least two endocannabinoid receptors (CB1 and CB2); endocannabinoid ligands, such as anandamide and 2- arachidonoylglycerol (2-AG); and enzymes implicated in the inactivation and degradation of these ligands, namely fatty acid amide hydrolase (FAAH) and monoacylglycerol lipase (MAGL) [1, 2].

The main functions of the ECS are the modulation of neurotransmission and the control of certain immunological processes; it is also implicated in metabolism and energy homeostasis, emotional states, and drug abuse [3, 4].

2.1. Endocannabinoid Receptors

To date, two endocannabinoid receptors have been identified and characterised. The CB1 receptor is one of the most abundant receptors in the mammalian brain [5, 6] and is highly conserved across species [7, 8]. These receptors are located mainly in the presynaptic terminals of the central and peripheral nervous systems, primarily in the cerebral cortex, hippocampus, basal ganglia and cerebellum [9]. High densities of the CB1 receptor are also found in pain pathways in the brain and spinal cord. This particular distribution is consistent with the capacity of cannabinoids to affect locomotor activity, alter cognition and memory and produce analgesic effects [10, 11]. CB1 receptors are also present in some peripheral tissues and non-neuronal cells, such as immune cells, the pituitary gland, gastrointestinal tissue, the heart, lung, bladder and adrenal glands [12, 13]. The CB2 receptor is less prevalent in the brain and is predominantly expressed in immune cells, where it modulates immune cell migration and cytokine release [14]. However, CB2 receptors have also been identified in neurons of the brainstem, cortex and cerebellum [15], although the role of these neuronal CB2 receptors remains unknown [16].

The endocannabinoid receptors belong to the superfamily of seven transmembrane-domain GTP-binding protein coupled receptors (GPCRs). Through signalling via Gi/o proteins, both receptors, when activated by an agonist, inhibit adenylate cyclase and stimulate mitogen-activated protein kinases (MAPKS) [17]. In addition, the CB1 receptor can couple to

Ca^{2+} and K^+ ion channels through Gi/o proteins, activating inwardly rectifying K^+ channels and inhibiting voltage-gated Ca^{2+} channels (VGCCs) of most types, such as the P/Q-, N- and L-type channels [18, 19]. Studies in the rat suggest that the type of Ca^{2+} channel to which the CB1 receptor is coupled depends on the brain area. CB1 receptors in the hippocampus seem to be coupled to N- and P/Q-type channels and to only the N-type in the stratum [20, 21]. The ability of the cannabinoid receptors to regulate ion channels is thought to be the mechanism by which the endocannabinoid system inhibits the release of neurotransmitters at the presynaptic site. Furthermore, the CB1 receptor can also couple to Gs proteins and thereby activate adenylate cyclase [22]. In the hippocampus, striatum and globus pallidus tissues, some studies have shown the co-localisation of Gi/o and Gs protein-coupled CB1 receptors [23, 24]. Recently, a study has demonstrated that the selective coupling of CB1 to Gs or Gi proteins is determined by a change in the amino-acid sequence in the second intracellular loop of the CB1 receptor [22]. In the last few years, studies have suggested a potential ability of the CB1 receptor to be modulated allosterically, that is, the receptor not only possesses an orthosteric target site for cannabinoid ligands, but it may also have one or more allosteric sites, where several ligands, such as some dopamine transporter inhibitors, can couple to modify the receptor's active state [25-27].

Although CB1 and CB2 are the best-characterised endocannabinoid receptors, there is much evidence for the existence of other potential endocannabinoid receptors. The transient receptor potential vanilloid type-1 (TRPV1) is one of these non-CB1 and non-CB1-like endocannabinoid receptors.

This cation channel receptor, implicated in mediating pain sensations, is also activated by anandamide, one of the main endocannabinoid ligands [28], as well as by other synthetic CB1/CB2 ligands, and is co-expressed with CB1 receptors in certain primary sensory neurons [7]. Although TRPV1 is not as selectively targeted by cannabinoids as CB1 or CB2, some authors have termed the TRPV1 the "ionotropic cannabinoid receptor" [16]. Another receptor suggested to be a potential endocannabinoid receptor is the orphan G-protein coupled receptor GPR-55 [29, 30].

Although it is one of the most-studied potential novel components of the endocannabinoid system, the reports of its ability to bind with cannabinoid ligands are controversial. This protein is phylogenetically different from CB1 and CB2 and shows very little sequence homology with them. However, it is very well established that AM251, a synthetic CB1 antagonist, acts as an agonist on GPR-55. The GPR-55 receptor is also activated by endogenous cannabinoid ligands, such as anandamide and 2-AG, as well as by some phytocannabinoids, such as delta-9-tetrahydrocannabinol (THC) and cannabidiol (CBD), but, as mentioned before, these results are conflicting and it seems that the binding properties of GPR-55 depend on the tissue and cell in which it is expressed [31]. Other possible targets for cannabinoid ligands have been proposed, such as some types of opioid, adrenergic, dopamine or 5-HT receptors, but the affinity of these receptors for cannabinoid ligands is very low [16].

2.2. Exogenous and Endogenous Cannabinoid Ligands

There is a great variety of cannabinoid ligands, which can be classified into three main categories: endocannabinoids, phytocannabinoids and synthetic cannabinoids (see Table 1).

Table 1. Summary of the main cannabinoid ligands

Type	Category	Compound	Description
Endocannabinoid Agonists		Anandamide (AEA)	CB1, CB2 and TRPV1 agonist
		2-Arachidonoylglycerol (2-AG)	Full CB1 and CB2 agonist
		2-arachidonyl glyceryl ether (Noladin ether)	Full CB1 agonist
		Arachidonoyl dopamine (NADA)	CB1 and TRPV1 agonist. Low affinity for CB2
		Virodhamine	Partial CB1 agonist. Full CB2 agonist
Phytocannabinoid Agonists		Delta-9-tetrahydrocannabinol (Δ^9-THC)	Partial CB1 and CB2 agonist
		Cannabidiol (CBD)	Low affinity for CB1 and CB2
		Cannabinol (CBN)	Week CB1 and CB2 agonist
Synthetic cannabinoids Agonists	Classical	HU-210	CB1 and CB2 agonist
		Nabilone	CB1 and CB2 agonist
	Nonclassical	CP55940	Full CB1 and CB2 agonist
		HU-308	Selective CB2 agonist
	Amino a lkylindoles	WIN 55,212-2	Full CB1 and CB2 agonist
		JWH-015	Selective CB2 agonist
	Eicosanoids	R-methanandamide (AM356)	Selective CB1 agonist
		Arachidonyl-2-chloroethylamide (ACEA)	Selective CB1 agonist
Synthetic cannabinoids Antagonists		Rimonabant (SR141716A)	CB1 inverse agonist/antagonist
		AM251	CB1 inverse agonist/antagonist
Synthetic Re-uptake blockers		AM404	Anandamide uptake blocker
		VDM11	Anandamide uptake blocker
Synthetic FAAH inhibitors		URB597	Irreversible FAAH inhibitor
Synthetic MAGL inhibitors		URB602	Selective MAGL inhibitor

The two best-studied endocannabinoid ligands are the lipids *N*-arachidonoylethanolamide (Anandamide or AEA) and 2-arachidonoylglycerol (2-AG). Anandamide was the first-discovered endogenous agent that coupled to the endocannabinoid receptors [32]. Although anandamide binds to CB1 and CB2, its binding affinity and efficacy is higher for CB1. Depending on the tissue and cell type in which anandamide acts, it can behave as a full or a partial agonist of CB1 receptors [7, 33]. Apart from acting on CB1 and CB2, anandamide can also activate the TRPV1 receptor at the same binding site that capsaicin does, an ability made possible due to the conformational flexibility of its N-alkyl chain [34].

Recent studies suggest that this interaction between anandamide and postsynaptic TRPV1 facilitates long-term depression (LTD) in the hippocampus and the nucleus accumbens [35]. Nevertheless, under certain conditions, anandamide may also bind to other non-cannabinoid receptors, such as GPR-55 and GPR119. Another very well-studied endocannabinoid ligand is 2-AG. This compound was discovered shortly after anandamide [36, 37] and was therefore the second endocannabinoid ligand described. The 2-AG compound is a full CB1/CB2 agonist, with approximately the same affinity for both receptors. In comparison to anandamide, 2-AG has greater potency and efficacy for the CB2 receptor and is present at much higher basal levels in the brain [37]. Therefore, many authors have proposed that 2-AG is the real natural ligand for CB1 and CB2 [38].

Both endocannabinoids are formed and released on demand, that is, they are not stored in vesicles like other neurotransmitters. Commonly, 2-AG and AEA are released from the postsynaptic cell and target presynaptic receptors, acting as retrograde signals that allow modulation of synaptic activity. After activation of the postsynaptic neuron, AEA and 2-AG are synthesised from different phospholipids inside the cell. The 2-AG signal is formed from the hydrolysis of 1,2-diacylglycerol (DAG) by *sn*-1 selective DAG lipases and is immediately released into the synaptic cleft [39, 40]. The biosynthetic pathway for AEA is not fully understood, and several different mechanisms for the formation of this endocannabinoid have been proposed. The most accepted hypothesis is that AEA is generated through the catalysis of N-arachidonoyl-phosphatidylethanolamine (NAPE) by selective phosphodiesterase (NAPE-PLD) [41]. Once 2-AG and AEA have exerted their action on the target receptor (CB1, CB2, or other potential cannabinoid receptors), they are re-absorbed by clearly identified elements into the pre- or postsynaptic cells to be degraded. It is known that 2-AG is mainly metabolised by MAGL, which is localised in the presynaptic neuron, to form arachidonic acid and glycerol, whereas anandamide is decomposed in the postsynaptic cell into arachidonic acid and ethanolamine by the FAAH enzyme [42]. Many other endocannabinoids have been identified, such as 2-arachidonyl glyceryl ether (noladin ether), arachidonoyl dopamine (NADA) and virodhamine, but their mechanisms of action, pharmacological profiles and characterisation require further investigation [18]. Phytocannabinoids are naturally occurring cannabinoids found in the *Cannabis Sativa* plant; over 60 of these different cannabinoid compounds have been identified and isolated. One of the most popular and best-studied phytocannabinoids is THC, which is the main psychotropic compound of cannabis and a partial CB1 and CB2 agonist [43]. In contrast, CBD, another frequently studied cannabinoid, has low to no affinity for any of the endocannabinoid receptors but still induces cannabimimetic effects. However, it has been shown that CBD displays a high ability to antagonise cannabinoid receptor agonists [39, 44].

The identification and characterisation of THC and the cannabinoid receptors has led to the development of numerous synthetic compounds that act as agonists or antagonists for both, or selectively for just one, of the cannabinoid receptors, although some can also target certain non-cannabinoid receptors. Most of these synthetic cannabinoids have a higher affinity, efficacy and metabolic stability than phyto- and endocannabinoids and are usually used for research and therapeutic purposes [45].

Synthetic cannabinoid agonists are classified into four different categories: classical, non-classical, aminoalkylindoles and eicosanoids [7, 12, 16]. The group of classical cannabinoids is composed of molecules that keep the tricyclic diterpene structure of THC. Included in this group are the synthetic analogues of THC, HU-210 and nabilone. Both compounds display higher affinity for both receptors than THC. Non-classical cannabinoids are characterised by bicyclic and tricyclic molecular analogues of THC that lack a pyran ring. CP55940 is one of the most well-known members of this group and has affinity for both endocannabinoid receptors, although this affinity is slightly lower in comparison to HU210 [16].

The aminoalkylindoles are less similar to THC and to classical and non-classical cannabinoids in their chemical structures. The main representative molecule of this group is WIN 55,212-2, which is also a dual CB1 and CB2 agonist, but with slightly higher affinity for CB2 [13, 16, 46]. Finally, eicosanoids are much more similar in their chemical structure to endogenous cannabinoids (such as anandamide and 2-AG) than to THC or aminoalkylindoles. Examples of members of this group are R-methanandamide (AM356) and arachidonyl-2-chloroethylamide (ACEA) [7]. Aside from the wide range of synthetic cannabinoid agonists, there are also a variety of synthetic antagonists. One of the best known compounds of this type is rimonabant (SR141716A). Although it can couple to CB1 and CB2, its affinity is much higher for CB1, on which it acts as an inverse agonist in a competitive manner.

In this sense, rimonabant not only reduces the capacity of the CB1 receptor to be activated by an agonist, it also induces some inverse cannabimimetic CB1-like effects [47]. Other known antagonists with a relatively high selectivity for CB1 are taranabant, AM251 and AM281.

There are other synthetic compounds that do not directly act on receptors but display agonistic functions, raising the levels of cannabinoids by inhibiting their degradation. These compounds are therefore called indirect agonists. The main indirect agonists that have been developed include re-uptake blockers and inhibitors of FAAH and MAGL, two enzymes that are responsible for the hydrolysis of cannabinoids such as anandamide and 2-AG [for review see 48, 49].

2.3. Endocannabinoid Enzymes

Once the endocannabinoid ligands have exerted their action on the receptors, they are inactivated by FAAH and MAGL. However, several recent studies have demonstrated that AEA and 2-AG can also be metabolised through oxygenation by cyclooxygenases (COX) into prostaglandin-ethanolamine and prostaglandin-glycerol ester, respectively, and by lipoxygenases (12- LOX and 15-LOX) to form 12- and 15-hydroperoxy derivatives [50, 45]. FAAH is a postsynaptic integral membrane protein that belongs to the amidase protein family.

This enzyme is responsible for the degradation of AEA into its two components, arachidonic acid and ethanolamine, although FAAH has been shown to also metabolise 2-AG *in vitro* [45].

In humans, FAAH is widely expressed in the brain and in some peripheral tissues such as the pancreas and kidneys [51, 42]. Moreover, the FAAH distribution in the brain is highly complementary to CB1 expression, as several tissues with an elevated expression of CB1 are also rich in FAAH [42], although there are also some areas with high FAAH but very low or no expression of CB1. This observation might be due to the presence of targets for anandamide other than CB1 (for instance, TRPV1). The existence of a second FAAH isoform was established in 2006 [52].

This protein is called FAAH-2 and is primarily found in cardiac tissue; it shares approximately 20% sequence identity with FAAH-1 [52]. MAGL is presynaptically located in the adult brain and is the primary enzyme for the hydrolysis of 2-AG, decomposing it into glycerol and arachidonic acid. Like FAAH, MAGL is highly co-expressed with CB1 throughout the brain, particularly in the hippocampus, cerebral cortex, anterior thalamus and cerebellum [53].

A third enzyme implicated in endocannabinoid inactivation is the N-acylethanolamine acid amidase (NAAA). However, although anandamide can be degraded by this protein, it is far from being one of the main active substrates. NAAA is practically inactive for 2-AG [54].

3. CANNABINOID-BASED THERAPIES FOR DRUG ADDICTION

Drug addiction is a complex problem. First, there are several addictive drugs that act differently in the nervous system; these include nicotine, alcohol, THC and cocaine, all of which are used in most parts of the world. Second, it is a problem characterised by its chronicity: addicted individuals remain in periods of abstinence, relapsing and experiencing perpetual craving feelings as well as maladaptive strategies. Third, addicted individuals suffer brain changes that, in many cases, become irreversible. Fourth, why some individuals become addicted and others regain control over the drug remains elusive. All of these factors, and others, explain the reduced number of drugs approved for the treatment of addiction; as an example, there are currently no medications specifically indicated for treating cocaine dependence.

The relatively recent discovery of the endocannabinoid system, its ubiquitous presence in the brain and its role in neurotransmitter release and other processes of cellular signalling pointed to this system as an excellent candidate pharmacological target for drug addiction. The hunt for molecules based on the endocannabinoid system had begun. Hundreds of researchers worldwide and the most important pharmacological companies had focused their efforts on the quest for cannabinoid-based therapies, among them, therapies for drug addiction. We will start this part of the chapter with a description of the rise and fall of rimonabant, a molecule that generated the greatest anticipation to date. Subsequently, published clinical trials covering the endocannabinoid system and nicotine, alcohol, THC and cocaine addiction will be reviewed. Finally, we will discuss the pharmacogenetics of the endocannabinoid system. This last subject is in accord with the expected pharmacology of the future, which will be based on personalised and preventive medicine using genetic biomarkers.

3.1. The Rise and Fall of Rimonabant

We consider it of interest to describe the "story" of rimonabant, as it was the first pharmacological treatment approved in Europe and in many other countries that was based on the blockade of the endocannabinoid system, specifically on the antagonism of CB1 receptors. This treatment was viewed as having great potential. The rimonabant molecule was patented in 1993, and its first description was in 1994 [55, 56]. Initially, the focus of the

French multinational pharmaceutical company Sanofi was to demonstrate that the use of rimonabant was effective for the treatment of obesity-related disorders. With this aim, Sanofi supported clinical trials in which more than 6,000 individuals were enrolled in Europe and North America (Rimonabant in Obesity – RIO studies).

In other clinical trials, Sanofi supported a series of studies to demonstrate the potential benefits of rimonabant for nicotine addiction. These studies, known by the acronym STRATUS (Studies with Rimonabant and Tobacco Use), were performed before 2007 and included two phase-III trials in which approximately 1,600 subjects participated, half of them in Europe and the other half in the United States. The results of these studies showed that rimonabant increased abstinence rates and reduced the weight gain that occurs after smoking cessation [57], but other results were never disclosed. When rimonabant was approved in Europe in 2006 for the treatment of obesity-related disorders, the indication of rimonabant for treating tobacco dependence was not included. Likely, Sanofi-Aventis was expecting that after the approval of rimonabant for obesity-related disorders and the conclusion of further experiments (STRATUS), it would be prescribed as an "off-label" medication [57]. The uses of rimonabant as a treatment for smoking cessation and the maintenance of abstinence were never included in the original submissions for approval in Europe and, as described below, the Food and Drug Administration (FDA) of the United States explicitly rejected rimonabant's use for these purposes.

However, in Europe, these potential uses for rimonabant were included in the Scientific Discussion Report submitted to the European Medicines Agency (EMEA) in 2006. There, the potential usefulness of rimonabant for the treatment of nicotine addiction was argued based on the results from animal models, and one experiment was described in which it was demonstrated that daily treatment with rimonabant for 8 days did not alter the pharmacokinetics of nicotine. Rimonabant was launched in 2006 for the treatment of obesity-related disorders as its only indication in many countries worldwide, including India, Argentina and several European countries. However, it was never sold in the United States, despite the high interest of the French pharmaceutical company. In April 2005, Sanofi submitted a new drug application to the Division of Metabolism and Endocrinology Products (DMEP) based on Zimulti (the American trade-name of rimonabant) in the United States. Its advisory panel raised several safety concerns. More than one year later, on 26 October 2006, Sanofi submitted a complete response addressing the panel's concerns and also including some new data. Finally, on 13 June 2007, the same advisory panel decided to vote against the approval of rimonabant for its original indication. The rejection of rimonabant for the treatment of smoking dependence was even earlier, in February of 2006. In Europe, the circumstances were vastly different.

Rimonabant was more or less successfully marketed in 13 European countries. Its pharmacological form was as 20 mg film-coated tablets, and its main excipient was lactose (115 mg). It was packaged either in blisters or bottles for oral administration. On 25 April 2005, Sanofi submitted an application for marketing authorisation to the EMEA for Acomplia (the Europe trade-mark of rimonabant). Approximately one year later, on 27 April 2006, Acomplia received a positive opinion from the EMEA's Committee for Medicinal Products for Human Use but with the request that Sanofi should monitor rimonabant-induced psychiatric side effects, particularly depression. On 19 June 2006, the European Commission approved a marketing authorisation for Acomplia to be indicated as an adjunct to diet and exercise for the treatment of obese or overweight patients. However, in the summary of the product, some warnings about mood alterations, depressive symptoms and the induction of depressive disorders could already be read. It seemed that cannabinoid-antagonism-induced weight loss was associated with Acomplia's central effects.

On 7 July 2007, in a first press release, the EMEA recommended contraindicating rimonabant in patients with on-going major depression or who were being treated with antidepressants. On 23 November 2008, in a second press release, the EMEA's Committee for Medicinal Products for Human Use concluded that the risk of depression was approximately doubled in patients taking rimonabant as compared with a placebo. As a result, the Committee stated that the benefits of rimonabant were no longer outweighing its risks, and the marketing authorisation should be suspended. Approximately three weeks later, Sanofi decided to voluntarily withdraw its marketing authorisation in the European Union, as was previously done in the United States. Finally, on 30 January 2009, the European Commission corroborated the decision to withdraw the marketing authorisation for rimonabant. Today, we can read on each rimonabant-document from the EMEA: "Medicinal product no longer authorised". It was not just rimonabant and Sanofi that followed this pattern of rise and fall. Other CB1 receptor antagonists were also withdrawn from Phase II and III trials, such as Otenabanat (from Pfizer), Ibipinabant (discovered by Solvay and licensed to Bristol-Myers Squibb) and Surinabant (also from Sanofi). This last molecule was similar to rimonabant, having only two differences between both molecules [58]. In reality, Surinabant was planned as a backup of rimonabant, with the intention of preserving the economic profit of the patent, due to the 20-year validity of patents and the fact that rimonabant was patented in the mid-1990s.

The final example is taranabant, a molecule patented by the German company Merck. Merck, like other pharmaceutical companies, was in competition with Sanofi for the development of treatments for obesity-related disorders based on the blockade of the endocannabinoid system. Similarly to Sanofi's molecule, taranabant is a CB1 inverse antagonist and is also able to reach the brain. Low/moderate doses (4-6 mg per day) cause approximately 30% receptor occupancy in healthy individuals [59]. In October 2006, taranabant entered Phase III trials for obesity, and by May 2008, Phase II trials for smoking cessation were completed [60]. However, on 2 October 2008, a Merck press release announced that they would discontinue all taranabant clinical trials and would not seek its FDA approval. Published studies [61] have reported that taranabant, most likely due to its ability to penetrate the central nervous system, caused an increase of psychiatric and gastrointestinal-related symptoms as well as flushing. The minor effect on abstinence from smoking was due, in many cases, to the nausea and feelings of illness that the participants reported. Again, as in the case of rimonabant, taranabant was effective at preventing weight gain, but its physiological and psychiatric effects did not outweigh its risks.

3.2. The Endocannabinoid System As a Pharmacological Target for THC, Alcohol, Nicotine and Cocaine Addiction: Clinical Trials

3.2.1. Cannabinoid Agonists As Replacement Therapy for Marijuana Dependence and Other Uses for Drug Addiction

Drug replacement therapies are characterised by a change of the main active chemical compound linked to the drug addiction phenotype to another compound that either causes a longer-acting but less euphoric effect (e.g., opioid replacement therapy with methadone), or to another route of administration, which consequently alters its pharmacokinetics and psychophysiological effects (e.g., nicotine replacement therapy with gum or patches). This pharmacological approach has also been used for cannabis dependence. Dronabinol, a synthetic and orally active form of THC, has been proven to be effective in preventing withdrawal symptoms in cannabis-dependent individuals, but it failed to prevent marijuana use or to achieve abstinence during a clinical trial of 12 weeks [62]. Similar results have been obtained in other trials and with human laboratory models after oral THC administration [63, 64]. Cannabis users reduce some of their withdrawal symptoms as well as mood parameters, such as anxiety and sleep troubles. Intriguingly, some withdrawal symptoms, irritability among them, remain unaltered by oral THC treatment. Therefore, as an overall conclusion, oral THC seems to be effective in preventing some withdrawal symptoms but may not be effective in reducing smoked cannabis or in improving abstinence [62-65]. This conclusion raises at least three concerns about oral THC replacement therapy: first, the improvement of withdrawal symptoms should be attributed to reducing negative reinforcement processes; the negative mood should be eliminated. Second, the typical cannabis-induced withdrawal symptoms are more subtle than other those of drugs such as opioids, alcohol and nicotine. Third, the heart rate is increased after cannabinoid agonist treatment.

The use of cannabinoid receptor agonists may also have other particularities that should be taken into account. As with any drug, there is the placebo effect, that is, a greater clinical benefit or response that cannot be attributed to the compound by itself. The opposite case is the nocebo effect. Both effects should be attributed, in part, to the expectancies of the subjects enrolled in the trial. Using THC or marijuana in clinical settings may have unpredictable outcomes. It has been demonstrated that manipulating the information given to the subjects, creating expectancies that they would intake THC, placebo or even another drug, changed the subjective and physiological effects of THC. Those participants who expected to receive THC reported greater pleasurable effects and a higher increase in their heart rate after THC oral intake [66-68]. This result suggests that subjective and physiological effects are modulated by expectancies, indicating that clinical and recreational settings of THC intake should be considered because in both contexts, there are dramatic differences in personal expectancies. As a conclusion, the patient's past experience and information about THC or marijuana may change the therapeutic or adverse effects of medicinal cannabinoid treatment. Supporting this idea, it has been reported that cannabis-dependent individuals display greater relaxation and social facilitation expectancies than non-addicted users, and that patients suffering different psychiatric disorders, such as depression, panic and anxiety disorders or psychosis, expected the worst effects after THC consumption [64, 70]. Even improved or impaired functioning has been associated with positive/negative expectancies [71].

Drug-addicted individuals show an attentional bias to drug stimuli. For example, they process these stimuli faster, reflecting an automatic or non-conscious processing [72, 73]. In other cases, the drug-related stimulus is able to provoke physiological changes, such as an increase of heart rate, skin conductance, and/or respiratory rate. All of these facts reflect that drug-addicted individuals are, to some extent, under the control of conditioned stimuli that, eventually, may induce drug use and relapse [74, 75]. Therefore, it seems that pharmacological treatment based on the endocannabinoid system should take into consideration this evidence. Interestingly, cannabis users show an attentional bias for food-related stimuli. This bias is linked to the repetitive demonstration that acute intake of THC causes an increase of appetite [76, 77]. CBD, which is one of the main constituents of the plant *Cannabis Sativa* and works as an indirect antagonist, has been proposed as a treatment for cannabis dependence as well as other addictive disorders [78]. CBD is able to reduce the attentional bias to drug and food stimuli after cannabinoid intake. This fact suggests that smoked cannabis could produce different results depending on the concentration of THC. Cannabis with a high content of THC would cause the expected drug-induced attentional bias, whereas Cannabis with a high content of CBD could reduce this effect. According to Morgan et al., [78] higher CBD may reduce the salience, or intensity of drug-related stimuli relative to other stimuli, thereby reducing the associative learning. These results were produced by analysing the levels of THC and CBD in the smoked cannabis of each cannabis user who participated in the study; this analysis showed a relationship between higher concentrations of CBD and lower attentional bias to drug- and food-related stimuli. A third main constituent of the plant Cannabis sativa, cannabinol, which functions as a cannabinoid agonist, increases the drugged, drunk, dizzy, and drowsy feelings of THC intake [79, 80].

THC in combination with Modafinil has been studied for the treatment of cannabis addiction (Modafinil is a psychostimulant compound approved for the treatment of narcolepsy and sleep-apnea). Due to methodological limitations, the results were inconclusive [81]. The authors hypothesised that due to cognitive impairments in cannabis-dependent individuals, a combination of THC with a medication enhancing cognitive function, such as Modafinil, may be useful for cannabis addiction [81, 82]. To the best of our knowledge, there have been no published clinical trials concerning the effectiveness of cannabinoid-based therapies on cocaine addiction. However, we consider it of interest to highlight two studies. First, Ghitza and colleagues [83] have shown that methadone-maintained patients who did not report THC use were associated with higher levels of cocaine consumption (77.6%) than individuals reporting THC use (65.7%). Based on their "unexpected" results, the authors concluded that non-reporting of THC use is a significant predictor of greater cocaine use in methadone-maintained patients. Second, Lukas et al., [84] demonstrated that THC increases plasma cocaine levels and subjective reports of euphoria. Cocaine use was also associated with a higher increase in THC-induced tachycardia than THC alone. This exacerbated tachycardia may explain why non-reporting THC use is a significant predictor of greater cocaine use. The mechanism that would explain the THC-induced higher rate of cocaine absorption is that THC-induced vasodilation of the nasal mucosa attenuates the vasoconstrictive effects of cocaine [84].

3.2.2. Cannabinoid Antagonists As Pharmacological Therapies for Drug Addiction

The orally active cannabinoid CB1 receptor antagonist, rimonabant, is effective in reducing the two most reliable biomarkers of THC consumption: heart rate and subjective effects (feeling high) [85]. Either an acute 90 mg/kg dose of rimonabant or chronic 40 mg/kg doses over 8 days can reduce smoked marijuana-induced tachycardia (approximately 60%) and marijuana's subjective effects (approximately 14-29%) [86, 87]. These effects do not seem to be related to changes in the pharmacokinetics of rimonabant, which has a long half-life that is estimated to be between approximately 6-7 days and a maximum of 32 [88]. Similarly, THC co-administration with respect to plasma levels of THC and its primary inactive metabolite THCCOOH also remain unaltered. However, the blockade of the THC-induced 'high' feeling by rimonabant disappears after 15 days. This result reveals that there are some effects that show tolerance to rimonabant, while others do not, suggesting that subjective effects are more sensitive. Therefore, if we consider that drug addiction is a chronic phenomenon in which the formation of pleasure memories and feelings of craving play a key role, it would be conceivable to conclude that rimonabant would not be effective in the treatment of cannabis dependence. Rimonabant at a dosage of 20 mg daily given for 9 weeks in combination with a nicotine patch is superior to rimonabant in combination with a placebo patch. It increases smoking cessation rates over rimonabant alone, and the adverse effects are similar between the placebo and nicotine patch groups. In a sample of more than 700 smokers, depression- and anxiety-related adverse events occurred in approximately 4% and 6% of patients, respectively [89]. Interestingly, and in accordance with previous reports, there was little post-cessation weight gain in either of the rimonabant groups. Other studies of the blockade of CB1 receptors and nicotine addiction were described in the previous section titled "the rise and fall of rimonabant".

A high number of preclinical studies have shown that the CB1 receptor modulates alcohol-related behaviours: (a) cannabinoid receptor agonists increase alcohol consumption in rats [90-92] ; (b) cannabinoid receptor antagonists reduce operant alcohol self-administration, alcohol intake, the motivation to consume alcohol, and prevent the acquisition of drinking behaviour and block the alcohol deprivation effect in rats [93]; (c) mice lacking the CB1 receptor show less preference for alcohol and higher concentrations of ethanol in the blood [94] as well as reduced alcohol self-administration and increased alcohol sensitivity [95, 96]. In humans, it is well known that THC and alcohol are often used together [97]. Alcohol increases plasma THC levels, resulting in an increase in the positive subjective mood effects [98]. However, despite the large number of preclinical studies revealing a robust relationship between alcohol and the entire endocannabinoid system, at present, only two clinical trials based on the blockade of the endocannabinoid system have been published. In the first study, the authors enrolled treatment-seeking patients (in this case, detoxified alcohol-dependent patients), and the patients received a double dose of 10 mg/day for twelve weeks. The authors reported only a modest effect with respect to the relapse rate, and more patients in the rimonabant group completed treatment compared to the placebo group, but statistically significant differences were not achieved [99]. In the second study, the authors enrolled non-treatment-seeking heavy alcohol drinkers, and the sample size was modest. Rimonabant was administered at a dosage of 20 mg/day for 2 weeks, and there was no observed effect on alcohol consumption [100].

These data reduced the positive expectancies with regards to the blockade or inverse agonism of CB1 receptors as effective pharmacological treatments for alcoholism. Nevertheless, that does not mean that the endocannabinoid system is not valid as a therapeutic target for alcohol-related disorders or other drug addiction disorders. The endocannabinoid system was only recently discovered, and there is still much to learn about it.

4. A BRIEF INTRODUCTION TO THE GENETICS OF THE ENDOCANNABINOID SYSTEM

In this subheading, we will focus on only two of the most relevant genes of the endocannabinoid system: the *CNR1* and *FAAH* genes. *CNR1* is the name approved by the HUGO Gene Nomenclature Committee (HGNC) for the CB1 receptor gene in humans. According to the Ensembl database (release 59), the *CNR1* gene is located on chromosome 6 (Figure 1a), in cytogenetic band 6q15. However, the HGNC and Entrez Gene – National Center for Biotechnology Information (NCBI, build 37) databases place the *CNR1* gene in cytogenetic band 6q14-15 [101]. The *CNR1* gene encodes the CB1 receptor (Figure 1b). There are three known isoforms that are produced by alternative splicing of the *CNR1* transcript. Isoform 1, also known as the long isoform, contains the 472 amino acids depicted in Figure 1b, and is considered the 'canonical' isoform. The CB1 receptor is a multi-pass transmembrane protein with eight topological domains (four extracellular and four cytoplasmic) that belongs to the superfamily of seven transmembrane domain proteins.

FAAH is the symbol approved by HGNC for the fatty acid amide hydrolase gene in humans. The *FAAH* gene is located on chromosome 1 in cytogenetic band 1p33 according to the Ensembl database (release 59) [101]. The HGNC and Entrez Gene (NCBI, build 37) databases place it in cytogenetic band 1p35-p34 (Figure 2a).

The *FAAH* gene encodes a transcript containing 15 exons that produces a homomeric single-pass membrane protein of 579 amino acids (Figure 2b). As can be observed, this enzyme has three topological domains (two cytoplasmic and one extracellular), one transmembrane domain, and a large intramembrane domain of 374 amino acids.

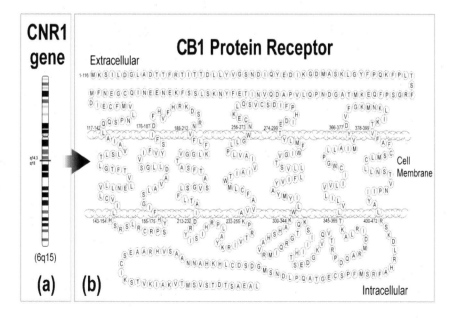

Figure 1. Molecular structure of the CB1 receptor.

Table 2. SNPs from the *CNR1* and *FAAH* genes and their characteristics according to the Entrez Gene human database

	Total Range	Total Length	MIM	Protein Product Length	Processed Length	mRNA Product Length
CNR1	88,849,583..88,855,056	5,474	114610			
mRNA- variant 1	88,849,583..88,855,056	5,474				5,486
mRNA-variant 2	88,849,583..88,855,056	5,474				5,307
protein isoform a	88,853,575..88,854,993	1,419		472		
protein isoform b	88,853,575..88,854,977	1,403		411	1,236	
FAAH	46,859,939..46,879,520	19,582	602935			
mRNA	46,859,939..46,879,520	19,582				2,105
protein isoform	46,860,021..46,879,247	19,227		579	1,74	

CNR1		
SNPs at isoform a	Allele	Total Length
rs1049353	A/G	1
rs1049355	A/T	1
rs1049356	A/C	1
rs12720071	A/G	1

FAAH			
SNP	Location	Allele	Total Length
rs12094805	mRNA	A/G	1
rs12094805	Protein	R	1
rs324419	mRNA	C/T	1
rs324420	mRNA	A/C	1

	Total Range	Total Length	MIM	Protein Product Length	Processed Length	mRNA Product Length
CNR1			**FAAH**			
SNPs at isoform a	Allele	Total Length	SNP	Location	Allele	Total Length
rs16880248	A/C	1	rs324420	Protein	T	1
rs2269	A/T	1	rs41305628	mRNA	A/G	1
rs35057475	A/G	1	rs61744669	mRNA	A/G	1
rs45516291	A/C	1	rs61744669	Protein	X	1
rs4707436	C/T	1	rs72480613	mRNA	A/G	1
rs62417860	A/C	1	rs72890799	mRNA	C/G	1
rs6911472	G/T	1	rs74783386	mRNA	C/G	1
rs73481138	G/T	1	rs75170991	mRNA	C/T	1
rs77016054	G	1	rs7524148	mRNA	A/G	1
rs7738931	A/C	1	rs7524148	Protein	T	1
rs78783387	E	1	rs75429705	mRNA	C/G	1
rs806368	A/G	1	rs75429705	Protein	G/T	1
INDEL rs11450775	-/T; deletion length=2	2	rs76972904	mRNA	C/T	1
INDEL rs34228304	-/G; deletion length=2	2	rs77101686	mRNA	C/T	1
INDEL rs34532735	-/C; deletion length=2	2	rs77101686	Protein	V	1
INDEL rs34669085	-/T; deletion length=2	2	rs77520097	mRNA	C/T	1
INDEL rs35947856	-/C; deletion length=2	2	rs77724956	mRNA	G/T	1

Table 2. (Continued)

	Total Range	Total Length	MIM	Protein Product Length	Processed Length	mRNA Product Length
CNR1			FAAH			
SNPs at isoform a	Allele	Total Length	SNP	Location	Allele	Total Length
INDEL rs71804102	-/A; deletion length=2	2	rs78072734	mRNA	A/G	1
INDEL rs72558793	-/T; deletion length=2	2	rs78551629	mRNA	A/G	1
			rs78726197	mRNA	C/G	1
			rs78726197	Protein	V	1
			rs78984535	mRNA	A/G	1
			rs79912673	mRNA	C/T	1
			INDEL rs34820226	mRNA	-/C; deletion length=2	1
			INDEL rs34820226	Protein	deletion length=0	1
			NAMED rs71694534	mRNA	(LARGE DELETION)/-	1
			NAMED rs71694534	Protein	-	1

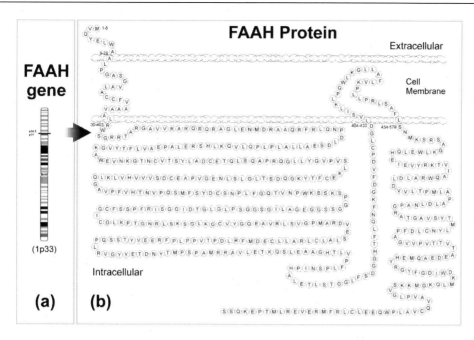

Figure 2. Molecular structure of the FAAH protein.

Amino acids 238–241 of the intramembrane domain make up the substrate binding site. The *CNR1* and *FAAH* genes have several Single Nucleotide Polymorphisms (SNPs). A SNP is a change in the DNA sequence that affects only a single nucleotide. In fact, a SNP is the smallest genetic variation that we can report and, depending critically on its position, a SNP can alter the functionality or expression of a protein. Table 2 summarises the SNPs of the *CNR1* and *FAAH* genes and their characteristics according to the Entrez Gene (NCBI, build 37) human database.

Table 3 summarises the SNPs from the *CNR1* and *FAAH* genes that have been studied since 2006, are available through PubMed and have been significantly associated at least once with drug addiction.

Table 3. SNPs from the CNR1 and FAAH genes that have been studied since 2006, are available through PubMed and have been significantly associated at least once with drug addiction

SNP	Phenotype	Authors	Finding
		CNR1	
rs12720071	Nicotine Dependence (ND)	X. Chen et al. (2008) [102]	Female-specific associations with ND
rs6454674	Cocaine dependence (CD)	L. Zuo et al. (2009) [103]	The interaction between this SNP (G/G or G/T) and rs806368 (T/T) significantly increases risk for CD
	Substance Dependence (SD)	L. Zuo et al. (2007) [104]	Risk for SD significantly increased with the number of "G" alleles,

Table 3. (Continued)

SNP	Phenotype	Authors	Finding
rs2023239	Cannabis dependence	F.M. Filbey et al. (2010) [105]	Carriers of the G allele had significantly greater neural response (fMRI) in reward-related areas of the brain during exposure to marijuana cues.
	Cannabis dependence and Alcohol consumption.	H.M. Haughey et al. (2008) [106]	T/C carriers report higher marijuana dependency scores, higher quantity and frequency of marijuana use and greater craving at abstinence, post-abstinence and post-cue exposure.
	CB1 receptor binding levels in postmortem brains. Brain activation and rewarding effects of alcohol.	K.E. Hutchison et al. (2008) [107]	Individuals with the C/T genotype demonstrated significantly greater CB1 binding in Brodmann areas 9 and 10, greater activation of mesocorticolimbic neurocircuitry and greater reward and positive affect after drinking.

	CNR1		
	Smoking Initiation (SI) and Nicotine Dependence (ND).	X. Chen et al. (2008) [102]	Sex-specific associations with SI and nominal association with ND
	Alcohol use and cue-reactivity after alcohol exposure.	E. van den Wildenberg et al. (2007) [108]	The C allele group tended to report more craving for alcohol during the alcohol exposure. The C allele participants low on baseline saliva production showed a larger beverage effect (due to a higher salivary reactivity after alcohol exposure).
rs1535255	Cannabis, cocaine, opioid, alcohol and polysubstance dependence.	A.I. Herman et al. (2006) [109]	Modest association with alcohol dependence (without comorbid drug dependence).
rs1049353	Cannabis dependence	C.A. Hartman et al. (2009) [110]	Nominal association between the C allele and cannabis dependence symptoms for the entire sample and Caucasian sample, but no for the Hispanic sample.

SNP	Phenotype	Authors	Finding
	Cocaine dependence (CD) and cocaine-induced paranoia (CIP)	L. Zuo et al. (2009) [103]	Nominally significant association with CIP
	Nicotine Dependence (ND).	X. Chen et al. (2008) [102]	Female-specific associations with ND
rs806380	Cannabis dependence	A. Agrawal et al. (2009) [111]	SNP significantly associated with cannabis dependence.
	Cannabis dependence	C.J. Hopfer et al. (2006) [112]	SNP significantly associated with developing one or morecannabis dependence symptoms, with the G allele having a protective effect. The SNP is significantly associated with problem cannabis use
rs806379	Cannabis dependence	A. Agrawal et al. (2009) [111]	SNP marginally associated with cannabis dependence.
rs806375	Antisocial drug dependence	R.P.Corley et al. (2008) [113]	Nominally significant.
rs806371	Cocaine dependence (CD)	L. Zuo et al. (2009) [103]	Significant association with CD

CNR1			
rs806368	Cannabis dependence	A. Agrawal et al. (2009) [111]	SNP significantly associated with cannabis dependence.
	Cocaine dependence (CD)	L. Zuo et al. (2009) [103]	The interaction between this SNP (T/T) and rs6454674 (G/G or G/T) significantly increases risk for CD .
	Smoking Initiation (SI) and Nicotine Dependence (ND).	X. Chen et al. (2008) [102]	Nominally significant in the women for the FTND
	Substance Dependence (SD).	L. Zuo et al. (2007) [104]	Significant interaction effects between this SNP (T/T) and rs6454674 (G/G or G/T) for comorbid DD and AD, for DD, and for AD.
rs754387	Cannabis dependence	A. Agrawal et al. (2009) [111]	SNP associated with cannabis dependence.

FAAH			
rs3766246	Amphetamine mood response	A.M. Dlugos et al. (2010) [114]	Association with higher self-reported arousal in response to amphetamine. Subjects with the C/C genotype showed significantly greater decrease in fatigue after 10 mg amphetamine administration.

Table 3. (Continued)

SNP	Phenotype	Authors	Finding
rs2295633	Amphetamine mood response	A.M. Dlugos et al. (2010) [114]	Association with higher self-reported arousal in response to amphetamine. Subjects with the C/C genotype showed significantly greater decrease in fatigue after 10 mg amphetamine administration.
rs324420	Cannabis dependence	F.M. Filbey et al. (2010) [115]	Carriers of the C/C genotype had greater neural response (fMRI) in reward-related areas of the brain during exposure to marijuana cues.
	Amphetamine mood response	A.M. Dlugos et al. (2010) [114]	Subjects with the C/C genotype showed significantly greater decrease in fatigue after 10 mg amphetamine administration.
	Marijuana Withdrawal	J.P. Schacht et al. (2009) [116]	C/C individuals reported more severe withdrawal symptoms than A/A and A/C individuals, after marijuana abstinence.

FAAH			
			Subjects with the C/C genotype displayed an increase in happiness after smoking marijuana. Craving did not differ between genotype groups.
	Marijuana Dependency and Alcohol consumption.	H.M. Haughey et al. (2008) [106]	The C/C group demonstrated a greater increase in craving post-abstinence.
	Drug use: tried, regular, and dependentIn all and those who tried cannabis: Cannabis dependence. Regular use of alcohol, hallucinogen, nicotine, opiate, sedative, stimulant.	R.F. Tyndale et al. (2007) [117]	Subjects with the A/A genotype who tried cannabis were significantly less likely to be cannabis dependent. Subjects with the A/A genotype were significantly more likely to report regular use of sedatives.
	Drug addiction	J.M. Flanagan et al. (2006) [118]	Significant contribution of the P129T homozygous (A/A) mutant carrier state to multiple drug addiction.

5. PHARMACOGENETICS BASED ON THE ENDOCANNABINOID SYSTEM

There are many differences among individuals in the ways that they respond to a drug, and this is presumably due to the fact that individuals are different. For example, the response to antidepressant treatment is mediated by genetic variants of the *CNR1* gene [119]. Therefore, genetic diversity would be one factor explaining the origin of differing responses to the same drug. The endocannabinoid system has genetic variants, specific genetic polymorphisms that can lead to changes in the expressed protein, such as the CB1 receptor or the FAAH enzyme. Genetic variants in the *CNR1* and *FAAH* genes cause alterations in their activity or their expression. For instance, the microsatellite polymorphism triplet repetition (AAT)n, located in a flanking 3' region of the *CNR1* gene, causes an alteration in gene transcription, ultimately leading to downregulation of *CNR1* gene expression. This change in transcription occurs when there are long alleles with high numbers of AAT triplets [120, 121]. This phenomenon suggests that pharmacological compounds based on the activation or blockade of the CB1 receptor, such as those described earlier in this chapter, would show different responses depending on the number of AAT triplets an individual possesses. It is plausible to assume that individuals with higher AAT triplet repetitions in *CNR1*, that is, with a downregulation of *CNR1* gene expression, would display lower undesirable effects under higher doses of cannabinoid receptor agonists/antagonists than individuals with a lower number of AAT triplets.

Two more examples can be found in *CNR1* SNPs. The *CNR1* rs1049353 SNP is a silent nucleotide change (1359G→A) that produces a threonine residue at codon 453 (Thr453Thr). Despite the fact that this SNP is synonymous, it could still affect mRNA stability or translation, resulting in an alteration of CB1 receptor function [122]. The *CNR1* rs2023239 SNP is an intronic SNP that consists of a T to C substitution that results in higher expression levels, causing an increase in the number of CB1 receptors in several areas of the brain [108]. The AAT triplet repetitions and *CNR1* rs1049353 and rs2023239 SNPs reveal that the pharmacokinetic properties of cannabinoid-based pharmacotherapy could vary between individuals. Therefore, in the near future, improved knowledge of functional genetic polymorphisms of the endocannabinoid system could increase the effectiveness of pharmacological treatments based on this system.

One can wonder if it is necessary to continue further pharmacological studies after psychiatric and other adverse effects appear. Usually, the most common strategy is to stop all of the experiments and forget about the drug. However, another option may be to segregate the population that is vulnerable to the side effects of the drug. Currently on the market, there are a small number of medicines with benefits that overcome their strong adverse effects. This effect is achieved by pharmacogenetic tests that evaluate the presence of a genetic variant (a genetic biomarker) that predicts the development of adverse effects. For instance, carbamazepine, approved for the treatment of epilepsy and bipolar affective disorder, causes harmful adverse effects in individuals carrying the HLA-B*1502 allele. Regarding the endocannabinoid system, Lazarus and colleagues [123] propose that because approximately 70% of studied patients treated with a cannabinoid receptor antagonist did not show psychiatric side effects, a significant proportion of the population could benefit from the treatment. This is an interesting proposal that may bring beneficial results. For instance, as depression and anxiety are the most frequent side effects induced by the blockade of the endocannabinoid system, genetic pharmacological tests of *CNR1* genes could segregate patients that could potentially benefit from cannabinoid antagonists. This potential suggests screening the population in two ways: (a) by performing a pharmacological genetic test that would reveal the genetic variants of the endocannabinoid system associated with the adverse effects; or (b) by applying behavioural/psychiatric tests that would reveal symptoms that can account for the failure of pharmacological treatment. Once again, the therapeutic benefits to the patients and the patient's health, personal and time costs should be weighed. Therefore, the knowledge of which genetic variants make a subject more vulnerable to drug addiction than others is worthy. This capacity to group individuals according to their susceptibility to becoming drug-addicted, for example, to marijuana, would allow for more efficient development of preventive strategies and, over the long term, a reduction of the health care burden of drug dependence-related disorders. That would represent preventive medicine that can be even more useful than personalised medicine, which treats (more efficiently) the symptoms instead of the causes.

Currently, there is a growing body of evidence that shows significant associations between genetic polymorphisms and drug addiction phenotypes despite one of the main problems of genetic association studies: the lack of replicability. To date, the most consistent evidence has been obtained with the triplet repetition (AAT)n of the *CNR1* gene and one SNP of the FAAH gene. Higher AAT triplet repetitions (n≥16) are associated in Caucasian populations with a vulnerability to drug dependence [124]. The rs324420 SNP of *FAAH* encodes a missense mutation that changes a cytosine to an adenine (385C→A or C385A), resulting in the substitution of a threonine residue (found in most of the population) for a proline residue (Pro129→Thr or P129T) [125]. The functional consequence of this SNP is that individuals homozygous for the A-allele exhibit reduced protein expression and half of the *FAAH* C/C protein activity due to a post-translational mechanism that precedes folding of the FAAH protein [126]. The C385A polymorphism has been associated with an increased likelihood to try THC but a reduced susceptibility to becoming THC dependent, with a significant over-representation of the 385 A/A genotype in indivuals addicted to cocaine, heroin, alcohol and methadone dependence, reduced craving among marijuana smokers, less severe marijuana withdrawal symptoms, lower happiness after smoking marijuana and a lower decrease in fatigue after amphetamine intake (for review, see [101]).

All of these studies suggest that personalised and preventive medicine based on genetic biomarkers of the endocannabinoid system can increase the effectiveness and safety of pharmacological compounds and reduce disease burden and health costs in the medium to long term. The endocannabinoid system seems to be a good candidate for the elucidation of genetic biomarkers that can predict the response to pharmacological treatment. The blockade/stimulation of the CB1 receptor or FAAH enzyme may benefit individuals but, in other individuals, may have no effect or even adverse side effects. The classical pharmacological dose-response curve, which is based on the average of multiple subjects, should be reviewed, taking into consideration meaningful genetic diversity parameters. This goal may be accomplished by reporting "*three-dose-response-curves*" corresponding to the three variants of an allele (e.g., AA/AB/BB).

CONCLUSION

The endocannabinoid system represents one of the strongest candidates for the development of pharmacological compounds for drug addiction. It is not strongly credible that one of the major regulators of brain neurotransmitters cannot serve as a pharmacological target for mood disorders and other psychiatric conditions. This system was only recently discovered, and it is plausible to speculate that it could go further than the dopaminergic and serotonergic systems in the field of pharmacological psychiatry. However, at the present time, there are many issues that need to be resolved. The nature of the psychoactive effects of cannabinoids represents a serious concern for many patients. It is necessary to increase the knowledge of the biochemistry of the entire cannabinoid system, from the functionality of all receptor binding sites and the molecules acting on them, to its interactions with other neurotransmitter systems and the development of drugs that modulate its components in more subtle ways. The use of genetic biomarkers would allow the segregation of patients, which would increase the effectiveness of drugs and reduce the side effects of medications based on the endocannabinoid system. As a general conclusion, the endocannabinoid system represents one of the most promising new targets for psychiatric-related disorders, particularly drug addiction.

REFERENCES

[1]   R.G. Pertwee. Cannabinoid pharmacology: the first 66 years. *Br. J. Pharmacol.* 147, 163 (2006).

[2]   D. Piomelli. The molecular logic of endocannabinoid signalling. *Nat. Rev. Neurosci.* 4, 873 (2003).

[3]   A. Serrano and L.H. Parsons. Endocannabinoid influence in drug reinforcement, dependence and addiction-related behaviors. *Pharmacol. Ther.* 132, 215 (2011).

[4]   A. Ameri. The effects of cannabinoids on the brain. *Prog. Neurobiol.* 58, 315 (1999).

[5]   M. Herkenham, A.B. Lynn, M.D. Little, M.R. Johnson, L.S. Melvin, B.R. de Costa and K.C. Rice. Cannabinoid receptor localization in brain. *Proc. Natl. Acad. Sci. USA.* 87, 1932 (1990).

[6]   L.A. Matsuda, S.J. Lolait, M.J. Brownstein, A.C. Young and T.I. Bonner. Structure of cannabinoid receptor and functional expression of the cloned cDNA. *Nature.* 346, 561 (1990).

[7]   M. Gómez-Ruiz, M. Hernández, R. de Miguel and J.A. Ramos. An overview of the biochemistry of the cannabinoid system. *Mol. Neurobiol.* 36, 3 (2007).

[8]   B. Lutz. Molecular biology of cannabinoid receptors. *Prostaglandins Leukot. Essent. Fatty Acids.* 66, 123 (2002).

[9]   K. Mackie. Distribution of cannabinoid receptors in the central and peripheral nervous system. *Handb. Exp. Pharmacol.* 168, 299 (2005).

[10] R.G. Pertwee, R.A Ross, Cannabinoid receptors and their ligands. *Prostaglandins Leukot. Essent. Fatty Acids.* 66, 101 (2002).

[11] R.G. Pertwee. Cannabinoid receptors and pain. *Prog. Neurobiol.* 63, 569 (2001).

[12] A.C. Howlett, F. Barth, T.I. Bonner, G. Cabral, P. Casellas, W.A. Devane, C.C. Felder, M. Herkenham, K. Mackie, B.R. Martin, R. Mechoulam and R.G. Pertwee. International Union of Pharmacology. XXVII. Classification of cannabinoid receptors. *Pharmacol. Rev.* 54, 161 (2002).

[13] R.G. Pertwee. Pharmacology of cannabinoid CB1 and CB2 receptors. *Pharmacol. Ther.* 74, 129 (1997).

[14] T.W. Klein, C. Newton, K. Larsen, L. Lu, I. Perkins, L. Nong and H. Friedman. The cannabinoid system and immune modulation. *J. Leukoc. Biol.* 74, 486 (2003).

[15] M.D. Van Sickle, M. Duncan, P.J. Kingsley, A. Mouihate, P. Urbani, K. Mackie, N. Stella, A. Makriyannis, D. Piomelli, J.S. Davison, L.J. Marnett, V. Di Marzo, Q.J. Pittman, K.D. Patel and K.A. Sharkey. Identification and functional characterization of brainsteam cannabinoid CB2 receptors. *Science.* 310, 329 (2005).

[16] R.G. Pertwee , A.C. Howlett , M.E. Abood, S.P. Alexander, V. Di Marzo, M.R. Elphick, P.J. Greasley, H.S. Hansen, G. Kunos, K. Mackie, R. Mechoulam and R.A Ross. International Union of Basic and Clinical Pharmacology. LXXIX. Cannabinoid receptors and their ligands: beyond CB1 and CB2. *Pharmacol. Rev.* 62, 588 (2010).

[17] A.C. Howlett, L.C. Blume and G.D. Dalton. CB(1) cannabinoid receptors and their associated proteins. *Curr. Med. Chem.* 17, 1382 (2010).

[18] V. Di Marzo. The endocannabinoid system: its general strategy of action, tools for its pharmacological manipulation and potential therapeutic exploitation. *Pharmacol. Res.* 60, 77 (2009).

[19] W. Twitchell, S. Brown and K. Mackie. Cannabinoid inhibits N- and P/Q-type calcium channels in cultured rat hippocampal neurons. *J. Neurophysiol.* 78, 43 (1997).

[20] J.M. Sullivan. Mechanisms of cannabinoid-receptor-mediated inhibition of synaptic transmission in cultured hippocampal pyramidal neurons. *J. Neurophysiol.* 82, 1286 (1999).

[21] C.C. Huang, S.W. Lo and K.S. Hsu. Presynaptic mechanisms underlying cannabinoid inhibition of excitatory synaptic transmission in rat striatal neurons. *J. Physiol.* 532, 731 (2001).

[22] X.P. Chen, W. Yang, Y. Fan, J.S. Luo, K. Hong, Z. Wang, J.F. Yan, X. Chen, J.X. Lu, J.L. Benovic and N.M. Zhou. Structural determinants of the second intracellular loop of the human cannabinoid CB1 receptor mediate selective coupling to G(s) and G(i). *Br. J. Pharmacol.* 161, 1817 (2010).

[23] M. Glass and C.C. Felder. Concurrent stimulation of cannabinoid CB1 and dopamine D2 receptors augments cAMP accumulation in striatal neurons: evidence for a Gs linkage to the CB1 receptor. *J. Neurosci.* 17, 5327 (1997).

[24] A. Jarrahian, V.J. Watts and E.L. Barker. D2 dopamine receptors modulate Galpha-subunit coupling of the CB1 cannabinoid receptor. *J. Pharmacol. Exp. Ther.* 308, 880 (2004).

[25] M.R. Price, G.L. Baillie, A. Thomas, L.A. Stevenson, M. Easson, R. Goodwin, A. McLean, L. McIntosh, G. Goodwin, G. Walker, P. Westwood, J. Marrs, F. Thomson, P. Cowley, A. Christopoulos, R.G. Pertwee and R.A. Ross. Allosteric modulation of the cannabinoid CB1 receptor. *Mol. Pharmacol.* 68, 1484 (2005).

[26] R.A. Ross. Allosterism and cannabinoid CB(1) receptors: the shape of things to come. *Trends. Pharmacol. Sci.* 28, 567 (2007).

[27] H.A. Navarro, J.L. Howard , G.T. Pollard and F.I. Carroll. Positive allosteric modulation of the human cannabinoid (CB) receptor by RTI-371, a selective inhibitor of the dopamine transporter. *Br. J. Pharmacol.* 156, 1178 (2009).

[28] V. Di Marzo , P.M. Blumberg and A. Szallasi. Endovanilloid signaling in pain. *Curr. Opin. Neurobiol.* 12, 372 (2002).

[29] R.G. Pertwee. GPR55: a new member of the cannabinoid receptor clan? *Br. J. Pharmacol.* 152, 984 (2007).

[30] E. Ryberg, N. Larsson, S. Sjögren, S. Hjorth, N.O. Hermansson, J. Leonova, T. Elebring, K. Nilsson, T. Drmota and P.J. Greasley. The orphan receptor GPR55 is a novel cannabinoid receptor. *Br. J. Pharmacol.* 152, 1092 (2007).

[31] H. Sharir and M.E. Abood. Pharmacological characterization of GPR55, a putative cannabinoid receptor. *Pharmacol. Ther.* 126, 301 (2010).

[32] W.A. Devane, L. Hanus, A. Breuer, R.G. Pertwee, L.A. Stevenson, G. Griffin, D. Gibson, A. Mandelbaum, A. Etinger and R. Mechoulam. Isolation and structure of a brain constituent that binds to the cannabinoid receptor. *Science.* 258, 1946 (1992).

[33] W. Gonsiorek, C. Lunn, X. Fan, S. Narula, D. Lundell and R.W. Hipkin. Endocannabinoid 2-arachidonyl glycerol is a full agonist through human type 2 cannabinoid receptor: antagonism by anandamide. *Mol. Pharmacol.* 57, 1045 (2000).

[34] L. De Petrocellis and V. Di Marzo. Non-CB1, non-CB2 receptors for endocannabinoids, plant cannabinoids, and synthetic cannabimimetics: focus on G-protein-coupled receptors and transient receptor potential channels. *J Neuroimmune Pharmacol.* 5, 103 (2010).

[35] V. Di Marzo. Anandamide serves two masters in the brain. *Nat Neurosci.* 13, 1446 (2010).

[36] R. Mechoulam, S. Ben-Shabat, L. Hanus, M. Ligumsky, N.E. Kaminski, A.R. Schatz, A. Gopher, S. Almog, B.R. Martin, D.R. Compton, R.G. Pertwee, G. Griffin, M. Bayewitch, J. Barg and Z. Vogel. Identification of an endogenous 2-monoglyceride, present in canine gut, that binds to cannabinoid receptors. *Biochem. Pharmacol.* 50, 83 (1995).

[37] T. Sugiura, S. Kondo, A. Sukagawa, S. Nakane, A. Shinoda, K. Itoh, A. Yamashita and K. Waku. 2-Arachidonoylglycerol: a possible endogenous cannabinoid receptor ligand in brain. *Biochem. Biophys. Res. Commun.* 215, 89 (1995).

[38] T. Sugiura, S. Kishimoto, S. Oka and M. Gokoh. Biochemistry, pharmacology and physiology of 2-arachidonoylglycerol, an endogenous cannabinoid receptor ligand. *Prog. Lipid. Res.* 45, 405 (2006).

[39] Z. Fisar. Phytocannabinoids and endocannabinoids. *Curr. Drug Abuse Rev.* 2, 51 (2009).

[40] N. Ueda, K. Tsuboi, T. Uyama, T. Ohnishi. Biosynthesis and degradation of the endocannabinoid 2-arachidonoylglycerol. *Biofactors.* 37, 1 (2011).

[41] J. Liu, L. Wang, J. Harvey-White, B.X. Huang, H.Y. Kim, S. Luquet, R.D. Palmiter, G. Krystal, R. Rai, A. Mahadevan, R.K. Razdan and G. Kunos. Multiple pathways involved in the biosynthesis of anandamide. *Neuropharmacology.* 54, 1 (2008).

[42] B.S. Basavarajappa. Critical enzymes involved in endocannabinoid metabolism. *Protein Pept. Lett.* 4, 237 (2007).

[43] R. Mechoulam and L. Hanus. A historical overview of chemical research on cannabinoids. *Chem. Phys. Lipids.* 108, 1 (2000).

[44] A. Thomas, G.L. Baillie, A.M. Phillips, R.K. Razdan, R.A. Ross and R.G. Pertwee. Cannabidiol displays unexpectedly high potency as an antagonist of CB1 and CB2 receptor agonists in vitro. *Br. J. Pharmacol.* 150, 613 (2007).

[45] V. Di Marzo and L.D. Petrocellis. Plant, synthetic, and endogenous cannabinoids in medicine. *Annu. Rev. Med.* 57, 553 (2006).

[46] V.M. Showalter, D.R. Compton, B.R. Martin and M.E. Abood. Evaluation of binding in a transfected cell line expressing a peripheral cannabinoid receptor (CB2): identification of cannabinoid receptor subtype selective ligands. *J. Pharmacol. Exp. Ther.* 278, 989 (1996).

[47] R.G. Pertwee. Inverse agonism and neutral antagonism at cannabinoid CB1 receptors. *Life Sci.* 76, 1307 (2005).

[48] K. Otrubova, C. Ezzilia and D.L. Boger. The discovery and development of inhibitors of fatty acid amide hydrolase (FAAH). *Bioorg. Med. Chem. Lett.* 21, 4674 (2011).

[49] M. Feledziak, D.M. Lambert, J. Marchand-Brynaert and G.G. Muccioli. Muccioli. Inhibitors of the Endocannabinoid-Degrading Enzymes, or how to Increase Endocannabinoid's Activity by Preventing their Hydrolysis. *Recent Pat. CNS Drug Discov.* 7, 49 (2012).

[50] M.L. Yates and E.L. Barker. Inactivation and biotransformation of the endogenous cannabinoids anandamide and 2-arachidonoylglycerol. *Mol. Pharmacol.* 76, 11 (2009).

[51] D.K. Giang and B.F. Cravatt. Molecular characterization of human and mouse fatty acid amide hydrolases. *Proc. Natl. Acad. Sci. USA.* 94, 2238 (1997).

[52] B.Q. Wei, T.S. Mikkelsen, M.K. McKinney, E.S. Lander and B.F. Cravatt. . A second fatty acid amide hydrolase with variable distribution among placental mammals *J. Biol. Chem.* 281, 36569 (2006).

[53] T.P. Dinh, T.F. Freund and D. Piomelli. A role for monoglyceride lipase in 2-arachidonoylglycerol inactivation. *Chem. Phys. Lipids.* 121, 149 (2002).

[54] N. Ueda, K. Tsuboi and T. Uyama. N-acylethanolamine metabolism with special reference to N-acylethanolamine-hydrolyzing acid amidase (NAAA). *Prog Lipid Res.* 49, 299 (2010).

[55] M. Rinaldi-Carmona, F. Barth, M. Héaulme, D. Shire, B. Calandra, C. Congy, S. Martinez, J. Maruani, G. Néliat, D. Caput, P. Ferrara, P. Soubrié, J. C. Brelière and G. Le Fur. SR141716A, a potent and selective antagonist of the brain cannabinoid receptor. *FEBS Lett.* 350, 240 (1994).

[56] G.G. Muccioli and D.M. Lambert. Current knowledge on the antagonists and inverse agonists of cannabinoid receptors. *Curr. Med. Chem.* 12, 1361 (2005).

[57] M.B. Steinberg and J. Foulds. Rimonabant for treating tobacco dependence. *Vasc. Health Risk Manag.* 3, 307 (2007).

[58] J.H. Lange and G.G. Kruse. Keynote review: Medicinal chemistry strategies to CB1 cannabinoid receptor antagonists. *Drug Discov. Today.* 10, 693 (2005).

[59] C. Addy, H. Wright, K. Van Laere, I. Gantz, N. Erondu, B.J. Musser, K. Lu, J. Yuan, S.M. Sanabria-Bohórquez, A. Stoch, C. Stevens, T.M. Fong, I. De Lepeleire, C. Cilissen, J. Cote, K. Rosko, I.N. Gendrano 3rd, A.M. Nguyen, B. Gumbiner, P. Rothenberg, J. de Hoon, G. Bormans, M. Depré, W.S. Eng, E. Ravussin, S. Klein, J. Blundell, G.A. Herman, H.D. Burns, R.J. Hargreaves, J. Wagner, K. Gottesdiener, J.M. Amatruda and S.B. Heymsfield. The acyclic CB1R inverse agonist taranabant mediates

weight loss by increasing energy expenditure and decreasing caloric intake. *Cell Metab.* 7, 68 (2008).

[60] B.A. Fremming and S.T. Boyd. Taranabant, a novel cannabinoid type 1 receptor inverse agonist. Curr Opin Investig Drugs. 9, 1116 (2008).

[61] M.F. Morrison, P. Ceesay, I. Gantz, K.D. Kaufman and C.R. Lines. Randomized, controlled, double-blind trial of taranabant for smoking cessation. *Psychopharmacology (Berl).* 209, 245 (2010).

[62] F.R. Levin, J.J. Mariani, D.J. Brooks, M. Pavlicova, W. Cheng and E.V. Nunes. Dronabinol for the treatment of cannabis dependence: a randomized, double-blind, placebo-controlled trial. *Drug Alcohol Depend.* 116, 142 (2011).

[63] M. Haney, C.L. Hart, S.K. Vosburg, J. Nasser, A. Bennett, C. Zubaran and R.W. Foltin. Marijuana withdrawal in humans: effects of oral THC or divalproex *Neuropsychopharmacology.* 29, 158 (2004).

[64] A.J. Budney, R.G. Vandrey, J.R. Hughes, B.A. Moore and B. Bahrenburg. Oral delta-9-tetrahydrocannabinol suppresses cannabis withdrawal symptoms. *Drug Alcohol. Depend.* 86, 22 (2007).

[65] C.L. Hart, A.S. Ward, M. Haney, S.D. Comer, R.W. Foltin and M.W. Fischman. Foltin and M.W. Fischman, Comparison of smoked marijuana and oral Delta(9)-tetrahydrocannabinol in humans. *Psychopharmacology (Berl).* 164, 407 (2002).

[66] J. Camí, D. Guerra, B. Ugena, J. Segura and R. de la Torre. Effect of subjective expectancy on the THC intoxication and disposition from smoked hashish cigarettes. *Pharmacol. Biochem. Behav.* 40, 115 (1991).

[67] J.M. Kirk, P. Doty and H. De Wit. Effects of expectancies on subjective responses to oral delta9-tetrahydrocannabinol. *Pharmacol. Biochem. Behav.* 59, 287 (1998).

[68] J. Metrik, D.J. Rohsenow, P.M. Monti, J. McGeary, T.A. Cook, H. de Wit, M. Haney and C.W. Kahler. Effectiveness of a marijuana expectancy manipulation: Piloting the balanced-placebo design for marijuana. *Exp. Clin. Psychopharmacol.* 17, 217 (2009).

[69] L. Hides, D.I. Lubman, J. Buckby, H.P. Yuen, E. Cosgrave, K. Baker and A.R. Yung. The association between early cannabis use and psychotic-like experiences in a community adolescent sample. *Schizophr. Res.* 112, 130 (2009).

[70] E. Guillem, C. Notides, F. Vorspan, M. Debray, I. Nieto, M. Leroux and J.P. Lépine. Cannabis expectancies in substance misusers: French validation of the marijuana effect expectancy questionnaire. *Am. J. Addict.* 20, 543 (2011).

[71] J.P. Connor, M.J. Gullo, G.F. Feeney and R.M. Young. Validation of the Cannabis Expectancy Questionnaire (CEQ) in adult cannabis users in treatment. *Drug Alcohol. Depend.* 115, 167 (2011).

[72] I.H. Franken. Drug craving and addiction: integrating psychological and neuropsycho pharmacological approaches. *Prog. Neuropsychopharmacol. Biol. Psychiatry.* 27, 563 (2003).

[73] M. Field and W.M. Cox. Attentional bias in addictive behaviors: a review of its development, causes, and consequences. *Drug Alcohol. Depend.* 97, 1 (2008).

[74] K. Wölfling, H. Flor and S.M. Grüsser. Psychophysiological responses to drug-associated stimuli in chronic heavy cannabis use. *Eur. J. Neurosci.* 27, 976 (2008).

[75] B.L. Carter and S.T. Tiffany. Meta-analysis of cue-reactivity in addiction research. *Addiction.* 94, 327 (1999).

[76] E.L. Abel. Effects of marihuana on the solution of anagrams, memory and appetite. *Nature*. 231, 260 (1971).

[77] E.M. Berry and R. Mechoulam. Tetrahydrocannabinol and endocannabinoids in feeding and appetite. *Pharmacol. Ther*. 95, 185 (2002).

[78] C.J. Morgan, T.P. Freeman, G.L. Schafer and H.V. Curran. Cannabidiol attenuates the appetitive effects of Delta 9-tetrahydrocannabinol in humans smoking their chosen cannabis. *Neuropsychopharmacology*. 35, 1879 (2010).

[79] I.G. Karniol, I. Shirakawa, R.N. Takahashi, E. Knobel and R.E. Musty. Effects of delta9-tetrahydrocannabinol and cannabinol in man. *Pharmacology*. 13, 502 (1975).

[80] R.E. Musty, I.G. Karniol, I. Shirikawa, R.N. Takahashi and E. Knobel, Interactions of delta-9-tetrahydrocannabinol and cannabinol in man. In: Braude MC, Szara S (eds). *The Pharmacology of Marihuana, Vol. 2*. Raven Press: New York, pp. 559–563. (1976).

[81] D.E. Sugarman, J. Poling and M. Sofuoglu. The safety of modafinil in combination with oral Δ9-tetrahydrocannabinol in humans. *Pharmacol. Biochem. Behav*. 98, 94 (2011).

[82] M. Sofuoglu, D.E. Sugarman and K.M. Carroll. Cognitive function as an emerging treatment target for marijuana addiction. *Exp. Clin. Psychopharmacol*. 18, 109 (2010).

[83] U.E. Ghitza, D.H. Epstein and K.L Preston. Nonreporting of cannabis use: Predictors and relationship to treatment outcome in methadone maintained patients. *Addict. Behav*. 32, 938 (2007).

[84] S.E Lukas, M. Sholar, E. Kouri, H. Fukuzako and J.H. Mendelson. Marihuana smoking increases plasma cocaine levels and subjective reports of euphoria in male volunteers. *Pharmacol. Biochem. Behav*. 48, 715 (1994).

[85] L. Zuurman, A.E. Ippel, E. Moin and J.M. van Gerven. Biomarkers for the effects of cannabis and THC in healthy volunteers. *Br. J. Clin. Pharmacol*. 67, 5 (2009).

[86] M.A. Huestis, D.A. Gorelick, S.J. Heishman, K.L. Preston, R.A. Nelson, E.T. Moolchan and R.A. Frank. Blockade of effects of smoked marijuana by the CB1-selective cannabinoid receptor antagonist SR141716. *Arch. Gen. Psychiatry*. 58, 322 (2001).

[87] M.A. Huestis, S.J. Boyd, S.J. Heishman, K.L. Preston, D. Bonnet, G. Le Fur and D.A. Gorelick. Single and multiple doses of rimonabant antagonize acute effects of smoked cannabis in male cannabis users. *Psychopharmacology (Berl)*. 194, 505 (2007).

[88] S. Turpault, V. Kanamaluru, G.F. Lockwood, D. Bonnet and J. Newton. Rimonabant pharmacokinetics in healthy and obese subjects. *Clin. Pharmacol. Ther*. 79, 50 (2006).

[89] N.A. Rigotti, D. Gonzales, L.C. Dale, D. Lawrence, Y. Chang and CIRRUS Study Group. A randomized controlled trial of adding the nicotine patch to rimonabant for smoking cessation: efficacy, safety and weight gain. *Addiction*. 104, 266 (2009).

[90] J.A. López-Moreno, G. González-Cuevas, F. Rodríguez de Fonseca and M. Navarro. Long-lasting increase of alcohol relapse by the cannabinoid receptor agonist WIN 55,212-2 during alcohol deprivation. *J. Neurosci*. 24, 8245 (2004).

[91] G. Colombo, S. Serra, G. Vacca, M.A. Carai and G.L Gessa. Endocannabinoid system and alcohol addiction: pharmacological studies. *Pharmacol. Biochem. Behav*. 8, 369 (2005).

[92] G. Colombo, S. Serra, G. Brunetti, R. Gomez, S. Melis, G. Vacca, M.M Carai and L. Gessa. Stimulation of voluntary ethanol intake by cannabinoid receptor agonists in ethanol-preferring sP rats. *Psychopharmacology (Berl)*. 159, 181 (2002).

[93] J.A. López-Moreno, G. González-Cuevas and M. Navarro. The CB1 cannabinoid receptor antagonist rimonabant chronically prevents the nicotine-induced relapse to alcohol. *Neurobiol. Dis.* 25, 274 (2007).

[94] F. Lallemand and P. de Witte. Ethanol induces higher BEC in CB1 cannabinoid receptor knockout mice while decreasing ethanol preference. *Alcohol Alcohol.* 40, 54 (2005).

[95] M. Naassila , O. Pierrefiche, C. Ledent and M. Daoust. Decreased alcohol self-administration and increased alcohol sensitivity and withdrawal in CB1 receptor knockout mice. *Neuropharmacology.* 46, 243 (2004).

[96] P.K. Thanos, E.S. Dimitrakakis, O. Rice, A. Gifford and N.D. Volkow. Ethanol self-administration and ethanol conditioned place preference are reduced in mice   lacking cannabinoid CB1 receptors. *Behav Brain Res.* 164, 206 (2005).

[97] K.M. Jackson, K.J. Sher and J.E. Schulenberg. Conjoint developmental trajectories of young adult substance use. *Alcohol Clin. Exp. Res.* 32, 723, (2008).

[98] S.E. Lukas and S. Orozco. Ethanol increases plasma Delta(9)-tetrahydrocannabinol (THC) levels and subjective effects after marihuana smoking in human volunteers. *Drug Alcohol. Depend.* 64, 143 (2001).

[99] M. Soyka, G. Koller, P. Schmidt, O.M. Lesch, M. Leweke, C. Fehr, H. Gann, K. F. Mann and ACTOL Study Investigators. Cannabinoid receptor 1 blocker rimonabant (SR 141716) for treatment of alcohol dependence: results from a placebo-controlled,double-blind trial. *J. Clin. Psychopharmacol.* 28, 317 (2008).

[100] D.T. George, D.W. Herion , C.L. Jones, M.J. Phillips, J. Hersh, D. Hill, M. Heilig, V.A. Ramchandani, C. Geyer, D.E. Spero, E.D. Singley, S.S. O'Malley, R. Bishai, R.R. Rawlings and G. Kunos. Rimonabant (SR141716) has no effect on alcohol self-administration or endocrine measures in nontreatment-seeking heavy alcohol drinkers. *Psychopharmacology (Berl).* 208, 37 (2010).

[101] J.A. López-Moreno, V. Echeverry-Alzate and K.M. Bühler. The genetic basis of the endocannabinoid system and drug addiction in humans. *J. Psychopharmacol.* 26, 133 (2012).

[102] X. Chen, V.S. Williamson, S.S. An, J.M. Hettema, S.H. Aggen, M.C. Neale and K.S. Kendler. Cannabinoid receptor 1 gene association with nicotine dependence. *Arch. Gen Psychiatry.* 65, 816 (2008).

[103] L. Zuo, H.R. Kranzler, X. Luo, B.Z. Yang, R. Weiss, K. Brady, J. Poling, L. Farrer and J. Gelernter. Interaction between two independent CNR1 variants increases risk for cocaine dependence in European Americans: a replication study in family-based sample and population-based sample. *Neuropsychopharmacology.* 34, 1504 (2009).

[104] L. Zuo, H.R. Kranzler, X. Luo, J. Covault and J. Gelernter. CNR1 variation modulates risk for drug and alcohol dependence. *Biol. Psychiatry.* 62, 616 (2007).

[105] F.M. Filbey, J.P. Schacht, U.S. Myers, R.S. Chavez and K.E Hutchison. Individual and additive effects of the CNR1 and FAAH genes on brain response to marijuana cues. *Neuropsychopharmacology.* 35, 967 (2010).

[106] H.M. Haughey, E. Marshall, J.P. Schacht, A. Louis and K.E. Hutchison. Marijuana withdrawal and craving: influence of the cannabinoid receptor 1 (CNR1) and fatty acid amide hydrolase (FAAH) genes. *Addiction.* 103, 1678 (2008).

[107] K.E. Hutchison, H. Haughey, M. Niculescu, J. Schacht, A. Kaiser, J. Stitzel, W.J. Horton and F. Filbey. The incentive salience of alcohol: translating the effects of genetic variant in CNR1. *Arch. Gen. Psychiatry.* 65, 841 (2008).

[108] E. Van den Wildenberg, R.G. Janssen, K.E. Hutchison, G.J. van Breukelen and R.W. Wiers. Polymorphisms of the dopamine D4 receptor gene (DRD4 VNTR) and cannabinoid CB1 receptor gene (CNR1) are not strongly related to cue-reactivity after alcohol exposure. *Addict Biol.* 12, 210 (2007).

[109] A.I. Herman, H.R. Kranzler, J.F. Cubells, J. Gelernter and J. Covault. Association study of the CNR1 gene exon 3 alternative promoter region polymorphisms and substance dependence. *Am. J. Med. Genet. B Neuropsychiatr. Genet.* 141B, 299 (2006).

[110] C.A. Hartman, C.J. Hopfer, B. Haberstick, S.H. Rhee, T.J. Crowley, R.P. Corley, J.K. Hewitt and M.A. Ehringer. The association between cannabinoid receptor 1 gene (CNR1) and cannabis dependence symptoms in adolescents and young adults. *Drug Alcohol. Depend.* 104, 11 (2009).

[111] A. Agrawal, L. Wetherill, D.M. Dick, X. Xuei, A. Hinrichs, V. Hesselbrock, J. Kramer, J.I. Nurnberger Jr, M. Schuckit, L.J. Bierut, H.J. Edenberg and T. Foroud. Evidence for association between polymorphisms in the cannabinoid receptor 1 (CNR1) gene and cannabis dependence. *Am. J. Med. Genet. B Neuropsychiatr. Genet.* 150, 736 (2009).

[112] C.J. Hopfer, S.E. Young, S. Purcell, T.J. Crowley, M.C. Stallings, R.P. Corley, S.H. Rhee, A. Smolen, K. Krauter, J.K. Hewitt and M.A. Ehringer. Cannabis receptor haplotype associated with fewer cannabis dependence symptoms in adolescents. *Am. J. Med. Genet. B Neuropsychiatr. Genet.* 141, 895 (2006).

[113] R.P. Corley, J.S. Zeiger, T. Crowley, M.A. Ehringer, J.K. Hewitt, C.J. Hopfer, J. Lessem, M.B. McQueen, S.H. Rhee, A. Smolen, M.C. Stallings, S.E. Young, and K. Krauter. Association of candidate genes with antisocial drug dependence in adolescents. *Drug Alcohol. Depend.* 96, 90 (2008).

[114] A.M. Dlugos, A. Hamidovic, C.A. Hodgkinson, D. Goldman, A.A. Palmer and H. de Wit. More aroused, less fatigued: fatty acid amide hydrolase gene polymorphisms influence acute response to amphetamine. *Neuropsychopharmacology.* 35, 613 (2010).

[115] J.P. Schacht, R.E Selling and K.E. Hutchison. Intermediate cannabis dependence phenotypes and the FAAH C385A variant: an exploratory analysis. *Psychopharmacology (Berl).* 203, 511 (2009).

[116] F.M. Filbey, J.P. Schacht, U.S. Myers, R.S. Chavez, K.E. Hutchison. Individual and additive effects of the CNR1 and FAAH genes on brain response to marijuana cues. *Neuropsychopharmacology.* 35, 967 (2010).

[117] R.F. Tyndale, J.I. Payne, A. Gerber and J. Sipe. The fatty acid amide C385A (P129T) missense variant in cannabis user: studies of drug use and dependence in Caucasians. *Am. J. Med. Genet. B Neuropsychiatry Genet.* 5, 660 (2007).

[118] J.M. Flanagan, A.L. Gerber, J.L. Cadet, E. Beutler and J.C. Sipe. The fatty acid amide hydrolase 385 A/A (P129T) variant: haplotype analysis of an ancient missense mutation and validation of risk for drug addiction. *Hum. Genet.* 120, 581 (2006).

[119] K. Domschke, U. Dannlowski, P. Ohrmann, B. Lawford, J. Bauer, H. Kugel, W. Heindel, R. Young, P. Morris, V. Arolt, J. Deckert, T. Suslow and B.T. Baune. Cannabinoid receptor 1 (CNR1) gene: impact on antidepressant treatment response and emotion processing in major depression. *Eur. Neuropsychopharmacol.* 18, 751 (2008).

[120] F.J. Barrero, I. Ampuero, B. Morales, F. Vives, J. de Dios Luna Del Castillo, J. Hoenicka and J. García Yébenes. Depression in Parkinson's disease is related to a genetic polymorphism of the cannabinoid receptor gene (CNR1). *Pharmacogenomics J.* 5, 135 (2005).

[121] G.P. Schroth, P.J. Chou and P.S. Ho. Mapping Z-DNA in the human genome. Computer-aided mapping reveals a nonrandom distribution of potential Z-DNA-forming sequences in human genes *J. Biol. Chem.* 267, 11846 (1992).

[122] P. Monteleone, M. Bifulco, G. Maina, A. Tortorella, P. Gazzerro, M.C. Proto, C. Di Filippo, F. Monteleone, B. Canestrelli, G. Buonerba, F. Bogetto and M. Maj. Investigation of CNR1 and FAAH endocannabinoid gene polymorphisms in bipolar disorder and major depression *Pharmacol. Res.* 61, 400 (2010).

[123] J. Lazar, G. Juhasz, L. Hunyady and G. Bagdy. Personalized medicine can pave the way for the safe use of CB_1 receptor antagonists. *Trends. Pharmacol. Sci.* 32, 270 (2011).

[124] A. Benyamina, O. Kebir, L. Blecha, M. Reynaud and M.O. Krebs. CNR1 gene polymorphisms in addictive disorders: a systematic review and a meta-analysis. *Addict. Biol.* 16, 1 (2011).

[125] J.C. Sipe, K. Chiang, A.L. Gerber, E. Beutler and B.F. Cravatt. A missense mutation in human fatty acid amide hydrolase associated with problem drug use. *Proc. Natl. Acad. Sci. USA.* 99, 8394 (2002).

[126] K.P. Chiang, A.L. Gerber, J.C. Sipe and B.F. Cravatt. Reduced cellular expression and activity of the P129T mutant of human fatty acid amide hydrolase: evidence for a link between defects in the endocannabinoid system and problem drug use. *Hum. Mol. Genet.* 13, 2113 (2004).

In: Emerging Targets for Drug Addiction Treatment
Editor: Juan Canales

ISBN 978-1-62081-913-5
©2012 Nova Science Publishers, Inc.

Chapter 9

THE ROLE OF METABOTROPIC GLUTAMATE 5 RECEPTOR IN ADDICTION

Jee Hyun Kim[1,2]* *and Andrew J. Lawrence*[1,2]

[1]Behavioural Neuroscience Division, Florey Neuroscience Institutes,
Parkville, VIC, Australia
[2]Center for Neuroscience Research, University of Melbourne, Parkville, VIC, Australia

ABSTRACT

A central problem facing the treatment of drug addiction is the enduring vulnerability to relapse by users, despite months or even years of abstinence. Therefore, it has been proposed that extinction, which involves learning to inhibit drug-seeking responses driven by drug-related cues and environments, may be more effective compared to abstinence as a potential treatment of drug addiction. Because extinction is an active learning process, it involves neurobiological substrates that subserve normal learning and memory, including increased transmission and plasticity at central glutamatergic synapses. In particular, accumulating evidence suggests that metabotropic glutamate 5 (mGlu5) receptors are functionally implicated in the extinction of drug-seeking behavior. Specifically, it appears that decreasing mGlu5 signaling impairs while increasing it facilitates extinction of drug-seeking behavior. We review the existing literature on mGlu5 receptors on reward learning and extinction and propose mGlu5 receptor signaling as a potential candidate for strengthening extinction memory that aids in the prevention of relapse to drug-seeking behavior.

INTRODUCTION

Reward-seeking is a necessary emotion to guide survival. However, it can lead to maladaptive behavior when expressed pervasively and interferes with everyday functioning, manifesting as addiction. Substance abuse is a major worldwide public health concern, and the World Health Organization (WHO) pin-pointed substance abuse as one of the three most

---

* Corresponding authors E-mail addresses: jeek@unimelb.edu.au; andrewjl@unimelb.edu.au

common mental disorders across the world, ranking it very highly as a cause of disease burden [1, 2]. In the recent United States National Comorbidity Survey Replication study, it was reported that 8.9% of adults met the 12-month Diagnostic and Statistical Manual of Mental Disorders (DSM-IV) criteria for a substance abuse [3]. Those staggering statistics also highlight the economic costs of anxiety disorders and substance abuse. For example, one estimate puts the yearly economic cost of substance abuse to be 3.5% of the gross domestic product within Western society [4]. Within Australia alone, the cost of alcohol and illicit drug abuse has been estimated to be $25 billion per year [5].

Despite the prevalence and the financial burden of substance abuse, research into finding effective treatments for drug addiction has received significant attention only in the past couple of decades. Nevertheless, research has led to the use of pharmacological agents as a standard, although not always effective, approach to ameliorate aspects of drug addiction [6, 7]; thus, the prevalence of substance abuse remains high. This is mainly due to the chronic and relapsing characteristic of drug addiction, even after prolonged abstinence and/or pharmacological treatments [8]. Indeed, it is widely agreed that the central problem facing drug addiction is extremely high rates of relapse [9-15]. Therefore, one focus of contemporary research in addiction is investigating the neural basis of cognitive-behavioral therapies combined with pharmacotherapy to improve treatment and prevent relapse in drug addicts [16, 17]. This is because there is much evidence supporting that learning and memory processes underlie the etiology of drug addiction and its relapse after treatment [9, 18-21]. Actions, cues and environments that are associated with the rewarding properties of a drug can trigger drug use in an individual [21-25]. That is, the many stimuli that surround the drug user (e.g., pub, club, sounds, people, paraphernalia) acquire powerful incentive motivational properties that can elicit drug-seeking behavior [18]. Thus, it has been suggested that cognitive-behavioral therapies involving inhibitory learning mechanisms may potentially lead to more effective treatments for drug addiction [16, 26]. Therefore, much effort has been placed into finding an effective pharmacotherapy to combine with cognitive-behavioral therapies to effectively treat these mental disorders with the aim of preventing relapse [27].

Cognitive-behavioral treatments for substance abuse rely largely on learning to inhibit drug-seeking behavior and drug-associated cues through a process called *extinction*. Extinction of instrumental behavior refers to the decrease in drug-seeking responses because the responses no longer deliver the drug reward. Extinction of a drug-associated cue refers to the decrease in drug-seeking behavior expressed to a stimulus due to repeated exposure to that stimulus without obtaining any drug reward. The stimulus can be a discrete cue (e.g., cigarette lighter) or a context (e.g., pub). Because extinction is an active learning process, it involves many of the neurobiological substrates that subserve normal learning and memory [28]. Rodent research has been pivotal in identifying many of those neurobiological substrates, which includes increased signaling and plasticity at central glutamatergic synapses in the neural circuitry underlying drug-seeking [29]. Metabotropic glutamate 5 (mGlu5) receptors, in particular, have received attention in drug addiction research in the last decade, both in relation to drug use / drug-seeking and the extinction of these behaviors. Therefore, it is the intent of this chapter to summarise the existing findings on the effects of decreasing or increasing mGlu5 receptor signaling on the acquisition, abstinence, extinction and relapse of drug-seeking behavior. We will first describe the most commonly used animal models of drug-seeking because the vast majority of what we do know about the effects of modulating mGlu5 receptor signaling on addiction-related behavior come from studies in animals.

ANIMAL MODELS OF DRUG USE / ADDICTION

Development of drug addiction and its relapse after treatment critically involves learning and memory retrieval processes [20, 30]. Specifically, the contexts in which drug taking occurs and the multiple cues that are present are initially neutral stimuli without any biological significance to the individual. However, classical conditioning occurs with repeated drug use, in which those contexts and cues become the conditioned stimulus (CS) through pairings with the drug (unconditioned stimulus, US). Classical conditioning can strengthen over repeated pairings, and as a consequence the CS gain greater potency to evoke powerful memories of the previous drug-taking experience that induce cravings, increases in drug-taking behavior, and relapse after treatment [31, 32].

Conditioned place preference (CPP) is a popular rodent model of drug-seeking behavior that is based on classical conditioning principles. CPP allows us to infer the rewarding or hedonic properties of a drug based on its ability to induce approach[33]. In CPP, animals are conditioned to associate a distinct context (i.e., CS) with a drug experience (i.e., US) [34, 35]. Drugs, such as cocaine, are injected immediately prior to the exposure to the context. Typically, a different context paired with saline/vehicle is used as a control context. After repeated conditioning trials, a drug-free test session is given, in which the animal is allowed free access to both contexts. CPP is indicated if the animal spends more time in a drug-paired context compared to the control context. Indeed, a variety of species will preferentially choose to spend more time in an environment where they have received an injection of drug over an environment where they have received vehicle for a variety of different drugs [34, 36-39]. Once acquired, CPP can be extinguished by simply placing the animal back into the drug-associated context without any drug injections.

Over the course of extinction, the animal will no longer display preference in time spent in the previously drug-associated context. Interestingly, relapse can be modeled in this paradigm by exposing the animal to 'stress' (e.g., pre-test footshock)[40] or 'drug prime' (i.e., pre-test injection of the drug) [41]. Such recovery in preference to the previously drug-associated context is referred to as *reinstatement*. As in the case with human drug users, relapse propensity also varies in rodents [35].

Although it is intuitive to expect that humans prefer the environments in which drug experience occurred [33], it should be noted that one of the shortcomings of CPP paradigm is that it fails to model one of the most important aspects of drug addiction displayed by humans. In CPP, drug presentations are externally controlled and the animal is the passive recipient, whereas humans clearly self-administer the drugs in most cases. Additionally, CPP does not involve learning to associate particular actions with reward outcomes, which is a critical component of drug abuse in humans. Therefore, the operant self-administration paradigm is widely accepted as a more ethologically valid animal model of drug addiction [42, 43] because it has both face and construct validity [44].

In this model, operant conditioning is employed in which a specific action (e.g. lever press, nose poke etc) is positively reinforced by an access to various types of rewards such as a sucrose pellet or a drop of alcohol. In the case of many drugs of abuse that are not administered orally, the reinforcer (drug) is typically infused through a chronic indwelling intravenous catheter. Animals will readily self-administer most drugs of abuse [10, 45-48]. Accordingly, the abuse potential of a substance in humans can be predicted from self-administration in rodents [49]. Additionally, the self-administration paradigm can assess the animals' motivation, or 'willingness', to obtain the drug by testing them on a progressive-ratio (PR) schedule. A PR schedule refers to the behavioral paradigm in which the response requirements for each successive reward increases in accordance with a predefined progression, so that the animal needs to perform more actions (e.g., lever presses) to obtain the same amount of reinforcer over the session. The most common index of assessing PR is the 'break point', defined as the highest response accomplished to obtain a single reward [50, 51]. Therefore, the break point can provide insight into the motivational strength of a reinforcer. The self-administration paradigm also can easily incorporate a Pavlovian conditioning component by introducing CSs that signal drug delivery with cues that are presented during drug-seeking [12, 52-54].

As with CPP, operant behavior and/or the CS associated with drug delivery can be extinguished when the behavior and/or the CS are no longer reinforced over repeated trials. Once extinguished, drug-seeking behavior can be reinstated by stress, drug prime, or presentations of the CS [55, 56]. Such reinstatement is clinically significant because in a typical reinstatement session, there is no access to the drug / reward, indicating that relapse can be triggered by mere exposure to the cues/contexts associated with drug use, even when the drug is unavailable. Both CPP and self-administration paradigms are widely employed to assess various aspects of drug abuse. Specifically, those paradigms allow neurobiological and pharmacological examinations of different stages of drug abuse, namely acquisition, consolidation, expression, extinction, abstinence and relapse of drug-seeking behavior.

THE EFFECTS OF GENETIC OR PHARMACOLOGICAL REDUCTION IN mGLU5 RECEPTOR SIGNALING ON REWARD-SEEKING BEHAVIOR

L-Glutamate is the primary excitatory neurotransmitter in the mammalian central nervous system and is the endogenous ligand for a number of ionotropic (e.g., N-methyl-D-aspartate; NMDA) and metabotropic (mGlu1-8) receptors. There is a clear role for glutamatergic mechanisms in aspects of drug addiction [57-59]. For example, the transition to cocaine addiction in rats has been suggested to reflect persistent deficits in synaptic plasticity at corticoaccumbal synapses [60]. Because of their specific synaptic and circuitry locations, metabotropic receptors have been implicated in the fine-tuning of synaptic efficacy and control of the accuracy of glutamatergic neurotransmission [61]. Among the metabotropic receptors is the mGlu5 receptor, which is one of a family of eight G-protein-coupled glutamate receptors within the central nervous system [62]. mGlu5 receptors are densely expressed in brain regions associated with reward-seeking, in particular, the nucleus accumbens (NAc), hippocampus and other cortical regions [63-65]. These receptors are predominantly localized to the perisynaptic annulus of postsynaptic dendritic spines, where they are positively coupled to NMDA receptor function and mediate various forms of synaptic plasticity [61]. Importantly, mGlu5 receptors are involved in NMDA receptor-mediated long-term potentiation (LTP) [66, 67] and long-term depression (LTD) [68], putative cellular mechanisms for learning and memory [60, 69]. For example, potentiation of mGlu5 receptor-mediated neurotransmission has been shown to enhance the induction of LTP and LTD in CA1 region of the hippocampus, an effect that is blocked by decreasing mGlu5 receptor activity via the mGlu5 receptor negative allosteric modulator MPEP (6-methyl-2-(phenylethynyl)-pyridine) [70, 71]. Importantly, daily systemic injections of cocaine over 1 week resulted in significantly increased levels of mGlu5 receptor mRNA expression in the NAc shell and dorsal striatum that persisted for three weeks after the cessation of cocaine administration [72]. The initial interest in the role of mGlu5 receptors in drug addiction arose due to the development of mice that are deficient of mGlu5 receptors. Chiamulera and colleagues first showed that mGlu5 receptor knockout (KO) mice apparently failed to acquire cocaine intravenous self-administration (IVSA) compared to their wildtype littermates (WT) across a variety of different doses of cocaine [73]. In that study, acquisition of an operant response to food reward did not differ between the KO and WT mice, showing that the IVSA acquisition deficit displayed by the KO mice was not due to a general inability of the KO mice to acquire the operant response. Additionally, the mice did not show any differences in their baseline locomotor behavior, however, injection of cocaine induced a significant increase in locomotor in WT mice only. The authors concluded that the reinforcing properties of cocaine were absent in KO mice. Surprisingly, microdialysis revealed that there were no differences in the basal extracellular dopamine (DA) levels as well as increases in DA levels in the NAc as a response to cocaine between the KO and WT mice. Furthermore, the distribution of DA receptors and DA transporter (DAT) also did not differ between the KO and WT mice. Therefore, from those findings it is yet unclear what mechanisms underlie the phenotype displayed by the mGlu5-KO mice. Nevertheless, that study sparked an ongoing interest in the role of mGlu5 receptors in drug-seeking behavior as evidenced by several follow-up studies from various different laboratories around the world, aided by the development of selective ligands for metabotropic glutamate receptors that have provided novel opportunities for investigating the role mGlu5 receptor in drug addiction.

Pharmacological studies using non-invasive, systemic injections are especially important in light of translational research because they suggest a potential pharmacological therapeutic target for the clinical population. Studies examining pharmacological antagonism of mGlu5 receptors consistently highlight the importance of mGlu5 receptor signaling on drug-seeking behavior. Specifically, pre-session systemic injection of the selective mGlu5 receptor negative allosteric modulator (NAM) MPEP [74] has been shown to decrease self-administration of cocaine [73, 75-77], nicotine [75, 77-79], heroin [47], ketamine [47], and alcohol [80-83] in animals. Furthermore, pre-session systemic injection of MTEP (3-[(2-methyl-1,3-thiazol-4-yl)ethynyl] -pyridine), an mGlu5 receptor NAM with greater selectivity and bioavailability than MPEP[84], decreases self-administration of cocaine [85, 86], methamphetamine [87, 88], nicotine [89], morphine [90] and alcohol [46, 91, 92] in animals. Microinfusion of MPEP into the NAc, but not the prefrontal cortex or the dorsomedial caudate also reduced alcohol self-administration [93], and microinfusion of MTEP into the NAc shell decreased alcohol self-administration [94]. Most of those studies also examined natural reward (e.g., sucrose) self-administration and locomotor activity and observed no effects of MPEP or MTEP. Taken together, it appears that the decrease in mGlu5 receptor activity is selectively affecting self-administration of drugs of abuse without significant non-specific motor effects. Despite the wealth of data highlighting a role for the mGlu5 receptors in drug self-administration, it is yet equivocal whether MPEP/MTEP works via reducing the hedonic aspects of drugs as initially suggested [73]. Studies have shown that systemic injection of MPEP or MTEP decreased break points in a PR schedule for cocaine, nicotine, methamphetamine and normal food, which suggest that MPEP/MTEP may be attenuating the motivation to consume nicotine, cocaine and food, rather than decreasing the hedonic value [87, 95]. Additionally, MTEP failed to affect the reinforcement enhancing effects of nicotine [89]. Furthermore, cocaine and nicotine usually lower intracranial self-stimulation (ICSS) reward thresholds, which is interpreted as a neural measure of the positive affective state associated with acute cocaine and nicotine consumption [96, 97]. If it is the case that MPEP/MTEP attenuates such positive affective state of drugs of abuse, such decrease in ICSS threshold due to cocaine should not be observed when the animal is injected with MPEP/MTEP. However, in Kenny et al. (2003), MPEP at doses that decreased cocaine and nicotine self-administration, did not affect cocaine's lowering action on ICSS threshold, suggesting that mGlu5 receptors actually do not regulate the hedonic/rewarding properties of cocaine [75]. Similar results were obtained with nicotine [97]. However, MTEP injection itself has been found to increase ICC threshold, although the mGlu5 receptor positive allosteric modulator (PAM) 3-cyano-N-(1,3-diphenyl-1H-pyrazol-5-yl)benzamide (CDPPB) had no effects [98]. Interestingly, recent studies indicate that MPEP itself can act as a positive reinforcer [99, 100]. Specifically, van der Kam et al. (2009) showed that rats that were stably self-administering ketamine or heroin continued to self-administer when MPEP was substituted in place of ketamine or heroin [99]. Additionally, drug-naïve rats acquired CPP to the context where MPEP was injected, and acquired IVSA when MPEP was used as the reinforcer [99]. Also, significantly lower doses of ketamine or heroin were required for the acquisition of CPP when MPEP was co-treated with ketamine and heroin, which led the authors to conclude that the attenuating effect of MPEP on ketamine and heroin intravenous self-administration is due to an increase, rather than a decrease, of the rewarding/reinforcing effect of these compounds [100]. These findings challenge the view that reducing mGlu5 receptor signaling interferes with the rewarding aspects of drugs of abuse, and strongly suggest that the effects of MPEP on self-administration is from satiation due to summation of rewarding aspects of MPEP and the drug. Findings on the effects of pharmacological increase in mGlu5 receptor signaling using the mGlu5 receptor PAM on drug-seeking behavior would be useful in further determining the role of mGlu5 receptor activity in drug-seeking, however, that research area is a gap in the literature that needs to be fulfilled in future. Finally, studies from our laboratory provide further evidence against the hypothesis that reductions in mGlu5 receptor signaling reduce rewarding properties of drugs of abuse. Specifically, we observed that mGlu5-KO mice acquire ethanol CPP similarly to their WT littermates, yet consume less ethanol with reduced preference [38]. This finding is consistent with the report that systemic MPEP injection had no effects on cocaine CPP in rats [101], but contrasts with our finding that MTEP prevented CPP to cocaine in mice [102]. We will discuss the complexities and potential explanations of these apparently conflicting findings more in detail in the later sections.

THE EFFECTS OF GENETIC OR PHARMACOLOGICAL REDUCTION IN MGLU5 RECEPTOR SIGNALING ON RELAPSE

The central problem facing drug addiction is the enduring vulnerability of addicts to relapse despite months or even years of abstinence [9-15]. This is at least partly because chronic, repeated drug use leads to the formation of powerful and lasting associations between the drug's effects, drug-specific withdrawal symptoms, and the environmental cues and contexts that are present at the time these drug-related effects are experienced. As a result, these stimuli become over-conditioned and over-learned. Therefore, it has been proposed that extinction, which involves an active learning to inhibit drug-seeking responses to drug-related cues and environments, is likely to be more effective compared to abstinence for the treatment of drug addiction [103]. Indeed, cue or drug-induced reinstatement of drug-seeking behavior is significantly reduced following extinction of the operant response compared to abstinence [104-106]. Further, extinction of cues present at the time of self-administration also significantly reduces cue-induced reinstatement compared to no-extinction controls [107]. Therefore, extinction can be conceptualized as cognitive-behavioral therapy, or 'rehabilitation', for substance abusers, where addicts may learn cognitive and behavioral strategies to control and/or inhibit drug-seeking habits and drug-associted cues.

The Role of mGlu5 Receptors in Relapse After Extinction

While there is a wide acceptance as to extinction's effectiveness in reducing relapse compared to abstinence, treatment approaches such as cue-exposure therapy that are used to desensitize the addict to the psychological and physiological responses evoked by drug-associated stimuli have shown only modest success rates [108, 109]. In the laboratory, relapse following extinction is still observed if the animal is exposed to the drug, drug-associated cue or context. Therefore, researchers have begun to examine the effects of modulating mGlu5 receptor signaling on relapse of drug-seeking behavior after extinction. As with the self-administration literature, the findings are largely consistent across several studies. For example, Backstrom et al. (2004) first trained rats to lever press for ethanol. Each delivery of ethanol was accompanied with a 3 s light-cue above the lever. During extinction, lever presses were no longer rewarded with ethanol, and rats showed a decrease in operant responding over the course of extinction. At reinstatement test, presentation of the light-cue alone evoked robust return of lever-pressing behavior, which was intensified when some ethanol was also presented with the light-cue. This reinstatement of ethanol-seeking was dose-dependently attenuated by a systemic injection of MPEP prior to the reinstatement test [81]. This finding was replicated with MPEP/MTEP in rats and mice using cocaine, methamphetamine, nicotine or natural rewards such as sweet condensed milk using a variety of different cues that were previously associated with drug delivery [77, 85, 87, 110-113]. Mutant mice with genetic deletion of mGlu5 receptors also displayed reduced cue-induced reinstatement to food reward [111]. Additionally, systemic injection of MTEP before a footshock stressor or drug prime also attenuated reinstatement of drug- and food-seeking [77, 86, 87, 114]. It should be noted that microinfusion of MPEP in the NAc had no effects on cue-induced reinstatement of cocaine-seeking, indicating that the locus of mGlu5 receptor's role in reinstatement may not be in the NAc in this instance [115].

There is a striking difference that emerges between the effects of mGlu5 receptor antagonism on self-administration versus reinstatement following extinction of drug-seeking behavior. That is, the effects of MPEP/MTEP on self-administration appear specific to drugs of abuse, rather than natural rewards such as sucrose. However, the same drugs affect reinstatement of extinguished operant response to both drugs of abuse and natural rewards. Therefore, while reducing mGlu5 receptor signaling may have effects (increasing or decreasing) on the hedonic properties of drugs of abuse such as cocaine while the animal is receiving the drug, its effects on reward-seeking behavior is more generalised across natural rewards and drugs of abuse during reinstatement sessions. This may be because during a typical reinstatement session, there is no drug/reward delivery following the operant response. Therefore, we propose that the role of mGlu5 receptor in relapse following extinction may be cognitive as well as (or instead of) perceptual and/or motivational. That is, pre-reinstatement injection of MPEP/MTEP may impair general memory retrieval of the previous CS-reward experience, thus attenuating relapse across different types of rewards, not just drugs of abuse. Such explanation is plausible because it is well-established that mGlu5 receptors play a critical role in NMDA receptor-mediated LTP and LTD [66-68, 70, 71], putative cellular mechanisms for learning and memory [60, 69].

The Role of mGlu5 Receptors in Relapse Following Abstinence

Unfortunately, only a small proportion of the millions of people suffering from addiction actually seek and/or can afford cognitive-behavioral treatment. For example, out of 23.5 million Americans who were considered to have an illicit drug or alcohol use problem, only 2.6 million (11.2%) received treatment at a specialty facility in 2009 [116]. Rather, many drug addicts attempt to overcome their addiction by simply attempting to abstain from drug use (known as going 'cold turkey'). Therefore, it is clinically relevant to examine relapse after abstinence as well as extinction. One of the major factors influencing such high relapse rates after abstinence in drug addicts is that craving induced by drug cues may actually increase over the first several weeks of the withdrawal period and remains elevated over extended periods of abstinence [117, 118]. Scientists have since discovered an analogous phenomenon in laboratory animals which has been termed 'incubation of craving'. For example, cue-induced drug-seeking behavior increases as the length of time of abstinence increases [119-121]. Incubation of craving is also observed with the natural reward sucrose [122], however, drugs of abuse cause incubation of craving that persists over a much longer time period compared to natural rewards [123]. In a typical abstinence-relapse study, the animal first undergoes a period of self-administration to acquire stable levels of drug administration. The animal then is forced into withdrawal for a period of time (typically a number of weeks) in the home cage [124, 125]. At the end of this period drug-seeking behavior is measured by re-introducing the subject to the operant chamber and measuring responding in the absence of drug. Cues that were present during the self-administration sessions are re-introduced, or the reward itself immediately before the session, to examine increases in relapse due to the drug/cue exposure.

To our knowledge, there are only two studies that examined the role of mGlu5 receptor in relapse following abstinence. Schroeder et al. (2005) initially showed that following prolonged withdrawal period from ethanol self-administration, rats showed high levels of operant responding when returned to the self-administration chambers. However, pre-test injection of MPEP significantly reduced operant responding in rats compared to vehicle injection [83]. Consistent with these data, our laboratory has shown that pre-test injection of MTEP combined with the selective adenosine A_{2A} receptor antagonist SCH58261 significantly attenuated cue-induced alcohol-seeking after 4 weeks of withdrawal from ethanol self-administration [52]. These findings are reminiscent of the effects of mGlu5 receptor antagonism on relapse following extinction, and we maintain the idea that the role of mGlu5 receptor in relapse following abstinence as well as extinction could reflect memory impairment as well as / rather than motivation.

MGLU5 RECEPTORS IN LEARNING AND MEMORY

The research described so far all highlight the importance of mGlu5 receptor signaling in different aspects and stages of drug-seeking behavior. However, most authors have interpreted the findings to be due to mGlu5 receptors influencing the motivational or rewarding properties of the drug or drug-associated cues.

Although such interpretation may well account for some of the findings, there are numerous data that cannot be explained by pure changes in motivation or hedonic properties of the reward. We propose an alternative interpretation of the findings – the effects of changes in mGlu5 receptor signaling significantly affects drug-seeking behavior through mediating learning, memory and retrieval mechanisms underlying drug addiction. Importantly, this hypothesis is not mutually exclusive from a putative role of mGlu5 receptors in the motivational/reinforcing properties of drugs of abuse. Indeed, it is quite possible that both mechanisms may contribute to the overall outcome. Additionally, mGlu5 signalling may affect learning and memory of the cue, action, and / or the incentive salience of the cue [126, 127].

Memory formation has long been thought to be sub-served by a mechanism called 'synaptic plasticity', which refers to molecular and morphological changes that occur in dendrites and axons that either enhance or reduce the effectiveness of electrical and/or chemical communication between neurons across synapses [128]. Research in the past 50 years has revealed that synaptic plasticity requires various molecular cascades that ultimately result in modifications of synaptic structure and efficacy [129, 130]. The best-studied mechanism that is widely believed to potentiate these changes is NMDA-dependent LTP [131]. LTP refers to a lasting enhancement of the strength of synaptic connection as a result of brief repetitive activation of that synaptic pathway [69]. Typically, excitatory synaptic signaling occurs chemically via presynaptic release of glutamate into the synapse.

Glutamate then binds to 2-amino-3-(5-methyl-3-oxo-1,2-oxazol-4-yl)propanoic acid (AMPA) receptors on the postsynaptic membrane, triggering the influx of positively-charged of sodium ions into the postsynaptic neuron [132]. Such influx of ions causes depolarization of the cell, called the excitatory postsynaptic potential (EPSP). Likewise, the induction of LTP begins with NMDA receptor activation that leads to an influx of positively-charged calcium ions through a ligand- and voltage-gated calcium channels into the postsynaptic neuron, causing depolarization [133].

If calcium influx does not reach a threshold, LTP fails to occur [134]. The rapid rise in intracellular calcium concentration initiates the short- or long-lasting activation of several proteins that appear to be necessary for LTP. For example, blocking phosphorylation (i.e., activation) of calcium/calmodulin-dependent protein kinase II (CaMKII) and protein kinase C (PKC) impairs the induction and maintenance of LTP [131]. Importantly, LTP disruption has been shown to impair memory consolidation in a region-specific manner [135-139]. In the hippocampus, for example, antagonism of NMDA receptors impairs both LTP induction as well as hippocampal-dependent spatial learning in rats [140].

Because antagonism of mGlu5 receptors can attenuate, or even prevent, NMDA receptor-mediated LTP [66-68, 70, 71], it is logical to expect changes in mGlu5 receptor signaling affects drug-seeking behavior through mediating memory processes. This account can, in theory, explain many of the behavioral findings described in the present chapter. Firstly, retardation of developing self-administration behavior may reflect mGlu5 antagonism disrupting learning, rather than changing the rewarding properties of the drug/reward. Secondly, reduction in already established self-administration may indicate mGlu5 antagonism interfering with the retrieval of operant conditioning memory. Lastly, attenuation of relapse following abstinence or extinction could reflect impaired retrieval of the drug experience or drug-associated cues and environments. This learning and memory theory on the role of the mGlu5 receptor is supported by the findings that MPEP decreases ethanol self-administration via a PKC-dependent mechanism in the NAc shell region [80, 94]. Also, intracerebroventricular infusion of MPEP significantly inhibited the up-regulation of PKC in the limbic forebrain of mice showing CPP to morphine [141]. As mentioned earlier, PKC is a protein critically involved in learning and memory [130, 142], and these findings strongly suggest that mGlu5 receptors could affect drug-seeking via learning and memory processes.

THE ROLE OF MGLU5 RECEPTOR IN THE EXTINCTION OF DRUG-SEEKING BEHAVIOR

Modulating learning and memory of drug-seeking behavior and its associated cues and contexts as a potential role for mGlu5 receptor signaling presents mGlu5 receptor antagonism as a double-edged sword for addiction therapeutics. That is, the ability of MPEP/MTEP in reducing drug self-administration and relapse has led researchers to suggest negative allosteric modulation of mGlu5 receptors as target for prevention of development and relapse of drug addiction [75, 76, 81, 85, 143]. However, if it is the case that mGlu5 receptor antagonism disrupts learning and memory, MPEP/MTEP should also interfere with extinction of drug-seeking behavior because extinction is a new learning.

Therefore, treating addicts with MPEP/MTEP putatively to reduce acute craving symptoms during cognitive-behavioral therapy sessions may significantly reduce the long-term efficacy of therapy because extinction learning is disrupted. Indeed, studies published to date indicate that mGlu5 receptors do indeed play a critical role in extinction of drug-seeking behavior. Olive and colleagues used the mGlu5 receptor PAM CDPPB (3-cyano-N-(1,3-diphenyl-1Hpyrazol-5-yl) benzamide) to assess the effects of elevated mGlu5 signaling on extinction of drug-seeking behavior. In the first study of its kind, they initially conditioned rats to express CPP using cocaine [144]. Rats then were systemically injected with either CDPPB or its vehicle 20 mins prior to daily extinction training. Pre-extinction injections of CDPPB dose-dependently facilitated the extinction of cocaine CPP, in that rats required significantly less days of extinction training to reach extinction criterion compared to vehicle injections [144].

The same group recently replicated this finding using cocaine intravenous self-administration [145]. Both pre- and post-extinction daily injections of CDPPB significantly reduced operant responding, and significantly reduced the number of days to reach extinction compared to vehicle injections. The post-extinction injection data are very important in ruling out any state-dependent explanation of mGlu5 receptor manipulation, which confounded many of the studies described earlier in the present chapter as most of them gave injections prior to the behavioral sessions. Taken together, the facilitating effects of CDPPB on extinction learning support the idea that mGlu5 receptors play a significant role in learning and memory mechanisms underlying drug addiction.

CONCLUSION

In summary therefore, we provide a review of the status of mGlu5-mediated signaling in various aspects of complex behaviors related to drug-seeking and drug-taking. There may be a role for mGlu5 receptors in gauging the reinforcing and motivational properties of drug (and natural) rewards. Nevertheless, we also posit that mGlu5 signaling mechanisms (and downstream cascades) may also be intimately linked to cognitive processes that underpin drug-seeking and extinction. Consonant with this hypothesis, there are convincing demonstrations that, in rodents at least, mGlu5 antagonism can prevent the associative learning processes necessary for the acquisition of the incentive value of a CS [126]. Moreover, mGlu5 receptors, specifically located on dopamine D1 receptor-positive medium spiny neurons of the striatal complex have been suggested to play a role in the incentive learning associated with cue-induced reinstatement of cocaine-seeking [127]. Accordingly, there is still great scope to unravel the precise mechanisms how, and circuitry where, mGlu5 signaling impacts upon reward-seeking, self-administration, extinction and reinstatement and more importantly, to interrogate the cognitive processes critical in these behaviors.

REFERENCES

[1]   WHO, Management of substance abuse: facts and figures. 2008, *World Health Organization*, Geneva.

[2]   WHO, The World Health Report - Reducing Risks, Promoting Healthy Life. 2002, *World Health Organization*, Geneva.

[3]   Kessler, R.C., et al., Prevalence, severity, and comorbidity of 12-month DSM-IV disorders in the National Comorbidity Survey Replication. *Arch. Gen. Psychiatry*, 2005. 62(6): p. 617-27.

[4]   Pouletty, P., Drug addictions: towards socially accepted and medically treatable diseases. *Nat. Rev. Drug Discov.*, 2002. 1(9): p. 731-6.

[5]   Collins, D.J. and H.M. Lapsley, The costs of tobacco, alcohol, and illicit drug abuse to Australian society in 2004/05. 2005, Canberra: *Department of Health and Ageing*.

[6]   Jupp, B. and A.J. Lawrence, New horizons for therapeutics in drug and alcohol abuse. *Pharmacol. Ther.*, 2010. 125(1): p. 138-68.

[7]   Boening, J.A., et al., Pharmacological relapse prevention in alcohol dependence: from animal models to clinical trials. *Alcohol. Clin. Exp. Res.*, 2001. 25(5 Suppl ISBRA): p. 127S-131S.

[8]   O'Brien, C.P., Progress in the science of addiction. *Am. J. Psychiatry*, 1997. 154(9): p. 1195-7.

[9]   Bossert, J.M., et al., Neurobiology of relapse to heroin and cocaine seeking: an update and clinical implications. *Eur. J. Pharmacol.*, 2005. 526(1-3): p. 36-50.

[10] Brown, R.M. and A.J. Lawrence, Neurochemistry underlying relapse to opiate seeking behaviour. *Neurochem. Res.*, 2009. 34(10): p. 1876-87.

[11] Capriles, N., et al., A role for the prefrontal cortex in stress- and cocaine-induced reinstatement of cocaine seeking in rats. *Psychopharmacology (Berl)*, 2003. 168(1-2): p. 66-74.

[12] Crombag, H.S., et al., Review. Context-induced relapse to drug seeking: a review. *Philos. Trans. R. Soc. Lond. B. Biol. Sci.*, 2008. 363(1507): p. 3233-43.

[13] Cruz, F.C., M.T. Marin, and C.S. Planeta, The reinstatement of amphetamine-induced place preference is long-lasting and related to decreased expression of AMPA receptors in the nucleus accumbens. *Neuroscience*, 2008. 151(2): p. 313-9.

[14] DeJong, W., Relapse prevention: an emerging technology for promoting long-term drug abstinence. *Int. J. Addict.*, 1994. 29(6): p. 681-705.

[15] Deroche-Gamonet, V., D. Belin, and P.V. Piazza, Evidence for addiction-like behavior in the rat. *Science*, 2004. 305(5686): p. 1014-7.

[16] Myers, K.M. and W.A. Carlezon, Jr., Extinction of drug- and withdrawal-paired cues in animal models: relevance to the treatment of addiction. *Neurosci. Biobehav. Rev.*, 2010. 35(2): p. 285-302.

[17] Taylor, J.R., et al., Targeting extinction and reconsolidation mechanisms to combat the impact of drug cues on addiction. *Neuropharmacology*, 2009. 56 Suppl 1: p. 186-95.

[18] Robinson, T.E. and K.C. Berridge, Addiction. Annu. Rev. Psychol., 2003. 54: p. 25-53.

[19] Robinson, T.E. and K.C. Berridge, Incentive-sensitization and addiction. *Addiction*, 2001. 96(1): p. 103-14.

[20] Childress, A.R., A.T. McLellan, and C.P. O'Brien, Role of conditioning factors in the development of drug dependence. *Psychiatr. Clin. North. Am.*, 1986. 9(3): p. 413-25.

[21] Franklin, T.R., et al., Limbic activation to cigarette smoking cues independent of nicotine withdrawal: a perfusion fMRI study. *Neuropsychopharmacology*, 2007. 32(11): p. 2301-9.

[22] Childress, A.R., et al., Limbic activation during cue-induced cocaine craving. *Am. J. Psychiatry.*, 1999. 156(1): p. 11-8.

[23] Childress, A.R., A.T. McLellan, and C.P. O'Brien, Nature and incidence of conditioned responses in a methadone population: a comparison of laboratory, clinic, and naturalistic settings. *NIDA Res. Monogr.*, 1986. 67: p. 366-72.

[24] Childress, A.R., A.T. McLellan, and C.P. O'Brien, Abstinent opiate abusers exhibit conditioned craving, conditioned withdrawal and reductions in both through extinction. *Br. J. Addict.*, 1986. 81(5): p. 655-60.

[25] O'Brien, C., et al., Conditioning mechanisms in drug dependence. *Clin. Neuropharmacol.*, 1992. 15 Suppl 1 Pt A: p. 66A-67A.

[26] Sutton, M.A., et al., Extinction-induced upregulation in AMPA receptors reduces cocaine-seeking behaviour. *Nature*, 2003. 421(6918): p. 70-5.

[27] Olive, M.F., Cognitive effects of Group I metabotropic glutamate receptor ligands in the context of drug addiction. *Eur. J. Pharmacol.*, 2010. 639(1-3): p. 47-58.

[28] Lattal, K.M., J. Radulovic, and K. Lukowiak, Extinction: [corrected] does it or doesn't it? The requirement of altered gene activity and new protein synthesis. *Biol. Psychiatry,* 2006. 60(4): p. 344-51.

[29] Myers, K.M., W.A. Carlezon, Jr., and M. Davis, Glutamate receptors in extinction and extinction-based therapies for psychiatric illness. *Neuropsychopharmacology,* 2011. 36(1): p. 274-93.

[30] Robinson, S., et al., Distinguishing whether dopamine regulates liking, wanting, and/or learning about rewards. *Behav. Neurosci.,* 2005. 119(1): p. 5-15.

[31] Jentsch, J.D., et al., Impairments of reversal learning and response perseveration after repeated, intermittent cocaine administrations to monkeys. *Neuropsychopharmacology,* 2002. 26(2): p. 183-90.

[32] Bouton, M.E., Context, ambiguity, and unlearning: sources of relapse after behavioral extinction. *Biol. Psychiatry,* 2002. 52(10): p. 976-86.

[33] Bardo, M.T. and R.A. Bevins, Conditioned place preference: what does it add to our preclinical understanding of drug reward? *Psychopharmacology (Berl),* 2000. 153(1): p. 31-43.

[34] Tzschentke, T.M., Measuring reward with the conditioned place preference paradigm: a comprehensive review of drug effects, recent progress and new issues. *Prog. Neurobiol.,* 1998. 56(6): p. 613-72.

[35] Brown, R.M., J.L. Short, and A.J. Lawrence, Identification of brain nuclei implicated in cocaine-primed reinstatement of conditioned place preference: a behaviour dissociable from sensitization. *PLoS One,* 2010. 5(12): p. e15889.

[36] Nathaniel, T.I., J. Panksepp, and R. Huber, Drug-seeking behavior in an invertebrate system: Evidence of morphine-induced reward, extinction and reinstatement in crayfish. *Behavioural Brain Research,* 2009. 197(2): p. 331-338.

[37] Abarca, C., U. Albrecht, and R. Spanagel, Cocaine sensitization and reward are under the influence of circadian genes and rhythm. *Proc. Natl. Acad. Sci. USA,* 2002. 99(13): p. 9026-30.

[38] Bird, M.K., et al., Metabotropic glutamate 5 receptors regulate sensitivity to ethanol in mice. *Int. J. Neuropsychopharmacol.,* 2008. 11(6): p. 765-74.

[39] Gass, J.T. and M.F. Olive, Positive allosteric modulation of mGluR5 receptors facilitates extinction of a cocaine contextual memory. *Biol. Psychiatry,* 2009. 65(8): p. 717-20.

[40] Lu, L., et al., Reactivation of cocaine conditioned place preference induced by stress is reversed by cholecystokinin-B receptors antagonist in rats. *Brain Res.,* 2002. 954(1): p. 132-40.

[41] Parker, L.A. and R.V. McDonald, Reinstatement of both a conditioned place preference and a conditioned place aversion with drug primes. *Pharmacol. Biochem. Behav.,* 2000. 66(3): p. 559-61.

[42] Macey, D.J., et al., Chronic cocaine self-administration upregulates the norepinephrine transporter and alters functional activity in the bed nucleus of the stria terminalis of the rhesus monkey. *J. Neurosci.,* 2003. 23(1): p. 12-6.

[43] Stretch, R., G.J. Gerber, and S.M. Wood, Factors affecting behavior maintained by response-contingent intravenous infusions of amphetamine in squirrel monkeys. *Can. J. Physiol. Pharmacol.,* 1971. 49(6): p. 581-9.

[44] Feltenstein, M.W. and R.E. See, The neurocircuitry of addiction: an overview. *Br. J. Pharmacol.*, 2008. 154(2): p. 261-74.

[45] McPherson, C.S., et al., Deletion of CREB1 from the dorsal telencephalon reduces motivational properties of cocaine. *Cereb. Cortex*, 2010. 20(4): p. 941-52.

[46] Cowen, M.S., E. Djouma, and A.J. Lawrence, The metabotropic glutamate 5 receptor antagonist 3-[(2-methyl-1,3-thiazol-4-yl)ethynyl]-pyridine reduces ethanol self-administration in multiple strains of alcohol-preferring rats and regulates olfactory glutamatergic systems. *J. Pharmacol. Exp. Ther.*, 2005. 315(2): p. 590-600.

[47] van der Kam, E.L., J. de Vry, and T.M. Tzschentke, Effect of 2-methyl-6-(phenylethynyl) pyridine on intravenous self-administration of ketamine and heroin in the rat. *Behav. Pharmacol.*, 2007. 18(8): p. 717-24.

[48] Kornet, M., C. Goosen, and J.M. Van Ree, The effect of interrupted alcohol supply on spontaneous alcohol consumption by rhesus monkeys. *Alcohol Alcohol*, 1990. 25(4): p. 407-12.

[49] Collins, R.J., et al., Prediction of abuse liability of drugs using IV self-administration by rats. *Psychopharmacology (Berl)*, 1984. 82(1-2): p. 6-13.

[50] Griffiths, R.R., J.V. Brady, and J.D. Snell, Progressive-ratio performance maintained by drug infusions: comparison of cocaine, diethylpropion, chlorphentermine, and fenfluramine. *Psychopharmacology*, 1978. 56(1): p. 5-13.

[51] Grasing, K., et al., A new progressive ratio schedule for support of morphine self-administration in opiate dependent rats. *Psychopharmacology*, 2003. 168(4): p. 387-96.

[52] Adams, C.L., J.L. Short, and A.J. Lawrence, Cue-conditioned alcohol seeking in rats following abstinence: involvement of metabotropic glutamate 5 receptors. *Br. J. Pharmacol.*, 2010. 159(3): p. 534-42.

[53] Jupp, B., et al., Discrete cue-conditioned alcohol-seeking after protracted abstinence: pattern of neural activation and involvement of orexin(1) receptors. *Br. J. Pharmacol.*, 2011. 162(4): p. 880-9.

[54] Aguilar, M.A., M. Rodriguez-Arias, and J. Minarro, Neurobiological mechanisms of the reinstatement of drug-conditioned place preference. *Brain Res. Rev.*, 2009. 59(2): p. 253-77.

[55] Shaham, Y., et al., The reinstatement model of drug relapse: history, methodology and major findings. *Psychopharmacology (Berl)*, 2003. 168(1-2): p. 3-20.

[56] Stewart, J. and R.A. Wise, Reinstatement of heroin self-administration habits: morphine prompts and naltrexone discourages renewed responding after extinction. *Psychopharmacology (Berl)*, 1992. 108 (1-2): p. 79-84.

[57] Kalivas, P.W., et al., Glutamate transmission in addiction. *Neuropharmacology*, 2009. 56 Suppl 1: p. 169-73.

[58] Knackstedt, L.A. and P.W. Kalivas, Glutamate and reinstatement. *Curr. Opin. Pharmacol.*, 2009. 9(1): p. 59-64.

[59] McFarland, K., C.C. Lapish, and P.W. Kalivas, Prefrontal glutamate release into the core of the nucleus accumbens mediates cocaine-induced reinstatement of drug-seeking behavior. *J. Neurosci.*, 2003. 23(8): p. 3531-7.

[60] Kasanetz, F., et al., Transition to addiction is associated with a persistent impairment in synaptic plasticity. *Science*, 2010. 328(5986): p. 1709-12.

[61] Spooren, W., et al., Insight into the function of Group I and Group II metabotropic glutamate (mGlu) receptors: behavioural characterization and implications for the treatment of CNS disorders. *Behav. Pharmacol.*, 2003. 14(4): p. 257-77.

[62] Hermans, E. and R.A. Challiss, Structural, signalling and regulatory properties of the group I metabotropic glutamate receptors: prototypic family C G-protein-coupled receptors. *Biochem. J.*, 2001. 359(Pt 3): p. 465-84.

[63] Bird, M.K. and A.J. Lawrence, Group I metabotropic glutamate receptors: involvement in drug-seeking and drug-induced plasticity. *Curr. Mol. Pharmacol.*, 2009. 2(1): p. 83-94.

[64] Romano, C., et al., Distribution of metabotropic glutamate receptor mGluR5 immunoreactivity in rat brain. *J. Comp. Neurol.*, 1995. 355(3): p. 455-69.

[65] Shigemoto, R., et al., Immunohistochemical localization of a metabotropic glutamate receptor, mGluR5, in the rat brain. *Neurosci. Lett.*, 1993. 163(1): p. 53-7.

[66] Lu, Y.M., et al., Mice lacking metabotropic glutamate receptor 5 show impaired learning and reduced CA1 long-term potentiation (LTP) but normal CA3 LTP. *J. Neurosci.*, 1997. 17(13): p. 5196-205.

[67] Jia, Z., et al., Selective abolition of the NMDA component of long-term potentiation in mice lacking mGluR5. *Learn Mem.*, 1998. 5(4-5): p. 331-43.

[68] Fitzjohn, S.M., et al., DHPG-induced LTD in area CA1 of juvenile rat hippocampus; characterisation and sensitivity to novel mGlu receptor antagonists. *Neuropharmacology*, 1999. 38(10): p. 1577-83.

[69] Bliss, T.V. and G.L. Collingridge, A synaptic model of memory: long-term potentiation in the hippocampus. *Nature*, 1993. 361(6407): p. 31-9.

[70] Rosenbrock, H., et al., Functional interaction of metabotropic glutamate receptor 5 and NMDA-receptor by a metabotropic glutamate receptor 5 positive allosteric modulator. *Eur. J. Pharmacol.*, 2010. 639(1-3): p. 40-6.

[71] Ayala, J.E., et al., mGluR5 positive allosteric modulators facilitate both hippocampal LTP and LTD and enhance spatial learning. *Neuropsychopharmacology*, 2009. 34(9): p. 2057-71.

[72] Ghasemzadeh, M.B., et al., Neuroadaptations in ionotropic and metabotropic glutamate receptor mRNA produced by cocaine treatment. *Journal of Neurochemistry*, 1999. 72(1): p. 157-65.

[73] Chiamulera, C., et al., Reinforcing and locomotor stimulant effects of cocaine are absent in mGluR5 null mutant mice. *Nat. Neurosci.*, 2001. 4(9): p. 873-4.

[74] Gasparini, F., et al., 2-Methyl-6-(phenylethynyl)-pyridine (MPEP), a potent, selective and systemically active mGlu5 receptor antagonist. *Neuropharmacology*, 1999. 38(10): p. 1493-503.

[75] Kenny, P.J., et al., Metabotropic glutamate 5 receptor antagonist MPEP decreased nicotine and cocaine self-administration but not nicotine and cocaine-induced facilitation of brain reward function in rats. *Annals of the New York Academy of Sciences*, 2003. 1003: p. 415-8.

[76] Platt, D.M., J.K. Rowlett, and R.D. Spealman, Attenuation of cocaine self-administration in squirrel monkeys following repeated administration of the mGluR5 antagonist MPEP: comparison with dizocilpine. *Psychopharmacology*, 2008. 200(2): p. 167-76.

[77] Tessari, M., et al., Antagonism at metabotropic glutamate 5 receptors inhibits nicotine- and cocaine-taking behaviours and prevents nicotine-triggered relapse to nicotine-seeking. *European journal of pharmacology,* 2004. 499(1-2): p. 121-33.

[78] Paterson, N.E., et al., The mGluR5 antagonist MPEP decreased nicotine self-administration in rats and mice. *Psychopharmacology,* 2003. 167(3): p. 257-64.

[79] Tronci, V., et al., The effects of the mGluR5 receptor antagonist 6-methyl-2-(phenylethynyl)-pyridine (MPEP) on behavioural responses to nicotine. *Psychopharmacology,* 2010. 211(1): p. 33-42.

[80] Olive, M.F., et al., The mGluR5 antagonist 6-methyl-2-(phenylethynyl)pyridine decreases ethanol consumption via a protein kinase C epsilon-dependent mechanism. *Molecular pharmacology,* 2005. 67(2): p. 349-55.

[81] Backstrom, P., et al., mGluR5 antagonist MPEP reduces ethanol-seeking and relapse behavior. *Neuropsychopharmacology : official publication of the American College of Neuropsychopharmacology,* 2004. 29(5): p. 921-8.

[82] Gupta, T., et al., Acute effects of acamprosate and MPEP on ethanol Drinking-in-the-Dark in male C57BL/6J mice. *Alcoholism, clinical and experimental research,* 2008. 32(11): p. 1992-8.

[83] Schroeder, J.P., D.H. Overstreet, and C.W. Hodge, The mGluR5 antagonist MPEP decreases operant ethanol self-administration during maintenance and after repeated alcohol deprivations in alcohol-preferring (P) rats. *Psychopharmacology,* 2005. 179(1): p. 262-70.

[84] Anderson, J.J., et al., [3H]Methoxymethyl-3-[(2-methyl-1,3-thiazol-4-yl)ethynyl]-pyridine binding to metabotropic glutamate receptor subtype 5 in rodent brain: in vitro and in vivo characterization. *J. Pharmacol. Exp. Ther.,* 2002. 303(3): p. 1044-51.

[85] Martin-Fardon, R., et al., Dissociation of the effects of MTEP [3-[(2-methyl-1,3-thiazol-4-yl)ethynyl]piperidine] on conditioned reinstatement and reinforcement: comparison between cocaine and a conventional reinforcer. *The Journal of pharmacology and experimental therapeutics,* 2009. 329(3): p. 1084-90.

[86] Lee, B., et al., Attenuation of behavioral effects of cocaine by the Metabotropic Glutamate Receptor 5 Antagonist 2-Methyl-6-(phenylethynyl)-pyridine in squirrel monkeys: comparison with dizocilpine. *The Journal of pharmacology and experimental therapeutics,* 2005. 312(3): p. 1232-40.

[87] Gass, J.T., et al., mGluR5 antagonism attenuates methamphetamine reinforcement and prevents reinstatement of methamphetamine-seeking behavior in rats. *Neur-opsycho-pharmacology,* 2009. 34(4): p. 820-33.

[88] Osborne, M.P. and M.F. Olive, A role for mGluR5 receptors in intravenous methamphetamine self-administration. *Annals of the New York Academy of Sciences,* 2008. 1139: p. 206-11.

[89] Palmatier, M.I., et al., Metabotropic glutamate 5 receptor (mGluR5) antagonists decrease nicotine seeking, but do not affect the reinforcement enhancing effects of nicotine. Neuropsychopharmacology : official publication of the American College of *Neuropsychopharmacology,* 2008. 33(9): p. 2139-47.

[90] Brown, R.M., et al., The mGlu5 receptor antagonist MTEP attenuates opiate self-administration and cue-induced opiate-seeking behaviour in mice. *Drug Alcohol Depend,* 2011.

[91] Cowen, M.S., E. Krstew, and A.J. Lawrence, Assessing appetitive and consummatory phases of ethanol self-administration in C57BL/6J mice under operant conditions: regulation by mGlu5 receptor antagonism. *Psychopharmacology (Berl)*, 2007. 190(1): p. 21-9.

[92] Sidhpura, N., F. Weiss, and R. Martin-Fardon, Effects of the mGlu2/3 agonist LY379268 and the mGlu5 antagonist MTEP on ethanol seeking and reinforcement are differentially altered in rats with a history of ethanol dependence. *Biological Psychiatry*, 2010. 67(9): p. 804-11.

[93] Besheer, J., et al., Metabotropic glutamate receptor 5 activity in the nucleus accumbens is required for the maintenance of ethanol self-administration in a rat genetic model of high alcohol intake. Biological *psychiatry*, 2010. 67(9): p. 812-22.

[94] Gass, J.T. and M.F. Olive, Role of protein kinase C epsilon (PKCvarepsilon) in the reduction of ethanol reinforcement due to mGluR5 antagonism in the nucleus accumbens shell. *Psychopharmacology (Berl)*, 2009. 204(4): p. 587-97.

[95] Paterson, N.E. and A. Markou, The metabotropic glutamate receptor 5 antagonist MPEP decreased break points for nicotine, cocaine and food in rats. *Psychopharmacology*, 2005. 179(1): p. 255-61.

[96] Markou, A. and G.F. Koob, Construct validity of a self-stimulation threshold paradigm: effects of reward and performance manipulations. *Physiology and behavior*, 1992. 51(1): p. 111-9.

[97] Harrison, A.A., F. Gasparini, and A. Markou, Nicotine potentiation of brain stimulation reward reversed by DH beta E and SCH 23390, but not by eticlopride, LY 314582 or MPEP in rats. *Psychopharmacology*, 2002. 160(1): p. 56-66.

[98] Cleva, R.M., et al., Differential Modulation of Thresholds for Intracranial Self-Stimulation by mGlu5 Positive and Negative Allosteric Modulators: Implications for Effects on Drug Self-Administration. *Frontiers in pharmacology*, 2012. 2: p. 93.

[99] van der Kam, E.L., J. De Vry, and T.M. Tzschentke, The mGlu5 receptor antagonist 2-methyl-6-(phenylethynyl)pyridine (MPEP) supports intravenous self-administration and induces conditioned place preference in the rat. *European Journal of Pharmacology*, 2009. 607(1-3): p. 114-20.

[100] van der Kam, E.L., J. De Vry, and T.M. Tzschentke, 2-Methyl-6-(phenylethynyl)-pyridine (MPEP) potentiates ketamine and heroin reward as assessed by acquisition, extinction, and reinstatement of conditioned place preference in the rat. *European Journal of Pharmacology*, 2009. 606(1-3): p. 94-101.

[101] Herzig, V. and W.J. Schmidt, Effects of MPEP on locomotion, sensitization and conditioned reward induced by cocaine or morphine. *Neuropharmacology*, 2004. 47(7): p. 973-84.

[102] Brown, R.M., et al., mGlu5 and adenosine A2A receptor interactions regulate the conditioned effects of cocaine. *Int. J. Neuropsychopharmacol.*, 2011: p. 1-7.

[103] Knackstedt, L.A., et al., Extinction training after cocaine self-administration induces glutamatergic plasticity to inhibit cocaine seeking. *J. Neurosci.*, 2010. 30(23): p. 7984-92.

[104] Kelamangalath, L., et al., The effects of extinction training in reducing the reinstatement of drug-seeking behavior: involvement of NMDA receptors. *Behav. Brain Res.*, 2007. 185(2): p. 119-28.

[105] Fuchs, R.A., R.K. Branham, and R.E. See, Different neural substrates mediate cocaine seeking after abstinence versus extinction training: a critical role for the dorsolateral caudate-putamen. *J. Neurosci.*, 2006. 26(13): p. 3584-8.

[106] Kelamangalath, L. and J.J. Wagner, Effects of abstinence or extinction on cocaine seeking as a function of withdrawal duration. *Behavioural pharmacology*, 2009. 20(2): p. 195-203.

[107] Krank, M.D. and A.M. Wall, Cue exposure during a period of abstinence reduces the resumption of operant behavior for oral ethanol reinforcement. Behavioral neuroscience, 1990. 104(5): p. 725-33.

[108] Conklin, C.A. and S.T. Tiffany, Cue-exposure treatment: time for change. *Addiction,* 2002. 97(9): p. 1219-21.

[109] Havermans, R.C. and A.T. Jansen, Increasing the efficacy of cue exposure treatment in preventing relapse of addictive behavior. *Addictive behaviors,* 2003. 28(5): p. 989-94.

[110] Kumaresan, V., et al., Metabotropic glutamate receptor 5 (mGluR5) antagonists attenuate cocaine priming- and cue-induced reinstatement of cocaine seeking. *Behav. Brain Res.*, 2009. 202(2): p. 238-44.

[111] Eiler, W.J., 2nd, et al., mGlu5 receptor deletion reduces relapse to food-seeking and prevents the anti-relapse effects of mGlu5 receptor blockade in mice. *Life sciences,* 2011. 89(23-24): p. 862-7.

[112] Iso, Y., et al., Synthesis and structure-activity relationships of 3-[(2-methyl-1,3-thiazol-4-yl)ethynyl]pyridine analogues as potent, noncompetitive metabotropic glutamate receptor subtype 5 antagonists; search for cocaine medications. *Journal of medicinal chemistry,* 2006. 49(3): p. 1080-100.

[113] Bespalov, A.Y., et al., Metabotropic glutamate receptor (mGluR5) antagonist MPEP attenuated cue- and schedule-induced reinstatement of nicotine self-administration behavior in rats. *Neuropharmacology,* 2005. 49 Suppl 1: p. 167-78.

[114] Martin-Fardon, R. and F. Weiss, (-)-2-oxa-4-aminobicylco[3.1.0]hexane-4,6-dicarboxylic acid (LY379268) and 3-[(2-methyl-1,3-thiazol-4-yl)ethynyl]piperidine (MTEP) similarly attenuate stress-induced reinstatement of cocaine seeking. *Addiction biology,* 2011.

[115] Backstrom, P. and P. Hyytia, Involvement of AMPA/kainate, NMDA, and mGlu5 receptors in the nucleus accumbens core in cue-induced reinstatement of cocaine seeking in rats. *Psychopharmacology,* 2007. 192(4): p. 571-80.

[116] SAMHSA, National Survey on Drug Use and Health 2007, *Department of Health and Human Services.*

[117] Gawin, F.H. and H.D. Kleber, Abstinence symptomatology and psychiatric diagnosis in cocaine abusers. Clinical observations. *Arch. Gen. Psychiatry,* 1986. 43(2): p. 107-13.

[118] Gawin, F.H., R. Byck, and H.D. Kleber, Desipramine augmentation of cocaine abstinence: initial results. *Clin. Neuropharmacol.,* 1986. 9 Suppl 4: p. 202-4.

[119] Shalev, U., et al., Time-dependent changes in extinction behavior and stress-induced reinstatement of drug seeking following withdrawal from heroin in rats. *Psychopharmacology (Berl),* 2001. 156(1): p. 98-107.

[120] Grimm, J.W., et al., Neuroadaptation. Incubation of cocaine craving after withdrawal. *Nature,* 2001. 412(6843): p. 141-2.

[121] Bienkowski, P., et al., Time-dependent changes in alcohol-seeking behaviour during abstinence. *Eur. Neuropsychopharmacol.,* 2004. 14(5): p. 355-60.

[122] Grimm, J.W., Y. Shaham, and B.T. Hope, Effect of cocaine and sucrose withdrawal period on extinction behavior, cue-induced reinstatement, and protein levels of the dopamine transporter and tyrosine hydroxylase in limbic and cortical areas in rats. *Behav. Pharmacol.*, 2002. 13(5-6): p. 379-88.

[123] Lu, L., et al., Incubation of cocaine craving after withdrawal: a review of preclinical data. *Neuropharmacology*, 2004. 47 Suppl 1: p. 214-26.

[124] Brown, R.M., et al., A differential role for the adenosine A2A receptor in opiate reinforcement vs opiate-seeking behavior. *Neuropsychopharmacology*, 2009. 34(4): p. 844-56.

[125] Reichel, C.M. and R.A. Bevins, Forced abstinence model of relapse to study pharmacological treatments of substance use disorder. *Current drug abuse reviews*, 2009. 2(2): p. 184-94.

[126] O'Connor, E.C., et al., The mGluR5 antagonist MTEP dissociates the acquisition of predictive and incentive motivational properties of reward-paired stimuli in mice. *Neuropsychopharmacology : official publication of the American College of Neuropsychopharmacology*, 2010. 35(8): p. 1807-17.

[127] Novak, M., et al., Incentive learning underlying cocaine-seeking requires mGluR5 receptors located on dopamine D1 receptor-expressing neurons. *J. Neurosci.*, 2010. 30(36): p. 11973-82.

[128] Konorski, J., *Conditioned Reflexes and Neuron Organization*. 1948, Cambridge: University Press.

[129] Kandel, E.R., The molecular biology of memory storage: a dialogue between genes and synapses. *Science*, 2001. 294(5544): p. 1030-8.

[130] Kandel, E.R., The biology of memory: a forty-year perspective. *J. Neurosci.*, 2009. 29(41): p. 12748-56.

[131] Sweatt, J.D., Toward a molecular explanation for long-term potentiation. *Learn Mem.*, 1999. 6(5): p. 399-416.

[132] Agranoff, B.W. and G.J. Siegel, *Basic neurochemistry: molecular, cellular, and medical aspects*. 1999, Philadelphia: Lippincott-Raven.

[133] Ascher, P. and L. Nowak, A patch-clamp study of excitatory amino acid activated channels. *Advances in experimental medicine and biology*, 1986. 203: p. 507-11.

[134] Lynch, M.A., Long-term potentiation and memory. *Physiol. Rev.*, 2004. 84(1): p. 87-136.

[135] Izquierdo, I., et al., Memory processing by the limbic system: role of specific neurotransmitter systems. *Behav. Brain Res.*, 1993. 58(1-2): p. 91-8.

[136] Malenka, R.C. and M.F. Bear, LTP and LTD: an embarrassment of riches. *Neuron*, 2004. 44(1): p. 5-21.

[137] Maren, S., Long-term potentiation in the amygdala: a mechanism for emotional learning and memory. *Trends. Neurosci.*, 1999. 22(12): p. 561-7.

[138] Wu, S.P., et al., Involvement of mitogen-activated protein kinase in hippocampal long-term potentiation. *J. Biomed. Sci.*, 1999. 6(6): p. 409-17.

[139] Zweifel, L.S., et al., Role of NMDA receptors in dopamine neurons for plasticity and addictive behaviors. *Neuron*, 2008. 59(3): p. 486-96.

[140] Morris, R.G., et al., Selective impairment of learning and blockade of long-term potentiation by an N-methyl-D-aspartate receptor antagonist, AP5. *Nature*, 1986. 319(6056): p. 774-6.

[141] Aoki, T., et al., Metabotropic glutamate receptor 5 localized in the limbic forebrain is critical for the development of morphine-induced rewarding effect in mice. *Eur. J. Neurosci.,* 2004. 20(6): p. 1633-8.

[142] Ahi, J., J. Radulovic, and J. Spiess, The role of hippocampal signaling cascades in consolidation of fear memory. *Behav. Brain Res.,* 2004. 149(1): p. 17-31.

[143] Paterson, N.E., et al., The mGluR5 antagonist MPEP decreased nicotine self-administration in rats and mice. *Psychopharmacology (Berl),* 2003. 167(3): p. 257-64.

[144] Gass, J.T. and M.F. Olive, Positive allosteric modulation of mGluR5 receptors facilitates extinction of a cocaine contextual memory. *Biological psychiatry,* 2009. 65(8): p. 717-20.

[145] Cleva, R.M., et al., mGluR5 positive allosteric modulation enhances extinction learning following cocaine self-administration. *Behav. Neurosci,* 2011. 125(1): p. 10-9.

In: Emerging Targets for Drug Addiction Treatment

Editor: Juan Canales

ISBN 978-1-62081-913-5

©2012 Nova Science Publishers, Inc.

Chapter 10

TARGETING TRACE AMINE-ASSOCIATED RECEPTORS IN THE TREATMENT OF DRUG ADDICTION

*Florent G. Revel[1], Marius C. Hoener[1], J. Renau-Piqueras[2] and Juan J. Canales[3]**

[1]Neuroscience Research, Pharmaceuticals Division,
F. Hoffmann-La Roche Ltd., Switzerland
[2]Biology and Cell Pathology, Research Center, La Fe Hospital, Spain
[3]Behavioural Neuroscience, Department of Psychology,
University of Canterbury, New Zealand

ABSTRACT

Drug addiction is a debilitating disease of the brain that poses a massive burden to society. There continues to be an enormous unmet need for prevention, treatment, care and support for those who suffer from drug addiction.

According to recent global epidemiological studies, stimulant abuse is particularly challenging to treat. Research into treatment for problematic stimulant abuse has yet to find a suitable pharmacotherapeutic agent to assist with detoxification, withdrawal, and relapse prevention. The newly discovered trace amine-associated receptor 1 (TAAR1) constitutes a novel receptor target for medication development with great potential to treat the pathological changes produced by chronic drug exposure, especially in stimulant abuse.

Here, we will review neurobiological and behavioral evidence to support the hypothesis that TAAR1 regulation by means of newly developed pharmacological tools offers a new avenue for the treatment of drug addiction.

* Email: juan.canales@canterbury.ac.nz

1. INTRODUCTION

Addiction represents one of the areas in medicine that is least understood, yet it generates a staggering burden on society due to costs for treatments and loss of productivity, in addition to the tremendous impact it causes on families, the educational and school system and the workplace. The search for pharmacotherapeutic agents for use in detoxification and relapse prevention in individuals dependent on drugs has been vigorous for decades, but so far largely unsuccessful. Such agents are needed to facilitate compliance and engagement in conventional psychiatric treatments, and to maximize their positive effects. Addiction to psychoactive drugs is a disease of the brain for which new medications are needed. Psychomotor stimulants, such as cocaine and methamphetamine, are highly addictive substances which consume a tremendous amount of resources to aid in recovery and treatment worldwide. The United Nations Office on Drug Control (UNODC) estimated that some 50 million people worldwide aged 15–64 used amphetamines-type substances, excluding ecstasy, at least once in 2009 [1]. It was estimated that methamphetamine use accounted for over 50% of all amphetamine-type stimulant use [1]. Also in 2009, the annual prevalence of cocaine use was estimated between 0.3 and 0.5% of the world population aged 15-64, or some 14.2 to 20.5 million people in that age range [1]. According to the *World Drug Report* [1], the number of cocaine users remains highest in the United States and has doubled in Europe in the last decade, increasing from 2 million in 1998 to 4.1 million in 2008, thus reaching record levels. With regards to the consequences of stimulant use, there is severe associated risk of dependence and mental health problems, including neurotoxicity, psychosis, depression, cognitive problems, risky sexual practices, nonpsychiatric medical problems and violence [2-4]. Stimulant addiction is recognized for its treatment challenges. Psychosocial/behavioral treatments for drug addiction are critical for promoting recovery and preventing recidivism, however the success of current programs is limited [5,6]. While several forms of non-specific pharmacology are currently in use, including anti-depressants and anti-epileptic drugs, there are no specific medications that can safely facilitate detoxification and promote quicker recovery from chronic stimulant abuse. Research into treatment for problematic methamphetamine and cocaine use has yet to find a suitable pharmacotherapeutic agent to assist with withdrawal, craving or blockade [7-10]. There is ongoing preclinical and clinical research into substitution treatment by means of agonist therapy, using dexamphetamine and methylphenidate [8,11,12] and other experimental medications [13-16]. To date such therapeutic approach appears to have been used with severely addicted people with the primary goal of harm reduction, neurochemical normalization and retention in treatment. Clinicians indicate that the availability of medications to reduce withdrawal symptoms in the early days and weeks of discontinuation of psychostimulant abuse would improve patient care [5,9]. Such medications could, in addition, facilitate compliance and engagement in psychosocial and behavioral treatments, multiplying the beneficial effects of these approaches. If such medications were developed, the clinical and social burden of chronic stimulant abuse could be significantly reduced worldwide.

Advances in the study of the brain mechanisms that contribute to drug addiction indicate that the classical biogenic amines, which include dopamine (DA), norepinephrine (NE) and serotonin (5-HT), are critical mediators. Biogenic amines play a fundamental role in modulating a wide variety of physiological and behavioral functions, including autonomic function, hormone regulation and motor control. In addition, DA, NE and 5-HT are believed to contribute critically to emotional and cognitive function, neurotoxicity and mental disease. Trace amines (TAs) represent a group of endogenous amines intimately related to these classical neurotransmitters [17-19]. In an attempt to identify new members of the 5-HT and DA receptor family, using a "cloning-by-homology" strategy, in 2001 two groups identified simultaneously a new family of G protein-coupled receptors [20] (see [19,21] for review). This family is now referred to as the trace amine-associated receptors (TAARs) [22], since members thereof were found to be sensitive to TAs. The newly discovered trace amine associated receptor 1 (TAAR1) is more than just another target for medication development in addiction and neuropsychiatry. Trace amines and their receptors have been found to be intimately related to the neurotransmitter systems involved in addiction, and are activated by some addictive drugs, especially stimulants, directly. Research efforts during the last decade have been devoted to understanding the function of TAAR1 and its mechanisms of action. Recent studies have shown a pivotal role of TAAR1 in monoamines regulation, and in acting as a substrate for the actions of several drugs of abuse, especially stimulants. We will review here evidence suggesting that manipulations of this system open new perspectives for the development of novel therapeutic strategies to treat addiction and addiction-related disorders.

2. THE TAAR FAMILY

TAs, such as p-tyramine (pTyr), β-phenylethylamine (PEA), octopamine, tryptamine and N,N-dimethyltryptamine, result from amino acids metabolism and share structural and metabolic similarities with classical biogenic amines, notably monoamines [18,23]. TAs are found in the brain, with a distribution generally matching that of biogenic amines, as well as in food such as chocolate, wine and cheese [18,19]. In the brain, TAs are characterized by their high rates of biosynthesis and catabolism, and are found only at trace concentrations (0.1-100 ng/g) - hence the name "trace" amines. Yet, TAs have been implicated in a wide range of neuropathological disorders, including schizophrenia, major depression, anxiety states, Parkinson's disease, attention deficit hyperactivity disorder, Tourette syndrome and obsessive-compulsive disorders (see [17,19,23] for review). In the absence of dedicated receptors, TAs were believed to exert their biological effects indirectly, through alteration of monoaminergic activity, and thereby were termed "false neurotransmitters" [18,19]. Cloning of the TAAR family significantly changed this view and suggested specific functions for TAs. Subsequent studies allowed identification of TAAR family members in various mammalian species, as well as construction of a uniform gene nomenclature (Table 1) [22-28]. As not all members of the family happen to be sensitive to TAs, the receptor family was termed trace amine-associated receptors [22] (TAARs). Remarkably, the number of TAAR genes and pseudogenes (ψ) was shown to vary significantly between species. There are 19 TAAR genes (2 ψ) in rat, 16 (1 ψ) in mouse, 9 each in human (3 ψ) and chimpanzee (6 ψ), and more than 100 in some fishes [29,30]. Phylogenetic and pharmacophore similarity analysis studies [22,25,26] revealed that the TAAR family forms a well-defined and coherent gene family, which can be subdivided into 3 subgroups (Table 1). Members of the different subgroups are likely to display different pharmacological profiles.

Table 1. Nomenclature of trace amine-associated receptors (TAARs). The 3 subgroups correspond to orthologues and group members correspond to paralogues. The nomenclature is based on the following rules: "TAAR" is followed by a number that designate the specific orthologue; a letter suffix may follow the number to distinguish paralogues; the suffix letter P then identifies pseudogenes. The old gene names are given when they had been previously reported (n.a.: no published old gene name available). For a comprehensive summary of the available sequence information for human, chimpanzee (Pan troglodytes), rat, and mouse TAAR genes, for details of the nomenclature system, and for a discussion of the proposed subgroup distinction, please refer to [22]

Generic name	Rat	Mouse	Human	Chimpanzee
Group 1				
TAAR1	TA1,TAR1,TRAR1	TA1,TAR1	TA1, TAR1, TRAR1	n.a.
TAAR2	n.a.	n.a.	GPR58	P (n.a.)
TAAR3	n.a.	n.a.	P (GPR57P)	P (n.a.)
TAAR4	TA2	n.a.	P (TA2P, 5-HT4P)	P (n.a.)
Group 2				
TAAR5	n.a.	n.a.	PNR	n.a.
Group 3				
TAAR6	TA4,TRAR4	n.a.	TRAR4, TA4	TRAR4
TAAR7			P (n.a.)	P (n.a.)
TAAR7a	n.a.	n.a.		
TAAR7b	TA12	n.a.		
TAAR7c	n.a.	P (n.a.)		
TAAR7d	TA15	n.a.		
TAAR7e	TA14	n.a.		
TAAR7f	P (TA13P)	n.a.		
TAAR7g	TA9			
TAAR7h	TA6			
TAAR7i	P (n.a.)			
TAAR8			TRAR5, TA5, TAR5, GPR102	P (n.a.)
TAAR8a	TA11	n.a.		
TAAR8b	TA7	n.a.		
TAAR8c	TA10	n.a.		
TAAR9	TA3	n.a.	TRAR3, TA3, TAR3	P (n.a.)

The mammalian TAARs share a range of common characteristics: all except one are encoded by a single exon of only ~1 kb in length, and all genes cluster to a narrow region (100-200 kb) of a single chromosome (6q23.1 in human). Interestingly, the sequential order of the various TAAR genes is highly conserved across species, a feature used to elaborate the TAARs nomenclature (Table 1) [22]. TAARs also have short N- and C-terminal domains, and all receptors display a predictive peptide fingerprint motif (NSXXNPXXY/HXXXY/FXWF) in their C-terminal domain that is absent from all other known GPCRs [22]. *In vitro*, when expressed in cells lines, only two TAARs have been shown to be sensitive to TAs, namely TAAR1 and TAAR4 [20,22]. The other receptors were unresponsive to TAs. The similarity of the predicted ligand binding pockets throughout the entire receptor family suggest that potential, as yet unidentified, ligands of the apparently TAs-insensitive TAARs might resemble small-molecular-weight compounds that are structurally and chemically similar to TAs [23]. In contrast, a range of TAARs have been shown to be sensitive to volatile amines, including natural components of mouse urine [26,31,32]. Coincidently, all TAAR genes except *Taar1* are expressed by subsets of olfactory receptor neurons in the mouse olfactory epithelium, similar to odorant receptors. For that reason, TAARs have been proposed to fulfil chemosensory functions, with roles in the detection of social cues in rodents [31,32]. Structural and functional evolution studies [26], as well as the expression of the TAARs in a number of peripheral organs including liver, kidney, spleen, pancreas, heart, gastrointestinal track and cells of the immune system [20,33-36,36], suggest that they may be involved in other biological processes, such as cardiovascular function [37,38]. Apart from TAAR1, the presence of other TAARs in the brain is still debated and awaits additional investigations. Since only TAAR1 and TAAR4 have been demonstrated to be TAs-sensitive [20,22], and given that TAAR4 is a pseudogene in primates, most studies so far have focused on TAAR1, as reviewed in the next sections.

3. TAAR1: EXPRESSION AND SIGNALLING

Expression of TAAR1 has been reported in monoaminergic brain regions [19-21,24,39,40] as well as in several organs of the periphery [20,21,34-36,41,42]. In mouse, *Taar1* mRNA, has been reported throughout the limbic system and in regions containing catecholaminergic cell bodies and their projections such as the locus coeruleus, substantia nigra, ventral tegmental area, dorsal raphe, striatum and basal ganglia [20]. However, inconsistent data have been reported in the brain, see e.g. [20,39,41] versus [32], depending on the study, method and species, presumably because *Taar1* expression levels are remarkably low. Using a line of mice where *Taar1* is replaced by the LacZ reporter gene (*knock-in*), *Taar1* expression has been identified reliably in a set of defined brain structures, including limbic and monoaminergic areas [32,39]. In particular, signal was detected in the ventral tegmental area (VTA) and dorsal raphe nucleus (DRN), as previously reported in mouse [19,20], rat [21] and monkey [24,40]. However, LacZ staining was not detected in certain key areas, which contrasted with previous studies, in particular in the substantia nigra [20,21,40], locus coeruleus [20,40] and cerebellum [19-21,40]. Unfortunately, while this line of mice enables the identification of *Taar1*-expressing cells, it does not provide information on the intracellular localization of the TAAR1 protein. In addition, currently available antibodies lack specificity and reliable antibodies against TAAR1 are still lacking. Development of such tools will be crucial to map TAAR1 projection sites, to determine its synaptic localization (*pre-* versus *post*-synaptic), and to decipher the cytological localization of TAAR1, which has been extensively debated. Nevertheless, the data currently available are consistent in showing that TAAR1 is expressed within monoaminergic areas, suggesting roles in modulating monoaminergic-related functions.

Of note, TAAR1 has been reported to colocalise with the dopamine transporter (DAT) in a subset of substantia nigra neurons in mouse as well as in rhesus monkey. Similarly, biochemical data generated in striatal and thalamic synaptosomes of mice and monkeys strongly suggest that TAAR1 also interacts with the 5-HT and norepinephrine transporters [43,44], although an histological demonstration of their putative colocalisation is still awaited. These observation are partly supported by electrophysiological recordings ex vivo which demonstrate the presence of functional TAAR1 in the DA and 5-HT neurons of the VTA and DRN, respectively, but not in the noradrenergic neurons of the locus coeruleus [45]. TAAR1 engages several signalling pathways. Upon activation, TAAR1 elevates intracellular cAMP levels via Gs [19,21,23]. *In vitro* measurements of cAMP levels in cell lines expressing TAAR1 showed that besides TAs, TAAR1 can be activated by a large palette of ligands. It includes endogenous molecules such as biogenic amines (including DA which activates TAAR1 with partial efficacy) [21-23,46], thyroid hormone-derivatives (e.g. 3-iodothyronamines, T_1AM) [47-49] and catechol-O-methyl transferase products (e.g. 3-methoxytyramine) [21,50,51], as well as synthetic substances such as amphetamine derivatives (e.g. *d*-amphetamine, methamphetamine, ecstasy) and ergolines (e.g. lysergic acid diethylamide, LSD) [21,24,40,50,52-55], as detailed below. However, these ligands also have TAAR1-independent effects via other targets, such as the monoaminergic transporters and receptors, or the sigma receptors [18,48,56,57]. Thus, TAAR1 appears to show "bidirectional polypharmacology": it is activated by multiple ligands, which themselves impact on multiple targets.

4. TAAR1 FUNCTION: IMPLICATIONS FOR ADDICTION

The lack of selective ligands has rendered the identification of TAAR1 biological functions particularly challenging. Recently, we have described the first selective TAAR1 antagonist, N-(3-Ethoxy-phenyl)-4-pyrrolidin-1-yl-3-trifluoromethyl-benzamide (EPPTB; RO5212773) [58]. EPPTB potently and selectively inhibits the PEA-induced cAMP production from human embryonic kidney (HEK)-293 cells transfected with mouse TAAR1. Use of EPPTB revealed that TAAR1 tonically activates inwardly rectifying K^+ channels (GIRKs) to reduce the basal firing activity of DA neurons in the VTA [58]. Furthermore, EPPTB increased agonist potency at DA D_2 receptors while reducing their desensitization rate, strongly suggesting a functional link between TAAR1 and D_2 receptors in DA neurons of the VTA. Whether TAAR1 interacts with D_2 directly or via other proteins, and how this interaction occurs, remain to be determined. Interestingly, DA itself can activate TAAR1, although only with partial efficacy (~50%) [21,22,40]. In DA synapses, the modulation of TAAR1 activity may thus result from the competitive binding of TAs and DA, according to their local concentration, forming complex feedback mechanisms on *Taar1*-expressing DA neurons. Further evidence of critical interactions between TAAR1 and D_2 receptors has been provided recently. Using a biosensor for cAMP, Espinoza *et al.* have shown that the D_2 antagonists haloperidol, raclopride and amisulpiride can increase TAAR1-mediated β-PEA-induced enhancement of cAMP in HEK293 cells co-expressing TAAR1 and D_2 receptors

[59]. The same study also revealed that TAAR1 and D_2 receptors can form heterodimers *in vitro* and, *in vivo*, haloperidol-induced c-Fos expression and catalepsy were attenuated in TAAR1 knockout mice. The study of TAAR1-D2 receptor interactions is important given the role of D2 receptors in mediating vulnerability to addiction.

Similarly, *in vitro* studies with HEK293 cells stably expressing TAAR1 and striatal synaptosome preparations have documented a reciprocal regulation between TAAR1 and the monoaminergic transporters, particularly the DAT [2, 4, 8, 23, 35, 41] [see 25 for review]. Monoamines transporters enhance TAAR1 activation, and may serve as conduits for TAs and amphetamines to enter cells where they could act as agonists of intracellular TAAR1 [8, 23, 25]. Conversely, TAAR1 appears to alter the functioning of monoamine transporters, by inhibiting monoamine uptake and by promoting monoamine efflux and transporter internalization [23, 25, 35, 41]. Xie and Miller (2009) have shown that methamphetamine-induced DA uptake inhibition is evident in cells co-transfected with TAAR1 + DAT, but it is absent in DAT-only or in striatal synaptosomes from TAAR1 knockout mice [60]. How this bidirectional regulation between TAAR1 and monoamine transporters occurs is still unclear, but it may involve the protein kinases A and C [25, 35, 42]. TAAR1-mediated regulation of DAT activity may be an important process sub-serving psychostimulat action. The ability of cocaine-like drugs to maintain self-administration in rodents is correlated with their potency in inhibiting the DAT [61]. Moreover, the self-reported "high" induced by stimulants in humans appears to be a function of both the rate of DAT occupancy by the stimulant and the speed of stimulant delivery into the brain [62]. Therefore, the functional regulation of DAT activity by TAAR1 suggests that these novel receptors could contribute to the long-lasting pathophysiological neuroadaptations produced by psychomotor stimulants.

The possible implication of TAAR1 in the physiological and psychopharmacological effects of stimulant drugs is further reinforced by the fact that several psychoactive substances, including amphetamine, methamphetamine, MDMA (3, 4-methylenedi-oxymethamphetamine; ecstasy), and lysergic acid diethylamide (LSD) are themselves agonists of TAAR1 [19, 21, 53]. Methamphetamine and amphetamine produce cAMP accumulation in concentration- and isomer-dependent manner in HEK293 cells expressing different species of TAAR1 [53]. Indeed, TAAR1 is a stereoselective binding site for amphetamines [53]. In a recent study, Lewin et al. (2011) have compared the agonist potency of ten pairs of enantiomeric amphetamines at primate TAAR1 and have determined that the S-configuration confers higher potency, the rank order of which parallels the stimulant action reported in humans. In the absence of selective ligands, understanding of TAAR1 biological function has advanced significantly with the engineering of mice that lack the receptor (*Taar1*$^{-/-}$ mice). Several lines have been generated independently. Surprisingly, the mutants have no overt phenotype and appear similar to normal wild-type littermates (WT) in most neurological and behavioural tests, except for the prepulse inhibition test for which a small deficit has been reported. However, the spontaneous firing rate of VTA DA neurons is clearly augmented in *Taar1*$^{-/-}$ mice, and only in the WT does pTyr decrease such firing activity [39,54]. Further application of the TAAR1 antagonist EPPTB not only prevents the pTyr-induced inhibition of firing frequency in WT, but also increases the firing rate to attain the frequency of untreated *Taar1*$^{-/-}$ mice. Importantly, *Taar1*$^{-/-}$ mice show hypersensitivity to the locomotor stimulating effect of *d*-amphetamine, which correlates with elevated striatal release of DA, noradrenaline and 5-HT following a *d*-amphetamine challenge [54]. Similar results have been obtained by Achat-Mendes et al. (2011) in locomotor activity assays and in the conditioned place preference (CPP) procedure, which measures drug-induced reward. *Taar1*$^{-/-}$ knockout mice acquired methamphetamine-induced CPP earlier than wild-type littermates, and retained it longer during extinction [42]. Altogether, these observations in mutant mice suggest that TAAR1 is a negative modulator of monoaminergic neurotransmission.

In vivo studies with TAAR1-selective ligands are eagerly awaited. Revel et al. [45] have engineered the first potent and selective TAAR1 agonist with optimized pharmacokinetic properties enabling *in vivo* experiments in mouse. We have conducted experiments with this compound, RO5166017, to study the regulation of cocaine-induced hyperactivity and conditioned place preference (CPP). The results have shown that RO5166017 dose-dependently blocked cocaine-induced locomotor activity but lacked stimulant effects when given alone within an ample dose range (0.3-20 mg/kg). In the CPP procedure, RO5166017 did not exhibit rewarding properties within the same dose range, while failing to alter cocaine-induced CPP (unpublished observations). These data suggest that RO5166017 does not show stimulant-like properties, reducing cocaine-stimulated hyperactivity, but not the rewarding-like effects of cocaine in the CPP paradigm. These data further indicate that the neuronal mechanisms by which TAAR-1 activation modulates cocaine-stimulated locomotor activity can be dissociated from those mediating cocaine-induced reward. Interestingly, studies with a partial agonist at TAAR1 have revealed that in rats with a history of consistent cocaine self-administration activation of TAAR1 drastically reduced cocaine intake (manuscript submitted). It is important that future studies investigate (1) whether such effects result from agonist or antagonist actions at TAAR1 (e.g., using specific agonists and antagonists), and (2) the extent to which these positive actions can be generalized to other stimulant drugs, such as methamphetamine. Furthermore, it is critical to test the therapeutic-like profile of TAAR1 manipulations in models of relapse (e.g. reinstatement and contextual relapse), which can be predictive of clinical efficacy.

A critical aspect of TAAR1-mediated regulation of DA neurotransmission is that while TAAR1 activation enhances DA efflux in DA terminal regions, including striatal synaptosomes [45,60], thereby mimicking the effects of amphetamine-like molecules [17], differential downregulation of the DA system has been reported in the somatodendritic DA regions. As indicated above, TAAR1 activation in the VTA decreases the firing rate of DA neurons and the release of DA by activating inwardly rectifying K+ channels [58]. In turn, blocking TAAR1 closes tonically active K+ channels, thus releasing DA neurons from tonic inhibition and increasing their firing rate [63].

CONCLUSION

The evidenced summarized in this chapter highlights the remarkable potential of TAAR1-related compounds to modulate the pathological neuroadaptations that abused drugs produce on the DA system. Indeed, chronic stimulant exposure is associated with long-lasting deficits in DA transmission, which may partially reflect the anhedonia and dysphoria that follows drug withdrawal [64, 65]. In this context, large efforts have been devoted to develop and evaluate stimulant-like medications (e.g., monoamine releasers or DAT inhibitors) that may act as a substitute, alleviate withdrawal symptoms, and prevent relapse. However, a major limitation of this approach is that many candidate medicines possess significant abuse liability. By contrast, in the light of the robust regulation of DA physiology and metabolism by TAAR1, the development and preclinical evaluation of TAAR1-related compounds may offer new leads for developing efficacious anti-addiction medications with minimal abuse liability.

REFERENCES

[1]   United Nations Office on Drugs and Crime (UNODC). World Drug Report. *United Nations Publication,* 2011, Sales No. E.11.XI.10.

[2]   Smout MF, Longo M, Harrison S, Minniti R, Cahill S, Wickes W, et al. The Psychostimulant Check-Up: A pilot study of a brief intervention to reduce illicit stimulant use. *Drug Alcohol. Rev.,* 2010, 29, 169-76.

[3]   London ED, Simon SL, Berman SM, Mandelkern MA, Lichtman AM, Bramen J, et al. Mood disturbances and regional cerebral metabolic abnormalities in recently abstinent methamphetamine abusers. *Arch. Gen. Psychiatry,* 2004, 61, 73-84.

[4]   Berman S, O'Neill J, Fears S, Bartzokis G, London ED. Abuse of amphetamines and structural abnormalities in the brain. *Ann. N. Y. Acad. Sci.,* 2008, 1141, 195-220.

[5]   Kampman KM. What's new in the treatment of cocaine addiction? *Curr. Psychiatry Rep.,* 2010, 12, 441-7.

[6]   Knapp WP, Soares BG, Farrel M, Lima MS. Psychosocial interventions for cocaine and psychostimulant amphetamines related disorders. *Cochrane Database Syst. Rev.,* 2007, CD003023.

[7]   Somaini L, Donnini C, Raggi MA, Amore M, Ciccocioppo R, Saracino MA, et al. Promising medications for cocaine dependence treatment. *Recent Pat. CNS Drug Discov.,* 2011, 6, 146-60.

[8]   Karila L, Reynaud M, Aubin HJ, Rolland B, Guardia D, Cottencin O, et al. Pharmacological treatments for cocaine dependence: is there something new? *Curr. Pharm. Des.,* 2011, 17, 1359-68.

[9]   Penberthy JK, Ait-Daoud N, Vaughan M, Fanning T. Review of treatment for cocaine dependence. *Curr. Drug Abuse Rev.,* 2010, 3, 49-62.

[10] Ross S, Peselow E. Pharmacotherapy of addictive disorders. *Clin. Neuropharmacol.,* 2009, 32, 277-89.

[11] Elkashef A, Vocci F, Hanson G, White J, Wickes W, Tiihonen J. Pharmacotherapy of methamphetamine addiction: an update. *Subst. Abus.,* 2008, 29, 31-49.

[12] Peng XQ, Xi ZX, Li X, Spiller K, Li J, Chun L, et al. Is slow-onset long-acting monoamine transport blockade to cocaine as methadone is to heroin? Implication for anti-addiction medications. *Neuropsychopharmacology,* 2010, 35, 2564-78.

[13] Velazquez-Sanchez C, Ferragud A, Hernandez-Rabaza V, Nacher A, Merino V, Carda M, et al. The dopamine uptake inhibitor 3 alpha-[bis(4'-fluorophenyl)metoxy]-tropane reduces cocaine-induced early-gene expression, locomotor activity, and conditioned reward. *Neuropsychopharmacology,* 2009, 34, 2497-507.

[14] Ferragud A, Velazquez-Sanchez C, Hernandez-Rabaza V, Nacher A, Merino V, Carda M, et al. A dopamine transport inhibitor with markedly low abuse liability suppresses cocaine self-administration in the rat. *Psychopharmacology (Berl),* 2009, 207, 281-9.

[15] Velazquez-Sanchez C, Ferragud A, Murga J, Carda M, Canales JJ. The high affinity dopamine uptake inhibitor, JHW 007, blocks cocaine-induced reward, locomotor stimulation and sensitization. *Eur Neuropsychopharmacol,* 2010, 20, 501-8.

[16] Velazquez-Sanchez C, Ferragud A, Renau-Piqueras J, Canales JJ. Therapeutic-like properties of a dopamine uptake inhibitor in animal models of amphetamine addiction. *Int. J. Neuropsychopharmacol.,* 2011, 14, 655-65.

[17] Berry MD. Mammalian central nervous system trace amines. Pharmacologic amphetamines, physiologic neuromodulators. *J. Neurochem.,* 2004, 90, 257-71.

[18] Burchett SA, Hicks TP. The mysterious trace amines: protean neuromodulators of synaptic transmission in mammalian brain. *Prog. Neurobiol.,* 2006, 79, 223-46.

[19] Grandy DK. Trace amine-associated receptor 1-Family archetype or iconoclast? *Pharmacol. Ther.,* 2007, 116, 355-90.

[20] Borowsky B, Adham N, Jones KA, Raddatz R, Artymyshyn R, Ogozalek KL, et al. Trace amines: identification of a family of mammalian G protein-coupled receptors. *Proc. Natl. Acad. Sci. USA,* 2001, 98, 8966-71.

[21] Bunzow JR, Sonders MS, Arttamangkul S, Harrison LM, Zhang G, Quigley DI, et al. Amphetamine, 3,4-methylenedioxymethamphetamine, lysergic acid diethylamide, and metabolites of the catecholamine neurotransmitters are agonists of a rat trace amine receptor. *Mol. Pharmacol.,* 2001, 60, 1181-8.

[22] Lindemann L, Ebeling M, Kratochwil NA, Bunzow JR, Grandy DK, Hoener MC. Trace amine-associated receptors form structurally and functionally distinct subfamilies of novel G protein-coupled receptors. *Genomics,* 2005, 85, 372-85.

[23] Lindemann L, Hoener MC. A renaissance in trace amines inspired by a novel GPCR family. *Trends. Pharmacol. Sci.,* 2005, 26, 274-81.

[24] Miller GM, Verrico CD, Jassen A, Konar M, Yang H, Panas H, et al. Primate trace amine receptor 1 modulation by the dopamine transporter. *J. Pharmacol. Exp. Ther.,* 2005, 313, 983-94.

[25] Vallender EJ, Xie Z, Westmoreland SV, Miller GM. Functional evolution of the trace amine associated receptors in mammals and the loss of TAAR1 in dogs. *BMC Evol. Biol.,* 2010, 10, 51.

[26] Staubert C, Boselt I, Bohnekamp J, Rompler H, Enard W, Schoneberg T. Structural and functional evolution of the trace amine-associated receptors TAAR3, TAAR4 and TAAR5 in primates. *PLoS One,* 2010, 5, e11133.

[27] Gloriam DE, Bjarnadottir TK, Yan YL, Postlethwait JH, Schioth HB, Fredriksson R. The repertoire of trace amine G-protein-coupled receptors: large expansion in zebrafish. *Mol. Phylogenet. Evol.,* 2005, 35, 470-82.

[28] Gloriam DE, Bjarnadottir TK, Schioth HB, Fredriksson R. High species variation within the repertoire of trace amine receptors. *Ann. N. Y. Acad. Sci.,* 2005, 1040, 323-7.

[29] Hashiguchi Y, Nishida M. Evolution of trace amine associated receptor (TAAR) gene family in vertebrates: lineage-specific expansions and degradations of a second class of vertebrate chemosensory receptors expressed in the olfactory epithelium. *Mol. Biol. Evol.,* 2007, 24, 2099-107.

[30] Hussain A, Saraiva LR, Korsching SI. Positive Darwinian selection and the birth of an olfactory receptor clade in teleosts. *Proc. Natl. Acad. Sci. USA,* 2009, 106, 4313-8.

[31] Liberles SD, Buck LB. A second class of chemosensory receptors in the olfactory epithelium. *Nature,* 2006, 442, 645-50.

[32] Liberles SD. Trace amine-associated receptors are olfactory receptors in vertebrates. *Ann. N. Y. Acad. Sci.,* 2009, 1170, 168-72.

[33] Chiellini G, Frascarelli S, Ghelardoni S, Carnicelli V, Tobias SC, DeBarber A, et al. Cardiac effects of 3-iodothyronamine: a new aminergic system modulating cardiac function. *FASEB J.,* 2007, 21, 1597-608.

[34] Fehler M, Broadley KJ, Ford WR, Kidd EJ. Identification of trace-amine-associated receptors (TAAR) in the rat aorta and their role in vasoconstriction by beta-phenylethylamine. *Naunyn Schmiedebergs Arch. Pharmacol.,* 2010, 382, 385-98.

[35] Ito J, Ito M, Nambu H, Fujikawa T, Tanaka K, Iwaasa H, et al. Anatomical and histological profiling of orphan G-protein-coupled receptor expression in gastrointestinal tract of C57BL/6J mice. *Cell Tissue Res.,* 2009, 338, 257-69.

[36] Nelson DA, Tolbert MD, Singh SJ, Bost KL. Expression of neuronal trace amine-associated receptor (Taar) mRNAs in leukocytes. *J. Neuroimmunol.,* 2007, 192, 21-30.

[37] Regard JB, Kataoka H, Cano DA, Camerer E, Yin L, Zheng YW, et al. Probing cell type-specific functions of Gi in vivo identifies GPCR regulators of insulin secretion. *J Clin Invest,* 2007, 117, 4034-43.

[38] Broadley KJ. The vascular effects of trace amines and amphetamines. *Pharmacol. Ther.,* 2010, 125, 363-75.

[39] Lindemann L, Meyer CA, Jeanneau K, Bradaia A, Ozmen L, Bluethmann H, et al. Trace amine-associated receptor 1 modulates dopaminergic activity. *J. Pharmacol. Exp. Ther.,* 2008, 324, 948-56.

[40] Xie Z, Westmoreland SV, Bahn ME, Chen GL, Yang H, Vallender EJ, et al. Rhesus monkey trace amine-associated receptor 1 signaling: enhancement by monoamine transporters and attenuation by the D2 autoreceptor in vitro. *J. Pharmacol. Exp. Ther.,* 2007, 321, 116-27.

[41] Regard JB, Sato IT, Coughlin SR. Anatomical profiling of G protein-coupled receptor expression. *Cell,* 2008, 135, 561-71.

[42] Achat-Mendes C, Lynch LJ, Sullivan KA, Vallender EJ, Miller GM. Augmentation of methamphetamine-induced behaviors in transgenic mice lacking the trace amine-associated receptor 1. *Pharmacol. Biochem. Behav,* 2011.

[43] Xie Z, Westmoreland SV, Miller GM. Modulation of monoamine transporters by common biogenic amines via trace amine-associated receptor 1 and monoamine autoreceptors in human embryonic kidney 293 cells and brain synaptosomes. *J. Pharmacol. Exp. Ther.,* 2008, 325, 629-40.

[44] Xie Z, Miller GM. Beta-phenylethylamine alters monoamine transporter function via trace amine-associated receptor 1: implication for modulatory roles of trace amines in brain. *J. Pharmacol. Exp. Ther.,* 2008, 325, 617-28.

[45] Revel FG, Moreau JL, Gainetdinov RR, Bradaia A, Sotnikova TD, Mory R, et al. TAAR1 activation modulates monoaminergic neurotransmission, preventing hyperdopaminergic and hypoglutamatergic activity. *Proc. Natl. Acad. Sci. USA,* 2011, 108, 8485-90.

[46] Navarro HA, Gilmour BP, Lewin AH. A rapid functional assay for the human trace amine-associated receptor 1 based on the mobilization of internal calcium. *J. Biomol. Screen,* 2006, 11, 688-93.

[47] Scanlan TS, Suchland KL, Hart ME, Chiellini G, Huang Y, Kruzich PJ, et al. 3-Iodothyronamine is an endogenous and rapid-acting derivative of thyroid hormone. *Nat. Med.*, 2004, 10, 638-42.

[48] Panas HN, Lynch LJ, Vallender EJ, Xie Z, Chen GL, Lynn SK, et al. Normal thermoregulatory responses to 3-iodothyronamine, trace amines and amphetamine-like psychostimulants in trace amine associated receptor 1 knockout mice. *J. Neurosci. Res.*, 2010, 88, 1962-9.

[49] Piehl S, Hoefig CS, Scanlan TS, Kohrle J. Thyronamines--past, present, and future. *Endocr. Rev.*, 2011, 32, 64-80.

[50] Barak LS, Salahpour A, Zhang X, Masri B, Sotnikova TD, Ramsey AJ, et al. Pharmacological characterization of membrane-expressed human trace amine-associated receptor 1 (TAAR1) by a bioluminescence resonance energy transfer cAMP biosensor. *Mol. Pharmacol.*, 2008, 74, 585-94.

[51] Sotnikova TD, Beaulieu JM, Espinoza S, Masri B, Zhang X, Salahpour A, et al. The dopamine metabolite 3-methoxytyramine is a neuromodulator. *PLoS One*, 2010, 5, e13452.

[52] Wainscott DB, Little SP, Yin T, Tu Y, Rocco VP, He JX, et al. Pharmacologic characterization of the cloned human trace amine-associated receptor1 (TAAR1) and evidence for species differences with the rat TAAR1. *J. Pharmacol. Exp. Ther.*, 2007, 320, 475-85.

[53] Reese EA, Bunzow JR, Arttamangkul S, Sonders MS, Grandy DK. Trace amine-associated receptor 1 displays species-dependent stereoselectivity for isomers of methamphetamine, amphetamine, and para-hydroxyamphetamine. *J. Pharmacol. Exp. Ther.*, 2007, 321, 178-86.

[54] Wolinsky TD, Swanson CJ, Smith KE, Zhong H, Borowsky B, Seeman P, et al. The Trace Amine 1 receptor knockout mouse: an animal model with relevance to schizophrenia. *Genes Brain Behav.*, 2007, 6, 628-39.

[55] Xie Z, Miller GM. Trace amine-associated receptor 1 is a modulator of the dopamine transporter. *J. Pharmacol. Exp. Ther.*, 2007, 321, 128-36.

[56] Fontanilla D, Johannessen M, Hajipour AR, Cozzi NV, Jackson MB, Ruoho AE. The hallucinogen N,N-dimethyltryptamine (DMT) is an endogenous sigma-1 receptor regulator. *Science*, 2009, 323, 934-7.

[57] Ledonne A, Federici M, Giustizieri M, Pessia M, Imbrici P, Millan MJ, et al. Trace amines depress D(2)-autoreceptor-mediated responses on midbrain dopaminergic cells. *Br. J. Pharmaco.l*, 2010, 160, 1509-20.

[58] Bradaia A, Trube G, Stalder H, Norcross RD, Ozmen L, Wettstein JG, et al. The selective antagonist EPPTB reveals TAAR1-mediated regulatory mechanisms in dopaminergic neurons of the mesolimbic system. *Proc. Natl. Acad. Sci. USA*, 2009, 106, 20081-6.

[59] Espinoza S, Salahpour A, Masri B, Sotnikova TD, Messa M, Barak LS, et al. Functional interaction between trace amine-associated receptor 1 and dopamine D2 receptor. *Mol. Pharmacol.*, 2011, 80, 416-25.

[60] Xie Z, Miller GM. A receptor mechanism for methamphetamine action in dopamine transporter regulation in brain. *J. Pharmacol. Exp. Ther.*, 2009, 330, 316-25.

[61] Ritz MC, Lamb RJ, Goldberg SR, Kuhar MJ. Cocaine receptors on dopamine transporters are related to self-administration of cocaine. *Science*, 1987, 237, 1219-23.

[62] Volkow ND, Wang GJ, Fischman MW, Foltin R, Fowler JS, Franceschi D, et al. Effects of route of administration on cocaine induced dopamine transporter blockade in the human brain. *Life Sci.,* 2000, 67, 1507-15.

[63] Revel FG, Bradaia A, Trube G, Stalder H, Ozmen L, Wettstein JG, et al. Modulation of dopaminergic activity in the mesolimbic system by trace amine-associated receptor 1 (TAAR1) modification. *European Neuropsychopharmacology,* 2009, 19, S273.

[64] Koob GF, Weiss F. Neuropharmacology of cocaine and ethanol dependence. *Recent Dev. Alcohol.,* 1992, 10, 201-33.

[65] Rothman RB, Partilla JS, Dersch CM, Carroll FI, Rice KC, Baumann MH. Methamphetamine dependence: medication development efforts based on the dual deficit model of stimulant addiction. *Ann. N. Y. Acad. Sci.,* 2000, 914, 71-81.

INDEX

Q

R

S